Shakespeare and Renaissance Drama

Hugh Mackay

Longman
is an imprint of

Harlow, England • London • New York • Bost
Sydney • Tokyo • Singapore •
Cape Town • Madrid • Mexico (

York Press

D0610490

In writing on this subject I owe a general debt to the guidance, suggestions and insights of teachers, colleagues and students, particularly to Professor Kathleen McLuskie at the Shakespeare Institute, Birmingham University, and to John Peacock at the University of Southampton. I would also like to thank Susan Mackay, and Rosie Carlton-Willis, who has provided a constant source of inspiration throughout.

Hugh Mackay

YORK PRESS
322 Old Brompton Road
London
SW5 9JH

PEARSON EDUCATION LIMITED
Edinburgh Gate
Harlow CM20 2JE
United Kingdom
Tel: +44 (0)1279 623623
Fax: +44 (0)1279 431059
Website: www.pearsoned.co.uk
First edition published in Great Britain in 2010

© Librairie du Liban *Publishers* 2010

The right of Hugh Mackay to be identified as author of this work has been asserted by him in accordance with the Copyright, Designs and Patents Act 1988.

ISBN 978-1-4082-0480-1

British Library Cataloguing in Publication Data
A CIP catalogue record for this book can be obtained from the British Library

Library of Congress Cataloging in Publication Data
Mackay, Hugh, 1969-
  Shakespeare and Renaissance drama / Hugh Mackay.
      p. cm. -- (York notes companions)
  Includes bibliographical references and index.
  ISBN 978-1-4082-0480-1 (pbk. : alk. paper)
  1. English drama--Early modern and Elizabethan, 1500-1600--History and criticism--Handbooks, manuals, etc. 2. English drama--17th century--History and criticism--Handbooks, manuals, etc. 3. Shakespeare, William, 1564-1616--Criticism and interpretation--Handbooks, manuals, etc. 4. Literature and society--England--History--16th century. 5. Literature and society--England--History--17th century. 6. Renaissance--England. I. Title.
  PR 651.M28 2010
  822.309--dc22
                            2010008351

All rights reserved. No part of this publication may be reproduced, stored in a retrieval system, or transmitted in any form or by any means, electronic, mechanical, photocopying, recording, or otherwise, without either the prior written permission of the Publishers or a licence permitting restricted copying in the United Kingdom issued by the Copyright Licensing Agency Ltd, Saffron House, 6–10 Kirby Street, London EC1N 8TS. This book may not be lent, resold, hired out or otherwise disposed of by way of trade in any form of binding or cover other than that in which it is published, without the prior consent of the Publishers.

10 9 8 7 6 5 4 3 2 1
14 13 12 11 10

Phototypeset by Pantek Arts Ltd, Maidstone, Kent
Printed in Malaysia, CTP-KHL

Contents

Contents

Part One
Introduction

The plays of Shakespeare are understood best when studied alongside those of his contemporaries. That is the premise of this volume on *Shakespeare and Renaissance Drama* – one designed to reflect much of the present-day critical thinking about the period's dramatic literature. There is a common, and understandable, assumption that the texts of Shakespeare's plays are able to 'speak for themselves', each one readily approached on its own terms. Studying a work over a period of weeks, or rehearsing for a production over a period of months, encourages an immersion in its poetry, narrative and characters which can foster a sense of the play's self-sufficiency and exclusivity. It is a measure of Shakespeare's achievement as a dramatist – his ability to craft works of powerful internal coherence – that such a sense of immersion is still possible after over 400 years of overwhelming familiarity with his plays. Yet for those who lived in late Elizabethan and early Jacobean London, and perhaps witnessed his plays in their very first productions, Shakespeare was only one among a number of high-achieving playwrights, writers who differed from one another in some respects but who also shared telling similarities in their approach to the writing of drama.

Shakespeare learned from earlier writers, adapting the poetic techniques and structural features of the plays of Christopher Marlowe and John Lyly as well as a host of other, now less well-known playwrights. Later writers such as Ben Jonson, John Marston and Thomas Middleton in turn borrowed liberally from Shakespeare and other dramatists, even as they strove to find their own distinctive approaches in an increasingly crowded marketplace for plays. One result of this is the sense of a continual dialogue going on between works written for the stage over this period: indeed, it has been pointed out that the great majority of literary allusions in the drama of this period are to contemporary plays and playwrights, and only secondarily to other kinds of literature.[1] Beyond this tightly knit world of mutual allusion and self-reference, other important social and historical forces helped to shape the environments in which the plays were written and performed, not the least of which was the development of a fully commercialised theatre, with playing companies, playhouses and regular theatre-goers. In sum, an emphasis on the immediate contexts of these plays is seen now not simply as desirable or informative, but as essential to a proper understanding of the plays. Contextual study, of one kind or another, has firmly established the trend in which critical discussions of the plays are conducted.

The present volume seeks to strike a balance between the close, single-text study often encountered in schools, and the broader picture which students will find themselves steered towards in university courses. Part Two of the book develops the argument for the appreciation of context which we have sketched out above, by taking as an example the production of one particular, non-Shakespearean play (*The Jew of Malta* by Christopher Marlowe) and using it to explore the various historical, literary and theatrical points of contact it would have shared with other plays from this period. The subject matter of the play is less important in this instance than what is going on around it – the business of its reception at a given historical and cultural moment and the sense we can get of the rich possibilities of meaning that could be read into this – and by implication any other – play-text. From here we can address a different kind of context in Part Three: that provided by theatrical genre. This is another, important area in which the connections between texts can be opened out and examined. By studying genres – literally, the 'kinds' of play offered to audiences in Renaissance England – we are studying the process by which individual works both resemble and distinguish themselves from one another. At the same time, we are asking why certain genres existed at certain times, and what might have been responsible for their popularity and durability.

We are familiar with the concept of genre from the many different kinds of media – fictional and non-fictional – which we are exposed to today, with their associated groupings and sub-groupings. Thus, there are disaster films, historical biographies, plays of ideas, postmodern theatre, television soaps, science fiction novels, role-playing games – all labels which create a clear expectation in their audiences of a particular kind of experience which will unfold in a generally understood format. Yet the subject is less self-explanatory than it might appear at first glance. What exactly do these labels describe – aspects of form, theme, content, style, or a blend of these? And how do we know for sure which labels apply in each case, given that an individual work may have features linking it to several possible groupings? (A disaster film may also be, for example, a science fiction film.) The problem becomes more pronounced when we realise that the concept of genre, which we take for granted, is a comparatively modern one which was not precisely articulated in Shakespeare's day. A good deal of Renaissance dramatic criticism, following classical precedent, formally recognised only two kinds of play: tragedy and comedy, which were conceived of as fairly static, unchanging categories. Yet we can see through discussions at the time that there was also an awareness of a much greater variety of informal groupings constantly being created through blending, hybridisation and departure from artistic precedent.*

Part Three of the volume examines six such groupings from the Elizabethan and Jacobean drama, while keeping a focus on what Lawrence Danson, in a helpful recent discussion, has distinguished as the *formal* and the *affective* (or emotional) aspects of genre.[2] The formal aspects of a dramatic genre or grouping, which can include the shape, structure and overall plotline or trajectory of the plays, can be identified from internal evidence – for example, whether the plays have happy or unhappy

---

* A famous case in point is that the first collected edition of Shakespeare's plays, the First Folio of 1623, was obliged to introduce a whole separate category for 'Histories' to accommodate a kind of play which simply did not fit in either of the critically sanctioned groups.

endings – and by making use of comparisons across a number of works. Persistent features in a number of plays suggest interrelatedness (as we will see, for example, in the cases of 'humours' and 'revenge' drama). It is also important to recognise that this modern analysis of genre should be balanced by an understanding of the historical and literary conventions at work in a play's construction. For example, we need to be aware that the five-act structure, derived from Roman drama, that we encounter in most edited versions of Renaissance plays often bears little relation to the actual structure of the plays as written for the stage: in Shakespeare's case act divisions were imposed by editors on what was originally a continuous succession of scenic units. At the same time, we need to acknowledge that classical and formal conventions were still operating at some level within the works of Elizabethan and Jacobean dramatists, with writers such as Ben Jonson more openly concerned to adhere to them.

In our assessment of what Danson terms the affective aspects of a play's genre we are on more difficult ground. What used to serve as a benchmark – our own emotional responses as audience and readers – is not now regarded as a reliable guide. Contemporary critical thinking has instilled a mistrust of 'trans-historical', or universalising, pronouncements about what people from earlier cultures may have thought or felt about a particular work. This may seem to cut right across our sense of the transcendent emotional power of some plays and the immediate, overwhelming effect they have on us. The denouement of *Othello*, for example, appears to generate in the modern audience the canonical emotions of pity and fear which have been associated with response to tragedy from Aristotle onwards (see Part Five: 'Further Reading'). The fact that 'pity' is on record as an Elizabethan audience reaction to the death scene of Desdemona suggests a broad continuity between their emotions and ours.[3] Yet we need to be aware that our present-day feelings towards the protagonist, Othello, will also be affected by the deeply troubled history of relations between white Europeans and black Africans, and the institutions of industrial slavery, racial 'science' and apartheid, which have intervened since the play was written. The sense of an injustice inflicted upon Othello as he is deceived and betrayed by Iago cannot therefore be equal for both historical groups. In the Elizabethan case, it would be tempered by the religious implications of his murder of Desdemona (the act must inevitably damn Othello). In the modern case, it is exacerbated by the prolonged historical narrative of the maltreatment of African people.

The chapters in Part Three therefore take an historical approach to the issue of theatrical genre in the period. When the first ever 'Complete Works of Shakespeare' appeared in 1623, only a few years after the dramatist's death, the fellow actors who had now become his editors settled on three generic divisions: comedy, history and tragedy. To these three we add three more: tragicomedy (an important, developing genre at the time which is particularly helpful for understanding Shakespeare's later plays), 'humours' comedy and revenge tragedy. These latter two categories were not formally recognised at the time, but are now seen as valid and important offshoots, or sub-genres, of the mainstream ones of comedy and tragedy. They are also chosen here because they can be seen as developing at something of a tangent to the classic Shakespearean genres (although as will be seen he provided an important stimulus to both of them). Each chapter begins with an example of response associated with the genre, wherever possible making use of contemporary anecdotal or theatrical records to provide an evaluation of the plays which may seem at some distance from our own. These records are points of departure only, and as might be expected they are very far from being unbiased. Some are wildly in favour of the plays they describe; some are wildly against them: none is neutral. They warrant inclusion, however, as flawed yet suggestive pieces of evidence in support of the view that the reception of plays could fall outside the range of the universal – indeed, that the idea of 'universal' responses to tragedy, comedy and other genres may be a misleading one.

One further benefit of taking the approach outlined here is that it can encourage us to shift our focus onto the underlying principle of *theatrical pleasure* in our assessment of the plays of this era. This in many ways provides the guiding interpretive framework of the volume. Whatever well-established contemporary critical concepts could be brought to bear on the writing and reception of plays in this period –

catharsis in the case of tragedy, for example, or moral correction in the case of comedy – these had to contend with the particular impulse which brought audiences to the theatres in the first place, and they can in many ways be seen as subordinate to that underlying impulse. Moreover, if, as many present-day critics argue, genres were not, and never have been, fixed categories but were constantly forming and re-forming, then this is because they found their identities in that roughly defined space between the consumers and the producers of plays. This volume suggests that the theatrical genres of Shakespeare's day need to be thought through in terms of the pleasures they offered, or purported to offer, to audiences. These theatrical pleasures could range from joy, fear, amusement and shock, to the pity at Desdemona's fate described earlier. They could also include the pleasures generated by pastoral and satiric forms, which are less familiar to us today. All of these were part of the complex entertainment provided by the Renaissance stage. This volume offers students an understanding of the way this process of interaction between theatre workers and play-goers helped shape not only individual plays but the development of the theatre industry as a whole.

The penultimate part of this of this volume, Part Four, looks at some aspects of the plays of the period which have excited the greatest amount of interest from a present-day critical point of view. Students, particularly at university level, are likely to encounter a large number of 'isms' as an important adjunct to their development of a broader perspective on Shakespeare and Renaissance drama: new historicism, feminism and cultural materialism are probably the most important to have affected Renaissance studies over the last thirty years, but there are many others available and being developed.* In many ways, critical perspectives such as these operate on a principle similar to that of the genres we have described, continually forming and adapting to take account of the plurality of possible interpretations which can be brought to bear on the texts – no one of these being 'right' in the sense of having exclusive explanatory validity. The stimulus has been immense, and in many respects has permanently changed the way the plays are read;

* See in particular the series on *Alternative Shakespeares* in 'Further Reading'.

but the critical landscape has as a result also become a more confusing one. Part Four, rather than reviewing these critical perspectives on an individual basis, will attempt to pick out those areas which have invited some of the most sustained and energising debate, allowing concerns with gender, subjectivity, rhetoric and national/racial discourse to guide the choice of plays and the shape of the discussion. The plays themselves, as throughout this book, will be the primary focus of attention, and Part Four merely shines a slightly different light on them than did Part Two and Part Three. All the chapters of this book share the assumption that no play of this period can be approached as an object detached from considerations of genre, politics and the informing standpoint of the observer. Yet these considerations can be seen as part of what made these plays so enjoyable to their first audiences, and still makes them enjoyable to us now.

Notes

1   Andrew Gurr, *Playgoing in Shakespeare's London* (Cambridge: Cambridge University Press, 1996), 2nd edn, p. 85.
2   Lawrence Danson, *Shakespeare's Dramatic Genres* (Oxford: Oxford University Press, 2000; repr. 2007), p. 3.
3   At a production of the play in Oxford in 1610 one observer, Henry Jackson, wrote of the performance of the boy player: 'Desdemona ... although she always acted her whole part supremely well, yet when she was killed she was even more moving, for when she fell back upon the bed she implored the pity of the spectators by her very face.' Translated from the Latin, in Gamini Salgado (ed.), *Eyewitnesses of Shakespeare* (London: Sussex University Press, 1975), p. 30.

Part Two
A Cultural Overview

1594: A Year in the Drama and Society of Elizabethan London

During the first half of 1594 the London theatres stirred into life after a year-and-a-half-long period of near-total closure. They had been shut down in the summer of 1592 as part of an enforced measure to limit the spread of an outbreak of bubonic plague in London. Now the threat seemed to have subsided enough to risk allowing crowds to reassemble in the confined spaces of the Elizabethan playhouse. A year is a long time in any business, and the result of the closures had been a kind of theatrical mass extinction among playing companies – those groups of actors, writers and investors who collectively made and staged dramatic performances for a paying public. A few sporadic performances in the London playhouses aside, they had been otherwise forced to survive by undergoing gruelling tours of the country. Now, where there had been several of these companies, only two remained in a properly functioning state, pieced together in some cases from the remnants of other companies that had collapsed. One of these, the Lord Chamberlain's Men, was the group joined by William Shakespeare, still a comparatively new playwright (and actor) making his mark with plays of English history, such as *Richard III*, of comedy, such as *The Comedy of Errors*, and of classical tragedy, such as *Titus Andronicus*. The other, the Admiral's Men, was at that time the pre-eminent theatre company in London, with the most prestigious actors and repertory. Despite the fact that the Lord Chamberlain's Men would soon eclipse them – hence this volume's focus on Shakespeare and the dramatists writing for the newer companies that sprang up over the next two decades – the Admiral's Men's fortunes as they returned to regular business provide an ideal standpoint from which to survey the theatrical and social terrain in Elizabethan London.

Top of the billing for the Admiral's Men following the enforced break was a play by a writer who had been killed (almost certainly assassinated) while the closure was in operation. The play was *The Jew of Malta*, the writer Christopher Marlowe, who had not yet reached thirty by the time he died.[1] The play had been written and first performed a good five years earlier, but in choosing to headline their re-opened business with a 'revival', rather than a new work, the Admiral's Men were showing that they could be keen assessors of business conditions at any given moment. On the one hand, the gesture speaks of continuity with a highly successful period just the other side of a disruption which had claimed many victims: it was 'business as usual', to rehearse the hackneyed but apposite sentiment. On the other hand, the play – which features a ludicrously villainous, grotesque Jewish schemer as its 'hero' – was well placed to chime with a political scandal which was currently enthralling London. A doctor of Portuguese nationality called Rodrigo Lopez, who was widely believed to be a practising Jew, was at that moment awaiting sentence following his conviction months earlier for the attempted poisoning of his most eminent patient, Queen Elizabeth herself.* For a theatre company just back on its feet, what better means of re-igniting attendance at the playhouse than by co-opting, channelling and casting into a pre-given mould such an incendiary public mood?

It might seem a cynical or tasteless move by the theatre company to capitalise on a set of currently heightened public expectations (about the theatre re-openings; about a forthcoming high-profile execution; about the circumstances of Marlowe's violent end). However, an Elizabethan Londoner would not have to approve of the theatre as an institution (and many did not) to feel compelled to have an opinion about *The Jew of Malta*'s latest staging, and to be caught up thereby in the theatre's

---

* Lopez was still waiting because the queen could not quite bring herself to sign the death warrant, only half-heartedly believing his guilt despite overwhelmingly hostile public opinion towards the elderly doctor.

ceaseless – and not infrequently irritating – efforts to place itself at the centre of life in the capital. The move also has a special value, however, in highlighting the conjunction between commercial and political factors at work in the theatre industry at the time Shakespeare was writing. In this chapter we will look at both these factors in greater detail, since the plays of this era were as much about these immediate social pressures – which all theatre professionals felt acting upon them keenly – as they were about the narratives, plots and characters which later ages have understood as timelessly enjoyable and rich in meaning. The writers and actors of this period loved to reflect openly, and over the course of their performances, on the actual circumstances of their trade. They paraded their opinions of themselves, their co-workers, their rivals and their audiences in numerous prologues, puns and asides, as well as overt references in the main body of the play. Macbeth's mordant summary of 'a poor player / That struts and frets his hour upon the stage, / And then is heard no more' (V.v.24–6) is only the most famous example of an idiom which was all too quick to draw attention to itself – regardless of whether this threw light or shade back upon the speaker. And while for the most part the business of playing (which was ultimately about entertainment) was well advised to steer clear of overt political comment, in practice a great many playwrights did offer such commentary via sometimes thinly disguised allusion, notwithstanding the threat of having to pay for it with imprisonment or physical mutilation.*

In what follows we can use this instance of the 1594 staging of *The Jew of Malta* as a window for a closer look at these aspects of Elizabethan and Jacobean culture. We will venture well beyond the particulars of this moment in order to gain a general overview of the public sphere in the period, but can return to it frequently to help fill out the claim above that these extrinsic factors were part of the very stuff of theatre. One of the most positive outcomes of critical thinking about Renaissance drama over the past three decades has been to render the whole area

---

* A play of 1604, *Eastward Ho* by Ben Jonson, George Chapman and John Marston, caused sufficient offence to the court of James I in its satire of Scottish courtiers to ensure that at least two of the writers ended up in prison and facing the prospect of having their ears and noses slit (a fate they managed to avoid, however).

of 'historical background' a less static or mechanistic one than it has sometimes seemed. Many of the readings available to us suggest that we are better off treating this background less as an inert mass of data which must be squared with the literary text in the foreground of our view, and more as a kind of 'background noise' which is constantly interfering with it. Indeed, both text and context can be taken together as part of a confusion of textual elements which coalesce to help form the substance of the play. And since a play is only ever realised in performance, that substance itself must be constantly changing. *The Jew of Malta* in 1594 was not quite *The Jew of Malta* in 1589; nor would either of these be the same as any of the numerous versions of the play staged over the following years. Over a more or less consistent verbal skeleton – the play-script; the part which survives today – many different kinds of theatrical 'body' would be imposed, each responding to shifting conditions in the public world surrounding the playhouse. Beginning with the political dimension, then, before moving on to explore the commercial one, this chapter will aim to show how both factors helped shape not just the world around these plays, but the plays themselves.

Discord and Debate: The Political Sphere

The queen, who, her followers thought, had so narrowly avoided being poisoned by the Portuguese doctor, was in her sixtieth year of life in 1594, and had been reigning in England for thirty-five of those. She was now on course to become the last of the Tudor dynasty – that family of monarchs who had come to power by conquest at the end of the previous century with Henry VII, and had run through Elizabeth's father, Henry VIII, her two half-siblings, Edward VI and Mary I, and then finally Elizabeth herself. Dynastic extinction was assured because Elizabeth had by her own choice avoided marriage and consequently children. It was a deliberate, if not wholeheartedly desired, policy on her part, which drew approval and anxiety in equal measure from her government and people. It avoided the conventional route of alliance with a foreign suitor: a route which had been taken earlier, with extremely unhappy consequences, by Elizabeth's elder sister, Mary, in her marriage with Philip II of Spain. Fears that England might become subject to another power were thereby calmed in certain sections of the country. But it created another problem by default: the queen had no natural heir, and as the prospect of competition for her hand had receded, that of competition for the throne after her death was in danger of growing. As a lone figure presiding over the demise of her dynasty, Elizabeth could on the one hand continue to enjoy the enormous cult of personality which had focused upon her 'Virgin' status; but on the other, the vulnerability she shared with any ageing monarch was thrown all the more sharply into relief.

The queen's presumed assassin, by contrast, would have found himself taking on the classic role of antagonist to the paragon of innocence created by the Cult of Elizabeth. No one will ever know whether or not Lopez was guilty of the crime for which he was finally hanged, drawn and quartered in July of that year: his 'confession' under torture would (one hopes) be considered extremely problematic today, and the queen's doubts are a crucial argument in his favour. However, we can be sure that he had secret ties to the kingdom which was at that moment England's most dangerous enemy: Spain. Once letters were intercepted revealing correspondence between the doctor and the same Philip II who had been married to Elizabeth's elder sister, his conviction became inevitable. Spain was both the greatest power in Europe in that period and the one most likely to launch an attempted invasion of England. It had already tried and failed once, spectacularly, six years earlier with the Armada fleet sent under Medina Sidonia, when a combination of Spanish imperial hubris, English tactical nous at sea and disobliging Channel weather saw the entire fleet thrown into disarray, with great loss of life.[2] Despite the humiliation inflicted on the Spanish king, there was every chance that the outcome would serve simply to increase hostility, and that Spain would resort to every method – whether invasion on an even grander scale, or covert attempts at assassination via the expedient of poison – to dispose of the queen. At the root of all this hostility lay religious disagreement, and the chafing national antagonism which was bred by it.

Spain was Roman Catholic, in the sense of upholding the one 'true and universal' creed which its followers assumed represented the only possible understanding of the Old and New Testaments. More than that, Spain, with its fabulous wealth and reserves of talent and industry, felt itself to be the standard-bearer for this ageless conviction in the face of new and bewildering threats to its validity. Beginning in Germany three quarters of a century before the historical moment we are discussing, dissatisfaction with the Catholic Church had become apparent both at the level of its practices and at the level of inward belief. A powerful priesthood, held to be essential for the salvation of souls, had led to a range of abuses, including the possibility of literally buying oneself back into favour with God via the purchase of pardons, whether from a priest or from a professional pardoner. And in emphasising 'works' – the world of religious action and ritual, often performed by means of such an intercessionary – over that of faith, Catholicism seemed to undermine the direct relationship with God that Christ's teachings had built towards. The principal troublemaker from the Catholic viewpoint was a German monk called Martin Luther, who urged a return to the Bible as the sole source of Christian authority, but there was precedent and widespread sympathy for his objections, which helps to explain the sheer speed with which this 'Reformation' in Christian thought and practice spread.* Loyal Catholics would have watched appalled as state after state, especially in the north of Europe, succumbed to the logic of this new and powerful idea, in what twentieth-century politicians called a 'domino effect' of ideological change.

England was one of the northern European states to succumb, although it did so in circumstances which had little to do with the idealism of the 'Protestants' – as reforming objectors to Catholicism were known. Elizabeth's father, Henry VIII, had at the start of his reign no time for the arguments of Martin Luther and his followers, but subsequently found the challenge to authority they implied extremely useful when it

---

* The most famous act in a complex historical process was Luther's nailing of a document, *The 95 Theses*, to the door of the chapel to the University of Wittenberg in 1517. These theses contested many of the perceived abuses of the Catholic church, including the sale of 'indulgences', that is, pardons for sin. Two of the most famous figures to emerge out of the English sixteenth-century drama, Hamlet and Doctor Faustus, are shown as students of the University of Wittenberg.

came to revising the terms of his marital contract. Afraid that his Spanish wife, Katherine, was unable to provide him with a male heir, he sought instead to divorce her and to marry the young English noblewoman Anne Boleyn. What stood in his way was not so much the ideology of the Catholic Church as the sensitivities of its most important institution: the Papacy. The pope, if he had chosen, could have granted Henry a divorce, but he felt (ironically enough) that the request went too close to treating the Papacy as a kind of marketplace for concessions. Henry's response – eagerly prompted by reformist sympathisers including Anne herself – was to sever all ties with the Papacy and make or unmake his own destiny in marriage by establishing himself as the Head of the Church in England in 1534. It was an expedient, partial adoption of Protestant thinking by a king who had no great affection for the cause; but once undertaken, there were too many far-sighted, ambitious individuals around Henry to allow the movement to halt at this point. Not least among the new opportunities were the vast reserves of wealth to be recovered from characteristically Catholic, but now obsolete, institutions all around England such as the monasteries: wealth which was now distributed among the courtiers and politicians who supported the changes.

It would be a great oversimplification to claim that England's hostilities with imperial Spain began with the rejection of Katherine in favour of Anne. Nevertheless, in the immediate aftermath of the break with papal supremacy England, in fear of an invasion, expanded its navy from a handful of warships to over a hundred and fifty, and built fortifications all around the coast as a precaution. That invasion was to wait another fifty years, during which time the consequences of the violent disruption initiated by Henry were borne by his children in a rapid series of changes of power. Henry's only son, Edward VI, although he died before reaching adulthood, pursued along with his councillors a far more assertive policy of fully Protestant Reformation, bringing into English worship many of those 'Lutheran' ideas which his father would have deemed heretical. His elder sister Mary, of mixed English and Spanish ancestry, being the daughter of Henry VIII and Katherine of Aragon, attempted on her succession to reverse these changes with equal vigour and ideological conviction, and to repair ties with the rest of Catholic Europe by marriage to the new king of Spain, Phillip II. In the confusion of contradictory religious impulses which characterised these years, one feature does emerge as a clear product of Henry's initial break with papal power: fear and distrust of 'the foreigner' was now a congenital response to change in most levels of English society outside the immediate circle around royal power, and the marriage was deeply unpopular. Reformist enthusiasm had also spread well beyond the intellectual elite to embrace many ordinary working people in the country who were powerfully animated by Protestant insistence on having both Bible and prayer books published in English rather than Latin. What in fact was being developed was a sense of national identity, and Mary's ferocious purges against these heretics could now be construed not as the restoration of a true religion by a rightful monarch, but as the imposition of an external, alternative form of worship by a half-Spanish, Spanish-married 'outsider'.

The beneficiary of this developing nationalist mood was to be Mary's younger half-sister, Elizabeth, who took the throne, aged twenty-five, on Mary's death in 1558. It may be becoming clear by this stage that the overlap between religion and politics – the governance of the state – helped shape each sphere in this period. We could think of each impetus as carrying along the other, but with their underlying positions continually switching. Henry's break with Rome was about political power – his desire to make his own decisions free from a central control – but the vehicle which carried this political imperative was to be found in certain concrete religious challenges to the pope's spiritual dominance. By the time of Edward VI, the imperative was by contrast a sincerely felt reforming impulse, carried out via a political programme for which an emphasis on use of the vernacular – the native language – in public life provided the vehicle. When at last Elizabeth came to power, this interplay between nation-building religious change and religious national self-definition was at a sophisticated stage – advanced enough to let an adept ruler appeal to both sides of the equation at once. Elizabeth's own Protestantism was as much or more about an independent England as it was about a specific creed. A case in point is provided by one of the most serious threats to Elizabeth's authority over the whole course of her reign: the presence of her cousin Mary, Queen of Scotland, after Mary was deposed and exiled into Elizabeth's care. As a Catholic monarch with a claim to the English throne, the Scottish queen, while kept in genteel confinement, provided a (largely willing) rallying point for Catholic nobles who sought Elizabeth's overthrow. The danger is unmistakably registered in a poem Elizabeth wrote in the late 1560s on her 'doubt of future foes'.[3] In these lines, she asserts:

> The daughter of debate, that discord aye doth sow,
> Shall reap no gain, where former rule still peace hath taught to know,
> No Foreign banished wight shall anchor in this port,
> Our realm brooks not seditious sects, let them elsewhere resort ...[4]

Written for Elizabeth's own private consumption, the lines nonetheless suppress any direct religious categorisation of her enemies, allowing the allusive phrase 'seditious sects' to mark a generalised threat, while linking the more explicit adjective 'Foreign' back to the gendered figure of 'debate' two lines earlier. That, we can readily gauge, is how Elizabeth is embodying the threat of Mary; and despite the fact that the two women were linked by blood just as Scotland and England were linked by land, it is via the conceit of an external, overseas danger – a ship anchoring itself in English harbours – that the poetic argument develops. The ominous tone in this piece was ultimately to Mary's disadvantage. In 1587 a conspiracy to put her on the throne following the planned assassination of Elizabeth was uncovered, and the imprisoned queen was beheaded – an act which helped galvanise Spain into its disastrous attempt to invade the country a year later.

By 1594, then, when another conspiracy seemed to loom in the shape of the Portuguese doctor, the responses of Elizabeth's subjects in the capital were strongly conditioned by a current of anti-foreign mistrust, one which served to superimpose itself upon the internal religious frictions which had fostered it. The sense of a national identity, concentrated in the life and well-being of the queen, lent a correspondingly clear and simple outline to complex external pressures, but also turned the eye away from fault lines that were constantly opening up beneath the nervous religious compromise – a denomination which sounded more or less Protestant, but looked rather more Catholic – put together by Elizabeth's councillors over the course of her reign. These fault lines sometimes become visible in Elizabeth's own court. The man most responsible for the discovery and prosecution of Lopez – the Earl of Essex, Robert Devereaux – was of a strongly Protestant persuasion often defined as 'puritan' in its wish to see religious reformation pursued to its limit. The man most responsible for trying to protect the doctor was the statesman Lord Burghley, of a more moderate reforming temper. In this instance, both men were playing power politics rather than following their religious convictions, but such convictions underpinned wider habits of mind – daring and caution respectively. Beyond the court, divisions within the reformed church continually fretted at the makeshift ties holding this compromise together. When eventually the Earl of Essex's accusations prevailed and the doctor's execution was ordained, it was little wonder that suppositions about his Jewishness should come to the fore. There were not meant to be any Jews in England at that time, while Portugal was at least an ally.* Here was an opportunity to focus the confusing details of the case onto one abiding exemplum of foreignness – of difference, of 'otherness'. Stephen Greenblatt relates the macabre story of Lopez's public execution. The doctor tried in vain to protest his innocence and his allegiance to the Protestant faith, but his vow upon the scaffold that he 'loved the Queen as well as he loved Jesus Christ' was met with the howls of derision reserved for one permanently thrust outside the national pale.

Consumer Society in Early Modern London

Members of the crowd who had gathered at Lopez's execution in June 1594, and who had perhaps gone to see Marlowe's play that May, would have comprised an eclectic group typical of metropolises. By this year the capital city had seen a rapid swelling of numbers to well over 200,000 – tiny by present-day standards, but more than double the number at the start of Elizabeth's reign. This reflected both an increase in England's population as a whole and the movement towards London from the

---

* The Jewish population of England had been expelled almost 300 years earlier (1290) by Edward I.

towns and villages of the countryside which this increase entailed. A cycle, which would have been largely invisible to the majority living at the time but which would have affected every aspect of their lives, was in motion. Greater numbers of people led to higher costs for basic goods; higher costs compelled recourse to the capital city, where the most work was to be found; and greater concentrations in the city forced up prices further. A proclamation from 1603, near the end of Elizabeth's reign, suggests the authorities' anxieties about the human and economic consequences of this influx. It warns of the 'great and manifold inconveniencies and mischiefs … unto the state of the city of London … by the access and confluence of people to inhabit the same'; people who could 'hardly be provided … for man's relief upon reasonable prices', and whose ever-growing poor underclass must live 'heaped up together and in a sort smothered' by the pressures of cheek-by-jowl existence in the city.[5]

The city was becoming a 'melting-pot', although less as we would understand that term today as connoting a mixture of native and non-native speakers, and more as a blend of social types from all over England. Although foreigners, especially refugees from religious persecution elsewhere in Europe (particularly France), certainly did resort to London, the capital's heterogeneous make-up was principally the result of the restless search by the English themselves, from all over the country, for labour, place, office or profit in a society becoming far more mobile than it had been in preceding centuries. This widespread sense of social moorings come adrift is best summed up in the Elizabethan designation 'masterless men' (although the problem applied with equal force to both sexes) for this newly mobile, potential workforce. A century earlier the assumption had been that many opportunities for employment would come from the great local landowner. Now, the steady dismantling of these traditional power bases – or 'great houses', as they were known – with the transfer of power to the monarch (ever the hidden agenda within the English Reformation) was removing such old certainties. To make matters much worse, lesser landowners were accelerating the rate at which land once farmed in common was being taken over (or 'enclosed') for sheep-farming, displacing many tenant families and creating a stratum of beggars and vagrants. Others who joined this influx may have had more prosperous backgrounds, or have been younger progeny of the landowning class: moneyed but without the property that had passed to their elder sibling. For most, however, who chose to take their chances with the city, a number of escape routes from poverty presented themselves. An unlikely, if always optimum, one would be to attach oneself to the entourage of one of the many officials attendant on the queen: to become, at however remote a degree, a functionary of her court. A more likely one was to fall back on one's own resources and to become part of London's thriving mercantile environment: to apprentice to a trade; to sell one's own labour, talent or learning as a service; or, if one had anything in the way of spare capital, to invest in new areas such as overseas trade. This second route was the option most were compelled to take; but it was the specific notion of investment – far less secure but at the same time with far fewer rules and restrictions to stifle progress – which promised the greatest returns.

Was this sense of opportunities opening up for the able and quick-witted alluded to in Marlowe's *Jew of Malta*? The play begins with the central character in a private moment, counting over the enormous quantities of wealth he has amassed through his trading 'venture[s]', and remarking on how:

> The needy groom, that never finger'd groat,
> Would make a miracle of thus much coin ...[6]

Incomprehension mixes with contempt for the hireling prepared 'for a pound to sweat himself to death'; yet Barabas, the Jew of the play's title, goes on to employ an image which suggests that such a grinding existence is far from inevitable, praising:

> The wealthy Moor, that in the eastern rocks
> Without control can pick his riches up ...

'Without control' – that is, without any fear of constraint – is oddly detached from a context, here. The Moor is blessed in having natural resources that strew precious stones in his path, and this happy state functions as a stark contrast to the 'needy groom' of seven lines earlier.

But it also functions as a rebuke. The 'control' from which the Moor is free does not appear to be of an exterior kind, and this makes the groom's 'restraint' appear self-willed, a failure of initiative in not taking hold of whatever advantages lie to hand. Servitude, Barabas seems to hint, is as much a product of the mind as of a lack of opportunity. He, by contrast, sets his own terms in dealing with the world:

> thus methinks should men of judgment frame
> Their means of traffic from the vulgar trade,
>
> And, as their wealth increaseth, so inclose
> Infinite riches in a little room.

Raising his opportunistic 'means of traffic' (the world of finance) above the 'vulgar trade' of those who sell their labour, Barabas also advocates the kind of 'enclosure' of resources which, as we have seen, caused huge disruption in the period. Such hoarding, such privatisation of wealth, is the logical outcome for a mind unfettered by a conventional morality. But the formulation Barabas uses – '[i]nfinite riches in little room' – is also something more. It functions as what present-day critical parlance refers to as a *trope*, a convention, whether this takes the form of figurative speech, as here, or of some kind of narrative device or structural motif.* For those who heard it uttered – among whom may have been many a 'needy groom' – a frisson of recognition of their own desires and potentials must have accompanied the programmed moral responses. To audiences crammed shoulder to shoulder with their fellow Londoners in the fully lit spaces of the public theatres, the extent of the city's human resources would be highly visible. The era's unprecedented concentration of humanity into the city brought great stresses with it – but, as Douglas Bruster puts it, it 'also enlarged the scope and extent of the market by enhancing economic activity with increased demand and opportunity for commercial exchange, legal and illegal alike.'[7]

---

* This use of the term 'trope' needs to be distinguished from the more technical sense of a *rhetorical* figure of speech which would have been familiar in early modern England. For the latter use, see Part Four: 'Rhetoric and Performance'.

The Theatre as a Commercial Space

One such area of commercial exchange – always precariously legal owing to the chronic attacks on its social worth – was the theatre itself. Beginning in earnest after 1576, when an open-air playhouse simply called The Theatre was erected in northern London, the performing of plays became a business answering in many particulars to the energy, enterprise and risk advocated by Marlowe's Barabas. The risk, however, was to be a collective one, beginning with the men who pooled their money to finance the building of The Theatre – such as James Burbage, a semi-professional actor who was by trade a 'joiner', or builder – and continuing with individuals such as Phillip Henslowe, who managed the Admiral's Men company in partnership with the actors, funded the writing of new plays for the stage out of the company's books, and (in the area which involved the serious money) purchased, stocked and hired out the clothes the actors wore on stage. The risk had to be collective: no one person could afford the sums necessary to set up and maintain a playhouse and the company who operated in it, and the nobles and monarchs who gave their names and liveries (or 'badges') to these companies were more important for 'the protection of the actors from harassment' by the authorities than for financial support.[8] The expense thus spread among 'sharers' (essentially shareholders in present-day, if slightly inexact, terms) within a company was due to a single, vitally important reason. Actors had hitherto been largely itinerant, indistinct in many people's eyes from the category of 'masterless men' or even beggars. They travelled from town to town taking their productions and props with them, mounting their performances in an ad hoc fashion wherever space became available – usually inns, which they had to hire, or marketplaces, in which performances had to be followed with a speedy round of the audience for remuneration. It had been effectively a large-scale, flamboyantly dressed 'busking' operation, allowing few certainties about the size of the audience or the financial return on their efforts. With the arrival of permanent, custom-built theatres, that situation was transformed utterly. Audiences now came to the actors on their own territory; money was regularly taken prior to the performance (the 'gate receipts'); effort could be expended in the knowledge that payment had already been forthcoming. All the risk now lay in the beginnings of the enterprise, the outlay of money to build and establish the playhouse. From then on, risk could be minimised and controlled, if never actually eradicated.

Barabas's felicitous trope about 'infinite riches in little room' thematises this shift towards a new commercial relationship between the players and paying public. That is, it makes use of the language of fantasy to draw on perceptions of a range of emergent factors – London's burgeoning population and the audience pool it created; the newly static ideology of performance space; the sense of a contract arising out of payment up front – and assists them into familiarity via the fictional world of the play. When Shakespeare came to write *Henry V* for the newly opened Globe theatre (the direct replacement for The Theatre) in 1599, the concluding words of the Chorus echo Barabas's formulation, and in a significant measure rework it:

> Thus far, with rough and all-unable pen,
> Our bending author hath pursued the story,
> In little room confining mighty men,
> Mangling by starts the full course of their glory.[9]

The trope of 'wealth' (in the form of kingly might) compressed into 'little room' is here combined with another trope – that of authorial self-deprecation. 'We [author and company together] are not worthy to attempt Henry's portrayal' is the gist of its laboured humility, rounding off similar sentiments uttered at the start of the play.[10] But anxieties about 'mangling' the subject of the play simply serve to reinforce the point about the ready availability of all things within the 'confines' of the playhouse. So excessively eager are the company to honour their contract with the audience, they seem to be saying, that they are prepared to break another kind of contract: that which should subsist between the representers and the glorious object of their representation, whereby fidelity of imitation should be guaranteed or not attempted at all. Yet it is the performers who choose to draw attention to this fact; and it is to the audience, not the spirit of the dead hero, that apologies are directed. The 'broken' representation the actors purport to offer (which, of course, will turn out to be no such thing) is at heart a gesture of good faith towards their paying public.

This idea of using notional, figurative 'contracts' with an audience was at heart a theatrical conceit having little real validity, and later playwrights such as Ben Jonson were to make fun of it (and by extension their audiences) in Prologues such as the one which precedes *Bartholomew Fair*.[11] However, relationships between theatre workers themselves – actors, writers and financiers – fully depended on a structure of contractual obligations. Because Henslowe's records happen to survive, and because he was so important for keeping money circulating through all channels of the theatre business, his case is of particular interest. Actors could be asked to sign detailed and binding agreements with him, which aimed to cover all contingencies where a default might occur – through the actor's drunkenness, through his failure to learn his lines or be costumed up in time for performances, or through his concurrent employment by a rival company – all of which were punishable by often heavy fines.[12] Henslowe had arrangements with the writers of plays, paying for and receiving works in instalments to minimise the risk of getting something unperformable (or getting nothing at all) and ensuring that, if need be, other scribal hands could complete or patch up the work. It was in no writer's interest simply to write a play and then try to sell it to a company. An 'outline' – or synopsis – was usually mooted first, and if accepted it would often be following suggestions or changes demanded by the company prior to actual composition. All this, it may be imagined, has rather severe implications for what we might want to think of as the 'integrity' of a literary work written in this period, and it is a problem we will be exploring in later chapters. The essential point to grasp is that play-writing and performing operated in this highly pressurised way because both fed into a particular system ensuring a regular turnover of new and/or perennially popular plays: the repertory system.

'Choice without Shame': The Repertory System

The repertory system – the rotation of plays over a roughly weekly cycle – was the only possible way for acting companies to meet the enormous demand for plays among the London public.[13] In a time when prices were rising without any apparent hope of relief, going to see plays in the public, open-air amphitheatres for little more than a penny a time represented, as Alfred Harbage put it, an 'almost unique opportunity' for low-income earners to get something for the money they had.[14] To keep prices as low as this, a constant output of new plays was required to ensure audience attendance figures of up to 3,500 a day at a single playhouse, and companies duly obliged with as many as forty new plays a year. This constant rotation and introduction of novelty into the system was the daily experience of theatre workers, who were responsible for a work rate and an output which can only be described as industrial. Highly active freelance writers such as Thomas Dekker could, through a mixture of single and co-authorship, be responsible for ten or more plays in a year, but freelance work was always uneven. Shakespeare, as an 'in-house' dramatist for the Chamberlain's Men, averaged a very regular output of two plays a year, alongside his other duties as actor and sharer.

This feature of theatrical production was to stamp itself onto the character of the artistic object itself, discernible in obvious ways such as the clown scenes which elongate the main action of *Doctor Faustus* (often argued to be by another hand than Marlowe's) and in less obvious ways such as the crafting of characters appropriate to particular performers in the company according to a type-casting no longer recoverable to us. As Andrew Gurr has argued, 'the repertory system was intense … and some systematisation would have been unavoidable'.[15] If novelty was in demand and willingly attained to by the theatre professionals, much elasticity would have accompanied it to persuade audiences that they were getting that purest of ideological justifications for an honest profit: choice. Stephen Gosson, a one-time playwright turned detractor of the theatre, tried as he saw it to expose the tawdriness he believed underpinned this system of 'choice without shame'; but in targeting the theatre itself on moral grounds he drew attention to the more abiding object of dread among social conservatives – that of a populace wielding its own purchasing power unchecked, and undirected.[16]

A writer who begins by taking money in an industry and who then turns on it so vituperatively appears harsh by our present-day standards, but there were specific reasons why such a standpoint could be embraced in Elizabethan England (as it was to be later by Ben Jonson in his poem 'Come leave the loathed stage'). An ideal of the value of literature was inculcated by a 'humanist' system of educating schoolchildren which had been in place since before the Reformation. Classical writers, historians and political theorists such as Horace, Livy and Cicero were now taught alongside the more familiar rote instruction from the Bible and the medieval philosophers, and among these an argument for writing as 'letters' – that is, as a practical contribution to the running of the state – was forcefully urged. The educational theorist Roger Ascham made this case in his programmatic text *The Schoolmaster* (1570); and although he had been tutor to the young Elizabeth, he envisaged the doctrine as one which might cascade downward a few levels socially:

> the youth of England, specially gentlemen, and namely nobility ... when they should be called forth to the execution of great affairs in service of their prince and country ... might be able to use and order all experiences ... according to square, rule, and line of wisdom, learning and virtue.

That initial, expansive gesture towards national inclusiveness ('the youth of England') narrows rather hurriedly towards the safer ground promised to an educational elite. Nevertheless, the grammar schools as well as the private tutors of the gentry and nobility shaped their educational strategies towards this ideal of 'service', and it fostered a complex sense of the relation between literary production and social worth.

A figure such as the courtier Sir Philip Sidney embodied the ideal at its purest. His prose works such as the *Arcadia* and his innovative sonnet sequence *Astrophil and Stella* began life as texts written for a close circle of friends and followers, subtly embedding political commentary and Protestant ideology within fantastic and often dazzlingly erotic narrative settings. These works were shared within this circle, copied out by hand, maintaining a resistance to the growing pull of the medium of print which might imply a profit motive.* But Sidney was rich and well placed and could afford to indulge in the image of the writer whose motives were public but whose coterie was private and whose stance remained amateur. At the other end of the scale in personal fortunes there was someone like Gosson: a university education cut short by lack of finances; an early literary career writing on a commissioned basis; striving to wrestle the staunchly humanist themes of plays such as his *Catiline's Conspiracies* (written to illustrate 'the necessary government of learned men in Cicero') through the free-running stream of tastes – the 'choice without shame' – of a market system.[17]

A dependence on this system was felt to be humbling by such reluctant professional writers, and the remedy most anxiously sought was a transference of that dependency onto a patron: a great man or woman who could afford them protection and some measure of financial support. Hence it was that Gosson was to dedicate his first stinging attack on the theatre (a print work entitled, with tartly humanist overtones, *The Schoole of Abuse*) to Philip Sidney himself, begging leave to 'present my Schoole, my cunning and my selfe to your worthy Patronage'.[18] Operating alongside the independent market for writing, this system of individual patronage kept itself quite distinct while at the same time continually intersecting with it, not least because new writers would be bidding for (and not just reaffirming) a patron's favours via the medium of such dedications. In Gosson's case the 'bid' backfired, and was to find itself on the receiving end of a corrective in the form of Sidney's more even-handed (and vastly more influential) *An Apology for Poetry* of 1595. A far more successful instance is provided by Ben Jonson's relationship to the Earl of Pembroke, William Herbert, whose willingness to act up to

---

* All these works did become available in print after Sidney's death.

the role of 'Maecenas' helped keep Jonson's career afloat financially and saved him from political danger when his writings edged into scandal.* However, as Kathleen McLuskie has argued, 'patronage transcended mere payment': it also supplied a way of sustaining cultural belief in a 'sacred vocation of poetry which was only accorded to those who knew they were true poets by virtue of having true patrons'.[19]

This opposition between the ideas of amateur and professional writers was to stiffen towards the turn of the century in relation to those who wrote for the theatre. Nonetheless, as the above scenario shows, it existed mainly in the imaginations of writers who saw it as a way of sustaining the ideal of an intellectual elite who wrote to advance the cause of learning rather than to earn a living. In practice, the economic realities of being a poet in a crowded marketplace dictated that almost everyone was 'professional' to some degree or other, and there were those, including Shakespeare, who not only embraced the category but thrived within it. In 1594, when Marlowe's *Jew of Malta* was beginning the new season at the re-opened Rose theatre and Shakespeare was just starting his long collaboration with the Chamberlain's Men, it was possible to find writers from many divergent backgrounds – university, the trade of acting, or simply self-taught and searching for an opening in a still-new vocation – catering for an audience pool of equally impressive social diversity.[20] In a subsequent chapter we will look in more detail at the phenomenon of the boy player companies – the 'little eyases' bemoaned by one of the characters in Shakespeare's *Hamlet* – that complicated this picture and lent some assistance to the increasingly confected status of the 'non-professional professional': the playwright who could carry on his trade in the security that he was not being seen as a tradesman. This phenomenon was several years off, however, and in 1594 the 'poet and the player' – that is, the learned writer and the industry craftsman – had as yet no need to go 'to cuffs' over the issue.[21]

---

* William Herbert is also a highly plausible candidate for the dedicatee of Shakespeare's Sonnets.

Before he was killed in 1593, Marlowe's career demonstrated how a writer could span the various positions that were later to emerge as contradictions. He had patrons, such as Lord Strange, who paid him to write *The Jew of Malta* for the company of actors, Lord Strange's Men, which operated under his name; but he had also earlier worked independently on plays such as *Tamburlaine*. He was university educated; but he was sent to Cambridge as a scholarship boy from a poor background, and by involving himself while still a student with the most conspiratorial domain of Elizabethan politics – infiltrating Catholic circles – he operated at the outer limits of the humanist ideal of state 'service'. He was deeply respected and widely imitated by other writers; but his fame also ensured that 'Marlowe' became a kind of brand name: a place where different textual fragments – controversial beliefs, outspoken views – could meet and be ascribed to him, as much as the place from which they were produced. This notorious function was to cost Marlowe his life, as the authorities, increasingly unnerved by the mishmash of inflammatory utterances laid at his door, had him ever more closely watched and (it seems a fair assumption) permanently silenced.[22] Some if not all of these utterances (atheistic, blasphemous, sexually transgressive) may well have been Marlowe's. What impresses from this historical distance is the powerful impetus his professional career as a playwright gave to the free circulation of textual matter through the society in which he lived: a more useful approach to the idea of authorship in this period, perhaps, than the ossified professional/amateur distinction some of the later playwrights attempted to install.

Two final points can be made here through a consideration of *The Jew of Malta*'s place in the literary and social world of late Elizabethan England. The first concerns the importance we need to accord *intertextuality*, in terms of the arguments offered here about the repertory system, and those which follow on from the writer's practical position as a mediator of texts in the period. William Shakespeare wrote *The Merchant of Venice* for his now-permanent employers, the Chamberlain's Men at The Theatre, a few years after the resumption of theatrical activity in London, perhaps as early as 1596 – adapting an Italian romantic prose source but enlarging its dramatic scope via 'the stupendous power of Shylock', the play's equivalent of Barabas.[23] It remains the most overt example in Shakespeare's canon of a reduplication of themes and character types; and that it was understood as such at the time is suggested by the fact that *The Merchant of Venice* is first recorded along with an alternative title, 'The Jewe of Venyce'.[24] We can plausibly assign a deliberate, commercial motive for the play, coming so soon after the historical events described earlier and performed while Marlowe's old favourite was still on the boards of a rival playhouse; and this should be encouragement to look out for other, less overt traces of such textual interactions; to think through their possible motivations, and how they might help us to materialise the work under scrutiny.

The second point concerns the issue of genre, a concept also examined in Part One: 'Introduction', but which can be introduced here via reflection on the resistance of modern-day critics to the Elizabethan categorisation of Marlowe's play as a 'tragedy'.[25] Internal evidence (the play's Prologue) as well as external (the first recorded reference to the play) shows consistency here, and yet no one today is comfortable with this designation, finding that by comparison with the tragedies of Shakespeare the play is at best a kind of super-cynical, bloody farce. Yet such problems are not just the product of a historical gap in tastes. An earlier play by Marlowe, the two-part *Tamburlaine*, is first recorded as a 'commicall discourse', but is later referred to as a 'Tragicall discourse', suggesting a degree of fluidity in reception of the dramatic text among Elizabethans themselves.[26] In the chapters which follow we will need to remain aware that while dramatic genres might have *represented* stable categories, they rarely prevailed as such when it came to the fashioning of the artistic object. This could result in a degree of tension between the ideal of the genre and its material manifestation: a tension reflected at the taxonomic level (by those whose job it was simply to record the play's category); the critical level (Sidney's *An Apology for Poetry* objects to, in his words, 'mongrel' genres like tragicomedy); and the commercial one (in *Hamlet*, Polonius's description of 'tragical-comical-historical-pastoral' plays is taken from a theatrical advertisement which appears to satirise its own efforts to please all-comers).[27] Keeping these levels in mind will help to test our own assumptions about how to read each particular play, and afford us a sense of the artistic opportunities opened up by an expanding market for theatre.

Notes

1   For *The Jew of Malta* as the first play to be performed at the re-opened Rose theatre in May 1594, see Henslowe's entry in *English Professional Theatre 1530–1660*, ed. Glynne Wickham, Herbert Berry and William Ingram, Theatre in Europe: A Documentary History (Cambridge: Cambridge University Press, 2000), record number 344, pp. 431–2.

2   For a lively and succinct account see Susan Brigden, *New Worlds, Lost Worlds: The Rule of the Tudors 1485–1603* (Harmondsworth: Penguin, 2000), pp. 290–4.

3   For a detailed analysis of the poem in full and its political connotations, see Marion Wynn-Davies, *Sidney to Milton 1580–1660*, Transitions Series (Houndmills: Palgrave Macmillan, 2003), pp. 1–7.

4   Queen Elizabeth I, 'The doubt of future foes exiles my present joy', in *The Penguin Book of Renaissance Verse 1509–1659*, ed. David Norbrook and H. R. Woudhuysen (Harmondsworth: Penguin, 1993), p. 95. Spelling modernised for this volume.

5   Quoted in Douglas Bruster, *Drama and the Market in the Age of Shakespeare* (Cambridge: Cambridge University Press, 1992), p. 20.

6   Christopher Marlowe, *The Jew of Malta* in *The Complete Plays*, ed. J.B. Steane (Harmondsworth: Penguin, 1969), I.i.1–37.

7   Bruster, *Drama and the Market*, p. 19.

8   Mary I. Oates and William J. Baumol, 'On the Economics of the Theatre in Renaissance London', *Swedish Journal of Economics*, 1972, pp. 136–60, p. 143.

9   William Shakespeare, *Henry V*, ed. T. W. Craik, Arden, 3rd series (London: Thomson Learning, 1995), Epilogue, ll. 1–4.

10   See the opening speech of the Chorus and request for audience pardon of 'The flat unraised spirits that hath dared / On this unworthy scaffold to bring forth / So great an object', *Henry V*, Prologue, ll. 8–11.

11   See the satirical 'Articles of Agreement, indented, between the spectators or hearers at the Hope on the Bankside', etc. in Ben Jonson, *Bartholomew Fair*, ed. G. R. Hibbard, New Mermaids (London: A & C Black Ltd, 1994), Induction, pp. 62 ff.

12   Stanley Wells, *Shakespeare & Co.* (London: Penguin, 2007), pp. 19–21, has a brief but fascinating account of Henslowe's dealings with actors. See entry

no. 197 in Wickham (ed.), *English Professional Theatre 1530–1660*, pp. 282–4, for an example of a contract drawn up by Henslowe.

13   See Roslyn Knutson, *The Repertory of Shakespeare's company 1594–1613*, 1991, p. 32, for an estimated turnover of a different play every day, five to eight days in a row, before resumption of the cycle.

14   Alfred Harbage, *Shakespeare's Audience* (New York: Columbia University Press, 1941), p. 64.

15   Andrew Gurr, *The Shakespearean Stage 1574–1642*, 3rd edn (Cambridge: Cambridge University Press, 1992; 1994), p. 105.

16   No plays of Gosson's survive, but a lengthy polemic directed at his one-time employer, the stage, does, structured – ironically enough – in five acts. See Stephen Gosson, *Plays Confuted in Five Actions*. As Gosson puts it, 'Mine eyes th[o]roughly behold the manner of Theatres, when I wrote plays myself, and found them to be the very markets of bawdry, where choice w[i]thout shame hath been as free as it is for your money in the Royal Exchange': for further discussion see Bruster, *Drama and the Market*, p. 6.

17   Stephen Gosson, *The Schoole of Abuse*, 1579, p. 23.

18   Gosson, *Schoole*, 'Epistle Dedicatory'.

19   Kathleen McLuskie, 'The Poet's Royal Exchange; Patronage and Commerce in early Modern Drama', in *Yearbook of English Studies, 1991* (21), pp. 53–62, p. 59.

20   Audiences remain a contentious area in scholarship of the Shakespearean period, with many disagreements of emphasis over social make-up. For a helpful review of the arguments, see Andrew Gurr, *Playgoing in Shakespeare's London*, 2nd edn (Cambridge: Cambridge University Press, 1996), pp. 3–5.

21   William Shakespeare, *Hamlet*, ed. Harold Jenkins, Arden, 2nd series (London: Routledge, 1982), II.ii.336–55.

22   For a detailed but highly readable account of the intrigue surrounding Marlowe's death, see Charles Nicholl, *The Reckoning: The Murder of Christopher Marlowe* (London: Cape, 1992).

23   Greenblatt, *Will in the World*, p. 271.

24   E. K. Chambers, *The Elizabethan Stage*, 4 vols (Oxford: Clarendon, 1923), vol. 3, p. 484.

25   For a review of this problem see James R. Siemon's introduction to the most recent New Mermaids edition of the play: Christopher Marlowe, *The Jew of Malta* (London: A & C Black, 1994), pp. xix–xxxviii.

26   For one possible explanation for this shift in designation see Lennard and Luckhurst, *The Drama Handbook*, p. 54.

27   Philip Sidney, *An Apology for Poetry*, in *The Norton Anthology of Theory and Criticism*, ed. Vincent B. Leitch et al. (London: W. W. Norton & Company), pp. 326–62, p. 357.

Part Three
Texts, Writers and Contexts

Comedies of Eros: *Galatea* and *A Midsummer Night's Dream*

> The ground work of Comedies, is love, cozenage, flattery, bawdry, sly conveyance of whoredome. The persons, cooks, queanes [i.e. prostitutes], knaves, bawds, parasites, courtesans, lecherous old men, amorous young men.
>
> Stephen Gosson, *Plays Confuted in Five Actions* (1582)

It seems rather unfair to start a discussion of comedy with a blast from one of the 'anti-theatrical' writers, especially one as bitterly reductive as this from Stephen Gosson (whom we encountered in the last chapter). Written in the early 1580s, a safe distance in time from the Shakespearean developments in comedy of the following decade, it nonetheless gives a sense of some of the core assumptions about dramatic comedy which were circulating in the Elizabethan period. In modern critical parlance we could say that they contributed to the 'horizon of expectations' about the genre. Gosson, an ex-playwright himself, frames his assessment in knowledgeable terms, purporting to make statements about generic structure (the 'ground work' of the plays) and of generic content (e.g. their 'persons'). Yet when it comes down to it, he chooses to focus – almost to the exclusion of other features – on the amorous (or, more specifically, sexual) content of the comic drama. Is this mendacious oversimplification? Or did he have some justification for doing so?

The comic in its broadest sense (as distinct from Comedy as a dramatic form) could encompass a very large range of situations and narrative permutations in the Elizabethan period, just as it does today. A glance through the posthumous, anecdotal jest book of Elizabethan London's most famous theatrical clown, Richard Tarlton (who was attached to the Queen's Men company of players and who died in the Armada year of 1588) gives a good sense of this range, and also shows that some of what Elizabethans evidently found funny matches up well with present-day approaches to the comic at both the practical and the theoretical levels. Take, for example, this reported encounter at a village fair between Tarlton and a recently married, rather eccentric young gentleman called Mr Sunbanke, who:

> had [t]his property with his necke, not to stirre it any way but to turne body and all. It chanced at the Faire end, he stood to pisse against a wall: to whom Tarlton came, and clapping him on the shoulder, God give you joy of your marriage, saies he, Mr Sunbanke, being taken pissing against the wall would have looked back to thank him, and suddenly turnes about body and all in the view of many, and shewed all ...[1]

When at the beginning of the twentieth century the philosopher Henri Bergson wrote his treatise on laughter (1900), he identified a universal human responsiveness to perceptions of what he called 'the mechanical within the living': humour is found in behaviour which momentarily reduces a person to the status of an automaton, an inflexible thing.[2] Behavioural inflexibility, exposure and humiliation are perennial comic tropes, thoroughly familiar from contemporary film and television comedy (the famous bar-propping disaster from *Only Fools and Horses* springs instantly to mind). They were to feature, as we shall see, in Shakespeare's dramatic treatment of some of his own comic characters, including Bottom and Malvolio. Other scenarios from *Tarltons's Jests* involving duelling, extemporal wit and interminable allusions to cuckoldry are perhaps less accessible to us now, but nonetheless attest to a readiness to find comic material within the most familiar business of day-to-day life. The stage was to make continual use of this kind of material, often felicitously working it into plots taken from classical dramatic narratives, prose romances or folk tales.

Comedy on the Elizabethan Stage

Imposing shape and order onto the teeming possibilities of this material was another matter, and leads us back to Gosson's seemingly reductive claims about the amorous 'ground work' of comedy. A vast number of Elizabethan and Jacobean comedies end in marriages – almost all of Shakespeare's do* – and this is often cited as one of the most reliable structural definitions for the genre in this period, at least where Shakespearean comedy is concerned. The conclusion in marriage was one of the legacies of the so-called New Comedy which classical drama bequeathed to Renaissance dramaturgy, developed by the Roman playwrights Plautus and Terence out of antecedents in the Greek drama (we will touch on Plautine comic themes in more detail in the discussion of *Twelfth Night*). The distinguishing feature of New Comedy was its movement away from a coarser, more ribald comic format, improving upon it by adding a strong spine of narrative interest in the shape of a romantic plot, usually involving a young couple who defy parental disapproval to marry. The 'love' element can be seen as providing the binding agent within a larger mix of elements which certainly included its share of licentious and scandalous material. It is most probably these that Gosson is alluding to when he rails against 'knaves', 'parasites' and 'courtesans' engaged in acts of 'bawdry' and 'cozening' (cheating). These were all stock character types from the Roman drama which were frequently reproduced in one form or another in the plays of the early modern period, mediated to it via the sixteenth-century theatrical innovation of the Italian 'Commedia dell'arte' (improvised, mask-based performances relying heavily on these roles). Their presence in the comic narrative thus reflects the one consistently held theoretical position about comedy deriving from classical discussions of the genre: that it shows people who are 'inferior', as Aristotle put it, to the moral norm, possessed

---

* The one Shakespearean exception, *Love's Labour's Lost* (1595), ends with a neat reversal of the convention, the ladies deferring marriage for a year until the men, previously hostile to courtship, have proved themselves sufficiently consistent to make worthy husbands.

of an intrinsic 'error and ugliness' that is, however, 'not painful', and who can be held up to ridicule as a result.[3]

The idea of ridiculing the morally defective might seem to recover a beneficial purpose for comedy, and in his *An Apology for Poetry* of 1595 Philip Sidney, despite his strong reservations about the genre, could rehearse the Aristotelian view that comedy was 'an imitation of the common errors of our life' presented in 'so ridiculous and scornful sort' that no 'beholder can be content to be such a one'.[4] Nonetheless, to comedy's critics the effect on the audience of putting amorous themes on the stage outweighed any moral benefits the adaptation of the New Comedy format might have. Like present-day 'moral panics' around the imitation of extreme violence in films, or the compulsive nature of computer games, we get a sense of the kinds of pleasure that were being associated with specific artistic forms in Gosson's argument that comedies could arouse 'carnal delight' – physical pleasure of a sort – which 'hindreth the course of reason' and 'whets us to wantonness'. Here it is not just the subject of the comedy which is carnal: its effect on the audience is imagined to be so, too, and this sense that comic themes could reach down from the stage to compel copycat behaviour among the audience is one which was frequently aired. Another writer, Gervase Babington, thought that the performative aspects of comedy were particularly at fault, suggesting a kind of chain reaction via the stage by which the actors 'corrupt the eyes with alluring gestures: the eyes, the heart: and the heart the body'.[5] A contemporary of Gosson's, Phillip Stubbes, makes this point even more explicit in his *Anatomie of Abuses* – a catch-all, sin-by-sin 'everything that's wrong with England today' tract, which gives generous space to the argument that, in the theatre:

> such wanton gestures, such bawdy speeches, such laughing and fleering, such kissing and bussing, such clipping and culling, such winking and glancing of wanton eyes, and the like, is used, as is wonderful to behold ... these goodly pageants being done, every mate sorts to his mate, every one brings another homeward of their way very friendly, and in their secret conclaves (covertly) they play the Sodomites, or worse.[6]

This last reference to 'Sodomites' introduces a special complication into ideas about the theatre's impact on society. Ostensibly it means anyone, man or woman, committing a sinful act of the kind Stubbes supposes inevitable among an audience inflamed by erotic spectacle. But we need to be aware, as a first rule of interpreting any statements about the performing of plays from this period, that only males were allowed to be actors on the public stage. Boys most usually, but younger men not infrequently, took the parts of all female characters in a play; and the practice, while attempting to sidestep the scandal of having women on stage, entailed another scandal – that of transvestism, or 'cross-dressing', explicitly prohibited by the Bible (Deuteronomy 22:5). There should be little doubt here that Stubbes allows a homoerotic form of pleasure in watching boys or men act the parts of women to be understood through the narrowly gendered lexis of the passage ('every mate sorts to his mate').

Feverish in tone as such claims may appear to be, they are nonetheless statements about theatrical pleasure; and while their broad front may be aimed at plays of all genres, the specific thrust of their attacks is the 'love' plots which they assume (with some justification) formed the core of the comic genre on the English stage. The anti-theatrical assault on the rewards of comedy ranges more widely than this, and Gosson in particular has much to say about the way the 'delight' conveyed by comedies encourages 'excessive laughter' which is an enemy to 'temperance', and about the addictive nature of the genre ('the more we gaze, the more we crave'). But it is the specific taint of 'wantonness' which supplies the most potent objection, since through it the subjects of comedies, the process of their enactment and the nature of their impact on the audience can all be lumped together in an argument which becomes self-reinforcing. Many of those plays which took the greatest risks with sexual and marital themes – Shakespeare's *Measure for Measure*, Middleton's *A Chaste Maid in Cheapside*, John Day's *The Isle of Gulls*, for example – were as yet more than a decade away. However, there was at this time a sphere of comedy in which such themes were broached quite freely and frequently, and which matches up in some respects to the accusations made by the anti-theatrical writers. Because this sphere was that of Queen Elizabeth and her court, however, and because the plays drew on classical myth and allegory to advance their subject matter, it could operate relatively free from the objections made to the products of the newly and fully commercial theatre of the suburbs. As an example of one such 'comedy of eros', we will look at John Lyly's *Galatea*.

Practising Impossibilities: Desire and Transformation in *Galatea*

John Lyly's *Galatea* (1585) is one of a small number of plays we will be looking at which were written for and performed exclusively by a boy's company: in this case, the Boys of St Paul's.* Since the great majority of characters in it are female, the play's production thus makes exemplary use of the special resource associated with the boy actors: female impersonation. The story centres on the fortunes of two young girls from a (highly allegorised) North of England setting, whose fathers both have the idea of disguising them as boys and forcing them to flee home to evade a custom of the community requiring the sacrifice of their most beautiful virgin to the god Neptune. Chance encounters in a woodland filled with supernatural beings, the comic crosses of true love, a gallery of rude-witted workmen, and a magical transformation all feature strongly among the ingredients. The play's formal structure, typical of Lyly's dramatic practice, elicits consideration from the outset. Three narrative strands unfold via regularly alternating scenes within the central locale of the woodland, but are fully brought together only in the play's final scene. The 'disguised virgin' strand is the longest by a slight margin, outlining the complications which arise as the two fugitives encounter one another while another girl, Hebe, is sacrificed in lieu of them (only to be rejected as not beautiful enough by Neptune's monstrous proxy, the Agar).

The play's second strand involves the prank played by Cupid upon the goddess Diana and her retinue of nymphs – the native inhabitants of the woodland which the girls flee into. Deciding on a whim to undermine

---

* Although the play was written in 1585, a number of delays meant that it did not see performance until 1588.

their sacred vow of chastity, the boy-god infiltrates their sect disguised as a girl and unleashes his arrows of desire among them. A marginally shorter strand, it has some claim to being the dominant one in narrative terms: for when Cupid is finally caught by the outraged nymphs, his resulting torture and enslavement brings in his mother, Venus, and sets the two goddesses, violently opposed in natures, against each other. The problem is resolved by the appearance of Neptune who strikes a bargain: if Diana will release Cupid, he will in turn soften his attitude towards the institution of virginity and rescind the sacrificial custom.

The third strand involves a trio of 'masterless men', comically distanced from the distressed class we looked at in the last chapter (even their starvation is rendered clownish), and their plan to find an employer. Masters are found, in the form of an Alchemist and then an Astronomer, but they prove to be so completely incompetent as to be unable to feed or pay their apprentices. Although seemingly subsidiary in comic matter, this strand is comparable in length with the others; and taken together the equal weighting of the narratives give the sense of a play held carefully and dextrously in balance.

The interleaving of these stories is, until the conclusion, very slight; but it hinges upon a crucial and unexpected dramatic development – that of same-sex love. When the two disguised girls encounter one another in the woods, their response (following an initial comic effort to learn patterns of 'male' behaviour from each other) is to fall promptly in love, each apparently charmed by the outward show of 'that fair boy's favour'.*,7 There follows a pair of soliloquies in which the two girls bemoan their bad luck and crave a resolution:

> GALATEA: Miserable Galatea, that, having put on the apparel of a boy, thou canst not also put on the mind. O fair Melibeus!
> ... Why did nature to him, a boy, give a face so fair, or to me, a virgin, a fortune so hard ... ?

---

* In the dialogues that follow we encounter Galatea hiding under the male alias of Tityrus, while Phillida hides under that of Melibeus.

[…]

PHILLIDA: Poor Phillida … Art thou no sooner in the habit of a
boy but thou must be enamored of a boy? … Go into the woods,
and transgress in love a little of thy modesty. I will – I dare not.
Thou must – I cannot … (II.iv–II.v)

While fully consistent at this stage with the language of thwarted
heterosexual love, the next encounter between the girls shows their
obsession with an unusually fair masculine 'favour' exerting interesting
pressures on their addresses to one another, as when Phillida exclaims:

It is a pity that nature framed you not a woman, having a face so
fair, so lovely a countenance, so modest a behaviour. (III.i.1.)

Phillida's 'regret' seems to work on a number of levels here. From the
standpoint of her male disguise, it is a piece of masculine bravado,
paying the licensed compliment of beauty to another boy ('if you were a
girl I'd *so* fancy you!'). From the standpoint of the fugitive girl beneath,
it is a more anxious declaration in favour of resolving the immediate
romantic crux ('I can't risk falling in love with a boy just now!'). But
from the standpoint of aesthetic principle, one which in this case views
the female body as the supreme object of erotic attention, it is a desire
already fulfilled ('you're too lovely to be anything but a girl!'). Galatea's
reply, 'I would not wish to be a woman, unless it were because thou art a
man', and Phillida's rejoinder, 'Nay, do not wish to be a woman, for then
I should not love thee' (ll. 8–11), develop the heterosexual flirtations
of the exchange by making use of the handy tradition of 'platonic love'
between men. But they too carry some ambiguities of sense: *unless it
were* because thou art a man'? Surely Galatea believes the other speaker's
'maleness' is a given? Cast in such conditional language, that belief is
in danger of sounding rather incidental to the primary issue of erotic
attraction growing between them. At the start of the dialogue both girls
are fully under the illusion that the other is a boy, but disguises start to
go awry as their simultaneous efforts to hint at their femininity to the
other become more urgent:

PHILLIDA [*aside*]: What doubtful speeches be these! I fear me he is as I am, a maiden!

GALATEA [*aside*]: What dread riseth in my mind! I fear the boy to be as I am, a maiden! (III.i.31)

The resulting 'quandary' is strictly irresolvable since neither can jettison their disguise to be sure of the truth. Yet it is striking that the new note of sexual uncertainty results neither in aversion nor in caution but in a kind of deflated acquiescence, not least in Phillida's closing invitation to Galatea: 'Come, let us into the grove, and make much of one another, that cannot tell what to think of each other' (III.i.63).

The love affair between Galatea and Phillida, central in terms of narrative interest, does not by itself drive forward any key narrative developments, as later scenes show them moping together in the woods, continuing to make 'much of one another' while approaching ever greater realisation of their true gender identities. It is the intersection of this static plot line with that of the more dynamic Cupid strand which will move the story towards its comic outcome, and it is once again the issue of (female) same-sex love which provides the impetus. Immediately after the scene in which the two disguised girls meet and feel the first stirrings of love, Cupid appears, threatening as part of his design against the nymphs to:

make their pains my pastimes, and so confound their loves in their own sex that they shall dote in their desires, delight in their affections, and practice only impossibilities. (II.ii.1–10)

Cupid's intention to 'confound' the nymphs' 'loves in their own sex' provides the play's most explicit evocation of erotic love between women, and it does so by placing it within an order of error different from that reserved thus far for the disguised girls. While the attraction between Galatea and Phillida can always be recovered as a heterosexual 'misunderstanding', the desires Cupid wants to inflict upon the nymphs belong, from his vengefully heterosexual standpoint, to the realm of 'impossibilities', that is to say strictly physical 'absurdities'. This needs to be read as a denial less of erotic possibilities than of dramatic ones, however. The spectacle of nymphs openly desiring one another could not be countenanced on the Elizabethan stage, and Cupid's objectives are sublimated as quickly as they are uttered via the handy expedient of having two beautiful 'boys' in the woods for the nymphs to focus their attentions on. As the nymphs squabble over who is to enjoy the love of which, the relationship between the two main narrative strands becomes clear. The erotic complications of same-sex desire so briefly raised by Cupid are fully absorbed by the Galatea–Phillida romance, which can perpetuate them in a more deniable form via the convenient 'disguise' motif.

Such deniability is the province of performance, with its priority on gesture, costume, and the sounds of words (creating multiple connotations) over their strict sense, all of which can be wrested into implying something other than they appear to. Yet it is especially striking that this 'deniability' of female same-sex love is carried on through an explicit expression of male-to-male desire, as the two girls attempt to prise the truth out of each other even while they push their suits of love:

> PHILLIDA: Seeing we are both boys, and both lovers, that our affection may have some show and seem as it were love, let me call thee mistress. (IV.iv.16–18)

Although this should be scarcely more admissible on stage than female same-sex desire, it is allowable here because it represents the form of feeling at the greatest degree of remove from the story: male-to-male desire is fully deniable by all the circumstances of the fiction. Yet it also manages to exercise the maximum amount of licence granted by the resources of the performance. The plays Lyly wrote for his courtly audience were all performed by boy actors, drawn from the ranks of choristers. What an audience would thus be witnessing in such a scene is two young male choristers impersonating the parts of two young girls in their own disguised roles of two young boys, indicating their female passion for one another in their looks and gestures while expressing their male passion for one another in their words. The layering of discrete roles is sufficient to make the homoerotic conceit 'safe', while the exact physical match between the characters and performers (boy actors playing 'boy' 'lovers') is enough to sustain its potency. The lightness of touch with which Lyly broaches such themes becomes most evident in the final scene, where all complications are resolved. As soon as Neptune has lifted the sacrificial burden on the land as part of his mediation between Venus and Diana, the two girls emerge from hiding and drop their disguises, to mutual dismay – each has indeed fallen in love with another girl. In the play's ideology of human affections female love is nigh undo-able, and this gives the girls the steadfastness they need to resist Diana's argument from nature:

> DIANA: Now things falling out as they do, you must leave these fond-found affections. Nature will have it so; necessity must.
> GALATEA: I will never love any but Phillida. Her love is engraven in my heart with her eyes.
> PHILLIDA: Nor I any but Galatea, whose faith is imprinted in my thoughts by her words. (V.iii.137–8)

Luckily the matter can be referred to the expert, Venus, who declares of their choice: 'I like well and allow it. They shall both be possessed of their wishes'; and it is only after leaving a good ten lines for everyone to digest this notion that she presents a resolution admissible to all. One of the girls will be transformed into a man, although '[n]either of them shall know whose lot it shall be till they come to the church door' (l. 151, l. 183). The solution *is* satisfying to the requirements of heterosexual convention because the girls have maintained all along that they were deceived by the other's male 'attire' (see ll. 127–31). But it is comically glib as well, given that it was the 'face of a maiden' that each has 'doted' on, and that Venus' expressed pleasure in their new-found love derives from its very repudiation of 'nature and fortune' (l. 124, l. 144).

Love in Translation: *A Midsummer Night's Dream*

The gender transformation which enables the comic conclusion of *Galatea* is borrowed by Lyly from one of the richest seams of classical narrative to be mined by Elizabethan writers: Ovid's *Metamorphoses*, of which an English translation by Arthur Golding had appeared as recently as 1567. These stories' appeal lay partly in the pleasure afforded by their habit of finishing an often outlandish tale with a dramatic, transformative ending rather than a moral or pious one, and Shakespeare was to make continual use of them, particularly at the start of his career as a dramatist. Sometimes this use took the form of direct and heavily signposted borrowings of narrative content rather than the magical conclusion itself, as in the Roman tragedy *Titus Andronicus*, where the character Lavinia – raped and with her tongue torn out – brings on stage an actual copy of the *Metamorphoses* to recall a story similar to hers and help reveal her assailants. Sometimes the debt could be exacted more in spirit, as it was to be in *A Midsummer Night's Dream*, where Ovid comes as much by Lyly's influence as by direct borrowing. The play was geared towards a much wider audience than Lyly's, possibly being performed at The Theatre soon after the reopening of the London theatres in 1594; but its setting involves a comparable blend of classical (i.e. ancient Athenian) and local English flavours. Chance encounters in a woodland filled with supernatural beings, the comic crosses of true love, a gallery of rude-witted workmen, and a magical transformation all feature strongly, once again, among the ingredients.[8]

These ingredients are similarly distributed among three dramatic spheres: the romantic, in the form of the two fugitive lovers Hermia and Lysander, who escape into a woodland to avoid Hermia's compelled marriage to Demetrius; the supernatural, in the form of the wood's (temporary) fairy inhabitants ruled over by the quarrelling Oberon and his queen, Titania; and the 'mechanical', to use a favoured Shakespearean term for an artisanal (rather than masterless) class of workmen, rehearsing a play in the woods for performance as a civic offering to Athens's ruler, Theseus, and his bride to be, Hippolyta. These distinct strands are more closely integrated than was the case in Lyly's play, with heterogeneity among plot lines as necessary for their resolution as for their complication within the single locale of the woodland. The story of the lovers in flight from the patriarchal control of marriage choice is initially complicated

---

* This duplication of romantic couples whose crossed allegiances form the basis of the comic intrigue is a persistent Shakespearean motif, introduced in one his earliest plays, *The Two Gentlemen of Verona*, where the debt to the conventions of Italian comedy is more overt.

from within, by having Hermia's spurned lover, Demetrius, pursue them with vengeful intent, himself followed by Helena, whom he has spurned for Hermia.* In *A Midsummer Night's Dream* it is, as Harold Brooks points out, taken through 'the complete range of permutations' (at least in terms of male-to-female attraction) as the result of the magical influence on their affections exercised by the fairy, Puck.* Commanded by Oberon to restore Demetrius' love for Helena through the application of a magic 'juice', he mistakenly applies it to Lysander as well as its intended target, with a full transferral onto Helena of the 'two-men-in-love-with-one-woman' scenario.[9] Active plot complication within – rather than gentle attenuation of – the romantic narrative distinguishes the Shakespearean handling of love's 'transformations' from the Lylyan one.

Although the dramatic possibilities of desire and rejection are exhaustively worked out among the Athenian lovers, it is possible to argue that they function as secondary to the spectacular realignment of affection in the Titania–Bottom 'romance'. The 'juice' applied to the lovers on Oberon's orders as a corrective to male inconstancy is intended primarily for his insubordinate wife, in an adaptation of a classic 'love-cure' technique by which one erotic fixation is driven out by another. The love-object here, however, is at first sight a maternal rather than an erotic one: a changeling child – an orphaned Indian boy – raised by Titania but now demanded by Oberon for his train. Oberon's attitude is moreover less corrective than it is malevolent towards his wife – 'thou shalt not from this grove / Till I torment thee for this injury' is his muttered response to her continued retention of the child. The odd sense of a disconnection between his grievance and his means of revenge is evident from his soliloquy:

> I'll watch Titania when she is asleep,
> And drip the liquor of it in her eyes:
> The next thing then she waking looks upon
> (Be it lion, bear, or wolf, or bull,
> On meddling monkey, or on busy ape)

---

* My thanks to John Peacock, who pointed out to me the mime version of the play staged by Lindsay Kemp (and filmed in 1985) which explored the same-sex erotic possibilities within the quartet of lovers.

She shall pursue it with the soul of love.
And ere I take this charm from off her sight
[...]
I'll make her render up her page to me. (II.i.177–85)

It is in fact difficult to ascertain whether the demand for the human property of a changeling boy is the root of their quarrel or the price exacted for the infidelities with which they accuse one another in their first angry exchange. The Indian child seems to sit at the intersection of several of Oberon's 'forgeries of jealousy' since, as Puck reports, his queen 'withholds the loved boy, / Crowns him with flowers, and makes him all her joy' (l. 81, ll. 26–7). In Oberon's plan these are precisely the favours he now wishes to see the drugged Titania bestow upon the bestial object of her affections, and it provides an important clue as to how he views her exercise of emotional independence. To Oberon (and his servant, Puck) the queen's love for the boy is a form of dotage – of irregular female desire which in this case confuses the erotic and the maternal, or perhaps fails to see a harmful connection between them. Titania herself gives a very different account of her love for the child, making it a matter of female solidarity with the human mother who died giving birth to it.[10] The play does not gainsay this, but it does present other instances where female dotage in desire is depicted as 'monstrous', as in Helena's entreaty to Demetrius, whom she has followed into the woods:

I am your spaniel; and, Demetrius,
The more you beat me, I will fawn on you.
Use me but as your spaniel, spurn me, strike me,
Neglect me, lose me; only give me leave,
Unworthy as I am, to follow you.
What worser place can I beg in your love –
And yet a place of high respect with me –
Than to be used as you use your dog? (II.i.203)

The speech and its nauseated rejoinder by Demetrius – 'I am sick when I do look on thee' – are overheard by Oberon immediately after his own plot to debase Titania to something bestial, and in showing him at once expressing his sympathy with the spurned woman the play neatly re-balances our evaluation of his motives in engineering the queen's own degradation. As the drug's effects take hold and the queen acts out Oberon's punitive fantasy, its success is so complete as to constitute a pyrrhic victory: the boy is delivered over and the queen enthralled by the half human, half ass monstrosity which Puck, on his own initiative, has conjured from the 'hempen homespun' Nick Bottom. 'Her dotage now I do begin to pity' is Oberon's proprietorial response to the sight of the queen decking the creature's 'hairy temples' with a 'coronet of fresh and fragrant flowers'; but not before he has 'at my pleasure taunted her', and been rewarded with the 'mild terms' begging patience which restore the optimum of moderate wifely submission (IV.i.46–60).

The physical transformation of Bottom into an ass while the artisans are rehearsing their play is Ovidian in its character; but it radically distorts Ovidian narrative trajectory by bringing the moment of transformation forward to the central point of the play (III.i.97 SD). In doing this the play interweaves a strict metamorphosis in shape with the more psychological forms of change displayed by the male Athenian lovers and the knock-on effects these have on the emotional stability of the women witnessing them. While Bergsonian comedy is generated by having the two men's affections jerked one way and then the other, the two women, whose friendship has been previously understood as 'two seeming bodies, but one heart' (III.ii.212), demonstrate their own inconstancy, without the need of a charm, by falling out with one another in a sequence of violent mutual accusations. Bottom's appearance with an ass's head acts as a literalising of this argument about human changeability, but also an important counterweight to it.

One possible way of thinking about this relationship between Bottom and the lovers is from the perspective of Renaissance rhetorical theory, an approach we are directed towards by the terrified exclamation of one of Bottom's fellow actors, Peter Quince: 'Bless thee, Bottom, bless thee! Thou art translated' (III.i.114). The term 'translation' was often used to define the rhetorical trope of metaphor, and its comic appropriateness here stems from the fact that metaphor is the dominant trope of 'alteration' in meaning. As the Elizabethan rhetorician Thomas Wilson puts it, it is 'an alteration of a word from the proper and natural meaning to that which is not proper and yet agreeth thereunto by some likeness that appeareth to be in it'.[11] Critics thus very properly point out the agreement of 'ass-ness' to 'Bottom-ness' in the changed person of the artisan, and the way Bottom thus becomes a 'walking metaphor' of himself.

Yet it could be argued that, judged by Wilson's criteria, Bottom makes an odd sort of a metaphor. His 'likeness' to an ass does not occur at the level of imaginative sympathy – of what 'appeareth' – so much as that of the bluntly physical: he is the thing itself, and there is no 'meaning' to be mined from him. Perhaps Bottom works better within a different class of rhetorical figure, that of the 'scheme', in which the actual physical properties of a language unit are 'altered either by speaking or writing, contrary to the vulgar custom of our speech without changing their nature at all'. Indeed, as soon as he has transformed Bottom, Puck employs an elaborate poetic scheme while chasing out the fleeing artisans (III.i.105–6), and the play as a whole is crammed with varieties of this kind of verbal patterning: sometimes poetic, as in the mouths of the fairies; sometimes comic, as in the many malapropisms of the artisans. The main point here is that in altering Bottom physically Puck effects no alteration whatever in his 'nature'. Showing indestructible poise during subsequent events, including his seduction by Titania, his self-identity remains continuous. This is in stark contrast to the Athenian lovers, whose emotional 'metamorphoses' translate into larger truths about the relationship of selfhood to appearance. Such is the conclusion Theseus reaches in his gloss on the reports of lovers' adventures: 'The lunatic, the lover, and the poet / Are of imagination all compact' (V.i.7–8).

Bottom is a stranger to imagination, so crucial to metaphorical thinking, and his plight is all the better for it. This does not mean, however, that he is installed as the play's unlikely hero, whose viewpoint we are encouraged to adopt. In making the artisans' play-offering the afterword to the comedy, long after all main narrative lines have been resolved, the play shows that it cannot let go of him as an object for its exuberant mockeries. As in the woodland scenes, these are focused on the dramatic and poetic deficiencies of the artisan performers, all of whom share (or abide by) Bottom's assumption that audience imagination is a dangerous force which must be managed with care:

> There are things in this comedy of Pyramus and Thisbe that will
> never please. First, Pyramus must draw a sword to kill himself;
> which the ladies cannot abide ... let the prologue seem to say we
> will do no harm with our swords, and that Pyramus is not killed
> indeed ... (III.i.8–18)

Although enthusiasts for the theatre, the performers of *Pyramus and
Thisbe* share with the anti-theatricalists an unsophisticated belief in the
capacity of dramatic representation to reach out to an audience and
work on its imagination unmediated by artifice or literary convention.
Their fiction therefore goes to inordinate – and hilarious – lengths to
undermine itself throughout (see, for example, the 'prologue' to the
Lion's entrance at V.i.214 ff.). It should not escape our notice that the play
makes violence, rather than sex, the subject of its last word on theatrical
illusion. In mocking the actors' presumption of the fearsome effects of
their 'most lamentable comedy' on the Athenian spectators, much of
the erotically transgressive material which has unfolded in the comedy
proper (*A Midsummer Night's Dream* has, after all, dealt with partner-
swapping, bestiality and rape, among other things) is discreetly removed
from its concluding vision. The very presence of gender confusions,
transformations of identity, female sexual initiative and transgressions of
social status within comedies such as *Galatea* and *A Midsummer Night's
Dream* suggests, however, that dramatic capital could always be found
(just as it is today) in giving pleasurable and surprising shapes to the
anxieties and perplexities of everyday life.

Extended Commentary: *Twelfth Night* (1601)

Charles I (r. 1625–49) was one early royal fan of Shakespeare in print,
owning a copy of *Shakespeare's Comedies, Histories and Tragedies* in its
Second Folio edition (1632), which he sometimes annotated with his
own comments. Against the title of *Twelfth Night* in the opening playlist
he wrote the name 'Malvolio', suggesting that, for Charles at least,
it was this particular stage figure that supplied the centrepiece of the

play.* That the humbling of Malvolio, which we will be exploring below, made a strong impression on audiences as well as readers is shown by an earlier reference to the play by the student and diarist John Manningham, writing in 1602 at the time of one of the play's performances at the London law schools known as the Inns of Court:

> At our feast we had a play called *Twelfth Night, or What You Will*; much like *The Comedy of Errors*, or *Menaechmi* in Plautus, but most like and near to that in Italian called *Inganni*. A good practice in it to make the steward believe his Lady widow was in love with him, by counterfeiting a letter, as from his Lady, in general terms, telling him what she liked best in him, and prescribing his gesture in smiling, his apparel, &c., and then when he came to practise, making him believe they took him to be mad.[12]

This is one of those nuggets of recorded opinion which provide tantalising hints about the theatrical pleasures associated with an Elizabethan comedy. Manningham brings a student's enjoyment to the moment of reception by identifying, even before discussing the play itself, its antecedents in the drama. This new play has a smack of Shakespeare's own early work (*The Comedy of Errors*); of a Roman comedy which had already inspired that earlier work and is now providing a template for this new one (*The Brothers Menaechmi* by Plautus); and most of all of an Italian comedy nowadays identified as *Gl'Ingannati*, or 'The Deceived'. Manningham is correct on all three counts. Shakespeare's tale of twins wandering a foreign land unaware of each other's co-presence, one of them a girl disguised as a boy, resonates strongly with these earlier plays. Manningham makes one small error which serves to thicken still further the tissue of literary derivations: in describing one of *Twelfth Night*'s key characters as a 'widow' rather than as a spinster mourning for her brother, he recalls a detail from an English narrative adaptation of the Italian play

---

* Curiously enough, Charles did the same with *All's Well That Ends Well*, penning the name 'Monsieur Parolles' next to its title, so giving pride of place to another celebrated victim of comedic humiliation: see Part Three: 'Tragicomedy'.

which did not survive into Shakespeare's comedy. His instinctive attempt to point to the sedimentary layers of dramatic and non-dramatic texts lying beneath *Twelfth Night* is worth pausing over here, since it speaks volumes about the play's fantastically rich formal inheritance.

Twelfth Night is indeed structurally similar to *Gl'Ingannati*, which was performed in 1531 and first published in 1538, and very widely translated, imitated and adapted thereafter. Essentially a member of the 'romantic comedy' sub-genre, this Italian play has as much or more to do with sex as with love, its scenes and dialogues coming closer than anything we have looked at above to the 'wanton' mode of comedy so excoriated by the anti-theatricalists.[13] A (very) young daughter of an impoverished merchant is due to be married off to a rich old neighbour, although she herself is in love with a youth who has since transferred his affections to that neighbour's daughter. The girl contrives to alter her fate by dressing in boys' clothes and serving as page to her one-time paramour, hoping thereby to frustrate the outcome of the wooing missions to her rival on which he sends her. It succeeds principally because her rival falls in love with her in her disguised persona, and it is only by the chance return of her long-lost twin brother that all the young romantic parties can pair off with the suitable partner. The sexual emphasis is partly evident in the handling of the homoerotic moments: a kiss between wooed daughter and disguised 'page' is enacted not once but three times, with only token resistance from the latter; and it is a norm among the male figures to sexually objectify young boys as much as young girls. This playing with the complication of cross-dressing represents *Gl'Ingannati*'s specific formal innovation over the Roman New Comedy traditions of romantic intrigue and identity confusion, traditions lying at the bedrock of subsequent dramatic 'strata'. However, it follows New Comedy in using a restricted location, stock character types (contemptible parents, gluttonous servants) and an element of sexual farce which intrudes continually into the play's 'marital' plot.*

---

* Although most of the examples of classical New Comedy come from Roman drama, the form ultimately designates a development in Greek drama which stressed careful plotting and corrective comedy over the often savage personal lampooning of the Old Comedy tradition.

An English theatre company's adaptation of such a plot line might seem to invite the objections of those who lambasted the depiction of amorous themes on stage as so much 'bawdry'. As we will see in what follows, however, *Twelfth Night* subtly brings its erotic, transgressive elements (suitably toned down) into a confrontation with some of the attitudes that oppose them, with the latter coming off worse. The play retains the core conceit of a disguised girl sent to woo on behalf of the man she secretly loves, but disencumbers it of parental and pecuniary motive or any prior romantic entanglement requiring resolution. Instead, a simple impasse in courtship between the Illyrian ruler Duke Orsino and the Countess Olivia – who has foresworn love for seven years and determined to remain veiled and cloistered in mourning for her brother – is brought into the narrative foreground. The arrival at Orsino's court of a shipwreck survivor, Viola, separated from her brother and disguised '*in man's attire*' (I.iv.1SD) for her own safety, creates the basis for the decisive comedic intervention into this impasse.

The play opens with Orsino's famous lines:

> If music be the food of love, play on,
> Give me excess of it, that surfeiting
> The appetite may sicken and so die. (I.i.1–3)

It is a characteristic of love melancholy to adopt a posture of bemoaning the sensation of desire while at the same time savouring it: however, this is no mere expression of debilitation on Orsino's part. He describes a dangerously restive, aggrandising quality to his love which resists all attempts to extinguish it, and which devours lesser objects such as the music he has asked for:

> O spirit of love, how quick and fresh art thou
> That, notwithstanding thy capacity
> Receiveth as the sea, naught enters there
> Of what validity and pitch soe'er
> But falls into abatement and low price
> Even in a minute. (ll. 9–14)

In his subsequent discussions with the disguised Viola about love, about Olivia, and about the nature of men and women, Orsino continues to draw upon what amounts to a rhetoric of immoderation to characterise his fixation upon the one 'constant image' which renders him '[u]nstaid and skittish in all motions else' (II.iv.18–20). As he declares to Viola, with more than a hint of self-congratulation:

> There is no woman's sides
> Can bide the beating of so strong a passion
> As love doth give my heart ...
> [...]
> Alas, their love may be called appetite,
> No motion of the liver but the palate,
> That suffers surfeit, cloyment and revolt.
> But mine is all as hungry as the sea,
> And can digest as much. (II.iv.93–101)

Orsino suggests a distinction between men and women in respect to love based on a belief about their constitutional differences. Women's passions can never amount to more than 'appetite' since by dint of physiological inferiority these quickly 'surfeit', while his own love he supposes inexhaustible. Yet the distinction collapses on recollection of his love as a 'sea' (l. 100), the same force of nature which in his opening speech he had found to inconstantly devalue all objects falling into it. As a consequence some weight is given to the jocular utterance of only a few lines before that men's 'fancies are more giddy and unfirm' than any woman's.

Orsino's passion is counterpoised by Olivia's display of mourning, which similarly defies moderation by putting her beyond the reach of feelings that might compromise her commitment to 'A dead brother's love, which she would keep fresh' (ll. 29–30).* Again, it is left to the debates she has with Viola to expose this resistance to the duke's entreaties of love as the product of a rather different underlying attitude, in particular a scorn for his extravagantly Petrarchan, 'by the book' conceits in wooing. As Viola

---

* See also the Sea Captain's summary of her behaviour in the next scene, I.ii.33–8.

quickly objects, 'I see you what you are, you are too proud' (l. 242), and she goes on to make short work of Olivia's defences by mimicking the direct and unformulaic approach which lies beyond Orsino's emotional grasp (ll. 256–68). It is this display of liberty ('are you a comedian?' Olivia asks), with its spontaneous edge of desire in the mock encomium which Viola delivers for Olivia, which conquers the countess's unsuspecting heart; and by her immediate succumbing to Viola's 'perfections' the shared malaise of both Illyrian nobles becomes evident. Each feeds upon a love based purely in the imagination: the duke because he is obliged to substitute 'fancy' for the sight of Olivia; the countess because she unwittingly substitutes a woman for a beautiful youth.

A different perspective on Olivia's commitment to mourning her brother is offered by the play's most purely physical figure of excess, her 'kinsman' the knight Sir Toby Belch, who asks: 'What a plague means my niece to take the death of her brother thus? I am sure care's an enemy to life' (I.iii.1–2). Sir Toby's outrageously self-descriptive surname, his unapologetic addiction to drinking, gourmandising and revelry in a household still in a state of mourning, anchor the play's romantic themes within the New Comedy traditions that underlie the Italian play and which Manningham's astute dramatic antennae had picked up: Toby is a complexly moulded version of the stock figure of the 'parasite' in Plautine comedy – the greedy hanger-on who consumes his noble's revenue. The play's intrusion of riotous good-living into the sombre setting of Olivia's household via the figure of Sir Toby and his confrères in revelry, Sir Andrew Aguecheek and the clown Feste, draws from a deeper well of comic energy than New Comedy and its Italian derivatives. While these comedies provided models for conscious emulation, being taught as part of an Elizabethan humanist education, another, more durable stratum was also available via the plebeian traditions of folk and festive entertainments which, being a part of daily life, were not committed to text.

The 'folk' side of this inheritance was examined by the critic and literary theorist Northrop Frye, who argued that Shakespeare's comedy was heavily indebted to a tradition of agrarian and seasonal ritual, the function of which was to celebrate the perennial supersession of death, decay and winter by spring, fertility and 'the green world'. Frye's analysis identified three components to this ritual progression, whereby forces hostile to life and generation are at first understood to be dominant, and are then challenged by a complicating/confusing impulse which ultimately overcomes them; this leads to a final stage of resolution and renewal.[14] The second, festival strand of plebeian comedy derives from an area first treated by C. L. Barber in his *Shakespeare's Festive Comedy*, and studied with particular interest by a contemporary, politically oriented criticism thereafter: the tradition of 'Misrule', whereby for a brief period associated with feast days normal social constraints are suspended and hierarchies upended. Servants become masters, men dress as women, feasting banishes the exercise of restraint, and a mock king – the 'Lord of Misrule' – presides in the overlord's place. The play's evocation of this tradition seems quite conscious: the very date which lends it its title, the last day of the Christmas revelries in the Christian calendar, had associations with precisely this kind of social inversion via its pagan antecedents in the 'Saturnalia' – the feast days dedicated to the Roman god Saturn during which slaves enjoyed temporary lordship over their masters.

The play's integration of classical and carnival comedic features becomes especially clear in the plot strand dealing with Malvolio, the steward of Olivia's household. In formal terms he functions in direct opposition to Sir Toby's 'parasite' role as an anti-pleasure, anti-comic impediment to the impulse toward excessive consumption. This structural capacity is apparent from *Twelfth Night*'s Italian predecessor, *Gl'Ingannati*, where an overeating, overdrinking servant is shown to be at loggerheads with a household tutor whom he generally refers to as a 'pedant'. In their slanging matches over the servant's drunken negligence, the tutor is accused of being an impostor, of harbouring a secret vice (sodomy), and of carrying himself above his humble station: 'can you ever be anything but the son of a mule-driver?'.[15] In *Twelfth Night* this opposition is rendered much less mechanically (there is, for example, more than just one antagonist to Malvolio) and Malvolio's character is developed along a very different trajectory; but traces of it surface in, for example, Sir Toby's retort after Malvolio has interrupted their night-time revels: 'Art any more than a steward? Dost thou think because thou art virtuous there shall be no more cakes and ale?' (II.iii.112–13). The exchanges between the revellers and Malvolio are fraught with a very specific set of tensions: Sir Toby's rebuke is delivered from his own, nominally much higher social position, lending a complicating class antagonism to the opposition between unrestrained pleasure and the moral 'preciseness' which would curb it. Saturnalian licence is now the province of those closely allied in degree (if not in manner) with the lady of the house, while the forces of control are their social subordinates. Sir Toby and his crew are the enactors of, in Malvolio's words, 'uncivil rule' (l. 120).

The stamp of Malvolio's opposition is not the stamp of pedantry, though that is absorbed into it when he is later described as 'like a pedant that keeps a school i' th' church' (III.ii.71). It is associated with 'virtue' of a stripe that Olivia's housekeeper, Maria, identifies when she describes him as being 'sometimes … a kind of Puritan' (II.iii.136). Maria's 'sometimes' makes of Malvolio a purely opportunistic practitioner of virtue, whose repudiations of pleasure are not the mark of religious purity but of a 'time-pleaser' whose primary wish is control for its own sake, as he 'cons state without book and utters it by great swathes' (II.iii.143–4). 'Puritan' in this broadly social sense more adequately describes someone like Stephen Gosson, whose attacks on collective pleasures such as the theatre were inextricable from his attempts to secure favour and patronage among the great. Such self-serving individualism is clearly effective when presented in the guise of moral uprightness; but, as Maria grasps, it would be unable to survive exposure to the counter-individualistic mirth of the crowd – to survive being transformed into a 'common recreation'.

Maria forges a cryptic love letter from her mistress that tempts Malvolio into believing its message to his own advantage. As a stratagem it relies for its success on his making the same excessive investment in the imagination that Olivia and Orsino do. All three worship its figments as substitutes for something existing in the world, and to fall in love with those figments is in a sense to fall in love with oneself. Whereas Olivia and Orsino's narcissism is born out of error or circumstance, however – doting on the self's fictions but not upon the self as imagination's object – Malvolio's is properly identified as 'self-love' (Olivia's phrasing at I.v.86), and revealed to be so in the 'private' moment he is overheard enjoying by those waiting for him to find the letter:

'Tis but fortune, all is fortune. Maria once told me she [Olivia]
did affect me, and I have heard herself come thus near ... Besides
she uses me with a more exalted respect than anyone else that
follows her ... To be count Malvolio. (II.v.21–32)

If the inadvertent 'self-loving' shown by Orsino and Olivia has led to a
kind of melancholy on the part of each, Malvolio's outright adoration of
the self-object leads, on his reading of the letter, to a kind of madness.
'[I]magination so blows him' that he is unable to submit its contents –
the commandment to wear 'yellow stockings ... cross-gartered' and to
'smile' in Olivia's presence – to reality-testing. Dedicated to maintaining
gravity and order within Olivia's household, it has all along been
Malvolio's 'secret wish', as Barber puts it, 'to violate decorum himself,
then relish to the full its power over others'.[16] It is an unregulated desire
to which the letter seems to promise absolute fulfilment in the form of
his elevation to the role of Olivia's spouse and the assumption of the
duties, and demeanour, of high office:

> I will be proud, I will read politic authors, I will baffle Sir Toby,
> I will wash off gross acquaintance ... I do not now fool myself to
> let imagination jade me ... (ll. 157–60)

Following his garishly amorous parade before Olivia, Malvolio is
incarcerated, at Sir Toby's behest, 'in a dark room and bound' (III.
iv.131), a standard method of dealing with the mad – the category into
which his sudden reaction from a habitually 'sad and civil' behaviour
now places him in his mistress's eyes (III.iv.5). If the play's guiding trope
has been that of inversion – of 'topsy-turvydom' – then it is Malvolio
who now bears its full brunt, as the revellers take their pleasure trying
to convince him of his madness by employing a form of reality-testing
turned inside out. Suppressed pagan notions of the soul, for example, are
used to discredit the fully orthodox opinions he holds:

> FESTE: What is the opinion of Pythagoras concerning wildfowl?
> MALVOLIO: That the soul of our grandam might haply inhabit
> a bird.

FESTE: What think'st thou of his opinion?
MALVOLIO: I think nobly of the soul, and no way approve [Pythagoras'] opinion.
FESTE: Fare thee well. Remain thou still in darkness. Thou shalt hold the opinion of Pythagoras ere I will allow of thy wits …
(IV.ii.49–8)

Malvolio's sanity is never placed in serious threat, but this is not because he himself is seen to undergo any comic re-enlightenment about the nature of his delusion. Rather, his obdurate self-esteem remains until the end of the play, at which point he is finally disabused of his belief about the letter's origins. In fact, that self-esteem outlasts the conclusion by which all the other characters' delusions are exposed and acknowledged, with his determination on his exit to be 'revenged on the whole pack of you'.

What kind of theatrical pleasure does the conclusion to *Twelfth Night* offer, then? We know that one early audience member found the duping of Malvolio to be a 'good practice' in general, and specifically included the 'den of madness' scene in his praise. Some audiences (and performers of the role) find something pitiable in the steward's treatment, and feel his victimisation spills into overkill, prolonged as it is even after Sir Toby's weariness with 'this foolery'. Perhaps one way of reconciling this combination of harsh dealing and romantic fulfilment is to look closer at that strange and contradictory figure of Saturn, the Roman god who is only vaguely alluded to in the play but whose influence bulks large, since it is his feast day that lies behind the structures of inversion and carnivalesque disorder. Saturn was on the one hand presider over the lost 'golden age' to which the Saturnalian feast paid homage; but on the other he was also the patron god of melancholy, and in particular of those 'sad and civil' men whose grave demeanour and solitary musings, while making them joyless companions, also fitted them for high office. In a breathtaking display of dramatic wit, the play extracts the Saturnalian from the Saturnine, forcing the logic of carnival onto the figure most opposed to its activities by appealing to all those fanciful and ambitious thoughts he harbours privately.

The means by which this logic is inflicted upon Malvolio is devastatingly appropriate. As the play's most recent editor, Keir Elam, points out, in abandoning decorum for an amorous display in yellow stockings, cross-gartered, Malvolio commits a sartorial 'transgression': a violation of the codes of socially appropriate dress for which both carnival and the institution of theatre were notorious in the minds of their opponents. The comparison between Viola's and Malvolio's transgressions in clothing is a deliberate one which offers a defence of the theatre's prerogative to practise these comic transformations. Both instances are voluntary and both are humiliating: Malvolio's becomes openly so, while Viola's disguise in her view makes of her a 'monster' of sexual indeterminacy which bars her from revealing her love to Orsino and her true gender to Olivia. It is significant that Viola describes the 'error' as one lying as much with the observer as the perpetrator: 'How easy is it for the proper false / In women's waxen hearts to set their forms' (II.ii.29–30). A feigned 'outside' has created an unexpectedly powerful response in Olivia; but it can only do so when the imagination is made apt to take by its absorption with absent objects. The final moments of the play, by contrast, show the proper, non-illusory effects of 'wonder' being achieved through the revelation of Viola's full theatrical presence. Her 'masculine usurped attire' remains on her past the ending, a still-disturbing, taboo force opposed to self-identity (she asks of her brother '[d]o not embrace me' until she can reclaim her 'woman's weeds'). But it is also revealed to be the instrument by which at least some of the bars to human and social relationships can be removed.

Notes

1   'Tarlton's Jest of a Bristow Man', from *Tarlton's Jests* (1628).
2   See Henri Bergson, *Laughter: An Essay on the Meaning of the Comic,* trans. Cloudesley Brereton and Fred Rothwell (London: Macmillan & Co., 1921), especially pp. 8–22.
3   See Aristotle, 'Poetics', trans. Richard Janko, in *The Norton Anthology of Theory and Criticism*, pp. 90–117, p. 94.
4   Philip Sidney, 'An Apology for Poetry', in *The Norton Anthology of Theory and Criticism*, pp. 326–62, p. 343.

5   Philip Stubbes, *Philip Stubbes's anatomy of the abuses in England in Shakspere's youth, A. D. 1583*, New Shakespeare Society Series, ed. Frederick J. Furnivall (London: Trübner for the Society, 1877–9), p. 83.

6   Stubbes, *Philip Stubbes's anatomy of the abuses in England*, p. 144.

7   John Lyly, *Galatea/Midas*, The Revels Plays (Manchester: Manchester University Press, 2000), II.i.65.

8   For a much more detailed, formal comparison of the two plays than can be offered here, see the chapter on 'Lyly and Shakespeare' in G. K. Hunter's *John Lyly: The Humanist as Courtier* (London: Routledge & Kegan Paul, 1962), pp. 298–349, pp. 318–23.

9   William Shakespeare, *A Midsummer Night's Dream*, ed. Harold F. Brooks, Arden, 2nd series (London: Routledge: 1991; 1979), II.ii.77.

10   For a reading which interprets Titania's fascination with the boy as erotic/ Oedipal, see Shirley Nelson Garnier 'A Midsummer Night's Dream: "Jack shall have Jill; / Nought shall go ill"', in *A Midsummer Night's Dream: Critical Essays*, ed. Dorothea Kehler (London: Routledge, 1998), pp. 127–43.

11   Thomas Wilson, *The Arte of Rhetorique*, Book 3.

12   See the Introduction to William Shakespeare, *Twelfth Night*, Arden, 3rd series, ed. Keir Elam (London: Cengage Learning, 2008), pp. 3–4; spellings modernised in the above.

13   Gl'Intronati di Siena, *Gl'Ingannati* ('The Deceived'). For a more detailed discussion of the complex provenance and sixteenth-century Italian dramatic context of the play, see John R. Ford, *'Twelfth Night': A Guide to the Play*, Greenwood Guides to Shakespeare (Westport, CT: Greenwood Press, 2006), pp. 20–6.

14   For this summary of Frye's tripartite reading of comic form see the reading given by Terence Hawkes in *Shakespeare's Comedies*.

15   Gl'Intronati di Siena, *Gl'Ingannati*, in *Five Italian Renaissance Comedies*, ed. Bruce Penman (Harmondsworth: Penguin, 1978), p. 249.

16   C. L. Barber, *Shakespeare's Festive Comedy: A Study of Dramatic Form and its Relation to Social Custom* (Princeton: Princeton University Press, 1959), p. 255.

Shakespeare's History Plays:
Richard III and *Henry IV Part 1*

The discussion of comedy in Part Three looks at some of the attacks on plays and actors which characterised responses to the growing popularity of theatre in the English capital. We will begin this discussion of the genre of the history play by looking at a defence of plays and play-going, penned by the professional writer and occasional dramatist Thomas Nashe in 1592. Nashe argued that plays in general were a benign example of the kinds of diversion which London's growing consuming class could enjoy in an afternoon's leisure. In fact, in comparison to drinking, gambling or brothel-haunting (Nashe is only concerned with male consumers here), play-going could be considered 'a rare exercise of virtue', given the typical 'subject' of the native drama:

> for the most part it is borrowed out of our English Chronicles, wherein our forefathers' valiant acts, that have lain long-buried in rusty brass and worm-eaten books, are revived, and they themselves raised from the grave of oblivion, and brought to plead their aged honours in open presence: than which, what can be a sharper reproof to these degenerate effeminate days of ours?[1]

Nashe's claim that the majority of plays shown on the London stages during the early 1590s were on the theme of English history is an overstatement; but it is a telling one. He chooses this class of subject matter to illustrate his point that plays have a 'virtue' in reproving a feckless and 'degenerate' populace. Our more warlike ancestors are brought back from the dead – 'revived' – to perform the work of toughening the nation's moral fibre in times of ease. This particular, ideological use of historical themes seems to mark out a genre distinct from comedy (where the aim is to delight) and tragedy (where the aim is to move the audience with serious emotions). What were its dimensions?

It is a good deal easier to generalise about the history play than to define it as a genre, since it enjoyed no prescriptive theory of the kind developed in classical times for tragedy or comedy. That Elizabethans could acknowledge 'history' as a distinct dramatic category is implied by its inclusion as one of three groupings in Shakespeare's First Folio, where it sits between comedy and tragedy. The 'contents list' of Shakespeare's history plays is carefully arranged in chronological fashion, from the earliest (*King John*) to the latest (*Henry VIII*), and follows a regular procedure of titling: either the 'First Part of King …'s Reign' for a series, or 'The Life and Death of …' for the majority of individual titles. An impression of interrelatedness and cohesion is given, which contrasts with the more idiosyncratic nature of the titles in the Tragedy and Comedy categories. Considerably earlier than the First Folio we find 'History' appearing as an allegorical figure alongside her dramatic companions in the induction to a play called *A Warning for Fair Women* (1599), carrying an appropriate generic garb: '*Enter at one doore, Hystorie with Drum and Ensigne: Tragedie at another … Comedie at the other end …*'.[2] Against these (rather meagre) suggestions of distinctiveness is the problem that 'history' as a tag could also be widely applied to many different kinds of play, with the straightforward connotation of 'story' or perhaps 'moral tale': as in *The Tragicall History of Doctor Faustus*. In this respect, 'history' is even more of an offender than 'comedy' in providing a catch-all term for 'dramatic representation'.

One could go further and point out that tragedy and history were bedfellows in ways that comedy and history were not. They often used the same sources, and both were involved in the depiction of serious actions frequently involving an important death at the conclusion. Does this mean that 'histories' were really just tragedies of a peculiarly local and particular type? To the modern critical eye an important distinction persists: Elizabethan history plays just do not seem to have had a specific form of their own. As one critic puts it, dramatic history had 'no identity to cut it off from tragedy' but at the same time 'it had some affinities with comedy'.[3] The plays often prove highly malleable in shape and tone, and present narratives in which marriages (albeit of a dynastic rather than romantic kind) conclude stories involving warfare and death (*Henry V*), or in which warfare and death crown stories with a strong focus on marriage (*Richard III*). History plays are, from this perspective, parasitic on other, more established dramatic forms: the classical ones of comedy and tragedy, but also more native traditions of drama, such as the sixteenth-century morality plays, which preceded the establishment of the commercial stage. The shape of any given history play will also be affected by its connections with previous plays in a sequence and, of course, by the events in the source material, since meaning is ultimately to be found *in* these events. So if dramatic form cannot serve to characterise the genre, what can?

This is where Nashe's claim about the instructive potential of plays 'borrowed out of our English Chronicles' becomes interesting. E.M.W. Tillyard's influential study of 1944 discussed Shakespeare's histories as purposive, conveying to Elizabethan audiences a moral argument, supposedly found in the sources Shakespeare drew on, for the guiding hand of God's providence in English history. God had a plan for every nation as well as for every individual, and both the study and the representation of history could reveal that plan. Later critics nuanced this idea. Irving Ribner, writing in 1957, thought that the 'didactic', providential evaluation of the plays, with its roots in medieval thinking, was counterbalanced by the new humanist emphasis on the political value of history.[4] History was interesting to the Renaissance mind for the practical service it could do as 'a guide to political behaviour'. It provided examples from the past to illuminate the present, and it complemented the sense of a divine plan with the idea that individuals 'might determine political success or failure' for themselves.[5] A more recent criticism, which we will draw on in what follows, finds a good deal less orthodoxy and unity in Elizabethan theorising about history than these readings did; but the basic idea of friction between a pragmatic human *use* of history and an overarching divine purpose for it remains a key one in reading these plays.[6]

It is a valid if crude argument to describe Shakespeare's dramas on historical themes as simply providing propaganda for the Elizabethan political status quo. But this does not do full justice to the arguments touched on above, and is a claim which could be made equally of a tragedy such as *Macbeth*, in which the lineage of the new king, James, is explicitly glorified, or even a comedy such as *A Midsummer Night's Dream*, with its allegorical allusions to Elizabeth I's chastity. Rather, political value as I am treating it here is implied by Nashe's use of the term 'virtue' when he refers to the civic value of these 'chronicle' dramas. When Nashe was writing, 'virtue' had a wider set of denotations than the simple one of 'moral goodness' which we understand today. It included a sense popularised by the Italian humanist Machiavelli to denote a kind of competence, readiness and acuity in public affairs. Virtue in this sense aimed at the goal of common good but did not mind about having to break a few bones while doing so. Virtue made use of 'Fortune', but was also proof against it. It could equate to a form of goodness, but not so much in the eyes of God as in the eyes of a secular history. Nashe called this the 'right of fame', and argued that plays above all could bestow it on the honourable dead. As he put it, 'there is no immortality can be given a man on earth' better than to be shown on the stage:

> How would it have joyed brave Talbot, the terror of the French, to think that after he had lain two hundred years in his tomb, he should triumph again on the stage and have his bones new embalmed with the tears of ten thousand spectators at least (at several times), who, in the tragedian that represents his person, imagine they see him fresh bleeding!*,[7]

---

* The 'brave Talbot' in question here was an English knight who had died in the territorial wars between England and France almost 150 years earlier, and the play in which he appeared was *Henry VI Part 1*, collaboratively written by a youthful William Shakespeare and, most likely, Thomas Nashe himself.

Historical Factors: *Richard III*

Like all the plays we will be looking at in this section, *Richard III* needs to be considered as part of a set of historical and dramatic relationships, rather than as a literary work in isolation. The play follows, and provides a conclusion to, the three-part sequence of Henry VI plays written at the start of Shakespeare's career as a dramatist. Henry VI's reign was a disastrous one for England, in which losses of territory in France (notwithstanding the efforts of 'brave Talbot') encouraged powerful nobles to take advantage of a weak, indeed mentally unstable, king in order to press their own, rival claims to the throne.* The salutary point about these rival claims is that they were good ones. Henry VI's grandfather, Henry IV, had come to power by deposing a legitimate king, his cousin Richard II. Richard himself had no issue, and in the tangled route map of claims to the throne that had been left by their own grandfather, Edward III (almost everyone in this story traces themselves back to him), Henry's seizure of power involved a forcible assertion of seniority for his own line of descent, that of the house of Lancaster, over other, arguably stronger, claimants within the family network: the lines of Mortimer and of York. As we shall see in more detail when we come to look at *Henry IV Part 1*, he was able to do so because of a mixture of personal grievances and public hostility towards Richard II, as well as his own political prowess – his 'virtue', if you like – in maintaining his hold on a shaky claim. When in his grandson Henry VI's reign that hold began to waver, the series of wars which followed between Lancastrian and Yorkist supporters concluded with the York line on the throne, albeit briefly.

The main problem for a later historian recounting these events lay in negotiating what was still a 'live' issue for the political settlement in Elizabethan times: the direct relationship of these events to the Tudor claim to the throne. Elizabeth's grandfather, Henry VII, had appeared from the margins of the royal lineage to defeat in battle and supplant

---

* The fact that Henry VI had succeeded to the throne as a minor (indeed, as a nine-month-old baby) and did not assume government until his sixteenth year had seriously exacerbated instability at the centre of power.

the last of the York lineage, Richard III himself. Tudor historians such as Hall, Holinshed and More dealt with Henry's even remoter claim to accession by bitterly attacking the moral right of Richard III to have been king; and dramatists drawing on this material were to do the same.

Stepping back from the mass of details, one can see how this long and bloody narrative lent itself to the avid philosophising about history so favoured in Shakespeare's era. The rightful ruler in terms of the succession is sometimes the least desirable one, but those willing to exercise political initiative in order to remove them must brace themselves for the incalculable consequences for future claims to legitimacy. The special interest of *Richard III* lies in the way it conjures an endgame out of this seemingly inexorable logic. Richard of Gloucester seizes kingship against the order of succession by murdering family members who stand in his way, ransacking the textbook of political expediency and manipulation in order to do so, and instituting a reign of tyranny over England. His career and eventual destruction are portrayed, however, less as the cause of a new history about to unfold than as the result and summing up of all that had gone before: *Richard III* is one long *consequence*. This is partly underlined by a notable shift in representational emphasis which the character undergoes from the *Henry VI* plays. Richard had already made an appearance in the last of these as the youngest of the three Yorkist brothers who defeated Henry VI and established their own line on the throne. In a series of remarkable, brazen soliloquies in this earlier play, Richard had conveyed to the audience his secret desire for the crown, relating his ambition directly to the fact of his own physical deformity. A hunchback and partly crippled, Richard is alienated from the natural boons of love and marriage, and can achieve a singular satisfaction only through the opportunity to 'command, to check, to o'erbear such / As are of better person than myself'.[8] In the opening soliloquy of *Richard III* these motives are recapitulated: Richard's deformity and temperament render him unsuited to the 'weak, piping time of peace' England now enjoys under the eldest brother, Edward IV; he is therefore, in a phrase nicely suggestive of his self-determining ideology of politics, 'determined to prove a villain'.[9] The intent he registered in the earlier plays, however, to gain the crown, is left curiously unarticulated here. Its existence is never in doubt, as Richard unfolds for us his 'plots', 'inductions', and 'deep intent' against his brother Clarence, second in line to the throne. The effect nonetheless is to take the immediate emphasis off the narrative's forward impetus, and to clear a space for the extensive revisitations of the recent past which occupy much of the play's first half.

To some extent, these revisitations find an organising principle in a figure already dead at the start of the narrative: the son of Henry VI, Edward Prince of Wales, stabbed to death by all three York brothers at the end of the previous play. All who had been complicit in his murder meet their destruction in *Richard III*, and the play relentlessly traces their downfalls back to this past event, most crucially through the repeated recollections of it offered by Margaret, Edward's mother. In a lengthy scene set in the court near the start of the play, Margaret intrudes as if stepping directly out from the earlier trilogy, again arresting the forward narrative movement which had been building up through political infighting between rival factions, and dragging attention back to the earlier plays via a series of 'frantic' curses against the assembled court (I.iii.158 ff.). Margaret has a multitude of grievances. The murder of her husband, Henry VI, at the instigation of Richard; the murder of her child, and her own deposition; and the curses and prophecies she utters here figure a complex set of exchanges which are worked out in the play's economy of retribution: a king for a king, a husband for a husband, and so forth. The slaying of her son simply serves to link the greatest number of her antagonists, either through direct blame (as in Richard's case) or in their role as bystanders (the lords Rivers, Dorset and Hastings), or for payment in kind (the fate she wishes upon the son of Elizabeth, the queen who has replaced her on the throne). Even some who fall outside her curses, such as the imprisoned Clarence, centre their misfortunes on this 'misdeed'. Indeed, when the moment comes for Clarence to confront his assassins, his murder is explicitly urged by them as divine vengeance for his complicity in the slaying of Margaret's son (see I.iv.190–9).*

---

* Margaret's unhistorical appearance in the narrative (she never returned to England after being ransomed from the Tower several years after Tewkesbury) is only the most prominent of a number of Shakespeare's departures from his historical sources (Thomas More's *History of Kyng Richard the thirde* being his principal source, but he also drew on the chronicle histories of Holinshed and Hall). These departures especially involve the roles of women in the play, such as Queen Anne and the Duchess of York, which are greatly expanded and set in a special antagonism with Richard.

Critics have remarked on the way Margaret's presence in the play powerfully affects its tone and structure, the sheer volume of her heavily patterned curses giving large stretches of the dialogue a kind of ritual intonation and quality. This jars so acutely with the impression of activity and scheming generated by Richard and his ally Buckingham that she is often cut out of productions completely, and to see the play in full is to be shocked at the kind of violence she inflicts upon its aesthetic. Margaret embodies an older form of drama – that of the Roman tragedies of Seneca, with their emphasis on formal rhetoric and the vengeance of the gods – and an older idea of history – that which sees a fatal, predetermined patterning to events. The tension set up between the competing positions of fatalism and personal initiative is neatly encapsulated when Margaret's cumulative curse upon Richard is turned back upon its speaker at the last moment by his substitution of her own name for his:

> MARGARET: Thou slander of thy heavy mother's womb,
> Thou loathed issue of thy father's loins,
> Thou rag of honour, thou detested –
> RICHARD: Margaret!
> [...]
> ELIZABETH: Thus have you breath'd your curse against yourself.
> (I.iii.231–40)

In the short term at least, self-determining ingenuity trumps the ritual endorsement of historical inevitability.

A similar tension emerges from the confrontation in I.ii between Richard and Anne, the widow of the murdered prince, but with an even greater emphasis on Richard's rhetorical and manipulative prowess, as he woos her in the presence of the dead King Henry's corpse. Again, an explicit rationale for his doing so is absent: he has spoken only of a 'secret close intent' to take her for his wife while leaving any direct political gain from this course oddly unstated. Richard's motives are less important than the vivid foregrounding of the immediate past, in the form of Anne's own curses against the murderer (Richard is portrayed as solely culpable, here) and in the bleeding of the corpse's wounds in Richard's presence. A more explicit instance of the dead 'revived' to instruct the present could hardly be urged, but the outcome is once more to demonstrate Richard in the act of repudiating historical inevitability. To the self-determining ambition of his soliloquies from the earlier plays Richard now adds a self-authoring facility: he quite literally translates each of Anne's accusations against him into favourable motives: 'He that bereft thee, lady of thy husband / Did it to help thee to a better husband'; ''twas I that stabb'd young Edward – but 'twas thy heavenly face that set me on' (I.ii.142–3, 185–6). As Anne's outrage gives way to perplexity and fascination, the play moots the capacity of one individual freely to rewrite recent history and thereby conquer the temporal logic which appears to bind everyone else. Again, given the purposelessness of the wooing and marriage, it is a resounding but empty victory for Richard, as his soliloquy on Anne's exit – taken up with self-parodying and comic expressions of vanity – suggests. The episode has functioned to underscore Richard's flair for revising the meanings of the past, and to act as a foil for the more politically relevant wooing-by-proxy of Elizabeth's daughter after Richard takes power.

Richard's manipulative skills and deft wordplay serve both to baffle his victims within the play, and to compel and delight the audience outside it via the soliloquies and asides he lavishes upon us. Reflecting on his own rhetorical prowess in the scene where he exchanges banter with the young princes who are to be his most notorious victims, Richard identifies a particular role for himself which critics find an apt one for his entire dramatic career: that of a 'formal vice' (III.i.82). The Vice was a non-realistic figure from an earlier, allegorical mode of drama (known as an 'Interlude') whose job it was to deceive and tempt the protagonist away from an equally personified set of 'Virtues'.*,10 The identification is significant in providing a moment of theatrical self-authoring to complement and deepen the political self-determination of Richard. The Vice had a number of characteristics which overlap with Richard's brand of stage villainy: in particular, a unique, 'liminal' position in the fiction which allows him to step between audience and play-world at will; and a mode of discourse which is constantly inverting and perverting the meanings of words. The product of a dramatic tradition which was fast

---

* Richard identifies himself with a specific one here, Iniquity, although by the later stages of Tudor drama the individual 'vices' had been rolled up into one composite figure.

becoming overtaken and replaced by that of the commercial drama, the Vice nonetheless survives into it because of his highly attractive characteristics of energy, invention and impudence, and because he brings with him characteristics of the Devil from medieval 'mystery' plays (an even earlier mode of drama). Richard, however, fleshes out this already compact theatrical persona with that of the arriviste professional actor. In the scene where he and Buckingham start to work on the Lord Mayor's sympathies for Richard's claim on the crown, they prepare themselves by exchanging tricks and techniques proper to the stage player – one who can 'Murder [the] breath in middle of a word, / And then again begin, and stop again', or 'Speak and look back, and pry on every side, / Tremble and start at wagging of a straw' (III.v.1–10). It is noticeable, however, that while it is Buckingham's claim that he can 'counterfeit the deep tragedian' – that is, act the part of the actor – it is Richard who reveals himself as past master of performance by attempting to instruct him in his role. Fully identified with the 'deep tragedian' via the bloody path he is carving through the narrative, Richard is again situated both inside and outside the world of the play: a maker of theatrical fictions, more than he is a product of them.

The tragedian's role, however, is constrained to end badly; and it is not long after Richard finally attains the crown that his part in the play becomes increasingly subject to the same narrative and generic logic suffered by the other characters. The deposed queen Margaret reappears at this point (IV.iv) to accuse him of being 'hell's black intelligencer, / Only reserved their factor to buy souls / And send them thither' (ll. 71–2). This underscores Richard's diabolic role, but at the same time it robs him of full agency. He is now seen as an employee of the supernatural order – a mere runner of errands in the farming of souls for Hell.

In the ensuing scene of Richard's attempt to win Elizabeth's consent to a match with her daughter, he is further robbed of control over events by Elizabeth's insistence that he must not swear an oath by the 'time to come', 'for that thou hast / Misus'd, ere us'd, by times ill-us'd o'erpast' (ll. 395–6). The past now shows resistance to his efforts at revision into a positive future: Elizabeth's capitulation to Richard's request at the scene's end is only apparent. It is a past subsequently figured in the most vivid fashion possible when, in the scene before doing battle with Richmond – heaven's 'minister of chastisement' – Richard is visited by the spirits of his victims. Senecan revenge tragedy and Tudor morality drama, two formal counterweights to the narrative of change and self-determination which Richard has championed, now fuse in the astonishing spectacle of ghosts processing across the stage to condemn the sleeping Richard on its one side and endorse the sleeping Richmond on the other (V.iii.118–77). Against the oppressive, formal patterning of the scene Richard is allowed one last, panic-stricken attempt at self-definition (ll. 178–207). But this serves only to identify him as a role – a 'murderer' – that has taken absolute possession of the performer.

'Vile Participation': *Henry IV Part 1*

Providing a concluding part to the civil war narrative of the three-part *Henry VI* plays, *Richard III* often gets grouped together with them as part of a dramatically cohesive 'tetralogy'. As a critical concept this is attractive, and we are culturally familiar with the idea of an extended three- and four-part narrative 'cycle' through such twentieth-century phenomena as Tolkein's *The Lord of the Rings*, the arrangement of which bears at least a few similarities to Wagner's massive four-part 'Ring' opera of the nineteenth century. Within the fast-moving and highly adaptive commercial environment of theatre in the early 1590s, however, it is stretching the point to apply this kind of planning to the earliest contributions of a young and relatively untried playwright, and there are doubts about the exact order in which the *Henry VI* plays were written.* More convincing is the claim for Shakespeare's 'second tetralogy', written in sequential order over the second half of the 1590s,

---

* The published version of the second of the *Henry VI* plays advertised it as the first of a 'civil war' two-part work in a similar format to Marlowe's *Tamburlaine*, suggesting a core set of works to which *Henry VI Part 1* later provided a preamble and *Richard III* a conclusion. On that basis, improvisational sequencing along the lines of George Lucas's *Star Wars* series seems the more appropriate filmic analogy.

and tracing the consecutive reigns of Richard II, Henry IV (to whom two plays are devoted) and finally Henry V. The format was by now in place for a sustained examination of historical themes stretching over several plays, and if the exact shape and composition of this could not have been evident as early as *Richard II*, it was one that could be retroactively imposed by the time of *Henry V*. To brace ourselves for the first of the chronological paradoxes we are likely to encounter, this 'second tetralogy' takes us backwards in time to the events which lay behind the first. If the sequence of plays ending with *Richard III* unearthed the most recent past that could be broached under Elizabethan censorship, the next sequence delved into the deep past behind it, finding a much more thoroughgoing and ominous causal logic developing out of the deposition narrative it tells.

We suggested that *Richard III* had a dead figure, Henry VI's son Edward, who in some measure haunted the play, acting as the emblem of a lost past. The greater part of this new series comes to be overshadowed by the figure of Richard II, killed at the conclusion of the play that bears his name but surviving in the next three plays as an exemplar of a distinct kind – that of the divine, or 'sacred', component in kingship which, irrespective of the monarch's own grievous faults, cannot be fully extricated from his person. His usurpation at the hands of Henry Bolingbroke (who becomes Henry IV) may have been construed as inevitable given Richard's intolerable actions against his subjects of all social classes, but it cannot unproblematically be called just. Henry's fundamentally political action in unseating Richard may at first pass unmolested by the divine authority that legitimates royal power, but in uncanny fashion that authority appears to reassert itself by interfering with the after-effects. Unlike in *Richard III*, however, this is due to 'secondary' and not supernatural causes. In part, these operate through the nobles who take exception to Henry's authority as soon as he begins to exercise it, most vocal among them the young Hotspur, who is quick to make a positive, revisionary example of the deposed Richard against 'this vile politician', this new 'king of smiles'.[11] The image which Hotspur keeps returning to (and which anticipates a similar usage in the case of the tyrant Macbeth) is that of a 'canker' – a weed* – set against the 'sweet lovely rose' of the legitimate king whom they have collectively 'put down' (l. 174). The organic metaphor is an incisive one: the troubling of Henry IV's reign is figured as something endogenous – an outgrowth of his own person – in the waywardness of his young son and heir, Prince Hal.

At the close of *Richard II* Henry had already tempered his newly acquired sense of a royal identity with the knowledge that '[i]f any plague hang over us' it is that of his son, the 'young wanton and effeminate' haunter of London's taverns and brothels.[12] The theme is reprised almost immediately at the start of *1 Henry IV*, when the contrast with Hotspur implied at the end of the previous play is made explicit by Henry's confessed envy of Northumberland (Hotspur's father) having 'A son who is the theme of honour's tongue', one who is 'sweet Fortune's minion and her pride' (I.i.82). Made in the awareness that Hotspur has scant respect for his kingship, the terms of Henry's praise are more double-edged than at first appears. 'Fortune's minion' may suggest someone favoured by destiny, or it may suggest a plaything of chance. It is against the latter contingency that the politician's understanding, and use, of history is supposed to offer protection.

When Henry upbraids his son about the rumours of his 'inordinate and low desires' (III.ii.12) which are dishonouring them both, he urges two forceful examples – a negative one drawn from the past (the deposed Richard) and a positive one from the present (Hotspur). Both of these demonstrate Henry's clear-sighted grasp of the centrality of perception (he uses the word 'Opinion', III.ii.42) in the gaining and maintaining of political power. It is a grasp inevitably affected by his personal prejudices, but one with a much closer fit to circumstance than Hotspur's wildly revisionary view of the deposed king Richard which we heard earlier. The example Richard had afforded was that of a legitimate monarch who had ruined his reputation by becoming 'a companion to the common streets'. Instead of maintaining an air of mystery (the crucial public relations stance for any monarch), his royal presence became

---

* In Shakespeare's period, 'canker' could denote both a weed (specifically the dog rose) and a corrosive disease – a range of meanings which Hotspur's insult brings together most effectively.

'stale' through familiarity. Richard had even seen fit to associate with common performers, 'shallow jesters and rash bavin wits', confident that the sacred nature of kingship could not be tainted by circumstance.*,[13] His rival, Henry, supplies this absence of royal behaviour by performing the majesty Richard takes for granted, although he himself remains oblivious to the contradiction between his scorn for performers and his enthusiasm for royal role-playing. Critics point out the revealing verbs Henry uses in recalling his own piece of acting – how it 'stole all courtesy from heaven' and 'dressed' him in 'humility' (ll. 51–2). By insisting that Hal fall in step with this hypocritical kind of performance the king threatens to lock them both into a display of power which will always seem aspirational, even after the kingship is secured. But there is a deeper irony for Henry. He is not to know that Hal has already pronounced his loose, Richard-like behaviour to be itself an act (see his soliloquy at I.ii.185–207), which is building towards a classic theatrical 'reversal' at the moment he becomes king, when he will 'dazzle' the world with the appearance of a miraculous 'reformation' in behaviour.

In producing Hotspur as a living example for Hal's admonishment (despite the fact that Hotspur is now in open revolt against him), Henry adds another slant to the practice of seeking political use-value in historical exempla. Hotspur is the embodiment of a chivalric ideal of glorious action which is both timeless and very much of his moment. He scoffs at the archaisms and quasi-pagan mysticism of his Welsh fellow rebel Glendower, but also carries with him a personal history of 'never-dying honour' – victories won, captives taken – which privileges martial endeavour in the ancient style (he is a 'Mars in swaddling clothes', according to the king, l. 112). He is the play's most abundant citer of

---

* Medieval and Elizabethan thinking dealt with this idea of a split between what the king does and what the king is in the doctrine of the king's 'Two Bodies'. The body natural was mortal and corruptible, like everyone else's, but the body politic was immortal and unchangeable: the manifestation of a divine sanction to rule. As such, the body politic could neither be forcibly removed nor contaminated by the actions of the natural body. Although the two bodies were conceived of as indivisible, a crisis of kingship could inevitably expose the gap between them, and Shakespeare's dramatisation of Richard II's deposition arguably focuses on just this.

history – its stand-in 'historian' – who nonetheless never cites a heroic predecessor as his model.[14] When Henry, thinking of his relationship to Richard II, claims 'as I was then is Percy [i.e. Hotspur] now' he in fact flatters himself, for Hotspur's assault, 'of no right, nor colour like to right', upon his kingdom is undertaken in direct repudiation of the kind of guile Henry had employed.

The fact that the play depicts events in a late-chivalric period should not blind us to Hotspur's idiosyncratic role within the narrative: history plays (it bears repeating) are not altogether re-creations of a particular historical moment but examinations of how that moment can become meaningful for later ones, and it is Hotspur's job to provide the more obviously 'Renaissance' mindsets of the king and Hal with a 'medieval' example of the code of honour on which to work. Hal's response to his father's bitter comparison is to declare that he will achieve the standard of honour embodied in Hotspur through a stroke of politic calculation: he will 'redeem' past behaviour 'on Percy's head', killing him 'in the closing of some glorious day' for an 'exchange' of '[h]is glorious deeds for my indignities'. The logic is faultless, fully consistent with a chivalric code of appropriating the honours of the vanquished party. But the idiom is chillingly pragmatic – a balancing of the books between Hotspur's glories and Hal's own shames, summed up in Hal's identification of Hotspur as a 'factor' whom he is allowing to 'engross up glorious deeds on my behalf' (ll. 147–8). If Richard III turned out to be a mere 'factor' for supernatural powers, a gatherer of souls within the domain of providence, then Hotspur is being groomed by Hal for a comparable role – a gatherer of honours – within the domain of statecraft. Hal's logic delivers something of a jolt, perhaps because it represents such a queasy reversal of the trope we have been examining in this section. The glorious dead are not here revived to frame an example; a living example is set up to be killed in order that his glory may be purloined.

The beneficiary of this strategy, however, is not Hal but the outlandish figure of Falstaff, who on the battlefield at Shrewsbury claims the credit for Hal's slaying of Hotspur. Hal's wresting of glories away from Hotspur has been a nuanced act of theft: these are 'proud titles' which he has fairly 'won' in combat even while he has 'robbed'

Hotspur of his youth (V.iv.76–8). By contrast, Falstaff's theft of glory from Hal is straightforward: one entirely in keeping with the career of petty stealing he has plied throughout. Why does the play give the fame of Hotspur's overthrow to him, with Hal's tacit endorsement? Falstaff is the walking antithesis of most values in the play – of honour, of self-sacrifice, of aristocratic bearing. He is quite possibly the antithesis of the genre, deriving as he does from the same comedic, Saturnalian stable as Sir Toby Belch is later to do in *Twelfth Night*, most particularly in his protracted mockery of Rule in the tavern scene, in which he plays the king to Hal's miscreant. It helps that he comes across as ahistorical, outside time: a knight of sixty-odd years who is governed by the urges of an infant, sleeping, eating and drinking in defiance of a reality principle that would confine these activities to a time and a place. The very first bit of dialogue we hear between himself and Hal establishes this:

> FALSTAFF: Now, Hal, what time of day is it, lad?
> PRINCE: Thou art so fat-witted with drinking of old sack, and unbuttoning thee after supper, and sleeping upon benches after noon, that thou hast forgotten to demand that truly which thou wouldst truly know. What a devil hast thou to do with the time of the day? (I.ii.1–6)

By the same token, one of his last acts is to proffer Hal a bottle of wine in place of a pistol in the heat of battle: 'There's that will sack a city', he declares, at which *The Prince draws it out, and finds it to be a bottle of sack* (V.iii.54–6). One argument is that by allowing Falstaff the credit of Hotspur's defeat, the reputation of Hotspur is thereby diminished: it is a calculated act which works to demean the rebel cause. But Hal himself is by public reputation not much Falstaff's superior: his one public gesture of chivalry, sending a challenge of single combat to Hotspur, is immediately withdrawn by his father, and no one remarks on it again. All the honours he goes on to win in battle are of a strictly private kind: rescuing his father from the assault of Douglas (with the king alone witness of this redemptive act), and the slaying of Hotspur, the honour of which he compassionately foregoes by refusing to take his colours. The play, then, does not show Hal paying 'the debt [he] never promised' by achieving public glory (that will be the outcome of the sequel, *Henry IV Part 2*). Here, his culling of honours for private reward leads towards a different kind of reversal, which sees Hal stepping outside the cycle of emulation almost everyone else seems so keen to perpetuate.

As we have seen here, and as will also be demonstrated by the extended discussion of *Henry V* below, Shakespeare's history plays do not just offer ways of moulding the narrative matter of the chronicles. Part of what made these plays sophisticated, ideologically valuable entertainments rather than theatrical potboilers was their continued negotiation with an idea of what history is and with how it could be used. It bears repeating that in terms of genre these lively confrontations with the dead were, at least until the appearance of formal tragicomedy, the freshest imaginable experience on the London stages.

Extended Commentary: *Henry V* (1599)

'An Imp of Fame'

Shakespeare's *Henry V* was written and performed a year or so after the two *Henry IV* plays, probably in early 1599. As the inaugural production for the new playhouse built by Shakespeare's company – the Globe theatre on the Bankside – *Henry V* was also to be the last of Shakespeare's chronicle history plays (or almost the last: there is a curious return to the history genre at the very tail end of his career with *Henry VIII*). The play's subject is fitting as a leave-taking to the genre. The first tetralogy had looked back over its shoulder at Henry V's reign as a bitter contrast to his son's: the opening lines of the first of the *Henry VI* plays acknowledge the passing of 'King Henry the Fifth, too famous to live long'.[15] The second tetralogy had led *up* to that theme of fame by making the early 'infamy' of the young prince its foremost object of consideration in dramatic terms. The dramatic tradition which Shakespeare inherited dealing with Henry V had also made fame and this particular king indissociable: the anonymous *The Famous Victories of Henry the fifth* had recently been performed and was published in 1598. Both this play and Shakespeare's *Henry V* made particular capital out of the most celebrated event of Henry's reign, his defeat of the French forces at the battle of Agincourt in 1415, announcing it in the subtitles as a major narrative focus (in Shakespeare's play it is the central one). As we shall see, however, the huge fame which accrues to Henry as a result of the victory is not registered by him as personal achievement but as an almost taboo subject – a triumph not to be credited to himself or his army but to God alone.*

As a depiction of the pivotal reign in Shakespeare's adaptation of the English chronicles, as well as the history play with the deepest generic back-story, we might expect *Henry V* to be more 'overdetermined' (in the sense of being overloaded with narrative input) than any other chronicle play in the canon. In fact, as several stage and screen versions have shown, the play is more than capable of standing alone, signalling its independence from the *Henry IV* plays in both historical and theatrical terms.[16] The play makes frequent reference to both the recent and the more remote past – the king's wild companions from his princely days and his father's usurpation of the crown – but the launching of a foreign war which forms the play's backdrop alters the context in which these familiar themes become negotiated. Most strikingly of all, the play makes use of a structural convention which is very uncharacteristic of the often realistic and episodic idiom of the history genre: a classical 'Chorus', to make an artificial division of the play into five consecutive acts. While the previous history plays had made occasional use of non-realistic figures (such as the emblematic 'Rumour', who sets the tone for *Henry IV Part 2*), nowhere in any Shakespeare play, in any genre,+ is there an ordering

---

* Shakespeare will follow his chronicle sources in Holinshed by showing Henry carefully ascribing victory all to God, but will surpass them in making Henry proscribe, on pain of death, any man to boast of it.

+ Both *The Tempest* and *The Comedy of Errors* observe, with varying degrees of fidelity, the neoclassical unities of time, place and action, and there are Chorus figures in *Pericles* and *The Winter's Tale*; but these do not become key structural motifs in the way that the *Henry V* Chorus does.

principle so pointedly deployed. It may seem possible, on the basis of what has been said above, to make some gratifyingly straightforward statements about the formal and affective properties of this particular history play. The miraculous English victory at Agincourt makes a direct emotional appeal to patriotism (one that remains stirring, even if some modern audiences feel highly resistant to that sort of thing), and the overt five-act structure augments the heroic tone and ritual presentation. Nonetheless, a question remains as to how far these facets of the play work together in support of Henry's 'famous victory', and how far they operate in conflict with one another to offer ironic commentary on a war of aggression which, while achieving spectacular military success, fails to secure a lasting peace.

A Necessary Victim?

The play's immediate job is to show the historical moment it represents as fully heroic rather than concerned with nostalgic – or bitter – reflection upon a supposedly superior past. It builds up a picture of the new king as in every way the embodiment of his martial ancestors: indeed, their memory is invoked less, as Nashe would have it, for the purposes of comparison, than for underwriting an absolute continuity with the past after the ignoble interruptions of previous generations of kings:

> Awake remembrance of these valiant dead,
> And with your puissant arm renew their feats.
> You are their heir, you sit upon their throne,
> The blood and courage that renowned them
> Runs in your veins … [17]

The play also has subtler means of invoking the dead for its purposes, however. In each of the history plays discussed so far we identified a particular figure who in some degree haunted the actions and politics of the present. *Henry V* makes ingenious use of this motif. The old, fat knight John Falstaff, who over the course of the two *Henry IV* plays had made a career of helping Hal misspend his youth, was banished from Hal's sight immediately after his consecration as king at the end of *Henry IV Part 2*. In *Henry V* he appears only by the report of others: first when he is announced as grievously ill, and second when he is pronounced dead. His pathetic, off-stage demise is traced directly back to his treatment at the hands of the newly crowned Henry, with the remnants of the Eastcheap group trying to reconcile their positive view of the new king with the belief that he 'hath killed his heart', and 'run bad humours on the knight' (II.i.88, 121).

In fact, the rejection of Falstaff is the rejection of all such 'humorous' instability and pursuit of the appetites which both Hal and Falstaff had laid claim to in the *Henry IV* plays. Hal's relationship to the pleasure seekers among the London taverns had all along been an (ultimately inextricable) combination of clever play-acting to disguise his true purposes and genuine self-indulgence, and by *Part 2* he was already expressing anxiety at his continued predilection '[s]o idly to profane the precious time' – in other words, to be subject to the play of events rather than an active participant in them. In his final exchange with his father at King Henry's death-bed he pointedly allays the latter's dread that his son's reign will be one of 'riot' from which the 'muzzle of restraint' will be removed, and in so doing confirms the earlier observation of the king's advisor, Warwick, that 'The Prince but studies his companions / Like a strange tongue', from which he may:

> in the perfectness of time,
> Cast off his followers, and their memory
> Shall as a pattern or a measure live
> By which his Grace must mete the lives of others
> Turning past evils to advantages. (*Henry IV Part 2*, IV.iv.68–78)

Warwick's faith in the capacity of the prince to read patterns in human behaviour stems partly from his own belief, expressed earlier in the play, that 'There is a history in all men's lives / Figuring the nature of the times deceas'd', which will, to the canny observer, quite literally 'hatch' into predictable action (III.i.81–5). This is an idea of historical process located somewhere in between the utterly impersonal 'revolution of the times' which Henry despairs of anyone ever understanding, and the strictly bodily, appetitive activities of Falstaff and his cronies which lurk outside the process of historical change. It is rooted in the individual, a product of their own motives and desires, but it is also symptomatic of a general pattern which can be understood with study, and describes a more positive understanding of the relationship of the here and now to past and future times.

The dead figure of Falstaff is to recur only once more in *Henry V*, rapidly receding into oblivion, when his name is 'forgotten' in conversation between the Welshman Fluellen and the Englishman Gower during a pause in the battle of Agincourt. Fluellen is offering an absurdly reductive, over-literalised version of Warwick's argument, claiming that 'there is figures in all things' throughout human history, and that Hal exactly resembles Alexander the Great in having killed 'his best friend'. For Hal:

> being in his right wits and good judgements, turned away the fat knight with the great-belly doublet: he was full of jests, and gipes, and knaveries, and mocks; I have forgot his name. (IV.vii.45–9)

Of this poignant semi-recollection of an indomitable wit (a forerunner of Hamlet's graveside meditation on Yorick, albeit far less flattering), Robert C. Jones has commented that it creates 'a simple inversion of the role of the dead hero who lives in remembrance to inspire the present', providing the play instead with a 'dead antihero whom the living hero must forget in order to fulfil his own role as leader'.[18] Although Gower briefly reminds Fluellen of Falstaff's name, we get a clear sense of that name now becoming dissociated from Henry's own, leaving only a kind of cipher – the girth and the mirth of the man – in its place. An earlier scene had already provided intimations of Falstaff's oblivion in the little eulogy given by the tavern hostess, Mistress Quickly: 'he's in Arthur's bosom, if ever man went to Arthur's bosom' (II.ii.9–10). A beautifully apposite confusion of 'Abraham's bosom' and the myth of King Arthur's resting place, 'Arthur's bosom' is, by way of malapropism, no place at all. The play seems to have the paradoxical habit of recalling Falstaff in order to make his memory fare a little worse each time – to deny him the capacity to 'haunt' the present the way we have seen previous figures do. Gower disputes Fluellen's idea that Henry's rejection 'killed' the knight, reinforcing the strong sense of antinomies – of contradictory positions – in the new king's behaviour. Falstaff's memory thus flags up the perplexing issue of Henry's personal responsibility now that he has assumed kingship, and it is one the play will return to again and again.

Playing the Blame Game

The play's opening business is all devoted to the launching of a war against France – not because the kingdom represents any threat to Henry's own but because of a claim, going back to his great grandfather Edward III's day, to 'some certain dukedoms / And generally to the crown and seat of France' (I.i.82). This sounds like a return to the ethical world of Hotspur – to titles, honour and renown sought purely for their own sakes – and Henry will protest his desire for honour during the course of the play. However, the build-up to the declaration of war betrays a very different set of motives. The initial impetus comes not from advisors or courtiers, but from the church, which feels imperilled by a renewed threat to church lands from the reforming policy of the Lancastrian dynasty. Their remedy is to distract the king by offering him a vast sum of money to pursue the territorial claims: a piece of unabashed policy which has the effect of removing from Henry himself any taint of the political manoeuvring which had attached itself to his father. Indeed, it had been Henry IV's dying advice to his son at the close of the previous play to 'busy giddy minds with foreign quarrels' – quite literally to displace the threat of civil conflict onto a foreign target – and the church's self-interest is now used to provide the operative means in this one (the play can have its cake and eat it here, associating the historical church of Henry V's time with pre-reformation ideals while obliquely affiliating Henry himself to reforming ones). In the council chamber, when the bishops put their almost comically obfuscated argument to the king, encouraging his claim to the French crown, it is Henry himself who forces them to square their argument with God's law – with 'right and conscience' – mindful of what the churchmen 'shall incite us to':

> take heed how you impawn our person,
> How you awake our sleeping sword of war:
> We charge you in the name of God take heed.
> For never two such kingdoms did contend
> Without much fall of blood … (I.ii.21–5)

The Archbishop of Canterbury obligingly falls in with this kingly act of self-exculpation, by openly insisting that the 'sin [be] upon my head' (l. 97).

This shifting of responsibility is more than just a moral clearing ground prior to the launching of war against France. It becomes a mode of action specifically associated with King Henry throughout the play. It reappears a little later in the scene, when the Dauphin's mocking gift of tennis balls provides the specific pretext for a war which has already been decided on, allowing Henry to claim that the Frenchman's 'soul / Shall stand sore charged for the wasteful vengeance' that will follow it (ll. 283–5). It appears in the next act, when the three conspirators against Henry's life – Scroop, Cambridge and Grey – find on the revelation of their plot that the 'mercy that was quick' in Henry only moments before, and which might have spared them the death penalty, is negated by their 'own counsel' to Henry that he put a lowly heckler to death (II.ii.79–80).

The long rebuke to Scroop which follows, complaining of his convincing show of loyalty, is doubtless a tour de force of betrayed sentiment; but it also works self-reflexively to bolster the sense that Henry now occupies a special sphere of moral innocence and integrity which puts him beyond all comprehension of deceit in others (ironic enough, given his history of dissimulation in the earlier plays): 'this revolt of thine', he tells Scroop, 'is like / Another fall of man' (ll. 141–2). The king's words may prompt recollection of an earlier exchange between the two churchmen on Henry's 'reformation' from wildness into piety – the assumption of a newly 'perfected' state which invites comparison with paradise before the Fall (I.i.25–69). Once on French soil, both the king's ambassadors and Henry himself continue to pursue this peculiar conceit of deflecting all blame for English aggression onto their opponents. The Duke of Exeter issues a warning to the French king that he himself must show compassion '[o]n the poor souls for whom this hungry war / Opens his vasty jaws':

> on your head
> Turning the widow's tears, the orphans' cries,
> The dead men's blood, the pining maidens' groans,
> For husbands, fathers and betrothed lovers
> That shall be swallowed in this controversy. (II.iv.105–9)

Most emphatic of all such instances is the hair-raising threat delivered by Henry to the French town of Harfleur, promising outright atrocities against the besieged inhabitants:

> What is it then to me if impious war,
> Arrayed in flames like to the prince of fiends,
> Do with his smirched complexion all fell feats
> Enlinked to waste and desolation?
> What is't to me when you yourselves are cause,
> If your pure maidens fall into the hand
> Oh hot and forcing violation? (III.iii.15–21)

The idiom is that of classical, pre-Christian warfare: the rape, infanticide and slaughter of the aged derive from Homeric motifs about the 'necessity' of war, while the threatened 'desolation' prefigures Mark Antony's desire in *Julius Caesar* to set 'the dogs of war' on Rome. But Henry himself remains utterly dissociated from the outcome and in a measure helpless to prevent it, declaring it 'bootless [to] spend our vain command / Upon th'enraged soldiers' (ll. 24–5). In his own construction he is a Christian king who has conquered his own appetites and rages, but who presides over an army operating out of a quite different ethical system.* If the effect is disconcerting, one of moral dissonance, it also provides the climax to the particular narrative arc which has followed the king's 'superhuman' surmounting of personal responsibility for bloodshed during the first half of the play. From this point on the play abruptly shifts its emphasis towards the 'sickness growing' in the English army, to the sudden diminishment of the king's power, to the threat of the French counter-attack, and to an increasing emphasis on the king's common humanity.+

---

* Cf. I.ii.242–4: 'We are no tyrant but a Christian king, / Unto whose grace our passion is as subject / As are our wretches fettered in our prisons.'

+ The sense of Henry's elevation above ordinary mortals is by no means lost, however, as witness the king's unmoved response to the execution of Bardolph, one of his erstwhile Eastcheap companions, at III.vi.106.

Agincourt: A New Way of Compassing Fame

The night before the battle of Agincourt Henry takes part in a discussion with some of the common soldiers of his army, all of whom fear and expect their destruction at the hands of the French forces the next day. If the Chorus has prepared us for the inspiring sight of Henry moving among his troops, comforting them with 'a little touch of Harry in the night', the idealism is swiftly undercut by what turns out to be a highly discomforting experience for the king himself. Deploying a little touch of subterfuge, Henry has concealed himself in an officer's cloak (ostensibly for a moment of private contemplation), but is drawn in to several unguarded conversations with his men. In the cagey set of exchanges with Bates, Williams and Court, both disguised king and soldiers attempt to 'feel other men's minds' – to sound one another out – about the parlous state of the army's chances. While the soldiers insist on the gap between the king's experience of their peril and their own, Henry – speaking 'on behalf' of the king – tries to close that gap. The distinction between king and subject is one of degree not kind, Henry argues, since:

> his ceremonies laid by, in his nakedness he appears but a man;
> and though his affections [i.e. his emotions] are higher mounted
> than ours, yet when they stoop they stoop with the like wing.
> (IV.i.105–8)

But the soldiers prove resistant to this notion, persisting in their opinion that the king is in a measure immune from the fate that is about to befall them, not least through the expectation of his being ransomed if captured in battle, an option not available to the common soldier (l. 122, ll. 189–90). Yet this gap the soldiers insist upon has further implications, developed by Williams out of Bates's argument that obedience to the king releases them from responsibility for the bloodshed in an unjust war:

> I am afeard there are few die well that die in a battle, for how
> can they charitably dispose of anything when blood is their
> argument? Now if these men do not die well it will be a black
> matter for the King, that led them to it, who to disobey were
> against all proportion of subjection. (ll. 141–6)

It is important to realise that no one here expresses concern with the justice of the war against France on a political level. They are only interested in the theoretical consequences of this for the individual soul, and Williams imagines that he has spotted a loophole: the larger crime of an unjust war, which would implicate the king alone, absorbs any and all lesser crimes of the men who die unabsolved in that war, effectively offloading them onto the king. Henry sees this argument directly for what it is, and successfully reasons Williams out of it – 'Every subject's duty is the King's, but every subject's soul is his own' – but Williams will not let go of the belief that the gap between king and subject remains insurmountable; that there is nothing 'a poor and private displeasure can do against a monarch' (ll. 196–7). After their dispute has elevated itself to the level of a 'quarrel', Henry in soliloquy vents his distress at the additional and, as he sees it, superfluous burden which Williams has tried to place on kingship:

> Upon the King! 'Let us our lives, our souls,
> Our debts, our careful wives,
> Our children and our sins lay on the King!'
> We must bear all. O hard condition,
> Twin-born with greatness, subject to the breath
> Of every fool whose sense no more can feel
> But his own wringing. (ll. 227–30)

The commoner Williams has, in Henry's view, found in the king's greatness a convenient repository for precisely those 'poor and private displeasure[s]' which should be his own responsibility. As Alexander Leggatt points out, the dispute with Williams caps the sequence by which Henry has been shifting the burden of responsibility (for war, for capital crimes, etc.) onto others.[19] Yet this seems to be more than just a case of Henry running out of means to evade this burden. Henry's tacit acceptance of the *unjust* responsibility Williams wishes on him implies a fulsome reversal in the play's logic: the king now takes on more than he feels he should, fully aware that his only return on it will be a hollow and profitless 'ceremony' – the impersonal trappings of his office. As the soliloquy shifts into Henry's prayer for his troops' safety (ll. 286–302), this stance of adopting excessive responsibility figures itself in his plea that God 'think not upon the fault / My father made in compassing the crown' (ll. 290–1). It is a prayer which will be unambiguously answered by the outcome of the battle itself, when 'God's arm' shows itself in the crushing number of French losses (ten thousand) against the miraculously small number of English dead (fewer than thirty). For this outrageous figure Shakespeare follows the least cautious of the estimates given in Holinshed.[20] In other areas, however, he tellingly departs from that source: in making it a capital crime to boast of the victory, as we noted above; but also in blatantly ignoring Henry's own tactical triumph of arraying sharpened wooden stakes in front of his archers to repel the French cavalry. Indeed, while *The Famous Victories* had made a point of praising Henry's 'pollicie' in doing this, *Henry V* makes a point of stressing the opposite – that never was a battle so won 'without stratagem / But in plain shock and even play of battle' (IV.viii.109–10). Both the play's protagonist and his playwright go out of their way to deny Henry the explicit claim to fame that was his by right in the chronicles.

It is part of the Chorus's job to supply this deficit in fame, through its safely artificial medium which provides a rhetorical, narrative-heavy counterpoint to the actions of the play. The Chorus, like much else about *Henry V*, has divided critical opinion as to its overall effect. In Part Two we touched on the way its protestations about the unrepresentable nature of the play's subject matter helped reassure audiences of the enduring good faith of the playing company. But it could be argued that the Chorus protests too much here – that it so repeatedly draws attention to this 'problem' that it threatens to be counterproductive to the theatrical enterprise. We might also feel suspicious that early published versions of the play (even if they appeared without the company's blessing) dispensed with the Chorus altogether, making for a lightweight but more generically conventional retelling of the story. Is the Chorus integral to the drama, or does its peculiar style make it somehow 'detachable'? Some commentators feel that the matter can be resolved by regarding the Chorus as working to create a critical detachment in the audience. Graham Holderness, for example, argues that its overinsistence on the poverty of theatrical representation checks the audience's full involvement in the fiction, employing a kind of Brechtian dialectic between 'empathy and objectivity', so that the play 'diminishes rather than enlarges the audience's readiness to receive it as true'.[21] Leggatt, pointing to the frequent mismatch between what the Chorus says will happen and what actually transpires on stage (such as putting us down in Eastcheap when we had been promised 'transport' to the fleet in Southampton, or narrating the journey to France after the army has been reported arriving there), also regards the choric device as inviting the audience to be 'self-aware' and to 'compar[e] our readings with his'.[22] Bringing such twentieth/twenty-first-century dramaturgical viewpoints to bear on the issue, a strong case can be made for seeing the Chorus as an unreliable narrator, and hence as a focus for the play's 'ironic' treatment of Henry's war against France.

However, as these readings also acknowledge, the excitement generated by the epic tone and rhetoric of the choric speeches introducing each act remains irresistible. They are, moreover, calculated to involve the audience as well as narrate the unperformable aspects of the story. From the opening plea for audience acceptance of the Chorus's operative function – 'Let us / On your imaginary forces work' – it increasingly extends, as Pamela Mason puts it, a sense of 'partnership' between itself and the audience that 'is characterised by work rather than play'.[23] By the beginning of the third act, emphasis on audience passivity has become reversed, with the listeners being asked actively to 'Grapple your minds to sternage' of the fleet leaving for overseas, and to 'Work, work your thoughts' in helping to 'mount' the siege of Harfleur (III.0.18, 25). There is an increasing emphasis on imaginative participation which, as critics point out, figuratively 'enlists' the audience in Henry's expedition. Perhaps we can therefore see the Chorus's role as one which is cleverly straddling the participatory and critically detached poles of audience experience. In doing so it mimics Henry's own tactic of shifting responsibility onto others. Initially entreating the audience 'patiently to hear, kindly to judge' the play which unfolds, it subsequently inveigles that audience into becoming an equal bearer of the narrative burden and a co-actor with Henry. On that reading the medium of the Chorus is a recognisable scion of 'media' activity in wars throughout history, using its position at the interface between the raw events of the story and its hearers to edge the latter from a state of objectivity to one of complicity.

Notes

1   Thomas Nashe, *Pierce Penniless his Supplication to the Devil*, in *The Unfortunate Traveller and other works*, ed. J. B. Steane (Harmondsworth; Penguin, 1985; 1971), pp. 112–13.

2   *A Warning for Fair Women: A Critical Edition*, ed. Charles Dale Cannon (The Hague: Mouton, 1975), Induction.

3   Kristian Smidt, quoted in Emma Smith (ed.), *Shakespeare's Histories: A Guide to Criticism* (London: Blackwell, 2003), p. 39.

4   Irving Ribner, *The English History Play in the Age of Shakespeare* (Princeton: Princeton University Press, 1957), p. 19.

5   Ribner, *The English History Play*, p. 18.

6   'The providential pattern of sacred dynastic succession and divinely ordered hierarchy, which E. M. W. Tillyard saw as a universally accepted belief common to the playwrights and their audience, is much more evident in the older chronicle sources and the official homilies than it is in the plays themselves, where the cause and effect of historical events is increasingly firmly centred in human choices and human actions', Margot Heinemann, 'Political Drama', in *The Cambridge Companion to English Renaissance Drama*, pp. 161–205, p. 179.

7   Nashe, *Pierce Penniless*, p. 113.

8   William Shakespeare, *King Henry VI Part Three* (Alexander Text), III.ii.166–7.

9   William Shakespeare, *Richard III*, ed. Anthony Hammond, Arden, 2nd series (London: Thomson Learning, 1981; 2003), I.i.1–40.

10   For a helpful summary of the characteristics and theatrical development drawn on here, see Peter Happé, *English Drama Before Shakespeare* (London: Longman, 1999), pp. 137–9.

11   William Shakespeare, *King Henry IV Part 1*, ed. David Scott Kastan, Arden, 3rd series (London: Thomason, 2002), I.iii.239, 243.

12   William Shakespeare, *King Richard II*, ed. Charles R. Forker, Arden, 3rd series, V.iii.3, 10.

13   See in particular E. H. Kantorowicz, *The King's Two Bodies: A Study in Mediaeval Political Theology* (Princeton, NJ: Princeton University Press, 1957).

14   On this point, see Robert C. Jones, *These Valiant Dead: Renewing the Past in Shakespeare's Histories* (Iowa City: University of Iowa Press), pp. 100–1. While agreeing in many details with Jones's lucid discussion of the role of 'history' in the history plays, we are offering here a slightly different reading of the way history is figured in the person of Hotspur.

15   William Shakespeare, *Henry VI Part 1*, ed. Edward Burns, Arden, 3rd series (London: Cengage, 2000), I.i.6.

16   Tillyard found the play to be 'as truly separated from the two parts of *Henry IV* as *Richard II* is allied to them', but his analysis was based on a rather redundant sense of 'inconsistencies' in the character of Henry over the three plays (Tillyard, *History Plays*, p. 309).

17   William Shakespeare, *Henry V*, ed. T.W. Craik, Arden, 3rd Series (London: Thomson Learning, 1995), I.ii.115–19.

18   Jones, *These Valiant Dead*, pp. 141, 143–4.

19   Alexander Leggatt, *Shakespeare's Political Drama The History Plays and Roman Plays* (London: Routledge, 1988), pp. 133–5.

20   Holinshed immediately follows this reported figure with the assertion that 'other writers of greater credit affirme, that there were slaine about five or six hundred persons'. For the estimates of a modern-day historian see Juliet Barker, *Agincourt: the King, the Campaign, the Battle* (London: Little, Brown, 2005), especially ch. 16, where a minimum number of 112 English dead is suggested.

21   Graham Holderness, *Shakespeare Recycled: The Making of Historical Drama* (New York: Harvester, 1992), pp. 109–11.

22   Leggatt, *Shakespeare's Political Drama*, pp. 123–5.

23   Pamela Mason, '*Henry V*: "the quick forge and working house of thought"', in *The Cambridge Companion to Shakespeare's History Plays*, pp. 177–92, p. 178.

Tyranny , Terror and Tragedy on the English Stage: *Doctor Faustus, Othello* and *Macbeth*

What might the average Elizabethan theatre-goer have understood by the theatrical genre of tragedy?[1] One answer to the question may be provided by briefly considering Marlowe's *Tamburlaine* of 1587, an experimental work which helped set the tone for the genre in the formative years of Elizabethan drama. An energetic, violent narrative of an all-conquering Scythian warlord, who rises with devastating ease from the rank of lowly shepherd to that of emperor over a mass of eastern kingdoms, the play was geared towards maximising the potentialities of the new London public stages, ushering onto them a whole new world of characters, settings, patterns of action and, above all, poetic language. The play's printed version from 1590 carried a subtitle on its title page emphasising Tamburlaine's 'tyranny, and terrour in Warre', for which he was 'tearmed the Scourge of God'. This intriguing set of attributes – which in its alliterative way reads rather like a hastily assembled theatrical strapline – goes some way to suggesting the composite nature of the tragic appeal the play was aiming at.

To take tyranny first, Phillip Sidney in his overview of dramatic genres in the *Apology for Poetry* thought that tragedy was 'most high and excellent' when it 'maketh kings fear to be tyrants, and tyrants manifest their tyrannical humours'.[2] Although a strong advocate for classical theories about dramatic form, Sidney's ideas about the conduct and fortunes of kings also carry overtones of a long-standing medieval tradition by which tragedy conducted an 'exposé of ruling-class corruption, for the ideological purpose of rendering the lives of high-living villains abominable to the populace'.[3] Such an emphasis 'on deserved rather than unmerited disgrace' could mesh with the broader notion of tragic narrative as showing a powerful individual who, as Chaucer's Monk defines it with some relish, 'stood in greet prosperitee / And is yfallen out of heigh degree / Into myserie, and endeth wrecchedly' – ostensibly due to the whim of Fortune but also (as many of the Monk's examples attest) to personal wickedness or defiance of God. If this 'rise and fall' shape bequeathed a rough idea of form to the Elizabethan stage, the notion of a deserved downfall due to a tyrannical misuse of power suggested the sort of narrative content that was preferred, one which chimed with Christian notions of virtue, humility and justice. In truth, tragedy here functioned as little more than an adjunct to the tradition of 'advice to princes' – poems, treaties and exempla on how to be a good ruler – and was distinguishable from other moral, cautionary narratives only in the social status of its protagonists and the spectacular ruin they suffered.

Marlowe's own approach to the format is instructive in its freshness: it takes a whole second part of *Tamburlaine* for the hero to reach that conclusion, which eventually comes about in speedy fashion after an explicit defiance of God (he burns a copy of the Koran). Marlowe is clearly more interested in the dramatic capital to be gained from Tamburlaine's tyrannies during the upward arc of Fortune's wheel than he is in the moral patterning of divine retribution on the way down.

The 'terrour' in the subtitle, by contrast, makes a statement about affect – about emotional response – which does seem to pay lip service to newly rediscovered classical conceptions of tragedy. The Greek philosopher Aristotle's only surviving work of literary criticism, the *Poetics*, argued that terror was one of the defining emotional pleasures of the genre. More specifically, a well-constructed work of tragedy should generate in the reader/auditor a complex effect derived from the combination of fear and pity in response to the protagonist's plight. The crowning example of such tragedy was, in Aristotle's view, Sophocles's *Oedpius Rex*, where both the craftsmanship of the drama (involving well-timed moments of 'reversal' and 'recognition') and its subject matter (the worthy king who had unwittingly slain his father and married his mother) combined to produce the canonical emotions. Here was a much more fully theorised idea of tragedy than had been provided by medieval writers, and for the humanist scholars who pondered it, it shifted the debate back towards technical and reception issues which had for long been obscured. It might be appropriate for tyrants to fear the wrath of divine justice or the fickleness of Fortune, but the idea that distressing emotions such as pity and fear could be pleasurable (and hence, in the case of a professional drama, marketable?) to a general audience was a new and potentially troubling concept.

Italian neoclassical critics, who did most of the thinking on this issue, were particularly exercised as to how to interpret Aristotle's original idea of the *catharsis* – or purgation (i.e. expulsion) – of these two emotions. From a Christian perspective, surely these were positive, necessary emotions, to be encouraged in the individual – fear of God on the one hand, Christ-like pity for the suffering on the other. How could it be a good thing to *expel* these emotions? In *Tamburlaine* the nod to the attractions of tragic terror occurs in the context of war and conquest, and becomes bound up with another concept that would stalk through many a tragic narrative on the English stages: that of the 'Scourge of God', or agent of divine wrath.* Tamburlaine, unlike Oedipus, is to be terrifying more for what he does than for what happens to him. However, since his conquests and cruelties are inflicted upon non-Christian kings and peoples, these terrors would be experienced at a safe remove for an Elizabethan audience, with a vicarious thrill rather than a moral lesson providing the emotional payoff.

Despite these claims to tragic status, the two parts of *Tamburlaine* would not strike us as tragedies in the sense in which we associate that term with Shakespeare's contributions to the genre, any more than they would have measured up to Aristotle's critical criteria (not to mention those of his zealous sixteenth-century neoclassical advocates). We would be more likely to bestow the label of 'true tragedy' on his subsequent *Doctor Faustus*, the first of the tragedies we will be looking at in this

* For an example of how Richard III, as 'heaven's factor', fulfilled a comparable role, see the discussion of this play in Part Three: 'Shakespeare's History Plays'.

section, which demonstrates a more recognisable emphasis on such favoured themes as choice, struggle, agonised debate, divided motives and emotional conflicts, all of which conspire to drag the protagonist to destruction. Yet in a way these apparently universal values are no less historically specific than the now irrecoverable pleasures of *Tamburlaine* and a host of other plays that would have passed for tragedy on the English professional stages.[4] In the discussion that follows we will try to see this trend towards psychological complexity in early modern English tragedy as a local and by no means inevitable outgrowth of the stage's appropriations of literary and theatrical materials from all around it – some of which were of a distinctly non-tragic kind.

One of these was the medieval notion of the 'psychomachia': the battle over – or within – the human soul, which persisted into Elizabethan times via morality dramas and Spenserian poetry.[5] What began as a pictorial and allegorical tradition with a specifically religious purpose – to show the Soul's suspension between Vices and Virtues and the inevitable fight between them – was reworked to great effect into those tragic contexts which emphasised the protagonists' particular agency in their own catastrophe. If *Doctor Faustus* first lays down the format for a fully interiorised psychomachia while retaining some of the morality drama's external trappings, *Othello*, *Macbeth* and *Hamlet* all go much further in integrating it as a dynamic feature of their dramas. These plays can hardly be reduced to this sort of structure, of course. But tracing its usage can give us a sense of just what is undergirding the peculiar power of these great tragedies – with their relentless focus on a central character, and the subjectively rich and drawn-out soliloquies which mark their progression towards disaster.

Finding Out the End: The Shaping Tensions of Marlowe's *Doctor Faustus*

Marlowe's tragedy *Doctor Faustus* may have received its first performance in 1592, the year before the playwright was killed.[6] Its story of a brilliant scholar who, desiring knowledge and power, enters into a contract with the Devil quickly established itself as a firm favourite on the Elizabethan stage, in the process becoming one of the period's most exhilarating theatrical experiences. The play's ultimate source is a German narrative of black magic and diabolic dealings, translated into English in 1592 as *The history of the damnable life, and deserved death of Doctor John Faustus*. The story as told in both source book and play has proved richly suggestive to critics and historians, who see in Faustus's *'damnable'* predicament a playing out of tensions between older, medieval and emergent modern-day values and beliefs. Thus spiritual well-being is set against material gain, intellectual orthodoxy against free-thinking independence, religion against science.[7] Certainly, the play seems to hover on the brink of a new world – one which valorises knowledge more than it desires obedience to God – and for that reason its doomed protagonist generates sympathy in many modern readers. But in fact we can see the play exploiting tensions between a variety of viewpoints and on a variety of levels, by this means producing its own kind of tragic experience for Elizabethan audiences.

Such tensions appear in aspects of the narrative, not least in the moment of the play's conclusion. In a clever twist on the theme of psychomachia – the allegorical representation of the conflict over the soul – the scholarly Faustus has contracted a bargain with Lucifer (via the mediation of his minion Mephostophilis) and exchanged his immortal soul for twenty-four years' worth of infernal powers. At the end of that allotted period Faustus finds himself unable to repent and thus receive God's mercy, and Lucifer reappears to claim his prize and drag Faustus to Hell. The doctor's damnation is presented as both inevitable and entirely deserved within a Christian moral framework. 'Faustus is gone. Regard his hellish fall', the Chorus demands in the epilogue to the play.[8] Yet a feeling of loss is allowed to accompany that sense of divine justice, and perhaps to qualify, even to disturb it. As it points the moral, the Chorus also laments 'Cut is the branch that might have grown full straight / And burned is Apollo's laurel bough / That sometimes grew within this learned man' (ll. 20–2). We might feel that two such distinctive registers – the admonitory and the plaintive – are at variance. Yet they are not necessarily experienced as being in conflict. They pull against each other with sufficient tension to create an emotional response of some complexity without forcing the experience of overt contradiction between them.[9] Such complex responses are the province of tragedy –

pity with fear, as classical theory demanded – but here at the conclusion of *Doctor Faustus* we also find an interplay of feelings approaching more specifically Renaissance values as well, as Faustus's desire for individual self-improvement is quashed by superhuman forces.

Tension of another kind is manifested in the play's use of dramatic form. We noted in Part Three: 'Shakespeare's History Plays' how, as *The Tragicall History of Doctor Faustus*, the play combines the episodic treatment typical of historical narrative with the more biographical slant of tragedy. The play follows its historical source quite closely in some of these episodes; in others it expands them greatly, but the emphasis remains on the individual fate rather than on political events. The comic scenes at the expense of the pope during the play's protracted mid-section were politically inflammatory enough to prompt censorship in earlier versions of the play; but the incidents themselves are more important for elaborating on Faustus's new-found magical abilities than for the papal satire they include. To this expansive, episodic approach the play adds elements from the tighter, but also more archaic, form of morality drama. In Shakespeare's *Richard III* the use of the morality format, while it may have been prompted by its usage in Marlowe's play, is nonetheless closely integrated with the historical narrative (see the discussion of Richard's self-identification as a 'formal vice' in Part Three: 'Shakespeare's History Plays'). In *Doctor Faustus* the repeated appearance of a Good Angel and a Bad Angel to exhort and tempt Faustus remains a much more obtrusive feature. As a result, the theatrical 'joins' between the tragical-historical and the allegorical modes are, perhaps deliberately, made more obvious. Functioning as two non-realistic, highly conventional dramatic figures, the Angels appear to Faustus in his most domestic, interior and realistic moments, typically when he is in his study, alone and in contemplation. There is therefore a productive tension of a psychological kind between these two dramatic modes: thought processes which reveal themselves through soliloquy in an 'episodic' fashion are rounded off, and thrown into relief, by the binary choices of a moral psychology symbolised by the two Angels.

Soliloquy and Salvation

In Faustus's first soliloquy we are made privy to a mind meandering among different intellectual positions, sifting and evaluating the learned professions of law, divinity, medicine, philosophy, and expressing a dissatisfaction with 'the end' – the ultimate goal – of each (I.i.4). All of these professions are of a scholastic kind well established from classical and medieval times, but although Faustus rejects them for the dark arts of necromancy he does not do so for reasons of their antiquity or redundancy. His enthusiasm for Aristotle remains undimmed – 'Sweet Analytics, 'tis thou hast ravished me' – or it does until he is brought up sharply against the finitude of philosophy's ambitions, which seems to offer 'no greater miracle' than to argue logically (ll. 6–10). The medley of Greek, Latin and vernacular tags with which Faustus sums up the attainment of each art expresses a mind impatient for new stimuli, and it carries him past the point of objective reflection (so perhaps arguing logically would have helped here after all).

Such a habit of mind starts to sound ominous when Faustus moves on to consider divinity: '"The reward of sin is death". That's hard.' (l. 40). Such a doctrine is 'hard' only because it is a partial reading of the passage in St Paul, one which stops short of acknowledging the countervailing claim in the same passage that redemption from sin is nonetheless freely bestowed on humanity by God. The effect of this argumentative missed step is twofold. It reinforces the irregular, episodic trend in Faustus's reasoning (one which marks a key development in the use of dramatic monologue to imitate the process of thought rather than simply summarise its content). But it also puts up an early marker of the association between Faustus and damnation – the fate which, the play frequently intimates, is to be his inevitable end. Suddenly, this whole, rather discursive business of choosing has become a terribly stark one, and now that he has decided to follow the 'metaphysics of magicians', the Good and Bad Angels appear to impose their binary morality upon that choice, neatly figured as an opposition between two very different kinds of deity: God, with his scriptures, and Jove, with his command of the elements (ll. 70–6).

As well as generating tensions through the use of contrasting dramatic forms, the play makes use of contrasting ideologies of salvation. This is seen most clearly in the vexing issue of the tragic 'inevitability' of Faustus's damnation. The Good Angel and its morality drama counterpart, the Old Man of the later scenes, seem to suggest that such an end is anything but pre-ordained and that, in accordance with orthodox Christian thinking, Faustus can make amends with God even after he has signed away his soul: 'Faustus repent; yet will God pity thee' (II.i.12); 'Yet, yet, thou hast an amiable soul / If sin by custom grow not into nature' (V.i.40–1). These exhortations, however, run up against a consistent strand in the play affirming that Faustus's 'nature' has already determined him in damnation, whether that be defined by what we nowadays think of as aspects of his 'character' (arrogant, aspirational, power-hungry), or by the more sinister transformation in 'nature' implied by his demand to be made 'a spirit' like Mephostophilis. Although the play obscures the precise outcome of this demand, the Bad Angel uses it to undermine Faustus's attempts to repent: 'Thou art a spirit; God cannot pity thee' (II.i.14). The Doctor's response to this points up the paradox of a 'will' which both is and is not free. Armed with the belief that God can pity even a repentant devil, he nonetheless finds that devil-hood and repentance are mutually exclusive: 'My heart is harden'd, I cannot repent / Scarce can I name salvation, faith, or heaven' (II.i.18–19). The more radical Calvinist doctrine of predestination, which holds that God has fore-ordained both the saved and the damned to their particular ends, is one possible route into the problem which the play sets of balancing responsibility with inevitability.[10] In a disconcerting way, the play manages to make both possibilities somehow true, as the Prologue describes him as a man 'swollen with cunning of a self-conceit', and likens him to the mythological Icarus whose 'waxen wings did mount above his reach' which 'melting, heavens conspired his overthrow' (Prologue, ll. 20–2). The 'heavens' reserve their unfathomable right to ordain the man to disaster, but make it a direct product of his ambition anyway.

What the play loses in terms of theological consistency it gains in tragic force, as Faustus's damnation starts to look as if it proceeds from all sources indifferently – Hell, Heaven and his own disastrous and misguided choices. In the final scenes the accent is placed increasingly on the role of pleasure in those choices, on an exchange of temporal and bodily satisfactions for the soul's immortal bliss, so that by the end he can summarise his career to his fellow scholars as that of one who '[f]or the vain pleasure of four and twenty years ... hath lost eternal joy and felicity' (V.ii.68–9). In fact, pleasure has all along been in a complicated relationship with knowledge, as Faustus's initial, giddy assessment of magic's potentialities attests: 'Shall I make spirits fetch me what I please? / Resolve me of all ambiguities?' (I.i.78–9). If in these earlier scenes knowledge has been sublimated into pleasure – an appetite to know new things which so many commentators have found characteristic of the Renaissance spirit of enquiry – in later scenes we find it under-propping carnal pleasure per se, as when Faustus obtains the sexual favours of the legendary 'Helen' whom he has earlier paraded as an object for scholarly admiration.*

It is left to the stock morality figures of the play – the Good and Bad Angels, Lucifer and his minions – not to mention the presence of hell-mouth gaping before him on the stage to reinforce the point about the World and the Flesh: 'His store of pleasures must be sauced with pain'; 'He that loves pleasure must for pleasure fall' (V.ii.17, 140). Yet the moralistic tenor of these concluding scenes is again thrown into confusion by Faustus's final speech as he awaits midnight and Lucifer's exaction of his bond (V.ii.143–200). In this harrowing tour de force of dramatic poetry, Faustus submits to the Christian justice of his doom while at the same time crying out for a form of relief that lies outside that system of justice. His panicked Latin invocation, imploring the horses of the night to run more slowly, is torn from (of all places) Ovidian erotic poetry, where a lover wishes to eke out the pleasures of love-making. His plea to 'the stars that reigned at my nativity' to draw him up into the higher reaches of the sky voices contentious astrological beliefs with a literalism sharpened by the terror of the moment. And his blasphemous and heretical desire for the soul's 'transmigration' into the body of a

---

* The figure of 'Helen' here and the figures of Alexander the Great and Darius conjured up earlier by Faustus are demons in the shape of the personages, not the historical figures themselves.

beast dares to prefer, even if it cannot effect, an alternative to the bitter fact of spiritual immortality. None of these expressions represents a direct challenge to Christian theology: they positively, if painfully, affirm it. But alternating throughout the speech with the despairing addresses to Christ, the tension they generate produces the play's final and most potent instance of tragic emotional complexity, as audiences are forced to confront the paradox of a comfortless Christianity.

Revenge and Reprobation: The Tragic Pleasures of *Othello*

Othello (1604), arguably the most emotionally powerful tragedy Shakespeare ever wrote, owes, as many critics point out, a great deal to the structures and plot elements of comedy. In this it is like another of his 'tragedies of love', the much earlier *Romeo and Juliet*, which sets out a fundamentally romantic-comic narrative of love triumphing over familial impediments, only to swerve from the happy ending which would be expected to conclude the narrative trajectory.[11] In *Othello*, the romantic love depicted was of a kind never shown before on the Elizabethan stage: that between a middle-aged Moor and a young European girl, both unquestionably virtuous (there had been black male/white female pairings on the stage before, but these involved villainous Moors with disreputable older women).

Despite this (for the time) outlandish romantic premise, the initial context might nonetheless have seemed strangely familiar to its early audiences. The violent disapproval to the match of Desdemona's father, the rich Venetian senator Brabantio, partly marks him out in the theatrically conventional role of the 'senex', or obdurate old man, whose bar to marriage the lovers must overcome. They themselves manage to do so in a public and socially sanctioned way which is also the province of comedy, gaining the approval of the Venetian hierarchy for the good fortune of the black general who is essential for the survival and well-being of their society in its wars against the Turkish empire. As the play develops, the comedy motifs shift into another context, that of the jealous and doting elderly lover riven with doubt about his young wife's faithfulness: here is a more bitterly satirical mode of comedy, but it is comedy nonetheless. During the latter half of the play, Othello becomes a figure poised momentarily between that of the uxorious husband and that of the abused patriarchal figure of domestic tragedy. It is the latter generic identity which the play finally, and devastatingly, assumes.

Attention to *Othello*'s crossing of tragic with comedic tropes can be satisfying on a number of levels, not least in testing our assumptions about the unique properties of tragedy as a form. It helps to suggest what might be thought of as the 'permeability' of tragedy's literary borders, even if, as one of the play's recent editors puts it, we do not 'consciously identify these routines as borrowed from comedy'.[12] Yet it is not quite the case, either, that the play suggests the marriage of Othello and Desdemona is the stuff of which happy endings would be made, were it not for the prejudice and unfathomable hatred of the play's villain-figure Iago, who falsely convinces his commander of Desdemona's infidelity and incites him to vengeance. At the end of the play, in the aftermath of Desdemona's murder at Othello's hands and with the mounting horror of Iago's malice becoming apparent to all, we are given the information that her father has already died of grief in response to what would have been the comedically fulfilling action of her marriage. According to Gratiano her 'match was mortal to him', so much so that the sight of her now, strangled in the marital bed, would drive him to desperation, 'Yea, curse his better angel from his side / And fall to reprobance'.[13] Take away Iago, take away his hostility to the couple's happiness and the fictive love triangle he conjures up to satisfy it, and the narrative would still be compromised by this anti-comic conclusion.[14]

The news of Brabantio's death is, whatever we may feel about him, uncomfortably volunteered in these final stages of the play. It enlarges the tragic ambit of the conclusion – the 'fallout zone' of the catastrophe – making use of a convention from classical tragedy, that of the 'Nuncius' or messenger figure who comes to report a key offstage event (just as the English ambassadors in *Hamlet* come to report the deaths of Rosencrantz and Guildenstern). But it also casts, retroactively, a pall over the otherwise fully realised romanticism of the love between Desdemona and Othello, while at the same time looking forward in figurative terms to the all-too-literal 'reprobance', or damnation, which Othello will suffer for the murder.

This damnation is a conclusion which neither the play, nor its protagonist, shies away from. Othello's fate is to be every bit as terrible as that which befalls Faustus, and it is one he willingly, if more courageously (or is it desperately?), invites at the tragedy's end: 'Whip me, ye devils from possession of this heavenly sight!' (V.ii.276). The play steers towards this conclusion in part by making use of morality drama themes and figures, as Marlowe's play had done. Where, however, *Doctor Faustus* had deliberately made these as overt as possible, in *Othello* there is sufficient variation and differentiation in the context to ensure the schema remains partially submerged. At the simplest level, such a reading would find in Othello an 'Everyman' caught in a psychomachia between Good and Evil symbolised in the personas of Desdemona and Iago.[15] Such a symbolic, 'Good Angel/Bad Angel' reading cannot fully account, however, for the shades of meaning and grey areas in the play's moral patterning in which, for example, both Othello and Iago invite 'diabolic' associations in the eyes of other characters. These are metaphorical in the case of Othello, a product of the long-standing medieval and early modern alliance between blackness and the devil, which Emilia makes explicit in her rebukes to Othello after the murder: 'O, the more angel she / And you the blacker devil!' (V.ii.129).

In the case of Iago something more disquieting is hinted at in the trappings of devil lore which attach to him – perhaps most strikingly, Othello's inability to kill him at the play's end. Are we to understand this as an invitation to read Iago's diabolical status literally? Germaine Greer, in her astute analysis of Iago's character function, argues that there is something patently 'more than natural' in his uncanny manipulations of characters and events, and puts this down to his occupying the conventional Vice's role from the morality template – throwing temptation in the path of others while frankly and energetically communicating his designs to the audience.[16] In a play in which the status of the 'natural' is thrown open to question, Iago more than anyone else embodies the resulting contradictions. His language is strongly naturalistic: a coarse, unadorned idiom which convinces everyone who hears of it of his soldierly sincerity, and which carries over into one-to-one communication with the audience via an informal manner well suited to his improvised stratagems and debased logic. Yet his shifts between different rationales in orchestrating his plot against Othello have been seen as non-naturalistic: the expression of something flying beyond acknowledged human motivation and into, in the notorious phrase, the realm of 'motive-hunting'.*

Ticking either or both of these characterological boxes (Vice and Devil were ultimately connected as figures) can take us only so far, then, in accounting for the disturbing effect which Iago generates. If his hostility to Othello gains some of its impetus from morality drama conventions, his motivation nonetheless remains a problem because the play keeps drawing attention to it: 'Will you, I pray, demand that demi-devil / Why he hath thus ensnared my soul and body?' (V.ii.298–9). One could address this issue not by appealing to a deep psychology in Iago but by pointing out that his apparently unconnected rationalisations all seem to devolve upon the act of theft: theft of position, theft of wife, theft of personal reputation.

In the soliloquy that first unfolds his antipathy to Othello, Iago employs an unusual and much-noted construction: 'I hate the Moor / And it is thought abroad that 'twixt my sheets / He's done my office' (I.iii.385–7). The use of 'And' instead of 'For' as a subordinating conjunction upsets the expected logic of the sentence: surely he means that he hates Othello because of the supposed cuckolding? By making the hatred parallel to the rationale, however, the soliloquy asks us to consider that rationale generically rather than specifically – to link it up with the numerous other instances of dispossession, real, imagined or planned, which appear and disappear without justification through the later soliloquies: 'For I fear Cassio with my night-cap too' (II.i.305).

Aristotle thought that tragedy was best when it focused on action instead of character: Iago is a character defined by and through a specific kind of action which sits at the obsessive core of his being, and it only defies rationalisation to the degree to which it is pervasive and supremely reductive of all human relations in which he has a share. It is an obsession which Iago successfully passes on to others by elevating Desdemona to

---

* The phrase is that of the poet and critic Samuel Taylor Coleridge, who saw in Iago's first soliloquy the expression of a psychological paradox: 'the motive-hunting of a motiveless Malignity'.

the supreme object of proprietorial desire and then playing on the terror of her loss. 'Zounds sir, you're robbed' is his first direct challenge to Brabantio, and it subsequently becomes Brabantio's to Othello: 'O thou foul thief, where hast thou stowed my daughter?' (I.i.85; I.ii.62). All this prepares for the successful indoctrination into precisely this possessive mentality of Othello, who, like Brabantio before him, adopts the lexis favoured by Iago as soon as he begins to doubt Desdemona: 'He that is robbed, not wanting what is stolen / Let him not know't, and he's not robbed at all' (III.iii.341).

Othello as Domestic Tragedy

The dramatic domain in which human, and particularly marital, relationships were presented in these proprietorial terms was that of domestic tragedy, which as a sub-genre had been around as early as the anonymous *Arden of Faversham*, published in 1592. *Othello* derives a number of key elements from it, although the debt here is more specifically formal than the one it took from morality drama. As with most plays in the sub-genre, a tensely anticipated spousal murder follows the breakdown of a marriage in which adultery, suspected or otherwise, is the motivating factor, the scenario itself being played out in a social context less elevated than that of the 'high estate' normally associated with tragedy.

Shakespeare's own company had a few years earlier performed a recent contribution to the genre, *A Warning for fair Women*, which described itself as a 'true and home-borne Tragedie', and which like *Arden of Faversham* before it had focused on the murder of a middle-class husband by an erring wife and her lover. *Othello* reverses the roles of victim and perpetrator, but keeps the emphasis on making everyday, and specifically feminine, objects and accoutrements important to the plot – such as having the murder pivot around the possession of a handkerchief. The plays' settings, too, are defined less by their geographical location – whether familiar England or exotic Cyprus – than by this world of feminine objects and space, and by the frightening emotional dissonance which the acts of violence create once they erupt among them.

Some very conventional links between women, domestic property, and women *as* domestic property are reinforced by these closely confined spatial parameters, but such links are also shown to be dangerously deceptive, not least because of the important status which women assume as controllers of that space. Othello's narrative 'enchantment' of Desdemona, we are told, occurs entirely within Brabantio's doors as she goes about her 'house affairs' (I.iii.148), and his subsequent wooing and their elopement from under her father's nose unwittingly reinforces the suggestion of a breach of domestic security which Iago so effectively cries up at the play's beginning. In the scene before the Venetian council, Desdemona is transferred, in conventional fashion, directly from familial to marital household, and shows in her entreaties to follow Othello to Cyprus that she will accept of no intermediate space.

Where Shakespeare deviates from these dramatic routines is in reworking them into a situation of otherness far removed from the English social contexts in which they had originated. *Arden of Faversham* and *A Warning for Fair Women* had both made limited use of class tensions in defining their narratives of sexual disloyalty, whether between aggrieved artisans and acquisitive property-owners or between city merchants and gentry 'cavaliers', often complicating sympathies for the protagonists in the process. Class becomes a factor, briefly, in Iago's opening expressions of antipathy to Othello ('I follow him but to serve my turn upon him', I.i.41) and to Cassio (one '[t]hat never set a squadron in the field', l.21), but this is quickly subsumed by tensions which we would nowadays understand as racial.

Othello's all-important 'difference' within the Venetian society – of which he is, as a Christian, nonetheless a full part – provides an alternative context for the theme of wifely rebellion which is construed as 'unnatural' (the term used to describe the wife's complicity in her husband's murder in *A Warning for Fair Women*). Again, Iago shows his dexterity in manipulating this new context as he lures Othello into doubt. Othello's fear that 'nature, erring from itself' might incline Desdemona to sexual revolt is taken up by Iago and translated from a social and marital commonplace into the theme of monstrosity which he has used privately to demean the attachment between them: 'Not to affect many matches of her own clime, complexion and degree ... One may smell in such a will most rank, thoughts unnatural' (III.iii.233–7).

Othello turns out to be peculiarly vulnerable to this suggestion, unable to separate the idea of Desdemona and sexual waywardness once it has been implanted by Iago. Perhaps this is because he himself has placed such emphasis upon the fascination of his own origins and his consorting with a world of monstrosities ('the Anthropophagi, and men whose heads / Do grow beneath their shoulders', I.iii.145–6) prior to service in Venice.[17] This clash of the highly exotic with the confined and home-bound functions to take the social and sexual problems of domestic tragedy out of their specific material context (Shakespeare's company, increasingly cultivating its gentlemanly audience, may have found it prudent to do so) and to essentialise the transgressions they explore – to make them a 'universal' problem of human jealousy.[18]

Othello accelerates through the stages of sexual jealousy with terrifying speed, unable to arrest the process at the cold comforts of 'ignorance is bliss' ('What sense had I of her stolen hours of lust?', III. iii.341), the promise of revenge upon Cassio, or the public humiliation of Desdemona. He seizes readily on the 'ocular proof' of the handkerchief: a 'first remembrance' to his wife which now he believes she has bestowed on Cassio (l. 363 ff.). To Iago, the handkerchief merely represents the reduction to a material, exchangeable object of the honour which he has, ironically enough, elsewhere defined as a priceless, essential thing. Othello, for his part, overloads it with meanings out of all proportion to its status as a simple domestic item: 'there's magic in the web of it ... And it was dyed in mummy, which the skilful / Conserved of maidens' hearts' (III.iv.71–7). Richly suggestive of the virginity both claimed and (in its 'spotted' patterning) taken by Othello, it becomes an emblem of the imponderable feminine 'otherness' of Desdemona as well as of his own exotic difference.

Othello's fixation upon the handkerchief thus serves, among several such indicators (e.g. his succumbing to a passion 'most unsuiting such a man', IV.i.78), to feminise him – to distance him ever further from his martial 'occupation' and make him a link in a chain otherwise made up of women (the Egyptian charmer, his mother, Desdemona) whose currency is that of spells, charms and love-tokens. But perhaps the key symbolic import of the handkerchief to Othello emerges during the 'bawdy-house' interrogation of Desdemona in IV.ii, when he (no doubt unconsciously) transfers its properties as a preserver of heart's-blood onto the person of Desdemona herself: 'there where I have garnered up my heart / Where either I must live or bear no life' (ll. 58–9). The conceit of the beloved as a vessel for – and hence an embodiment *of* – one's own soul is a conventional one, most often associated with Petrarchan love poetry. In this play the idea takes on a frightening literalness, as Othello first unjustly 'blackens' and finally murders that embodiment. In the particular dramatic 'psychomachia' that *Othello* traces, the protagonist's treatment of his loved one precisely mirrors the treatment of his own immortal soul, delivered no less wilfully and by his own hands into the 'second death' of eternal damnation than was Faustus's.

'Bloody Instructions': Revisiting Tragic Tyranny in *Macbeth*

On the face of it, Shakespeare's *Macbeth* (1606) provides an ingenious perspective on Sidney's idea that tragedy should make 'kings fear to be tyrants, and tyrants manifest their tyrannical humours'. It tells the story of an eleventh-century Scottish thane who, despite his own initial reluctance, is prompted by supernatural agents and the ambition of his wife to murder the king, Duncan, who is his guest and kinsman, and to claim the crown for himself. It has a strong emphasis in its second half on the exercise and overthrow of tyranny, when Macbeth's kingship dissolves into a series of bloody purges against perceived threats to his safety. Its central scene even shows the sort of thing Sidney might have had in mind in forcing 'tyrants [to] manifest their tyrannical humours', when Macbeth is confronted in public by the ghost of one his victims, and becomes visibly unhinged with terror, arousing the suspicion of everyone around him.

From this point of view, the play brought together tyranny and terror into one of the most potent mixtures the English stage had seen. But if Sidney's recommendations about tragedy were aimed at providing a cautionary tale to monarchs about not letting power get to their heads, Shakespeare's representation of tyranny functioned rather differently. The play acts as a piece of flattery to the Scottish king, James VI, who had ascended the English throne in 1603 to become James I of England and Ireland, and whose own royal ancestor Banquo is represented in the play as Macbeth's key victim (as well as the ghost who subsequently terrorises him). At the heart of *Macbeth* is a mysterious prophecy, uttered by three witches to both men at its start, foretelling that while Macbeth shall *be* king, Banquo shall *beget* kings. When James I saw the play performed at court, then, he was seeing a story about the providential triumph of his own dynasty over tyranny and usurpation.

In addition to this topical interest, *Macbeth*'s torrid depiction of violations of nature and custom in high places, and its emphasis on tyranny and the supernatural, would all have ensured the interest of the new monarch, who had himself authored books on the divine right of kings (of which tyranny would be an egregious perversion) and witchcraft.[19] Yet in terms of genre the play can also be seen as a development of the claustrophobic environments of domestic tragedy which Shakespeare had already used so effectively in *Othello*. There are echoes, both narrative and verbal, from *Arden of Faversham* and *A Warning for Fair Women*.[20] It is from the intimacy of husband and wife in their criminal career, however, that domesticity (of a kind) arises most powerfully, as Lady Macbeth compels her husband to obtain by foul means the crown which 'fate and metaphysical aid' have promised him. Their relationship is perhaps the most complex and elusive feature of the play.

Actors of the play today (as they must surely have done in Shakespeare's time) have to come to some decision as to how to present the peculiar 'chiasmus' within this relationship – that is, the crossing-over of their respective psychological trajectories from Macbeth's repugnance towards murder and Lady Macbeth's steadfastness towards it to the reverse of these positions in the play's latter half.* From the perspective of genre,

---

* Freud became fascinated by this development and supposed that husband and wife could represent the splitting of a single character into two, where guilt transfers itself from him to her, culminating in her somnambulistic 'hand-washing' and subsequent – presumed – suicide.

we could try to look at it this way: if domestic tragedy performs a parody of the sanctified union of marriage, overturning gender norms in the act of spousal murder, Macbeth provides a parody at a still further remove, showing a reversal of norms in a couple united in murder.* As that unity begins to unravel during the play, this reversal is itself reversed, with the husband's dominance re-asserted, albeit without an accompanying return to a natural order

If Lady Macbeth gives herself over readily to what fate seems to have planned for her husband and herself (see her speech at I.v.40–1 where she communes with the 'Spirits / That tend on mortal thoughts'), Macbeth embodies through his soliloquies a more recognisable scenario of struggle. We are back in Faustian territory once again, where an individual's collusion with the dark powers becomes the pretext for a psychomachia in which the protagonist finally succumbs and secures his damnation. If the scenario itself is familiar, however, its parameters in *Macbeth* are noticeably different from those of *Doctor Faustus* or even *Othello*. Hearing the witches' prophecy that he shall 'be King hereafter', his response is remarkable for the way it shrugs off the conventional demarcation of good from evil: 'This supernatural soliciting / Cannot be ill; cannot be good' (I.iii.130 ff.). This isn't just a case of mistaking good for bad, but a rejection of the whole framework. Oppositions cancel one another out, so that 'nothing is but what is not'. His companion, Banquo, is less convinced of the neutrality of the witches, identifying them as the 'instruments of Darkness' whose habit it is to 'tell us truths' – in effect, to equivocate – in order to lure us to destruction.[+] He is right, of course, as Macbeth himself will much later realise; but that is not quite the point here. Rather, the psychological battle – the 'torment of the mind' – which Macbeth undergoes is one which takes place outside a concern for the spiritual consequences of his actions. In the soliloquy in

---

* In *Arden of Faversham* and *A Warning for Fair Women* the wife murders, directly or indirectly, the husband. In *Othello*, it will be recalled, Desdemona was the 'fair warrior' in the face of Othello's unmanly passion. Compare also the similarly domestic, but more benign, idea of feminine usurpation in *Othello*, where Iago comments that 'Our general's wife is now the general' (II.iii.309–10).

[+] On the political significance of equivocation in the play, see the discussion of Macbeth in Part Four: 'Nation-Building'.

which he ponders the consequences of murdering Duncan, the inward tug of war is caught as never before in dramatic language:

> If it were done, when 'tis done, then 'twere well
> It were done quickly: if th' assassination
> Could trammel up the consequence, and catch
> With his surcease success; that but this blow
> Might be the be-all and the end-all – here,
> But here upon this bank and shoal of time,
> We'd jump [i.e. risk] the life to come. – But in these cases
> We still have judgment here; that we but teach
> Bloody instructions, which, being taught, return
> To plague th'inventor ... (I.vii.1–10)

What Macbeth means by 'the life to come', as the next lines go on to suggest, is not a life after death but a mysterious action of futurity by which violence will return to its originator. By the time of the prelude to his next murder, that of Banquo, Macbeth has long since accepted the fact that he has given his 'eternal jewel ... to the common Enemy of man' (i.e. his soul to Satan), and regrets only that damnation devalues the rule that he has won for himself by murdering Duncan (III.i.60–9).

The latter half of the play concentrates on bringing together the psychological and political consequences of Macbeth's seizure of the crown. He has attempted to pre-empt the threat of Banquo's future succession by murdering him, but Banquo's Ghost now returns at a feast to take Macbeth's own seat at the table. This terrifying gesture is as prophetic for Macbeth's hold on power as anything the witches have told him. In the final stages of the play, as Macbeth contemplates the oncoming English army, now swelled with defecting Scottish nobles, he declares 'This push will cheer me now, or disseat me ever' (V.iii.21). The two balanced clauses within this line add up to something richly suggestive and seem, like so much else in *Macbeth*, to equivocate their meanings to the point of mutual cancellation. 'Cheer' has often be taken to denote, or at least to quibble upon, 'chair', in logical opposition to 'disseat'; while the latter term, a Shakespearean coinage, is ambiguously spelt in the First Folio ('dis-eate') and in later editions becomes 'dis-ease', in opposition to the 'cheer' of proper health. The overall sense of the line thus seems to hover uncertainly between a sense of political unrest and psychological disturbance, while never settling on either of these outright.

His confidence bolstered by the Weird Sisters' prophecies that he cannot be harmed by any 'man of woman born' (IV.i.80–1), Macbeth is unable to make the commonplace link between a diseased ruler and a diseased body politic that the audience inevitably does. Nor can he himself fully grasp the psychomachia he is undergoing between 'cheer' and despair. We, however, can see that struggle unfolding before us, as he lurches from bravura to nihilism; from 'fly, false Thanes / And mingle with the English epicures' to 'I have liv'd long enough: my way of life / Is fall'n into the sere, the yellow leaf' (V.iii.7–8, 22–3). The final revelation that the witches have all along been equivocators (his nemesis, Macduff, was not 'born' but delivered via Caesarean section), and he himself nothing more than a bloody tyrant, make of Macbeth's inward struggles the darkest examination of futility in the Jacobean drama.*

Extended Commentary: *Hamlet* (1600)

Questions of Genre

Faustus, *Othello* and *Macbeth* were all fresh to the stage in terms of subject matter, moulded from scratch by their dramatists into tragic material from various well-known narrative sources. In the case of *Hamlet*, we have something more substantial in the way of a theatrical 'back-story'. It may seem surprising to us now, but in writing this, the most theatrically and linguistically inventive of all his plays, Shakespeare was providing his company with a 'remake' (or 're-imagining', as Hollywood might put it) of a 'Hamlet' play which had been on the stage perhaps ten years earlier. This earlier play is lost, and the author of it unknown.+

---

* The word 'tyrant' is used of Macbeth almost routinely by his opponents in the second half of the play; see in particular the conversation among the Scottish exiles in the English court, IV.iii.

+ He is frequently assumed to be Thomas Kyd, who had written the highly successful *Spanish Tragedy* of 1587.

There are, however, a couple of contemporary references to it which anticipate, albeit in less flattering kind, the sort of reception history which Shakespeare's *Hamlet* was to have.

In the first of these references Thomas Nashe, inveighing against the English enthusiasm for modelling plays on Seneca, scoffed that 'if you entreat him fair in a frosty morning he will afford you whole Hamlets, I should say handfuls of tragical speeches'.[21] The comment is both unfair (Seneca himself had nothing to do with a Hamlet story) and highly revealing. Even before the Shakespearean version, it would seem, the story's central figure has become a kind of dramatic cliché within the genre: notorious for his inordinate speechifying, but already in some way representative of the 'tragical' form itself. The second reference comes from the writer Thomas Lodge in 1596, and is more disparaging still in its arch recollection of the 'ghost which cried so miserably at the Theatre, like an oyster-wife, *Hamlet, revenge*'.[22] Unlike Nashe's comment, Lodge focuses the issue of genre for us in a more pointed way, identifying this pre-Shakespearean *Hamlet* as an early contribution to the highly successful and widely adapted revenge tragedy sub-genre.

Revenge was the central fact of the narrative source which lay behind the stage versions of *Hamlet*. The story first appears in written form in a twelfth-century Norse saga about a young Danish prince, Amleth, who exacts vengeance upon the uncle who murdered his father, married his queen mother and seized the kingdom, feigning madness as a cover for his revenge. It was retold in the Elizabethan period by the French writer Belleforest in a manner which de-emphasised some of the more obviously pre-Christian elements of the story while retaining the central appeal of an intra-familial narrative of retribution.

Neither of these versions contains a Ghost of the murdered king who appears with a demand for vengeance, and we can assume that it was this highly theatrical, Senecan component which provided the early play's sensational contribution to the narrative. The Shakespearean 'remake' does not shy away from this sensationalism, but it also gives sufficient stage- and speech-time to the Ghost to ensure that it becomes a fully integrated dramatic character, humanising and even rendering pitiable its demand for vengeance upon the fratricidal Claudius. Indeed, if the Ghost in Shakespeare's play had just wailed 'like an oyster-wife' for revenge we might have had only another version of the bloody but straightforward story which was Shakespeare's inheritance. Instead, Hamlet's traumatic encounter with his father's spirit becomes the starting point for a fully fledged psychological drama which focuses at unprecedented length on the protagonist's tortured mental condition.

In fact, the play opens out into so many unexpected (and unexplained) avenues that the initial impetus towards revenge is frequently obscured altogether. *Hamlet* could almost be described as an anti-revenge play within its revenge genre since it portrays, as Harold Jenkins puts it, 'a man with a deed to do who for the most part conspicuously fails to do it'.[23] How and why does this development come about?

Mood Swings: Melancholy and Psychomachia

To expand a little on the 'psychological drama' which takes over the *Hamlet* narrative, an argument can be made out that the play shows the protagonist undergoing a particular kind of inner struggle over the ethics of revenge itself, one which impedes his determination to carry out the deed demanded of him. In her analysis of what she calls Hamlet's 'heroic doubt', Germaine Greer points to the play's reflective aspects and the hero's deferment of the act of killing as marking his shunning of the cyclical morality which vengeance always involves.[24] In that cycle, the wild justice wielded by the revenger must inevitably be returned on his or her own head. Hamlet's sceptical energies, his relentless probing and questioning, are instead directed towards exposing the hypocrisy and pretence within Denmark which allows a man like Claudius to seize power in the first place. In a discussion along similar lines, R. A. Foakes nuances this moral dilemma as a movement, traceable throughout the play, from a pre-Christian ethic of vengeance to one of Christian abhorrence of the 'irascible' emotions that in classical times were held to be virtues (Hamlet himself glosses these when he accuses himself before Ophelia of being 'very proud, revengeful, ambitious', etc.).[25]

The call for revenge is thus merely the pretext for a more searching examination of Elizabethan culture's moral fault lines, as it attempts to negotiate between the twin inheritances of classical and Christian tradition. Such readings persuasively place *Hamlet* within the broader religious and philosophical tensions of Renaissance England. But, as with almost any argument one can make about the meaning of the play, they often succeed by suppressing other key aspects. Hamlet himself may briefly doubt the provenance and truthfulness of the Ghost, but he never explicitly calls into question the pagan ethic of slaying Claudius. And arguing that Hamlet's personal mission is to expose falsehood and deceit at the court of Elsinore avoids the problem of Hamlet's own performing and role-playing as a madman, which occupies so much of the play.

Another way of understanding the psychological drama which *Hamlet* puts centre stage is to see the task of revenge as imposed upon someone who belongs in a historically specific character niche: that of the melancholic.[26] Melancholy, which we would nowadays gloss as a state of mind akin to depression, occupied in Elizabethan medical thought a wide spectrum of mental disorders, from fleeting sadness to full-blown madness. Revenge drama itself was heavily populated by mad and melancholy characters: the genre's prototype revenger from *The Spanish Tragedy* became notorious as 'mad Hieronimo', and in *Hamlet* insanity will of course be Ophelia's fate. Such instances of complete or partial breakdown tend to unfold logically out of the calamitous events of the revenge narrative. Hamlet's own melancholy, by contrast, is figured as prior to them, and this allies him with melancholic characters more usually found in comedy than tragedy, further estranging him from the type of the revenger.

When we first encounter Hamlet, his hallmarks are scholarly (he is urged not to go 'back to Wittenberg' – Faustus's university) and asocial (he is 'too much in the son'), attributes which Shakespeare had already fleshed out in some detail with characters such as the melancholy Jacques from *As You Like It*.[27] But perhaps the closest comparison is a character like the aristocratic Dowsecer from George Chapman's comedy *An Humourous Day's Mirth* (1597). Dowsecer is given a series of long soliloquies moralising on the vanity of living, and at the thought of marriage he expresses a quasi-suicidal desire to 'creep into this stubborn earth / And mix my flesh with it'.[28] In true comedic fashion his

113

melancholy musings are overheard by other characters who debate their cause but who soon manage to cure him of his affliction by prompting him towards true love. In fact, Dowsecer would be a great parody of Shakespeare's Hamlet were it not that he appears on stage several years before him. Shakespeare, it seems, has once again performed the same comedy-into-tragedy trick we have seen him do in *Othello*.

A convention of performance[29] establishes Hamlet's melancholic condition on his first entrance via his 'nighted colour' and physical isolation from the court: a display of mourning which in the opinion of the king and queen has gone too far. Hamlet's first soliloquy allays suspicion of pathological grief for his father's death, only to replace it with another: his morbid horror of his mother's remarriage to Claudius. In Hamlet's mind this figures not merely as immodest but as monstrous: an 'incestuous' union with her husband's brother (l. 157). The shock of it – which he alone seems to register – is enough to drive him to suicide, and here the melancholic's desire to compound his flesh with the elements and avoid the taint of sexuality emerges in deadly earnest:

> O that this too too sallied flesh would melt,
> Thaw and resolve itself into a dew,
> Or that the Everlasting had not fixed
> His canon 'gainst self-slaughter. (ll. 129–32)

The speech that follows is reminiscent of Faustus's first soliloquy in presenting not just a set of contents but a structure which helps establish the speaker's peculiar habits of mind. In Hamlet's case, the train of thought develops by means of *resistance* to an intrusive idea, as he tries to fight off the implications of his mother's 'wicked speed' in remarrying:

> That it should come to this,
> But two months dead, nay, not so much, not two.
> So excellent a king that was to this
> Hyperion to a satyr, so loving to my mother,
> That he might not beteem the winds of heaven

Visit her face too roughly. Heaven and earth,
Must I remember? Why, she would hang on him
As if increase of appetite had grown
By what it fed on, and yet, within a month –
Let me not think on't. Frailty, thy name is woman. (ll. 137–46)

The back and forth movement of thought recalls the convention of the psychomachia; but where Faustus's soliloquies retain the spatial parameters of the morality tradition – good on the one side, evil on the other – with Hamlet those parameters become temporal, as he finds himself torn between an idealised past and a fallen present. What is at stake in this inner struggle is not the speaker's spiritual condition, but his imaginative one. Even as he perceives the true nature of his uncle's depravity, Hamlet shows the melancholic's dangerous propensity towards distortion and exaggeration, towards 'moralising' from the particular: 'How weary stale flat and unprofitable / Seem to me all the uses of this world', he declares, ominously contradicting his earlier rebuke to his mother: 'Seems madam? Nay it is, I know not "seems"' (l. 76). His subsequent encounter with the Ghost will both confirm his worst suspicions of Claudius and exacerbate this exaggerating propensity: as Horatio observes of him as the prince follows the Ghost alone, he 'waxes desperate with imagination'.

Hamlet's immediate response to the Ghost's revelations and the awesome task he imposes upon him suggest for a moment that he has teetered over into madness proper, as displayed in his bizarre manner towards the spirit's subterranean commands: 'you hear this fellow I'the'cellerage?' (l. 151). In fact this turns out to be an early manifestation, or trial run, of his use of 'antic' behaviour as a deliberate disguise (one of the few purposive actions we see him take). Hamlet's decision to 'put an antic disposition on' is one of the play's major puzzles (l. 170), perhaps more so even than his so-called 'delay' in taking revenge (which can in part be accounted for by a convention within the genre of throwing impediments and doubts into the path of the hero).* Feigned madness[30] was a key plot

---

* Foakes's term 'neglect' seems a more accurate description of Hamlet's failure to take a timely revenge.

constituent from the original Amleth/Hamlet narrative, where the hero was in danger from the moment of his father's very public slaying, but it is devoid of any such structural rationale in Shakespeare's play, and is much more obviously counter-productive in drawing unwanted attention to him. Most critics assume it is there to reveal something about Hamlet's inner state of mind, or to act as a 'safety-valve' for an intolerable emotional strain. If its function is ultimately unexplained in the play, however, its form can still be analysed in terms of its comic – and specifically satiric – style and content.

A grotesque ('antic') manner suggests the buffoonery and lampooning of rough satire, while Hamlet himself establishes the tenor of his 'mad' speeches in his first exchange with Polonius, where he indicates he will be taking a leaf out of the 'satirical rogue['s]' textbook (II.ii.193). 'Comicall satyre' had not only taken the London stages by storm over the very period in which *Hamlet* was written, but it was also understood as one of the era's cacophonous 'voices of melancholy', particularly where it aimed to strike a harsh and wounding note.[31] As Bridget Gellert Lyons points out, Hamlet's mad talk takes the form of a series of satiric reductions – of the Ghost to a stage figure, of Polonius to a 'fishmonger', of the king to a morality vice-figure. In thus attempting to 'turn the action of the play into a comedy', Hamlet is taking a measure of control over events – even if it is not the kind we expect him to take.[32] In a spectacular shift away from the presentation of the melancholic as typical *object* of comedy (as Dowsecer had been), Hamlet has become a *subject* – or producer – of it.

That strategy may seem appropriate for a 'time' that is 'out of joint' – as Hamlet ruefully reflects after the Ghost's departure – but his preference for acting out the time's disjunctions, projecting them back onto the court at Elsinore, begins to compromise his capacity to redress them. An encounter with the players provides another shock to the system, abruptly confronting him with the fact that 'performing' can indeed issue in 'action' – at least as far as the violent physiological responses associated with tragic emotion are concerned:

> Is it not monstrous that this player here
> But in a fiction, in a dream of passion
> Could force his soul so to his own conceit

That from her working all his visage wann'd
Tears in his eyes, distraction in his aspect
And his whole function suiting with forms
To his conceit? And all for nothing,
For Hecuba! What's Hecuba to him
Or he to her that he should weep for her? (II.ii.486–94)

The player's emoting is 'monstrous', in Hamlet's unflattering assessment, in part because it adheres to a style of theatrical performance which he consistently rejects over the course of the play, and which he will try to 'reform' when he comes to stage his own conscience-catching drama. Full-blooded, stalking, and aspiring to outdo the hyperbolic terms of the speech itself, that acting style would have been recognisable to *Hamlet*'s Elizabethan audience as belonging to an earlier phase of the London professional stages which was now under sustained attack by satirists on the one side and agitators for decorum on the other (Hamlet himself demonstrates both tendencies). Yet it is also clear that, from Hamlet's perspective, this old-fashioned style retains an enviable facility for making 'saying' tantamount to 'doing', whereas he himself finds he 'can say nothing' for a murdered father. His attempts to remedy the deficiency merely end up producing a risible performance of his own, in which he is led 'like a whore' to 'unpack [his] heart with words', and then castigate himself for cowardice. The humiliation for Hamlet lies in the player's naive, unproblematic identification with both a theatrical and a legendary past (in the form of the archaic narrative of Pyrrhus' revenge), one which points up how far Hamlet himself is dissociated – 'disjoined' – from them, for all his promise to the Ghost to 'remember'.

The struggle, or psychomachia, within *Hamlet*, then, continues to work itself out over this issue of the hero's relation to a different time frame, pointing up his alienation from that heroic and martial world of past action which is prompting him to his revenge. In Hamlet's next soliloquy, as he contemplates the outcome of taking a potentially life-destroying action (he never specifies exactly what, despite the widespread assumption he means suicide), the locus of that debate is shifted forwards, towards what may lie in the future:

To be or not to be, that is the question.
Whether 'tis nobler in the mind to suffer
The slings and arrows of outrageous fortune
Or to take arms against a sea of troubles
And by opposing end them. To die, to sleep –
No more; and by a sleep to say we end
The heartache, and the thousand natural shocks
That flesh is heir to: 'tis a consummation
Devoutly to be wished. (III.i.55–63)

The life after death seems momentarily to have more allure than the present, offering both a kind of continuity and a termination in the perpetual rest of the soul. If a rationale is being sought for the act of revenge Hamlet has earlier accused himself of failing to take, then the future functions as a worthy substitute for the promptings of the past (the memory of King Hamlet, we should note, has just been compromised by Hamlet's suspicion that the Ghost may have a diabolic origin). Or it does, at least, until 'thinking too precisely on th' event' (as he will describe it in a later soliloquy, IV.iv.40) persuades him that even the disembodied soul may be disturbed in its sleep through whatever 'dreams may come / When we have shuffled off this mortal coil'. This crippling realisation, which Hamlet formulates in suggestively Faustian terms as 'the dread of something after death', has the effect once more of undermining 'enterprise' and trapping him in the here and now. 'Conscience' – in the broadest sense of the mere capacity to think – is responsible for the impasse, reprising the age-old motif of the soul fluctuating between contrary positions, but here making a mockery of the protagonist's capacity to choose between them.

Just one of the potentially limitless critical approaches that could be taken to *Hamlet*, then, would be to see it as the introduction of a Faustian-style ethical dilemma, with its emphasis on the ultimate fate of the soul, into a revenge tragedy framework, with its typically worldly interrogations of justice and political corruption. Yet the result we see is something far more than just a clever crossing of such familiar tragic tropes. The play's numerous reflections on theatricality, performance and genre (tragical-comical-historical-pastoral, not to mention satirical) help to make it what we might call a tragedy of self-reflection. *Nosce teipsum* – the classical demand to 'know thyself' – had once again become the great philosophical catchword of the age; but *Hamlet* shows that such a process of looking inward can be terrifying in some instances, opaque in others.

The key scene in which Hamlet stages 'The Murder of Gonzago', the playlet designed to show Claudius the terrible image of his own crime, is a case in point. The play not only succeeds spectacularly in achieving this end but also deeply discomforts Gertrude in showing her the action of a fictional queen protesting too much against remarriage, before succumbing to seduction (in his subsequent encounter with her Hamlet will take advantage of this discomfort to set up before his mother 'a glass / Wherein you may see the inmost part of you'). Both king and queen are forced to join Hamlet as fellow sufferers in the traumas that self-reflection can bring about. But the 'play-within-a-play' scene also moves us away from transparency and towards increasing mystery over Hamlet himself. The scene is bracketed by a set of conversations between the prince and others, opening with a tribute to the stability of the self (Hamlet praises the Stoic Horatio as 'that man that is not passion's slave'), and closing with a declaration of the self's endless mutability (Hamlet speaks of the inaccessible 'heart of my mystery', which changes like a cloud). At the scene's close we see him transformed with shocking suddenness from witty equivocator in his conversations with Rosencrantz and Guildenstern to diabolic revenger ('Now it is the very witching time of night'), before then moving on to unleash his fury on his mother, generating increasing doubt as to whether Hamlet's self can ever be truly known, either to him or to us.[33]

Like protagonist, like the play as a whole: a curious hollowness is felt to sit at the centre of *Hamlet*. It breaks with the revenge tragedy convention of placing the play-within-the-play at the conclusion of the drama, and brings it forward to provide its protracted mid-section instead – the imitation of an action rather than an action proper. Both Hamlet and *Hamlet* are thus alike products of the same brilliant innovation in tragic form – each a vast canvas of activity, intrigue, emotion, discourse and opinion, stretched around a pointedly absent centre.*

---

* William Empson imagined the play's sense of inner absence was a 'purely technical' decision on Shakespeare's part in the act of revision, a clever reversal of expectations which enlarged the embarrassing gaps and stubborn contrivances of the original *Hamlet* play rather than filling them in with more persuasive content.

Notes

1   Both medieval and neoclassical understanding of the tragic protagonist shared an emphasis on the high-born member of society as the hero; Aristotelian theory was not specific on this, but most of the precedents Elizabethan writers would have known (in particular from Roman drama) would have involved the higher classes. Aristotelian theory did stipulate, however, in an important formulation, that the hero should be good, and indeed 'better than us' (*Poetics*, 4.2.1–3). Readers of Elizabethan drama can usefully consider how far the plays of this period – and those of Marlowe in particular – deviated from these stipulations.

2   Philip Sidney, *An Apology for Poetry*, in *The Norton Anthology of Theory and Criticism*, ed. Vincent B. Leitch et al. (London: W. W. Norton & Company), p. 344.

3   Terry Eagleton, *Sweet Violence: The Idea of the Tragic* (Oxford: Blackwell, 2003), p. 12.

4   The theme of conflict, for example, does not appear before the nineteenth century as a generic criterion, and only then as a result of centuries of absorption of a specifically Shakespearean model which seemed to support a new, Hegelian interpretation of human development. For the specific application of this idea of tragedy as conflict to Shakespeare's dramas, see Bradley's *Shakespearean Tragedy*.

5   In an entertaining discussion on modern poetry, Jay Rogoff points out how the concept retains some purchase today in 'popular cultural parodies: Daffy Duck dithers between a miniature Daffy-angel and Daffy-devil, one at each ear', etc. 'Pushing and Pulling', *Southern Review*, vol. 41, no. 1, Winter 2005, pp. 189–209, p. 189.

6   The play's first performance cannot be dated with any accuracy. A number of stories, however, attest to its enduring effect on audiences, particularly through the on-stage presence of the 'devils', who purportedly caused terror in both audiences and (in what may amount to a clever bit of marketing) the actors themselves (see Chambers, *The Elizabethan Stage*, vol. 3, pp. 423–4).

7   For a good reading of the play in relation to these intellectual and historical themes, see Robert N. Watson's discussion of 'Tragedy' in *The Cambridge Companion to English Renaissance Drama*, pp. 334–7.

8   Christopher Marlowe, *Doctor Faustus*, Epilogue, 23, in *The Complete Plays*, ed. J.B. Steane (Harmondsworth: Penguin, 1969).

9   For a reading which stresses the more 'openly contradictory' aspects of *Doctor Faustus*, see Dollimore, *Radical Tragedy*, pp. 109–19.

10   Terry Eagleton nicely sums up the paradox: 'Faustus has so hardened his heart, or perhaps had it hardened for him by a Calvinist God, that [repentance] has been thrust out of reach' (*Sweet Violence*, p. 114).

11   In the view of Chiwetel Ejiofor, who played the title role at the Donmar Warehouse in 2007, *Othello* functions almost as a 'sequel' to *Romeo and Juliet*. www.guardian.co.uk/film/2009/apr/26/chiwetel-ejiofor-interview

12   William Shakespeare, *Othello*, ed. E. A. J. Honigmann, Arden, 3rd series (London: Thomson, 1999), Introduction, p. 77.

13   Shakespeare, *Othello*, ed. E. A. J. Honigmann, V.ii.203–7.

14   On this point see Dympna Callaghan, *Woman and Gender in Renaissance Tragedy: A Study of 'King Lear', 'The Duchess of Malfi' and 'The White Devil'* (London: Harvester Wheatsheaf, 1989), pp. 59–60. Brabantio's continued hostility has been in some measure anticipated by Desdemona at IV.ii.45–8.

15   See Watson, 'Tragedy', p. 338.

16   See Germaine Greer, *Shakespeare* (Oxford: Oxford University Press, 1986), pp. 44–8.

17   On the argument for Othello's vulnerable identity created by his own practice of 'narrative self-fashioning', see Stephen Greenblatt, *Renaissance Self-fashioning* (Chicago: University of Chicago Press, 1980), ch. 6, 'The Improvisation of Power'.

18   Patricia Parker speaks of a 'central chiastic crossing of foreign and domestic, exotic and sexual in the play', 'Fantasies of "Race" and "Gender"', p. 92.

19   James I, *The Trew Law of Free Monarchies* (1598) and *Daemonologie* (1597).

20   Motifs which cluster around the central murder of King Duncan – qualms of conscience beforehand, knocking at the doors afterwards – recall the compression of similar events in *Arden of Faversham*. A line from *A Warning for Fair Women* of many years earlier – 'Oh sable night, sit on the eye of heaven / That it discern not this black deed of darkness' – seems to contain in germinal form such entreaties from Macbeth as 'Come, seeling Night / Scarf up the tender eye of pitiful Day' before murder is done. William Shakespeare, *Macbeth*, ed. Kenneth Muir, Arden, 2nd series (London: Routledge, 1984), III.ii.46–7.

21   Chambers, *Elizabethan Stage*, iv, 235. Spelling modernised.

22   Shakespeare, *Hamlet*, ed. Harold Jenkins, Introduction, p. 83.

23   Shakespeare, *Hamlet*, ed Jenkins, p. 140.

24   Germaine Greer, *Shakespeare* (Oxford: Oxford University Press, 1986).

25   R. A. Foakes, 'Hamlet's Neglect of Revenge', p. 91.

26   See in particular A. C. Bradley's discussion in *Shakespearean Tragedy: Lectures on Hamlet, Othello, King Lear and Macbeth*, Introduction by John Russell Brown (Houndmills: Macmillan, 1985; 1990), pp. 96–102. Although Bradley's character-based analyses, now over a century old, are not representative of current critical method, these particular comments stand up well.

27   William Shakespeare, *Hamlet*, ed. Ann Thompson and Neil Taylor, Arden, 3rd series (London: Thomson Learning, 2006), I.ii.113, 67.

28   Chapman, *An Humourous Day's Mirth*, vii.173–9.

29   Romeo is another Shakespearean tragic hero whose first entrance draws on a complex of features associated with melancholy – solitariness, weeping, secret sorrow. Indeed, his concerned father Montague only just stops short of specifying the condition: 'Black and portentous must this humour prove / Unless good counsel may the cause remove' (*Romeo and Juliet*, Alexander Text, I.i.139–40). For a similar use of the trope in comedy, see Antonio's entrance at the beginning of *The Merchant of Venice*, where the inexpressible sorrow suggests, we may surmise, his romantic longing for Bassanio.

30   While Hamlet is unusual in making a whole play out of the theme, feigned madness was a favourite plot device in Elizabethan and Jacobean drama, important in the sub-plots of *King Lear* and *The Changeling* (both discussed in this volume) and in many other plays. *Hamlet* also has the distinction of generating a great amount of debate as to just how 'feigned' the prince's pretence of madness really is. For a helpful summary and review of its place in the Hamlet story, see the discussion on 'An antic disposition' in the Introduction to *Hamlet*, ed. Ann Thompson and Neil Taylor, Arden, 3rd series, pp. 64–70.

31   See Bridget Gellert Lyons, *Voices of Melancholy: Studies in Literary Treatments of Melancholy in Renaissance England* (New York: W. W. Norton & Company, 1975).

32   Lyons, *Voices of Melancholy*, p. 94.

33   Postmodern and post-structuralist critics have taken particular interest in this theme: e.g. Francis Barker argued that the prince symbolises the 'unfulfilled interiority' of the transition from medieval to modern personhood – the moment at which a bourgeois ideal of fully coherent inner self was being reached out for but could not quite yet be grasped (Francis Barker, *The Tremulous Private Body: Essays on Subjection* (London: Methuen, 1984)). In a recent, extensive, scene-by-scene analysis of the play, Jan H. Blits has seen Hamlet as fatally abandoning the crucial 'centre-ground' of moral action in favour of thinking on the one hand and 'theatrical' acting on the other, Jan H. Blits, *Deadly Thought: 'Hamlet' and the Human Soul* (Lanham, MD: Lexington Books, 2001).

Tragicomedy: *All's Well that Ends Well* and *Philaster*

Tragicomedy could well be regarded as the major Renaissance contribution to the history of theatrical genre. Its very label describes a process of mingling or crossover, and seems appropriate to a period which witnessed a greedy assimilation of literary forms (especially the newly rediscovered Greek and Roman ones) and their combination with more familiar ones. We have already encountered, via the famous piece of publicity-speak read out by Polonius, the Elizabethan recognition that acting companies would inevitably bring together different kinds of genre – tragedy, history, comedy, pastoral – in order to maximise theatrical appeal. We have also seen that scripts and records of performances at this time variously recognised 'tragicall comedies', or 'A Lamentable Tragedie mixed full of pleasant mirth' (the subtitle for *Cambyses*),[1] or plays which were listed as tragedies in one place and as comedies in another. But the term 'tragicomedy' implies something more than just such a pragmatic process of hybridisation. It implies a bringing into relation of distinctly opposite registers, mirth and sorrow, which by rights ought to be incompatible. Considered in those terms, the idea could give rise to a certain amount of ideological tension.

Taking a closer look at Polonius's formulation, 'tragedy, comedy, history, pastoral, pastoral-comical, historical-pastoral, tragical-historical, tragical-comical-historical-pastoral', it is noticeable that the union of tragedy and comedy occurs only at the very end of the list, and even then merely as part of a larger compound word, which helps to soften the shock of contradiction.*,[2] Philip Sidney's comment on tragicomedy in *An Apology for Poetry* expresses outright the sort of distaste this yoking together of opposites could provoke, when he complains of plays that 'be neither right tragedies, nor right comedies, mingling kings and clowns ... so as neither the admiration and commiseration, nor the right sportfulness, is by their mongrel tragi-comedy obtained'.[3] Sidney's objection to tragicomedy has a dual aspect here. The offence against decorum, the classical notion of keeping things in their appropriate place, is both of an artistic kind (the 'commiseration' of tragedy and the 'sportfulness' of comedy are both compromised) and a social one (the high- and low-born should be kept apart in art as they are in life). The resultant mingled form is therefore something 'mongrel', which is to say, without an identity of its own.

Yet not long after Sidney wrote these objections there were, on the Continent, some equally well-informed attempts to promote tragicomedy as a form with an identity. The most important of these, in terms of subsequent impact on the English drama, was formulated by the Italian playwright Giambattista Guarini in a spirited defence of his own tragicomedy *Il Pastor Fido*, or 'The Faithful Shepherd' (1585). For Guarini, neither the artistic nor the social criticisms of tragicomedy held up. On the one hand, the writer's aim was not to conjoin 'two entire plots, one of which is a perfect tragedy and the other a perfect comedy', but to create 'from the two a third thing that will be perfect of its kind'.[4] On the other, he adduced plenty of evidence that even the purest of classical tragedies 'united in a play persons of high rank and those of low station'. The point was that, properly handled, tragicomedy could provide a 'mingling of tragic and comic *pleasure*' (my italics) which arose from a kind of exchange between comic and tragic elements, for example by taking a good deal of tragic matter (its serious themes, its great personages, its narrative dangers) and working it through a comic

---

* The final four-part categorisation only occurs in the Folio version, published after Shakespeare's death, so the earlier Quarto versions of Polonius's list omit the combination of tragedy and comedy altogether.

form towards a pleasurable, rather than terrifying, ending. This was, in fact, the best kind of play of them all, Guarini reasoned, for a civilised, Christian society, since we are shown a story that is 'tragic in possibility but not in fact', moving us but ultimately delighting and reassuring us.

That the development of a formal tragicomedy as Guarini describes it here had an important impact on English drama is not in doubt, but the exact process by which this occurred is complex and open to debate. For the purposes of what follows, we can note that Guarini's play *Il Pastor Fido* (although not the defence that went with it) appeared in translation in England in 1602, just around the time that the sub-genre of romantic comedy was going into decline. As we have seen elsewhere, satire and humours were now all the rage in comedy, and love stories with happy endings were looking decidedly passé in this new climate. There would not for several years be a point at which one could say romantic themes had definitely returned in the guise of the newly respectable tragicomedy, but it may be no coincidence that in the early years of the seventeenth century Shakespeare wrote some comedies that were decidedly dark, even distressing, in tone.

Troilus and Cressida (1602), *All's Well That Ends Well* (1603) and *Measure for Measure* (1604) were all written and performed around the time of the transition from Elizabeth's rule to that of King James in 1603 (a point not lost on historicist readings of these plays). The nineteenth-century label 'problem comedy', for a long time applied to them, is now increasingly rejected in favour of their identification as tragicomedies: Verna A. Foster's recent discussion groups them under the specific heading of 'Ironic tragicomedy'.[5] Part of the irony lies in the way formal elements from the earlier romantic sub-genre of comedy are reproduced. All three plays treat the subject of love, and the later two end in marriage; but the comic satisfactions granted by the union are much compromised by the absence of any satisfactory process of wooing in the build-up to them.* The resolutions in these later two plays are particularly complex and strenuous, and seem designed almost to defer the comedic conclusion past the point of audience delight and

---

* *Troilus and Cressida* has plenty of wooing, leading to a consummation, but then moves rapidly towards a conclusion directly opposite to a marital one.

into that of mere relief.[6] We will look at these aspects in more detail in our discussion of *All's Well That Ends Well* below.

Foster also talks about a later phase of Shakespearean tragicomedy associated with the last group of plays he wrote (at least as a solo author), which she calls 'romantic tragicomedy'. The term 'romantic' here does not signify in quite the same way as it does in the phrase 'romantic comedy', and highlights the tendency of these plays to draw on the same kind of narrative themes that prose romances such as Sidney's *Arcadia* did: tales of adventure and chance discovery, often set in far-off lands but always with a strong hint of fantasy and improbability (critics have referred to these plays as Romances, but the label, as Foster points out, is a bit weak in terms of defining dramatic form).

As with the earlier group, the 'tragicomic' label was not itself applied to these plays at the time Shakespeare wrote them. After his death the First Folio scattered them in a bemused fashion throughout its categories: grouping them either under Comedy, as it did with *The Winter's Tale* and *The Tempest*, or under Tragedy, as it did with *Cymbeline, King of Britain*, or in one case leaving them out altogether, as it did with *Pericles, Prince of Tyre*. Nonetheless, these plays need to be seen as engaging to some degree with the trend towards writing formal tragicomedy which began towards the end of first decade of the 1600s. Two of Shakespeare's fellow playwrights in the King's Men, Francis Beaumont and John Fletcher, were enthusiasts for Guarini's ideas and became strongly associated with this trend (we will examine their contribution more closely in *Philaster*, below), and their plays and Shakespeare's show a number of resemblances around this time.

To the above point, a further consideration can be added. All the writers for the King's Men shared a vested interest in capitalising on a new development in theatrical space that had opened up for their company in 1608. They now finally had the use of an indoor theatre, the Blackfriars, to add to their outdoor one of the Globe. Not only did this provide them with the opportunity for putting on plays the whole year round, switching between the Globe in summer and the Blackfriars in winter, but it allowed them to cater more directly for the wealthier, educated class of customer who tended to patronise London's indoor playhouses.*,7 There can be few better ways to capitalise on a new acquisition of theatrical space than by offering up a whole new diet of theatrical fare to go with it. When we come to look at *The Tempest* in the final part of our discussion below, we can usefully bear in mind the appropriateness of formal tragicomedy to the intimacy and exclusivity of the new venue.

For a literary period in which discussions of genre are often disorganised or absent altogether, tragicomedy is unusual in the amount of discussion and theorisation it invited from contemporary commentators. All three plays in the chapter that follows – *All's Well That Ends Well, Philaster* and *The Tempest* – are chosen because they exhibit some kind of response to that discussion, although they do so in markedly different ways.

Tragicomical Minglings: *All's Well That Ends Well*

As well as reflecting ironically on the romantic comedies that came before it, *All's Well That Ends Well* supplies an ironic response to the whole issue of mingling high- and low-born characters which Sidney found a problematic aspect of 'mongrel tragi-comedy'. This response occurs not so much at the level of dramatic decorum (we could take our pick from any Shakespeare play in any genre to see that mixing social types is hardly an issue for him)+ as at that of what might be considered narrative decorum. Love between the social classes, of a cruelly unreciprocated kind, is the major theme of *All's Well That Ends Well*, and from this the play generates a good deal of dissonant emotional effect as well as painful

---

* As an insight into the unstable world of theatre in Elizabethan England, it's worth knowing that the company Shakespeare belonged to had actually built the Blackfriars theatre in the first place in 1596 with precisely this plan of seasonal use in mind, but had then been forbidden to use it because of objections by the local residents. The boy companies had rented it for a decade, after which opposition to the idea of adult company use had died down.

+ There are, nonetheless, two scenes in *All's Well That Ends Well* in which a clown is pointedly thrust into the company of the countess (I.iii and II.ii), and the accent on the social affront which this produces here seems a little stronger than in *Twelfth Night*. As the countess points out, the clown is no respecter of persons, least of all at court: 'what place make you special, when you put off that with such contempt?' (II.ii.4–5).

narrative development. In the province of Rossillion in France a young count, Bertram, and a young ward under the countess his mother's care, Helena, have each been bereaved of a father. Bertram's desire to follow his companions to the wars in Italy is frustrated by the French king's determination to keep him safe at the Paris court, while Helena's unspoken love for the young count is frustrated by her sense of her lowly origins as the daughter of a physician. Making use of her own skill in medicine and prescriptions left by her father, however, Helena cures the king of a mortal illness in exchange for choice of whichever husband she pleases. In an elaborate sequence (which seems to invert the casket-choosing scene from *The Merchant of Venice*), she passes respectfully over a number of eligible men before lighting on Bertram – who promptly refuses a match which he claims is dishonourable and demeaning to his status. The king enforces it; but Bertram's capitulation is at once followed by his flight to Italy before consummation can occur. Worse still, he vows in a letter to Helena that he will not recognise her as a wife until she can obtain the ring on his finger and show him a child begotten by them both – self-evidently 'impossible' tasks. Helena, distraught and in deep penitence for what she has done, leaves for Italy on a pilgrimage and an early death. There, however, a chance meeting with a young woman, Diana, whom Bertram is attempting to seduce, provides the opportunity to procure both ring and child by means of a deception – the substitution of herself for Diana in the sexual encounter. While this machination is put into effect, we see the exposure and humiliation of Bertram's braggart companion Parolles, who by means of a trick 'interrogation' is revealed to be a coward. A drawn-out and convoluted finale sees the return to France of all parties and the revelation of the consummation of the marriage between Helena and Bertram – to which he now assents.

We can pause over these details for a moment to consider how they are handled in terms of dramatic structure. For obvious reasons the 'bed-trick' or sexual substitution (which is used again under similar circumstances in *Measure for Measure*) could not be directly staged in Elizabethan times, although, like the cure of the king, it receives a great deal of discussion and comment from the characters.[8] Each provides an important focal point for substantial passages of debate, and contributes to the play's shape and tone, which is often described as that of a sour, sardonic fairy tale. Yet in terms of what actually unfolds on stage, the play's dramatic emphases must lie elsewhere. These can be divided between the charting of an upward trajectory in the representation of Helena's erotic ambition and a downward one in the social presumption of Parolles, who is a hanger-on of Bertram's. Parolles, a 'miles gloriosus' – that is to say a braggart soldier, familiar from Greek and Roman comedy and the more contemporary Commedia dell' arte – is Shakespeare's principal addition to the details he took from the prose source, the ninth story of the third 'day' from Boccaccio's *Decameron*. Despite its happy conclusion the Helena plot line can be seen as tragic in terms of its tone and narrative structure, while the Parolles plot line is comic, although making use of a harshly satirical form. The two characters are linked early on in the play, exchanging some banter which helps establish their parity as well as their animosity. Yet the two story lines only intersect in incidental details (such as Parolles' role in encouraging the count in his later attempts to debauch Diana), thus pointedly keeping apart what formal tragicomedy was supposed to meld together into an artistically perfect whole.

The play's opening notes of loss and mourning establish a sombreness to the play which is more pervasive and long-lasting than that of *Twelfth Night*. Helena's opening soliloquy follows, as critics have pointed out, a similar pattern to Hamlet's in exposing an idiosyncratic grief which is masked by the public display of mourning:

> I think not on my father,
> And these great tears grace his remembrance more
> Than those I shed for him. What was he like?
> I have forgot him; my imagination
> Carries no favour in 't but Bertram's.
> I am undone: there is no living, none,
> If Bertram be away; 'twere all one
> That I should love a bright particular star
> And think to wed it, he is so above me.

[...]
> ... he's gone, and my idolatrous fancy
> Must sanctify his relics.[9]

Helena's admission that Bertram has fully displaced her sorrow for her father might deliver a jolt, but is consistent with Elizabethan notions of female duty in transferring affection from the paternal to the (in this case wished-for) marital overlord. Aspects of her diction are revealing of the sheer strength of Helena's sexual longing for Bertram, selecting from the language of gestation and childbirth when she speaks of an imagination which '[c]arries' Bertram's 'favour'. Helena here unconsciously indulges a wish-fulfilment fantasy of virginity lost even as she consciously acknowledges its impossibility. She is 'ahead of herself', in a manner recalling Rosalind in *As You Like It* when she speaks of a sorrow divided between that for her father and that for Orlando, her 'child's father'.[10]

Helena is defeated by a class gap (which was certainly not Rosalind's problem) and as if to exacerbate the sense of that gap she characterises her love for Bertram as 'idolatrous'. While to the countess and those of her retinue Helena is a 'gentlewoman', even if that term implies having a servant status, Helena herself insistently speaks of being Bertram's polar opposite socially, 'poorer born', 'humble' in origins and labouring under 'baser stars'. The fact of her background does seem to leave her vulnerable to the assumptions of others about her precise social status, as shown in the exchange with Parolles, who begins by hailing her as a 'queen' (quibbling on 'quean', period slang for prostitute), and impressing on her the general idea of virginity as a 'commodity' (I.i.97–160). This is the satirical banter – in fact, this is briefly the world – of the newly developing 'city comedy' intruding itself to dissonant effect into the fairy-tale setting of the play. In her soliloquy immediately after Parolles leaves Helena outlines a personal philosophy which dispenses with the ugly notion of a marriage for profit, but also makes use of the 'politic' thinking Parolles has urged her to exercise about getting a husband:

> Our remedies oft in ourselves do lie,
> Which we ascribe to heaven; the fated sky

Gives us free scope; only doth backward pull
Our slow designs when we ourselves are dull.
[...]
The mightiest space in Fortune nature brings
To join like likes, and kiss like native things. (ll. 212–19)[11]

This is already a big development away from Helena's opening soliloquy: all of a sudden, Helena has decided that nature (i.e. her own desire) has priority over sanctioned rank; and it is noticeable that this new attitude does not stop to consider whether marriage between two such socially diversified 'likes' (as she wishfully construes them both) will diminish or ennoble the parties involved. She is, as it were, going to get her man.

The play deals with this problem of Helena's ambition – of a desire she believes transcends social status but which also pointedly ignores the potentially levelling outcome on its object – by keeping up a constant friction between these two issues. Her personal merit is continually stressed in the scenes which lead up to her marriage with Bertram, and the countess fully endorses and encourages the match. When Helena overcomes the king's initial disbelief in her healing prowess, she does so both by the power of her words (she employs a highly elevated, semi-mystical style in her dialogue with him which matches and then surpasses his own royal style) and (in a hint of potential narrative danger) by the offer of her own life and reputation in exchange for failure. Yet the scene in which she makes choice of the eligible lords as her reward sees her rejecting each in turn with the gentle caution that marriage to her would demean their status: 'I'll never do you wrong, for your own sake ... in your bed / Find fairer fortune if you ever wed!' (II.iii.90–2). Maidenly humility? This is no doubt part of the effect; but equally there can be no doubt that when Bertram savagely rebuffs her after the choice falls on him – 'A poor physician's daughter! Disdain / Rather corrupt me for ever' (II.iii.115–16) – he has the backing of her own words on the matter. It is only at this point that the king reveals the option that he can 'build up' her status, while stressing that honour is an adjunct of personal virtue: 'Good alone

/ Is good, without a name' (II.iii.118 ff.). In terms of narrative decorum, however, it is too late to dispel the threat that Helena has represented, and in response to the king's entreaties Bertram's opposition shifts to simple hate: 'I cannot love her nor will strive to do it' (l. 145).

Bertram's subsequent flight from this presumed disgrace to his aristocratic status is abetted and encouraged by his hanger-on Parolles. This captain of the wars represents another kind of presumption to social parity with the count, as shown by his blustering riposte to the suggestion from the old lord Lafew that Bertram is his 'lord and master' (II.iii.186 ff.).* For all his self-importance, it is significant that mere encouragement is all Parolles provides, and his role in the play, like his role in society, seems oddly inflated throughout. Although he shoulders much of the blame for being a bad influence on Bertram, he is not a significant agent in any of the painful narrative developments which follow in the second half, which include Helena's anguished pilgrimage, her reported death (deliberately circulated by her), and Bertram's resort to the practices of evasion and seduction in his pursuit of Diana.

Parolles' name, the French for 'words', reinforces the view that he is a mere 'bubble' of honour which has a purely verbal derivation, and in the stratagem played upon him by the French officers and soldiers on campaign in Florence that 'bubble' is decisively pricked when they decide to expose him as a coward by pretending to take him captive into the enemy camp. The play makes a lot of dramatic capital out of this sequence, with the ambushing of Parolles in IV.i and his exposure and humiliation in IV.iii straddling the very time period in which Bertram is seducing (as he thinks) Diana while in fact consummating his marriage with Helena. One could perhaps account for such a strong dramatic investment as a 'symphonic device', which parallels in comic form the unravelling, layer by layer, of Bertram's own personal honour which his behaviour towards Helena and Diana reveals.[12] Yet it is equally tempting to see this episode as having value in generic, rather than narrative, terms by recalling Sidney's points about decorum.

---

* See also Lafew's rebuke at II.iii.256–8: 'You are more saucy with lords and honourable personages than the commission of your birth and virtue gives you heraldry.'

In having the business with Parolles supply the gap for the bed-trick which is being performed off-stage, the play ensures that any irresolvable tensions arising from the sexual 'mingling' of high- and low-born characters in the main narrative are displaced onto the secondary one, where we see the play's most egregious social pretender relegated to the position of a clown and ejected from the company of the great. For Parolles emerges not just as a coward in front of the 'lords and honourable personages' of the army, frantically volunteering the secrets of his camp in order to preserve his life, but as an outright 'Fool' (IV.iii.95), even playing the fool's part in ridiculing (unwittingly) his social betters when he satirises Bertram's lusty escapades. When the stratagem is revealed to him he seems to accept this new identity with a note of self-discovery: 'Simply the thing I am / Shall make me live … being fool'd, by fool'ry thrive' (IV.iv.322–7). The next we see of him he is begging at Rossillion, a shabby, broken figure, slighted by the palace clown (V.ii).

The play's final stages strengthen the movement towards turning the narrative into a 'mingled yarn, good and ill together' (IV.iii.68), and in doing so they perform a kind of stress-testing on the capacity of mixed tragic and comic elements to provide audiences with theatrical pleasure. The tone becomes more sombre than ever, with the court of Rossillion, and the countess in particular, in mourning for the supposed death of Helena. Bertram has returned, officially forgiven and finding some measure of rehabilitation by agreeing to an arranged marriage with Lafew's daughter, 'Maudlin'.* While the audience knows that a reconciliation is being engineered by Helena, in league with Diana, a sequence of reversals keep deflecting the play away from that comic ending and generating suspense instead.

Helena's hopes receive a blow when she arrives at the wrong court while seeking the king. The marriage ceremony of Bertram and 'Maudlin'

---

* In perhaps the most blatant example in Shakespeare's dramas of a 'MacGuffin', or expedient plot device not important for anything other than moving the narrative forward (Alfred Hitchcock's term), we never hear of 'Maudlin' prior to this moment, yet Bertram claims he has loved her all along; we never see her on stage despite the fact that she is being lined up to marry him; nor is she referred to again after Lafew has retracted his offer of marriage once suspicions about Bertram begin to mount. She is, in every sense of the notion, a placeholder for Helena until her appearance at the scene's conclusion.

gets underway, but an exchange of rings that had taken place during the earlier bed-trick now comes to light when Bertram is spotted wearing Helena's ring, leading the appalled king to suspect the young count of murdering her. The entry of Diana, declaring herself to be Bertram's jilted wife-to-be, further confounds matters as she claims both to have given and not given him the ring. As the king threatens her with death to get the truth, she at last enacts the play's reversal, ushering Helena into the presence with a conundrum: 'Dead though she be she feels her young one kick / So there's my riddle: one that's dead is quick' (V.iii.294–7).

The revelation that Helena is alive, is pregnant, and has successfully beguiled Bertram of his ring, fulfilling all the tasks, now issues in full forgiveness and acceptance between the principals. Yet the play's final sentiments remain strongly couched in the conditional mood. As the king puts it, 'All yet *seems* well, and *if* it end so meet, / The bitter past, more welcome is the sweet' (ll. 327–8, my italics). Such concluding uncertainties further the sense of *All's Well That Ends Well* as an experimental work, one drawing on precisely those ideas about tragicomedy as a genre that its theoretical commentators found most uncomfortable, and daring to give them dramatic shape.

'Things Possible and Honest': *Philaster* and Formal Tragicomedy

Philaster, or, Love Lies a-Bleeding was a collaborative work by Francis Beaumont and John Fletcher, written probably in 1609 for performance by the King's Men. It has good claim to being the first successful attempt to introduce into English Renaissance drama the formal approach to tragicomedy developed by Italian writers such as Guarini. This approach is well summed up in a Preface written by John Fletcher to an earlier solo effort, *The Faithfull Shepherdess*:

> A tragie-comedie is not called so in respect of mirth and killing, but in respect it wants deaths, which is enough to make it no tragedie, yet brings some neere it, which is enough to make it no comedie ...[13]

The 'bringing near' to death of a play's characters is a positive statement about the structuring of events in the story, which serves to distinguish the genre from the recognised ones of comedy and tragedy. At the same time, tragicomedy is defined negatively, by an absence of actual deaths in the outcome, but also an absence of the assurances of life in the lead-up to it.

There is an important nod to Guarini in the claim that tragicomedy is not a kind of theatrical double-header – that is, it is not two stories rolled up into one to offer audiences a bit of mirth and a bit of killing, thus pleasing all comers. Guarini had argued that from the judicious mixing of comic and tragic elements a new form would arise which was coherent in itself, with its own distinctive pleasures and rewards. Fletcher's debt to Guarini can be gauged by the fact that *The Faithfull Shepherdess* also adapted aspects of his practice, working this comparatively new form through the pastoral milieu and characters that was the Italian's preferred setting for tragicomedy ('pastoral' referring, essentially, to the lives and loves of shepherds).[14] However, this had emphatically failed to give the Blackfriars' audience the hoped-for pleasure, seemingly because the pastoral tag had led them to expect precisely the kind of robust, mixed-bag entertainment that Guarini had decried.

Yet the joint-authored *Philaster*, employing the same tragicomic form and a smattering of pastoral elements, was a major success and went on to help shape the future repertoire of plays for the King's Men. In part this was because of the willingness of the collaborators to seed the new approach to tragicomedy in more familiar theatrical soil for contemporary audiences, adapting in particular motifs from Shakespeare's *Hamlet*, *Othello* and *Twelfth Night*.

Philaster, the play's title character, is a prince of Sicily, loved by the nobles and citizens for his reputed character and virtue, but regarded with trepidation by the King of Calabria who has conquered the kingdom the prince was heir to. Unable to imprison or exile Philaster for fear of popular rage, the usurping king perceives a solution to securing his succession by marrying his daughter Arethusa to a foreign prince, the Spanish Pharamond. She, however, like the rest of the court, is contemptuous of the bombastic Spaniard and loves Philaster instead. To maintain a secret communication between them Philaster sends a young orphan boy, Bellario, whom he had rescued from a life in the wilds, to wait on her. Arethusa manages to expose Pharamond as a lecher who is having an affair with one of the court women, Megra, but this revelation, instead of releasing Arethusa from the marriage, sees her falsely accused by the vengeful Megra of fornication with Bellario. The accusation is embraced with alarming unanimity throughout the court, and some of the nobles seize upon it to provoke Philaster (who has a Hamlet-like circumspection when it comes to action) into revolt against the imposition of the Spanish lord. From this point on the play arranges a sequence of meetings between the three principals, Philaster, Arethusa and Bellario, each of which (after the fashion of *Othello*) reinforces the hero's belief in the princess's sexual betrayal while testing the loyalty of the accused parties to destruction.

The encounters develop in a way which suggests the intermingling of tragic and comic pleasures afforded by formal tragicomedy. Episodes are of a highly contrived nature, often setting up a situation from which unfortunate consequences follow with almost mechanical immediacy. So, for example, in III.ii the king commands Arethusa to rid herself of the boy whom all hold responsible for her ruined reputation. This prompts a conventional complaint in soliloquy from the princess on the world's hostility to a maiden's good name, which has barely run its course before Philaster appears. Their encounter shows him veering from an initial effort to console her towards seizing on her sorrow as proof of her disloyalty. No time is allowed for the principals to move through the gradations of suffering and conflicted response by which agency is suggested in tragedy. Characters stumble into one another's dramatic space and at once reach conclusions polarised from the facts, suggesting a comic cause of misunderstanding.[15] But a tragic effect is nonetheless moulded onto each encounter via the expansive emotion and studied rhetoric of the speeches. Thus Arethusa's response to Philaster's entreaties to be rid of the boy is richly patterned, moving from hypnotic repetition into free-flowing, overlapping lineation to create variation within the mood of rhetorical questioning:

Who shall now tell you how much I loved you?
Who shall swear it to you, and weep the tears I send?

Who shall now bring you letters, rings, bracelets?
Lose his health in service? Wake tedious nights
In stories of your praise? Who shall sing
Your crying elegies, and strike a sad soul
Into senseless pictures, and make them mourn?[16]

Philaster's response to what he perceives as Arethusa's continued erotic attachment to the boy has an equally literary tone (a 'sad text', he later calls it). This mediates his (again, very Hamlet-like) misogynistic anguish and emotional instability through a pastoral vision of retreat into '[s]ome far place', where he may:

dig a cave, and preach to birds and beasts,
What woman is, and help to save them from you;
How heaven is in your eyes, but in your hearts
More hell than hell has; how your tongues, like scorpions
Both heal and poison; how your thoughts are woven
With thousand changes in one subtle web
[...]
How all the good you have is but a shadow,
I' th' morning with you, and at night behind you
Past and forgotten ... (ll. 125–36)

Tragic structure is maintained because each subsequent encounter develops and deepens the suffering of the protagonists. But there is a distancing between action and emotion in the unfolding of events, with the rhetorical extremes reached by the characters appearing to outstrip in order of magnitude the sequences of events which give rise to them.

Philaster combines this distancing between action and emotion with further distancing effects between the audience and the fictional world of the play. This becomes most evident in what is perhaps the play's key scene, IV.v. Philaster, fleeing into the wilds to avoid the sight of either Arethusa or Bellario, accidentally stumbles across the boy cradling the princess in his arms. She has merely fainted, but the sight of this tableau elicits the now expected response from Philaster, complete with the kind of volte-face ordinarily encountered in comedy (he has just entered regretting his harsh judgment of Arethusa): 'I will be temperate / In speaking, and as just in hearing – [*Sees them.*] / O monstrous! Tempt me not, you gods! (IV.v.18–21).

In the sequence that follows, the protagonists all attempt to outdo one another in proving their love and loyalty, with the negotiation of an act of violence as the central proof. This is the moment at which the tragicomedy now brings its protagonists near to death. Arethusa will not submit to Philaster's demands that she kill him with his own sword, but Philaster does assent to do as much for her, and has already begun to sheathe his blade in her flesh when they are interrupted by the appearance of a country-fellow, who brings a shatteringly new perspective onto the scene:

COUNTRY-FELLOW: Hold, dastard, strike a woman? Th' art a craven I warrant thee
[…]
PHILASTER: Leave us, good friend.
ARETHUSA: What ill-bred man art thou, to intrude thy thyself Upon our private sports, our recreations?
COUNTRY-FELLOW: God 'uds me, I understand you not; but I know the rogue has hurt you.
PHILASTER: Pursue thine own affairs; it will be ill To multiply blood upon my head, Which thou wilt force me to.
COUNTRY-FELLOW: I know not your rhetoric, but I can lay it on if you touch the woman. *They fight.* (IV.v.86–99)

The audience has up to this point been guided by the 'rhetoric' rather than the deeds of the central characters, accepting their emotions at the level of pathos rather than that of tragic terror. Now the narrative threatens to pull that action up to the level of the rhetoric and into genuine tragedy, a new form of distancing is employed by having a representative of the pastoral mode enter to dispute the language and assumptions of the two royal figures. This affects audience interpretation of the events on stage. The scenario's sexual undertones (the sword, the wound, the princess's

willing submission) are now made explicit in Arethusa's peevish rebuke
to the country-fellow that he has intruded into their 'private sports',
dragging the couples' seemingly inevitable progress towards tragic status
down into bathos. At the same time, the countryman's bafflement over
their elevated language and unfathomable motives works to bracket the
entire scenario, making it appear somehow unreal, even unnecessary.
In the fight which ensues he overcomes Philaster, who slinks offstage
muttering 'The gods take part against me, could this boor / Have held me
thus suddenly else?' (IV.v.103–4). Despite this ignominy the scene is not
meant to align our point of view with the country-fellow's against that
of the prince's. We cannot quite ignore Arethusa's pleas to the gods for
Philaster's safety during the fight (l. 100), and the man's boorishness is
underlined by his follow-up line to the rescue of the wounded Arethusa:
'I prithee wench, come and kiss me now' (ll. 107–8). Sympathy for
any one individual in the action is less important than the privileged
perspective which the audience is afforded through the decentring of
each character's point of view.

This separation of audience perspective from that of the characters
is maintained in the scene immediately afterwards, in which the prince
comes across Bellario sleeping on the ground and takes advantage of the
opportunity to stab his supposed rival. In the soliloquy leading up to this
deed Philaster's qualms of conscience over his treatment of Arethusa are
balanced by a mean-spirited emphasis on his own self-preservation: 'She
may be abused / And I a loathèd villain; If she be / She will conceal who
hurt her' (IV.vi.12–14). This sets up a disparity between sentiment and
motive which is furthered in the manner of his wounding of Bellario.
The nature of the action is comparatively petty: Philaster is not moved
to strike a killing blow because the wounds he himself carries are not
fatal: 'I ha' none I think / Are mortal, nor would I lay greater on thee'
(ll. 24–5). But his interpretation of this gesture to Bellario, once the
youth awakens, shows Philaster still thinking in terms of tragic suffering:
to be merely wounded rather than honourably killed is in his view a fate
'worse than death' (l. 30). Now finding Bellario's loyalty and love utterly
convincing, Philaster swings back towards the pole of tragic despair:
'Then I shall die for grief, if not for this / That I have wounded thee'

(ll. 44–5). Once again, however, dramatic rhetoric and dramatic action are put in unfortunate juxtaposition, as Philaster creeps into a nearby bush to hide from his pursuers. He emerges from his hiding place only once he has heard Bellario taking all the blame for the princess's injuries and being carried off to torture, at which point he finally volunteers to shoulder the appropriate responsibility – but even then, his Marlovian outpourings as he praises Bellario maintain his rhetorical isolation from everyone else in the scene.

What has been said here about the handling of action and characterisation in *Philaster* can suggest the following way of looking at the play's tragicomic effect. Philaster does not (despite some powerful critical arguments to the contrary) lose sympathy as his behaviour grows ever more hysterical and damaging to those around him.[17] Rather, the gaps which the play opens up between action and rhetoric, audience and character perspective, undermine his credibility instead. His unswerving adherence to a tragic idiom come what may, coupled with an inability to exercise any kind of self-control, simply make his plight less and less believable over the course of the play, even though his status as its hero remains explicitly upheld.

Beaumont and Fletcher's plays were commended in the period for their tales of 'wronged Lovers' who could 'perswade [audience] eyes to weepe into the streame, and yet smile when they contribute to their owne ruines', and *Philaster* fits this description rather well: someone who is both emotionally affecting and liable to raise a smile. It is not a characteristic confined to him alone in the play. His antagonist the King of Calabria, distraught at the loss of his daughter, exasperates his courtiers with his desire to exercise godlike control over events, at which point they urge him to demand things 'possible and honest' instead. In *Philaster*, however, the hero's depreciating credibility is neatly underwritten by the play's even less credible resolution, in which Arethusa's name is finally cleared (and Philaster's jealousy banished for good) by the revelation that Bellario has all along been a young woman named Euphrasia. Secretly in love with Philaster from before the start of the play's action, she has chastely entered his service by means of a male disguise, and the three now agree to exist happily ever after as a trio of husband, wife and romantically disinterested maidservant. As the final contrivance in a highly contrived theatrical experience, the revelation turns out to be beautifully apposite rather than trite. And to the mix of dramatic pleasures already offered by this venture in tragicomic form, the play has added the potent fantasy of a suffering female loyalty, doubled.

Extended Commentary: *The Tempest* (1611)

The plays which Shakespeare wrote for the King's Men following their move into the Blackfriars in 1608 have similarities with both kinds of tragicomedy we have looked at above, but important differences as well. Like the earlier tragicomedies, *Pericles*, *Cymbeline*, *The Winter's Tale* and *The Tempest* all end happily for their protagonists, yet their tone is very different from that of Shakespeare's earlier romantic comedies. We often find them suffused with a sense of loss and injustice which for much of the narrative resists any clear sense of how it will be dispersed. Plays in both groups frequently entertain a movement between a tragic first half and a comedic second half which restores a person and/or situation that was assumed dead or lost. Large gaps of time and space often intervene before that conclusion is reached. Where Helena in *All's Well That Ends Well* had gone on a pilgrimage, from which distance she could effect the decisive break with the unhappy course of events that had preceded it, both *Pericles* and *The Winter's Tale* invoke a huge interval of fourteen and sixteen years respectively between the first and second parts of the action, enough time for infants to become young adults and bring about the crucial reconciliations. To this *The Winter's Tale* adds a major shift in location, from Sicily to Bohemia, and then back again.

The process of restoration, which often takes in those of forgiveness and reconciliation as well, sometimes includes the impression, if not the actuality, of resurrection and miracle: Helena's reappearance in the court of Rosillion initially beggars the belief of Bertram and the court, while in *The Winter's Tale* Hermione, wrongly accused of adultery and thought to have died of grief, appears at the end as a statue brought to life. Both occurrences are ultimately the product of artifice, not true miracle

(Hermione's 'statue' has marks of age on it, enough to suggest that it is her natural body and that she has been in hiding up until this moment), but the effect of a miracle is nonetheless carefully aimed at, particularly in the later play where the audience are not privy to the stratagem leading up to it.

The deliberate challenge to realism at the end of *The Winter's Tale* is, however, a product of the much greater emphasis on artifice that marks the second group of tragicomedies, and which aligns their approach more closely with the experiments in formal tragicomedy being undertaken by Shakespeare's colleagues. Through it we experience the same kind of involvement 'from a distance' that Beaumont and Fletcher's play had so effectively conjured, even when the plays become tragic in more than possibility, as when secondary characters meet their deaths – sometimes quite violent ones – in the course of the story rather than merely being brought close to them.* This deliberate foregrounding of artifice can be seen as part of the set of formal elements which the King's Men introduced at this time to give tragicomedy a distinctive identity, and in particular to define a more gentlemanly set of audience responses which operated midway between the poles of terror and laughter that characterised tragicomedy's parent genres, thus making it suitable for a Blackfriars clientele.[18] The pastoral mode also finds inclusion in these later plays, helping to provide a tonal 'third way' which again provides an estranging perspective on the (over-) excitements of tragic narrative.+ This use of artifice is most apparent in what was probably Shakespeare's last solo-authored play, *The Tempest* of 1611. The play is notable for its adherence to neoclassical strictures about unity of time, place and action, in marked contrast to the expansiveness of some of the earlier and later tragicomedies. This has the particular effect, as we shall see, of running the tragic and comic strands of the narrative in tandem, rather than treating

---

* In the case of both *Cymbeline* and *The Winter's Tale* important deaths, those of Cloten and Antigonus respectively, occur as part of the story arc, but take place offstage. A kind of sublime horror, peculiar to these tragicomedies, is attained in each case, by having the report of Antigonus being feasted on by a bear and by the introduction on stage of the head and then the headless trunk of Cloten.

+ So *Cymbeline* has the 'family' of hideaways in a Welsh mountain, while *The Winter's Tale* has the extended sequence of the sheep-shearing feast.

them consecutively as Shakespeare had done previously. But it is above all through its focus on the 'art' of its central character, Prospero, that the play's exploration of dramatic artifice is given a coherent narrative framework.

The Tempest starts with a catastrophe – a shipwreck caused by the tempest of the title – and works its way towards a comedic conclusion. In terms of content this play is arguably the most fantastic of all Shakespeare's works, since no sooner has the audience witnessed the calamity at sea which takes down a ship full of nobles, including Alonso, the King of Naples, and his chief courtiers, than we are introduced to the idea that one man is the author of it: the magician Prospero, who lives as a castaway on a nearby island with his young daughter, Miranda. There was magic aplenty in *A Midsummer Night's Dream* and *Macbeth*, but not of this order, and human beings were not responsible for it.

The play's seamless shift in perspective, from close-up involvement in human suffering in I.i, through Miranda's distressed commentary on it from a safe distance at the start of I.ii, to Prospero's detached explanation of his reasons for causing the storm, is in many ways an exercise in miniature of the tragicomic effect of emotional distancing. Through it we learn that twelve years earlier Prospero had been usurped (to reprise a theme from *Philaster*) as ruler of Milan and cast out onto the waves by his brother, Antonio, in league with the very king whose vessel he has just sent to the seabed. '[P]rovidence divine' had then brought Prospero and the baby Miranda safely to the island, and now 'bountiful fortune' has brought his enemies directly to these shores.[19] The shift in Prospero's use of terms here is significant: where twelve years ago he had been dependent upon a benevolent power, 'providence', to preserve him, now he is very much the active party, scanning his 'auspicious star' to ensure that this is the moment for him to seize his fortune and settle his accounts with his betrayers.

The 'art' of magic which Prospero has perfected in the twelve long years of exile have made him an all-powerful ruler of this island, exercising complete control over its inhabitants. These include the spirit Ariel and the strange, primitive Caliban, both of whom he treats as slaves (the latter is described in the dramatis personae as '*a savage and deformed slave*'). While Ariel does his bidding in recompense to Prospero for reversing a spell of captivity upon him, and on the promise of future freedom, Caliban's attempted rape of Miranda has demoted him from the level of adopted child to that of resentful drudge, fit only to do menial chores about the 'cell' where Prospero lives.

The scenario flags up several important themes, partly unfolded through the exchange with Ariel, when the spirit momentarily chafes at his servitude (I.ii.242–300). This broaches in a new way a persistent concern of Jacobean tragedies and tragicomedies with issues of absolutism – of the prerogative of rulers to exercise power without any say from their subjects. The plays of the King's Men generally adopted a conservative attitude towards this political issue, unsurprisingly given their regular performances at court and the fact that their patron, James I, had authored a tract upholding the divine right of monarchs to be answerable to God alone rather than to the people they ruled.[20]

Although *Philaster* had obliquely satirised this viewpoint, in the form of the King of Calabria's childish demand for instantaneous performance of his most outrageous requests (*Philaster*, IV.iv.30 ff.), the attitude of these writers is more clearly exemplified in the plot of *The Maid's Tragedy* (c. 1610) in which a nobleman finds out that he has been married off to a woman who is the king's secret mistress. Goaded by her on their wedding night with the revelation, the nobleman nonetheless immediately expresses the doctrine of absolute obedience and consent, despite his injury at royal hands: 'In that sacred name / The King, there lies a terror; what frail man / Dares lift his hand against it?'[21]

Rather than engaging head-on with such political issues, however, *The Tempest* can be seen as rolling together two powerful tragicomic themes, usurpation and absolutism, and sublimating them in the magical powers of Prospero. Unlike the usurping King of Calabria in *Philaster*, compelled to muse pathetically on the fact that 'when we [kings] come to try the power we have / There's not a leaf shakes at our threatenings' (IV.iv.57–8), the deposed Prospero is able to 'Put the wild waters in [a] roar' and split the pine in which Ariel had been imprisoned. The extent of his powers as they are unfolded over the course of the play seems like a direct answer to the Boatswain's rebuke to the courtiers on board the stricken vessel: 'What care these roarers for the name of king?' (I.i.16–17). Dominion over nature has replaced that of rule over human subjects, but is used as a testing ground for these same theories of obedience, as Prospero shows when he cajoles Ariel first via threat (to return him to his dreaded place of captivity, I.ii.294–6) and then via reward (he shall be free after two days, l. 299).

The Tempest's blend of tragic and comic pleasures is experienced in the unfolding of Prospero's deep purpose in sinking the ship and bringing its occupants within his grasp. The play leaves open the possibility that his powers may yet be used for revenge on the shipwrecked survivors. His 'art' has brought them intact onto the island's shores, but we do not yet know what for; only that, as he repeatedly tells Miranda, he is doing 'all in care' of her. Yet now, from the scattered retinue of the Milanese expedition, Ariel retrieves the King of Naples's son, Ferdinand, and delivers him to Prospero, who shows Miranda the handsome young man, the first European other than her father that she has ever seen. As Prospero watches from afar, he comments approvingly on the fact that '[a]t the first sight / They have changed eyes' (l. 441) – that is, they are falling in love – and all 'goes on … As my soul prompts it' (ll. 420–1).

This is merely the first part of his plan, revealed in stages over the course of the play, to reverse the usurpation. In keeping with the emphasis in the late plays on redemption, this is to be done not simply by restoring the old order, replacing himself in power at the expense of his brother Antonio, but by building an improved future out of the wreckage of the present, uniting the previously hostile states of Naples and Milan in a marriage between the young couple. This benevolent aim, however, is to be achieved through the same kind of manoeuvring between tyrannical control and generous acquiescence that had characterised his earlier exchange with Ariel. He enslaves Ferdinand on an absurd charge of treason and puts a spell on him when he tries to resist, brusquely quashing Miranda's entreaties the while. The sexual and political rewards which Prospero is lining up for the two must be earned, it appears, 'lest too light winning / Make the prize light' (I.ii.452–3), and that will involve absolute submission on the part of each of them to his whims.

This comic trajectory, tending towards a marriage, which *The Tempest* signals from its early stages, does not issue in a comic mood, however, since the play sustains a sense of threat, both in the grief felt by the survivors over the apparent loss of their number and through the hatching of a series of murderous conspiracies against those in power. In this it achieves its successful superimposition of comic upon tragic narratives which distinguishes it from the consecutive development of these two modes in earlier examples of Shakespearean tragicomedy. Both Ferdinand and his father, Alonso, are convinced that the other has drowned in the storm; and Prospero's powers, through the agency of Ariel, exacerbate that belief by what amounts to a kind of psychological torture. Luring Ferdinand into the magician's presence, Ariel's hypnotic music and song persuade the young man that:

> Full fathom five thy father lies,
> Of his bones are coral made;
> Those are pearls that were his eyes,
> Nothing of him that doth fade
> But doth suffer a sea-change
> Into something rich and strange. (I.ii.397–402)

By the same token, in the play's central scene, III.iii, Ariel appears to the king and his followers and offers the starving company a mirage for a banquet, before snatching it away and terrifying the wrong-doers among them with threats of punishments present and future:

> The powers delaying, not forgetting, have
> Incensed the seas and shores – yea, all the creatures –
> Against your peace. Thee of thy son, Alonso,
> They have bereft, and do pronounce by me
> Ling'ring perdition, worse than any death
> Can be at once, shall step by step attend
> You and your ways … (III.iii.73–9)

Prospero, again watching from afar, now leaves them in their 'distractions' and their 'fits', satisfied that they are thoroughly 'in [his] power', and returns to the young lovers waiting in his cell. As with problem plays such as *All's Well That Ends Well*, there is an emphasis on the prolongation of mental suffering and a mood darkened by the belief in another's death. At the same time, there is a shift in perspective of the kind employed by formal tragicomedy which relieves the audience from too close an empathy with this suffering.

The twin narrative trajectories of tragic threat and comedic renewal narrow onto the play's key scene of a wedding celebration for Ferdinand and Miranda (IV.i). The '*slave*' Caliban has earlier fallen in with two of the survivors, Stephano and Trinculo, and, sampling some of the wine the two men have salvaged from the ship, elects them as new overlords with the power to release him from bondage to Prospero via the expedient act of murdering him. The two drunkards, with their evident origins in commedia dell' arte buffoons, do not in themselves pose a serious threat; but the malice of Caliban has more resonance, since it directly targets the 'art' of Prospero by which, Caliban insists, the erstwhile duke has cheated him of the island: 'First … possess his books, for without them / He's but a sot, as I am' (III.ii.91–2).

Knowledge of this threat informs audience reception of Prospero's use of his powers in the ceremony which shortly follows. From one perspective, that art is seen at its most powerful and miraculous, as Ferdinand comments with amazement on the spectacle of the goddesses Iris, Juno and Ceres being conjured up to bless the forthcoming union between himself and Miranda (IV.i.60–124).* The form of the spectacle reproduces that of the masque: a courtly and aristocratic entertainment, immensely popular at the court of James I, which involved lavish costume and scenery and which put the accent on music and dance and the ruler's godlike power to impose order on proceedings. The commercial drama sometimes invoked masques as narrative components, but in ways that subtly critiqued these claims for monarchical authority. For example, in the fifth act of *Philaster*, the king mistakes for a masque what turns out to be a ceremony of marriage uniting, against his wishes, his daughter and the play's hero.

---

* The goddesses are, like Faustus's apparitions of Helen and Alexander, spirits in disguise, but this very fact is meant to reflect upon the extent of the magician's powers.

This use of the masque to shatter a ruler's illusions about his own power is similarly traced in *The Tempest*. At the height of the spectacle Prospero suddenly remembers the 'foul conspiracy' of 'the beast Caliban and his confederates / Against my life' (IV.i.139–41), whereupon the elaborate pastoral dance he is presenting between nymphs and reapers disappears *'with a strange hollow and confused noise'* (l. 139 SD). Prospero has been similarly 'disillusioned', but the check to his power is here one of defining a limit to what his 'art' can achieve (a rather more tactful one from a royal perspective). That art can, it seems, perform any natural and supernatural action his mind desires, but it cannot produce an improvement in the nature of Caliban, as Prospero himself goes on to acknowledge bitterly:

> A devil, a born devil, on whose nature
> Nurture can never stick; on whom my pains
> Humanely taken – all, all lost, quite lost! (ll. 188–90)*

The moment is a key one not just in terms of narrative action but in terms of the play's handling of its own formal and generic influences. While the threat of Caliban and his confederates is easily dispersed, it is by recourse, as it has always been, to physical torture (see the list of agonies commanded by Prospero at ll. 258–61). Tragicomedy, via the dramatist's seemingly omnipotent interventions, may engineer improbable recoveries, but it does not assume, as the masque does, that all chaotic and destructive matter within the narrative can be manipulated towards a concluding vision of harmony. In the play's final scene, then, Prospero decides to relinquish his art, to 'abjure' his 'rough magic' (ll. 50–1). For his part, Caliban, in a poignant moment, is given the expression of redemptive longing so characteristic of the genre: 'I'll be wise hereafter / And seek for grace' (V.i.295–6). But the play leaves us in little doubt that he must remain a 'thing of darkness' only acknowledged in his continuing servitude to the arbitrary rule of his master (l. 275).

---

* This theme of Caliban's obduracy has been present from the start of the play, most notably in the case of the language taught him by both Prospero and Miranda, of which Caliban himself declares that his only 'profit on 't / Is I know how to curse' (I.ii.364–5).

Notes

1   Robert Preston, *Cambyses. A Lamentable Tragedie, mixed full of pleasant mirth, containing the life of Cambyses King of Persia* ... (c. 1561). Sometimes described as a 'hybrid morality', since it adapted the morality format to a portrayal of historical narrative and characters, its subtitle likewise suggests an amalgamation of different kinds of theatrical appeal: see Cox and Kastan, *A New History of Early English Drama*, p. 340.

2   William Shakespeare, *Hamlet*, Arden, ed. Harold Jenkins, 2nd series (London: Routledge, 1982), II.ii.392–5.

3   Sidney, *An Apology for Poetry*, in *The Norton Anthology of Theory and Criticism*, p. 357.

4   Giambattista Guarini, 'The Compendium of Tragicomic Poetry', in Albert H. Gilbert, *Literary Criticism: Plato to Dryden* (New York: American Book Co., 1940), pp. 507–22.

5   Verna A. Foster, *The Name and Nature of Tragicomedy* (Aldershot: Ashgate, 2004), pp. 53–4.

6   The 'harsh ironic juxtapositions of tonalities and generic structures' of this group of plays make them 'modally tragicomic', Robert Henke, *Pastoral Transformations: Italian Tragicomedy and Shakespeare's Late Plays* (London: Associated University Presses, 1997), p. 51.

7   See Gurr, *The Shakespearean Stage*, p. 46, for the story behind the acquisition of the indoor (or 'hall') playhouse, and the same author's *Playgoing in Shakespeare's London*, pp. 73–80, for discussion of the clientele.

8   Critical analysis of *All's Well That Ends Well* has nonetheless often focused on these particular story components. W. W. Lawrence showed in the 1930s that each derived from a repertoire of folk-narrative forms: the self-explanatory 'Healing of the King' tale, transposed by Shakespeare's prose source from a male healer-hero to a female one; and the 'Fulfilment of the Tasks', a subset of the 'Clever Wench' tales in which a wife answers the challenge of her husband to become pregnant by him without his knowing. See William Witherle Lawrence, *Shakespeare's Problem Comedies*, 2nd edn (New York: Ungar, 1931; 1960).

9   William Shakespeare, *All's Well That Ends Well*, ed. G.K Hunter, Arden, 2nd series (London: Routledge: 1967; 1995), I.i.76–96.

10   William Shakespeare, *As You Like It* (Alexander Text), I.iii.10–11.

11   Compare Helena's words with those of Cassius in *Julius Caesar*, I.ii.138–40: 'Men at some time are masters of their fates: / The fault, dear Brutus, is not in our stars / But in our selves, that we are underlings.' Both speakers assert the individual's capacity – under certain circumstances – to determine their own destiny, but Helena's acknowledgment of free will is tempered by a

sense that failure to seize the initiative might return one to the controlling power of fate.

12   A. P. Rossiter, *Angel with Horns: Fifteen Lectures on Shakespeare*, ed. Graham Storey (London: Longman, 1961), p. 91.

13   Francis Beaumont and John Fletcher, *The Faithfull Shepherdess*, Preface.

14   On pastoral as the dramatic 'mode' which especially accompanied the genre of formal tragicomedy see especially Robert Henke, *Pastoral Transformations*.

15   Finkelpearl finds this to be an effect of character, by which Philaster's personal inadequacies are shown up: 'Philaster conforms to Bergson's classic description of comic figures in the machinelike predictability of his response', Philip J. Finkelpearl, *Court and Country Politics in the Plays of Beaumont and Fletcher* (Princeton, NJ: Princeton University Press, 1990), p. 156. But the same form of response is visible (if to a lesser degree) in other characters, too; for example, the princess in her rapid transition in this same scene from endorsement of Bellario in Philaster's presence to bitter repudiation of the boy shortly afterwards.

16   Francis Beaumont and John Fletcher, *Philaster, or, Love Lies a-Bleeding*, ed. Andrew Gurr, The Revels Plays (Manchester: Manchester University Press, 1969; 2003), III.ii.74–80.

17   See Finkelpearl, *Court and Country*, ch. 8.

18   See in particular Lee Bliss, 'Pastiche, burlesque, tragicomedy', in *Cambridge Companion to English Renaissance Drama*, pp. 237–61; and Robert Henke, '"Gentleman-like Tears": Affective Response in Italian Tragicomedy and Shakespeare's Late Plays', in *Comparative Literature Studies*, vol. 33, no. 4, 1996, pp. 327–49.

19   William Shakespeare, *The Tempest*, ed. Virginia Mason Vaughan and Alden T. Vaughan, Arden, 3rd series (London: Thomson learning, 1999), I.ii.159, 178.

20   See James VI and I, 'The Trew Law of Free Monarchies', excerpted in *Divine Right and Democracy: An Anthology of Political Writing in Stuart England*, ed. David Wootton (Harmondsworth: Penguin, 1986), pp. 99–106. The tract was written in 1598 while James was still King of Scotland only, but was widely published and read in England before he came to power there in 1603.

21   Francis Beaumont and John Fletcher, *The Maid's Tragedy*, in *Four Jacobean Sex Tragedies*, ed. Martin Wiggins (Oxford: Oxford University Press, 1998), II.i.287–9.

Comedies of Humour, Comedies of Pain: *Every Man in His Humour* and *The Fawn*

'We have here a new play of humours in very great request, and I was drawn along to it by the common applause, but my opinion of it is (as the fellow said of the shearing of hogs), that there was a great cry for so little wool.' Such was the view of London gossip and letter writer John Chamberlain in 1597 of George Chapman's *An Humourous Day's Mirth*, huffily dismissing the latest big thing in the craze-dominated world of Elizabethan public theatre. He may have disapproved, but Chamberlain had a sharp eye for contemporary trends and was correct in pinpointing the inception of a new genre. This was the second play by Chapman to push the idea of 'humours' at audiences as a distinctive theatrical commodity ('variable humours' had been a title-page description of his previous play, *The Blind Beggar of Alexandria*) and it did so by enlisting the term as a kind of generic buzzword.

We can perhaps imagine audiences being invited to go and see a 'humours' play much as one could sample the varieties of 'exploitation' films they used to have in the 1970s, or the 'reality' staple of TV shows a few decades later. The 'play of humours' thus inaugurated was to be picked up and developed by other writers – most notably Ben Jonson – and to make a major contribution to the shape and tone of comedy as a whole over the next ten years. But it was not, for reasons we will look at below, a genre which Shakespeare worked within, even when his own company was promoting it. While the humours theme was something he made constant use of in his plays (the Henry IV plays are full of references to them), as a theatrical format it remained distinctively non-Shakespearean.[1]

151

What were they, then, these comedies of humours (they were always comedies) which excited all this 'common applause'? The idea sounds tautologous to us – surely a comedy *is* (or at least *has*) humour by definition? But the broad equivalence we make between 'humour' and what is funny is a development of the word's use which post-dates Elizabethan times. As the tendency to use the plural suggests, humours were things as much as qualities in the discourse of the time, a feature of long-standing ideas about the body, the world around it, and the relationship between the two. They were commonly understood as bodily fluids, mixed up together and doing the overall job of nourishing and irrigating the limbs and organs.* There were four of them – blood, phlegm, black bile and yellow bile – and the trick in terms of sustaining physical health was to keep them in balance with one another. However, there were factors which complicated this task.

The humours were thought to share their qualities (hot, cold, wet and dry) with the four elements – air, moisture, earth and fire – which made up the surrounding world. Thus one could become 'humorous' when dietary habit or even atmospheric conditions encouraged one or other of these internal fluids to predominate in the bodily system. A conversation early on in *An Humourous Day's Mirth* has some fun with this commonplace idea, when a character remarks, 'The sky hangs full of humour, and I think we shall have rain.' 'Humour' here means moisture generally, but it leads him quickly to conclude that 'we may chance to have a fair day, for we shall spend it with so humorous acquaintance as rains nothing but humour all their lifetime'.

The idea that the humours could be floating about in the form of vapours, ready to precipitate themselves into people who then proceed to act under their influence, is presented as a joke, but one with a strong material basis in the medical beliefs of the time. The predominance of a particular humour was always signified as a behavioural as well as a physical

---

* This was before anyone knew about the oxygenation and circulation of the blood.

symptom. To a way of thinking that did not make a rigorous distinction between psychology and physiology – mind and body, character and constitution – a person *was* what they ate, drank and breathed.

The new genre, then, suggests that it will specialise in 'humorous' examples of this kind, people whose personal inclinations – sadness, irascibility, cupidity and so forth – are the product of a particular blend of bodily humours. To some extent the various writers who followed Chapman's lead will do this: Dowsecer in *An Humourous Day's Mirth* and Downright in *Every Man in His Humour* are embodiments of their humoral types, melancholy and choler, respectively. A favoured format was to subordinate narrative to the parading of a succession of such types through the play, getting the appropriate comic value from each in turn.

Yet the dramatists were too creative to restrict themselves to mere character studies constrained by medical theory. We tend to find the humours theme being applied less literally, impacting on the dynamics of individual behaviour or even on the dynamic of the play itself. Dramatic capital could be generated, for example, out of the notion of fluidity which derived from the medical theory. Ben Jonson acknowledges as much in the Prologue to the second of his humours plays, *Every Man out of His Humour*, when he lectures audiences on the proper signification of the word 'humour':

> [W]hat soe'er hath fluxure, and humidity,
> As wanting power to contain itself,
> Is Humour. So in every human body,
> The choler, melancholy, phlegm, and blood,
> By reason that they flow continually
> In some one part, and are not continent,
> Receive the name of Humours. Now thus far
> It may, by *Metaphor*, apply it self
> Unto the general disposition:
> As when some one peculiar quality
> Doth so possess a man, that it doth draw
> All his affects, his spirits, and his powers,
> In their confluctions, all to run one way,
> This may be truly said to be a Humour.[2]

153

Thus the humours, or more specifically their symptoms, 'wanting power to contain' themselves, could issue forth in a 'flood' of mannerisms, quirks and verbal excesses from the characters, at times threatening to 'overflow' the narrative, and 'burst the bounds of propriety'.[3] Or they could be seen to inundate the faculty of reason, with sensual addictions and bodily appetites overcoming the rational self-mastery and moral constancy required of civilised behaviour.

As if to balance out this notion of fixed character traits, a still further kind of 'humorous' character emerged who was highly adaptable and an expert in manipulation and disguise. This provided another application 'by *Metaphor*' of the medical theory, for the bodily fluids were understood as unstable entities readily transformable into one another, producing sometimes startling shifts of character and mood within a single individual.[4] Thus alongside the pathological humorists, and sometimes acting as their antagonist, we find a highly performative character who could, as Chapman's 'blind beggar' boasts, 'assum[e] the humour' of anyone they chose, and then as quickly put it off and adopt another.*

It should not be too big a leap from here to realising that the use of medical terminology to mock fixed behaviours could lend itself to the practice of satire. Comedy was from ancient times generally concerned with the idea of moral correction, and the Renaissance revival of this ideal meant that many plays devoted themselves to exposing and redressing individual error. Chapman's plays, and the first of Jonson's 'humours' comedies *Every Man in His Humour* (discussed later in this chapter), kept this corrective aim within a fairly benign temper, inflicting some ignominy on the idiotic and the wicked but venturing nothing lasting or painful. With the subsequent *Every Man out of His Humour*, however, Jonson's comic programme undergoes a shift, with an emphasis on making

---

* Prince Hal exemplifies this mode of behaviour in one of the tavern scenes of *Henry IV Part 1* when, having tormented a poor 'drawer' (barman) by forcing him into absurd repetitions of the slogan of his trade, he declares, 'I am now of all humours that have showed themselves humours since the old days of goodman Adam' (II.iv.90–1). What Hal does briefly in this scene encapsulates one of the *modus operandi* of the humours genre: using one kind of 'humorous' behaviour to expose the inconsistencies, contradictions and pathological fixations in the temperaments of others.

the correction as harsh as possible, delivering a sting in the tail which psychologically and sometimes even physically wounds the miscreants.[5] It is no longer enough to shrug tolerantly at people 'in' their humours; they must be driven uncompromisingly 'out' of them. Such an approach could correspond in a fairly obvious way to the medical practices of phlebotomy (blood-letting) or purgation (induced vomiting) by which the doctors of this period attempted to rid the body of what they thought of as excessive and harmful humours. Making comedy harshly corrective, as satire aimed to do, was a literary application of some of these key tropes of medicine, forcing audiences to confront, through the laughter, some tough and often unpalatable truths about themselves and their society.

There were two other reasons why Jonson introduced a vein of satire into the humours form, both closely interlinked. The first was a response to the appearance on the literary scene of a number of specialist satirists (usually working in verse), in particular John Marston, who cleverly adapted this harsh new tone to some otherwise self-consciously lightweight comedies (Marston and Jonson were to become both rivals and collaborators over the next ten years). The second was the chance to write these satirical plays for companies who were composed exclusively of boy actors (who were usually also trained choristers). We may marvel at the rush among learned writers to pen dramas for such companies given the array of talent available in the adult groups; but their origins in an academic, non-professional tradition, and their patronage by the wealthier class of consumer, is precisely what made them so attractive to dramatists like Jonson, who were constantly concerned about being labelled as purely commercial writers.

From his secure position with a prestigious adult company, Shakespeare watched these developments and, a few gestures aside, kept aloof from them. This was partly because the combative approach to audiences was anathema to a responsible company man such as himself, and partly because the whole humoral-satirical fad was becoming the province of boy players who posed, if only for a while, a serious commercial threat to the adults. Indeed, his own play *Hamlet* famously enlists the prince himself as a plaintiff in the adult players' cause, when he expresses astonishment at the success of the boy actor phenomenon which was threatening to drive the established companies out of business.[6] Yet Hamlet's interview with Rosencrantz and Guildenstern over the 'little eyases' is itself, of course, a little snippet of satire, suitably unforgiving, which grudgingly colludes in the high-profile craze for dramatic satire which had taken over the London theatre scene at the close of the sixteenth century.

'A Gentleman-like Monster': *Every Man in His Humour*

Ben Jonsons's *Every Man in His Humour* was first performed in 1598 by the Lord Chamberlain's Men. Shakespeare himself took one of the main roles in the play (he is named on Jonson's 1616 Folio cast list as among its 'principal comedians'), and there is even an anecdote, dating from the eighteenth century, that Shakespeare had encouraged the company to accept this play from the younger, less well-known playwright when they were at the point of rejecting it. If so, then the company were rewarded with a highly successful comedy which firmly established the humours genre as the fashionable interest of the day.

Part of the appeal lay in the fact that the play was among the first of Elizabethan and Jacobean comedies to focus exclusively on contemporary city life, giving priority to situation and setting over the story-telling that dominated much public theatre drama. In its earliest version – the one Shakespeare would have performed in – the action was located in Florence, Italy. Only later in his career did Jonson decide to make overt what had been implicit all along, rewriting the play to substitute English character and place names for the façade of Italian ones that he had used in the first version (the version used in this discussion).

By the time Jonson put together the 1616 folio of his collected works, a trend towards realism in drama had become well established, offering city audiences the theatrical pleasure of narratives involving instantly recognisable, everyday types, who seemed almost as if they had stepped onto the stage from the street, and were ready at any moment to step back out again. In the Prologue Jonson added to this later version he made a point of rejecting as old-fashioned the histories and romances of an earlier period, insisting that plays should show, as his will show, 'deeds, and language, such as men do use'.[7] However, the realism this implied was very far from the documentary kind we are familiar with from television soaps or chamber pieces for theatre today. Jonson's plays attempted, to a far greater degree than those of any of his contemporaries, to make immediacy of place and person operate through the structures and conventions of classical drama – the unities of place, time and action and established character types. This made his comedy an early standard-bearer for neoclassical dramatic practice, a dazzling fusion of London's quotidian here-and-now with revered ancient forms.

Every Man in His Humour portrays the interlinked fortunes of two 'gallants' – fashionable, well-to-do, single young males of the city – and the various encounters they undergo during their leisurely experience of daily life in the capital. The play signals its relationship to its genre by including only the barest minimum of romantic comedy plotting, keeping the focus instead on the succession of 'humorous' types whose attitudes and foibles are exposed as a result of their contact with the two young men. At the same time, the play slyly promotes an awareness of the genre's new-found fashionableness by continually stressing a connection between humours *and* fashion over the course of the play itself. As we will see, it does this by critiquing that link, holding up to particular ridicule those characters who mistake fashions for humours and humours for fashions. The confusion between the two was something Jonson was to dismiss explicitly in the prologue for his next play, *Every Man out of His Humour*, where he scoffs at those who equated 'humour' with a mere 'apish or fantastic strain' or who thought to 'affect a humour' by wearing the latest French fashion in clothing. Here, in *Every Man in His Humour*, such unlearned views form an integrated part of the action, with inferior sorts of gallants labouring under the assumption that they can simply 'don' a humour to become more interesting to others. By the same token, the play shows its two heroes triumphing over the suspicious attitudes of an older generation who react to their youthful pursuits, including an interest in the arts, as if those pursuits were some kind of morbid affliction.

The first strand of the action involves Ed Kno'well, whose youthful promise as a student and a poet must contend with the overzealous concerns of his father, who disapproves of his son's passion for poetry. The elder Kno'well is a sympathetic character in his own right, a kindly father concerned for his son's welfare and determined to ensure that he is not forced 'by any violent mean' to give up his interests, but is rather won 'by love / And urging of [...] modesty' to see the error of his ways (I.i.203–15).* Nonetheless, the audience is alerted from the start to the self-deception which attaches to this standpoint. As the older man declares in a soliloquy at the play's opening:

> Myself was once a student; and, indeed,
> Fed with the self-same humour, he is now,
> Dreaming on nought but idle poetry,
> That fruitless and unprofitable art,
> Good unto none, but least to the professors,
> Which, then, I thought the mistress of all knowledge:
> But since, time, and the truth have waked my judgment,
> And reason taught me better to distinguish,
> The vain, from th' useful learnings. (I.i.15–18)

We have all come across well-meaning double standards like the one offered here, arguments that what was good enough for oneself is not good enough for one's own progeny. The elder Kno'well effectively admits the premise that he then goes on to deny, that a fascination with poetry is an entirely predictable outcome of a student culture which was classical and humanist in its emphasis. Yet he now revises his own youthful preference for poetry as an artefact of mere 'humour': which is to say, an error of judgement, a dangerous predilection. It is not simply that poetry is a mere transitory thing, a passing interest without the universal value that poetic theorists argued for it. On his argument it is not even properly cultural, being relegated to the level of bodily disposition in direct opposition to the 'reason' which characterises 'useful learnings' (l. 23).

---

* The elder Kno'well's frequently long-winded advice to the younger makes him a possible precursor of Shakespeare's Polonius: see especially his speech, complete with gnomic utterances, to Stephen at 62–86 in this scene.

Both the absurdity and hypocrisy of this position are nicely underlined by the soliloquy's diction and form. The elder Kno'well makes heavy use of the self-reflexive pronoun ('myself was once a student'; 'self-same humour') to invite us to accept his evaluation of poetry as the normative one, but this succeeds principally in reflecting its arguments about humoral errors of judgement back upon the speaker. It is an impression comically reinforced by the fact that, in a play dominated by prose, he utters these anti-poetic sentiments in blank verse.[8]

With the objectivity of this standpoint undermined even as it is put forward, the play's intrigues can begin, with the elder Kno'well intercepting a letter to his son from one of his companions, the free-living gallant Wellbred. On prying into its contents he finds the rationale he needs to bolster his suspicions about declining standards among the youth of the day, 'petulant, jeering gamesters' (l. 189), in comparison to former (i.e. his own) times, and determines to win his son away from such influences.

The second strand of the plot mimics the outline of the first, focusing on the groundless sexual jealousy of the recently married merchant Kitely towards Wellbred, who is temporarily residing in his household. With similarly telling over-insistence, Kitely paints the picture of a young man who, at first appearing 'perfect, proper, and possessed', has now through contact with London society become 'loose, affected, and deprived of grace' (II.i.46 ff.). Most alarmingly, he is now transforming his house into a 'mart' (market), a 'theatre, a public receptacle / For giddy humour and diseased riot'. A standard antipathy is being worked out here between the figure of the honest merchant, with his puritan work ethic and his neat separation of public from private spaces, and the carnivalesque domain of 'common' spaces. The analogy of the theatre is particularly telling, for here 'riot' goes indoors and privacy is turned into public property. Such anxieties draw on wider fears about the debauchment of London's female citizenry via their exposure to plays and spectacles for, as quickly becomes apparent, it is Kitely's secret conviction that Wellbred's free and attractive manner must inevitably tempt his young wife.

The theme of 'giddy humour' – a thing that ought, on the analogy of the bodily fluids, to be subject to containment and control but has now become openly displayed – thus works as the elder Kno'well's does, to reflect back upon Kitely's over-anxious standpoint. Over a series of

159

episodes we watch him struggle, unable to contain and at the same time unable to reveal his anxieties, morbidly venturing and then quashing them in a set of inadvertent public 'performances' which leave others around him astonished and bewildered. He resorts to exasperating circumlocutions to entreat the 'plain squire' Downright to have a word with Wellbred on his behalf, pathetically excusing himself on the grounds that the young gallants in his circle might suspect him of jealousy. His feverish efforts to master his fears in front of his wife and sister prompt Dame Kitely to think he is suffering from some 'new disease' (l. 209), and in soliloquy he does go so far as to admit to a 'pestilence' which is breeding the 'black poison of suspect' in his brain. Finally, in a hilarious interview with his servant, Cash, we find him on the brink of revealing the terrible 'secret' of his anxiety about his wife, only to retreat into the mundane concern of day-to-day business – the collection of receipts etc. – instead. Cash is left marvelling at the potency of a malady which threatens to sweep everyone else along with it:

> Best dream no longer of this running humour,
> For fear I sink! The violence of the stream
> Already hath transported me so far
> That I can feel no ground at all! (III.ii.141–4)

Both Kitely and the elder Kno'well are constructed as 'humorous' in part through their fixation on the supposed humours of others; but this is only one way in which the play as a whole will put the watching and observing of other people's behaviours at the centre of its comic dynamic. Although disorders of the humours are not 'catching' as Cash's conceit might imply, there does seem to be something mimetic about them, in the sense that they can invite imitation (invariably for the worse). This is made particularly clear in the case of the play's lower stratum of 'gulls' – individuals whose folly makes them ripe for the mockery of their betters – as each tries to establish an acceptable social identity for himself.[9]

Ed Kno'well's cousin Stephen aspires to gentlemanly behaviour, but can only produce vacuous parodies of class status; while Matthew, a self-proclaimed poet, has only a tissue of plagiarisms from other writers to show for his efforts. Both are enthralled by Captain Bobadill, whose self-elevation to model soldier, gentleman and arbiter of literary taste goes unquestioned in the teeth of his bragging style. A sort of chain of imitations, or more specifically imitations of imitations, opens up between them, with Stephen's parody of 'gentleman-like' melancholy (at one point he asks for a 'stool … to be melancholy upon') eagerly adopted by Matthew as appropriate for a poet, while Stephen himself goes on to ape Bobadill's affected choler.* All three characters function schematically to set off the more substantial examples of humour in the play (Bobadill is exposed as a hollow version of the genuinely choleric Downright when the latter beats him into submission) or the relaxed, ideal behavioural stances of the young gallants (a proper gentleman and a proper poet respectively).

This idea of the absurd affectation of humours was not invented by Jonson: previous playwrights Lyly and Chapman had both used it to comic effect. However, Jonson goes further in making these imitations the basis for a critique of social pretension, putting in the mouth of the servant Cash a class-based definition of the term 'humour': 'it is a gentleman-like monster, bred, in the special gallantry of our time, by affectation; and fed by folly' (III.ii.164–6). We have already seen how Kno'well and Kitely made of themselves 'humorous' comic objects through their self-defeating attempts to place themselves outside the poetic and the theatrical spheres. Here we find disorder at the other end of the pole within a set of failed performances, which produce a 'gentleman-like' monstrosity rather than an image of the gentleman proper.[10]

Counterbalancing these inept social performers is the figure of Brainworm, the servant in Kno'well's household, who employs a variety of disguises to foil his master's efforts at reforming his son. Brainworm is not associated with any specific humour, but he clearly emerges out of the tradition popularised via Chapman's *Blind Beggar* as one who fashions himself to the humours of others. It is a function he combines with other, more specifically classical roles: the wily slave from Roman Comedy, but also (as his name implies) the 'parasite', or hanger-on –

---

* Choler is the humour which predominates in the irascible temperament, and was therefore appropriate to the soldier.

161

although here he is parasitic upon other people's identities rather than their purses.

If his recourse to disguise is not strongly motivated in plot terms, it can perhaps be seen as part of the excess of hilarity, propelled by its own energy into a kaleidoscopic array of forms, which abounds within the healthy, sanguine humour. It is a move, moreover, which sees him stepping into the place vacated by the artistically and theatrically inept, taking on the joint role of actor and constructor of plots: as he reflects with glee in the first disguise as a maimed soldier, he has been 'translated … from a poor creature to a creator' (II.ii.1–2). As Anne Barton points out, it is a wholly amoral and exuberant kind of creative activity, one which Jonson was in later plays to subject to a more severe ethical scrutiny. Here, however, it is given generous licence, as Brainworm switches from disguise to disguise (he later describes it as 'the day of my metamorphosis') until all the characters are corralled under one roof and forced into embarrassing confrontations of one another's humours.

At the play's final 'unmasking', as Judge Clement is forced to untangle the knot of accusation and counter-accusation that has resulted from Brainworm's various conspiracies, the servant is not only excused but commended for 'the wit o' the offence' (V.i.178). Wit – active in the case of Brainworm, passive in those of the young gallants – has indeed triumphed over monomania, and Clement rewards it accordingly with an invitation to feast at his house (Jonson was very fond of having a legal expert presiding over the denouements of his comedies). To this the genuinely 'humorous' characters are also invited, after the judge has first 'conjure[d]' them to 'put off their discontents'. If this amiable conclusion seems to fall short of a correction, that was something Jonson was himself to rectify in his subsequent comical satires.*

---

* In Jonson's first version of the play, published in 1601, all the characters, foolish or witty, are invited to the final feast, in the fashion of a typically forgiving comic ending. In the later, revised version of 1616, Jonson excludes the gulls Stephen, Matthew and Bobadill from the feast and has some of them sit outside cold and hungry – a more punitive ending, designed to purge the foolish, which reflects the intervening years of dramatic satire.

'Immoderate Heat': *The Fawn*

If the parasite was implicitly the hero of *Every Man in His Humour*, this is explicitly the case in John Marston's *The Fawn* of 1604 (its alternative title is *Parasitaster*). Here, however, we find the parasite responsible for conducting a morally corrective agenda throughout the play's action rather than simply exercising wit for wit's sake, as Brainworm had.

The Fawn sits at a fascinating confluence of generic types: satire and humours comedy together, but also the comic sub-genre of 'disguised duke plays', which enjoyed a brief popularity shadowing the transition from Elizabeth's to James's rule. Shakespeare's *Measure for Measure* is the best-known example, in which a Viennese ruler absents himself from government on a temporary pretext, but returns in secret to sound the depths of the corruption and abuse in his dukedom which would otherwise be hidden from him. This type of scenario traced itself to an earlier work by Marston called *The Malcontent*, although in that play the duke has been deposed and assumes a new identity to recapture his dukedom. *The Fawn* provides its own variation on the formula.

The Duke of Ferrara, Hercules, leaves his country in disguise to follow his son, Tiberio, to the court of Urbino, where the young man has been sent to negotiate a match between his father and the fifteen-year-old princess Dulcimel. Hercules, however, is hopeful that this ploy will encourage the two young principals to fall in love instead, thus resolving the problem of his son's reluctance to marry. Going by the pseudonym Faunus, the duke lurks in the court of Urbino keeping an eye on their growing attraction, while becoming an increasingly feted figure there owing to his policy of flattering all and sundry (the parasitic behaviour of the play's title).* Court life as presided over by Dulcimel's father, the self-important but foolish Gonzago, is utterly corrupt, particularly in sexual matters, and Hercules sets himself the task of reforming it not by attacking its corruption openly (it is not, after all, his court) but by 'flattering all / In all of their extremest viciousness', encouraging vice to

---

* The 'fawn' designation plays upon the idea fawning/flattering also intimated in the 'parasite' label.

the point at which it destroys itself through its own excess.[11] It is a variant application of the medical-humoral metaphor: let the sores filled with noxious humours swell until they burst, rather than lance them directly as the protagonist of *The Malcontent* elected to do, or purge them as Jacques in *As You Like It* boasted he would do. A denouement sees the young lovers secretly betrothed while a court entertainment staged by Hercules – a masque utilising the late medieval theme of the 'Ship of Fools' – holds up to ridicule all those who have sinned against the natural course of love.[12] Chief among them is Dulcimel's father Gonzago, who has been witlessly facilitating the match while attempting to obstruct it.

Both main plot and sub-plot of *The Fawn* thus devolve upon the figure of the flatterer, as the disguised duke unites in himself what one critic has described as the 'saturnalian' and the satiric functions: he attempts to secure love, marriage and future heirs for his dukedom while cleansing a corrupted polity.[13] Healthy versus debased desire is the play's presiding theme, and Urbino's courtiers function as 'walking humours' to illustrate the point: Herod is cuckolding his own brother, the impotent Sir Amorosa, and sponging off his estate; 'Nymphadoro' is a court serial monogamist, whose tally of sixty-nine mistresses has vitiated his capacity for real ardour; and Don Zuccone, the familiar humoral comedy figure of the irrationally jealous husband, displays an almost wilful attachment to the idea of being made a 'notorious' cuckold by his wife Lady Zoya.[14] Such men are sickly parodies of the ideal of romantic love which had become associated with the court of Urbino via Baldassare Castiglione's enormously influential *The Courtier*, a book which provided the key Renaissance conduct manual for courtly behaviour.[15] The ridiculous ease with which Hercules goes about puffing up their respective foibles rests partly on his own debasement of the humanist ideal of eloquence, deploying rhetorically contradictory positions and praising his targets in the same breath for being married and for not being married, for having children and for not having children, and so forth.

However, the play's attitude to the theme of sensuality is more complex than this corrective agenda alone would suggest. In his first soliloquy, as he prepares to cross into Urbino, Hercules casts off the outward trappings of rule with the pronouncement '[n]ever shall those manacles of form / Once lock up the appetite of blood' (I.i.40–1). The practical requirement to don a disguise has unexpectedly become a much larger gesture pointing towards a symbolic and, beyond that, a kind of physiological liberation. With studied sourness, he reflects on the 'exorbitant affects' and 'wild longings' which he has been forced by his high office to forego:

> He that doth strive to please the world's a fool.
> To have that fellow cry, 'O mark him, grave,
> See how austerely he doth give example
> Of repressed heat and steady life,'
> Whilst my forced life against the stream of blood
> Is tugged along, and all to keep the god
> Of fools and women, Nice Opinion … (ll. 53–9)

The power he has wielded hitherto, in other words, has relied on the appearance of a cold and bloodless virtue which belies the ferment of desires which lie within (we may think of Angelo in *Measure for Measure* as a particularly tormented instance of this conflict). Now, at this belated stage of his career, Hercules determines to overturn these social constraints and allow 'affection … desired rule' (l. 52). It is an almost carnivalesque pronouncement, a ruler actively seeking to have his heart rule his head and to give his passions free reign, in a period when this was almost the definition of bad government.

It is possible (if uncomfortable from a modern perspective) to read these sentiments as the revitalisation of an older man through the prospect of marriage to a much younger girl. But the plan to bring Tiberio and Dulcimel together seems to be shaping in Hercules's mind from the start, and as critics point out, while the language of desire is used throughout the soliloquy ('affect', 'appetite'), it does not seem to take any specific object. In fact, the 'blood' which Hercules twice refers to seems curiously redolent of the Freudian concept of the *libido* – that formless mass of urges which subsequently becomes split up into separate drives – and there is a kind of structural similarity to the concept in humours theory, in that the blood was the basic bodily fluid from which all the others arose and to which they were all ultimately 'reducible'. But the blood was also retained as one of the humours after their separation in the body, comprising the most vital and noble of the four. It would thus be an appropriate humour for a ruler to be dominated by, and once he has sampled court life at Urbino Hercules finds the appropriate object upon which to expend its excessive vigour, vowing to 'waste this most prodigious heat / That falls into my age like scorching flames' in flattering others towards excesses of their own.[16]

Hercules thus joins the humorous characters of the play, but also stands above their imbalance and rigidity, describing himself as 'on a rock, from whence I may discern / The giddy sea of humour flow beneath' (II.i.575 ff.). His own 'stream of blood' is nothing like the 'sanguine complexion' which Nymphadoro blames for making him 'enforcedly in love with all women' (III.i.1–4), and is much more like the 'free heat' or 'Enthusiasm' to which Gonzago pathetically lays claim. However we choose to understand the vital heat which has gripped Hercules from the moment he jettisons the robes of state, he shows himself adept at channelling it towards a rhetorical, moral purpose:

> Another's court shall show me where and how
> Vice may be cured; for now beside myself,
> Possessed with almost frenzy, from strong fervour
> I know I shall produce things mere divine:
> Without immoderate heat, no virtues shine. (II.i.592–6)

Hercules's strategy for manipulating personalities and events at Urbino thus complicates the opposition between witty youth and suspicious, self-deluding age which the play carries over from a humours comedy like *Every Man in His Humour*. If the latter character type appears in the shape of Gonzago, who tries to keep the young lovers apart and ensure that his daughter marries Hercules, the former is represented by Dulcimel, who runs rings round her father, having him communicate her desire for Tiberio under the pretext of delivering them as rebukes to the young man. Hercules represents a triangulation of this arrangement, temporarily suffused with youthful vitality but mature enough to channel it in a political rather than a biological direction. A biological resolution to his 'immoderate heat' is achieved vicariously, instead, via the marriage between the two lovers and its speedy consummation in the play's final act. While Hercules has been largely a bystander in this part of the narrative, the blessing he pronounces as he watches Tiberio climb a tree into Dulcimel's chamber demonstrates his understanding of the way biology can require a helping hand from political expediency:

Let it be lawful to make use, ye powers,
Of human weakness, that pursueth still
What is inhibited, and most affects
What is most difficult to be obtained (V.i.15–18)

His 'too cold son', in other words, has been enflamed by the prohibition which has been placed on Dulcimel by her father, a reaction which ties up precisely with her own half-serious admission to a friend that she loves Tiberio for 'only a woman's reason: because I was expressly forbidden to love him' (III.i.242–3). Both of these eroticised responses to debarment obviously recall Hercules's initial rush of blood once released from his ducal capacity, the only difference being that his is belated and acknowledged as erotically redundant.

Desire – at its most basic, bodily, appetitive and humoral level – is thus seen as having something social, rather than purely natural, about the way it is produced in the first place. The play fits its recognition of this theme around the basic premise of the genre that all the world is 'humorous' – that everyone is irregular, twisted, eccentric to some extent – and allows for a sophisticated and tolerant standpoint which emerges despite the emphasis on exposing and correcting folly and vice.

Marston's *The Fawn* can be regarded as building on the correctional project of dramatic satire, but modifying it to make the keynote one of latitude; morally and literally letting characters swell in humoral excess till they burst. Marston, the specialist satirist, may have decided to take his drama in this new direction partly because of his feud with Jonson during the 'poets' war' which had scandalised the stage in the first years of the seventeenth century. The feud had come to a head with Marston himself being mortifyingly lampooned on stage by his rival playwright – perhaps the worst possible fate for a self-conscious worker in satire – as his fictional counterpart in *Poetaster* was administered a purge which caused him to vomit up examples of his idiosyncratic diction. But dramatic satire had also found a dangerously juicy target in King James himself, the self-anointed philosopher prince whose manner, both bookish and boorish, as well as his habits of favouritism and endowment of his Scottish followers, had attracted caustic allusion in plays almost from the first year of his reign. A number of writers (Marston included) had landed themselves in serious trouble, indeed in jail, as a result. Placing a wise duke alongside a foolish duke would help blunt the ridicule that could otherwise have associated James with Gonzago, with his relentless attempts to call attention to his own wisdom and eloquence, and might even have coaxed the monarchical observer/reader into succumbing to precisely the kind of flattering self-delusion that Hercules so delights in encouraging. There should be little doubt, however, in which of the two a knowing early seventeenth-century audience would be most tempted to identify the features of their new ruler.

Extended Commentary: *Volpone* (1606)

Volpone, or The Fox, first performed in 1606, was neither a humours comedy nor a 'comical satire' in any precise, Jonsonian definition of those terms (the 1616 collected edition of his works simply classes it as a 'comedy'). Nonetheless, the play owes much to these two dramatic forms, and in return it cleverly fashions a new dramatic context for the themes and tropes it borrows from them. We saw in the last two plays discussed how use was made of familiar comic conventions in the naming of characters, making them either semi-allegorical or satirically representative of a particular humour or virtue: Wellbred, Brainworm, Nymphadora, and so on. *Volpone* takes this convention to another level, insinuating the fabulous in among the realistic. Characters are not now mere moral types but become synonymous with their proverbial animal counterparts.

In fact, the play seems to derive almost all its characters from an Aesopian bestiary. Volpone, the Fox of the title, is a rich Venetian inflicting an ingenious scam upon his fellow citizens: he languishes at home pretending to be at death's door while promising his wealth as inheritance to anyone and everyone who brings him lavish gifts. In this he is assisted by his servant Mosca (the Fly), whose powers of persuasion allow him to dupe several victims at one time with repeated promises of their imminent success: the lawyer Voltore (the Vulture), the ageing Corbaccio (the Raven) and that perennial satiric standby, the fanatically jealous husband Corvino (the Crow).

The main action is thus self-consciously emblematic in its patterning: in an early scene Volpone describes himself as 'a fox / Stretched on the earth, with fine delusive sleights / Mocking a gaping crow' (I.ii.94–6). This hard veneer of fable becomes romantically (or at any rate sexually) enriched, however, after Mosca relates the beauty of Corvino's wife, Celia, to his master, prompting him to venture out from self-imposed confinement into the city in disguise (as a quack doctor) to gain a glimpse of her and to contrive how to seduce her. A sub-plot follows a self-important Englishman abroad in Venice, Sir Politic Would-Be, and the exposure of his pretensions to espionage and state intrigue. It touches the main plot principally via the attentions bestowed on the malingering Volpone by Sir Politic's wife, whose garrulous social effrontery drives him to distraction.

Volpone cleverly adapts the practice in humours comedies of parading eccentric or foolish characters one after another before an audience and putting them into revealing or mortifying predicaments. Where this could be developed in a rather leisurely, incidental fashion in a play like *Every Man in His Humour*, with characters taking part more in a rogues' gallery than a co-ordinated action, in *Volpone* the practice is fully integrated into the play's narrative and moral structure. Each of the dupes is brought before the Fox as he feigns the extremity of sickness on his couch, and each is led to expose the self-serving and self-deluding motives which sustain his 'generosity', sometimes with Mosca providing a chorus, sotto voce, to drive home the point:

> VOLTORE: How fare you sir?
> VOLPONE: I thank you, Signior Voltore.
> Where is the plate? Mine eyes are bad.
> VOLTORE: *Putting it into his grasp*   I'm sorry
> To see you thus still weak.
> MOSCA: *Aside*   (That he is not weaker.)[17]

In the play's opening scenes the procession of what Volpone calls his 'birds of prey / That think me turning carcass' through his room is an overlapping one, rather in the manner of farce, with characters shuffled in and out following knocks on the door, narrowly missing one another but forced into an edgy awareness of each other's rivalry for Volpone's favour. This tightly organised, 'revolving doors' pattern allows Mosca scope for some outrageous satirical licence at the expense of their naked self-interest, as for example in his reassurances to the lawyer, Voltore:

> I, oft, have heard him say, how he admired
> Men of your large profession
> [...]
> That, with most quick agility, could turn,
> And re-turn; make knots, and undo them;
> Give forkèd counsel; take provoking gold
> On either hand, and put it up: these men,
> He knew, would thrive, with their humility. (I.iii.52–60)

Mosca is speaking with feigned admiration of the lawyer's dexterity in forging out of legal cases a labyrinthine plot for personal gain; but he might just as easily be talking about his own 'agility' in bamboozling the gift-givers and playing them off against one another.

The discipline and continuity achieved in the play's opening act goes some way to fulfilling the author's boast in the Prologue that his play will present:

> a comedy refined
> As best critics have designed;
> The laws of Time, Place, Persons he observeth
> From no needful rule he swerveth. (Prologue, ll. 29–32)

However, as much as Jonson preached the centrality of these neoclassical 'laws', his dramatic invention is simply too powerful to be constrained by them. The narrative complication of Volpone's lust for Celia ensures that the action of later scenes moves out into the streets of Venice and then back again into his rooms before shifting into the court rooms, reprising the motif of characters grown too 'humorous' to stay in one place and instead seeming to ebb and flow from one locale to another. The 'laws of Time' seem similarly redundant, here. As some critics have pointed out, the scam Volpone and Mosca put into practice could continue indefinitely, just so long as the fox maintains his near-death façade. Even when the whole charade nearly comes unstuck through his pursuit of Celia, events are so managed by Mosca that by the beginning of the fifth act the situation has returned more or less to where it was at the start of the play – a repeating loop in which the process of deception threatens to be never-ending.

While the 'birds of prey' are all motivated by straightforward material greed, the fox and the fly are more complexly represented. On the one hand they are the agents of satire in the play, exposing and commenting upon the mendacity and greed of their victims, and frequently marvelling, as Mosca does here, in their complicity in their own gulling:

> Too much light blinds 'em, I think. Each of 'em
> Is so possessed and stuffed with his own hopes
> That anything unto the contrary,
> Never so true, or never so apparent,
> Never so palpable, they will resist it – (V.ii.23–7)

The satire can be more general in tone, too, as in Mosca's jocular counter (borrowed from Erasmus's *Praise of Folly*) to Volpone's claim that it is impossible to be learned:

> O, no: rich
> Implies it. Hood an ass with reverend purple,
> So you can hide his two ambitious ears,
> And he shall pass for a cathedral doctor. (I.ii.110–13)

In a key departure from the classic satiric format, however, these observations proceed from individuals who are every bit as amoral as their dupes; and master and servant are further allied to the gulls via the logic of humoral *excess* which, as we shall see, leads them towards a humiliating conclusion. Here, narrative point of view and alignment of audience sympathy with Volpone and Mosca is established by emphasising that success is primarily a reward for their own genius in duplicity and impersonation. In an early exchange between the two, Volpone begins by saluting his 'saint' – the gold that is already heaped up, Jew of Malta-style, in his room – before going on to remind Mosca that:

> I glory,
> More in the cunning purchase of my wealth,
> Than in the glad possession; since I gain
> No common way: I use no trade, no venture ... (I.i.30–3)

What Volpone means by the 'common way' of gaining wealth in Venice is a blend of traditional modes of exploiting the environment and the newly emergent forms of financial accumulation – banking, money-lending – for which the Italian Renaissance was already famous. He distances himself from these pursuits, delighting instead in exploiting the exploiters; but rather than this turning him into a noble profiteer – a sort of Robin Hood of the piazzas – the 'purchase of ... wealth' lends his enterprise an oddly tautologous, even redundant character. This works partly as a comment on the sterility behind the new financial ethos, whereby money breeds money, but it also reproduces the peculiar behavioural arc of characters such as Hercules, in *The Fawn*, who subscribe to action for action's sake, following their momentary urges and needing no prior rationalisation for them. Indeed, despite their polarised moral positions, both characters demonstrate a similar interplay between the appearance of old age (feigned in the case of Volpone, genuine in that of Hercules) and the superabundant vigour which is hidden by it. This is shown most spectacularly when, having inveigled Celia into his bedroom with the connivance of her husband Corvino, Volpone springs from his couch and begins his seduction of her, enacting a brilliant theatrical fantasy of rejuvenation:

> Why art thou mazed, to see me thus revived?
> Rather applaud thy beauty's miracle;
> 'Tis thy great work: that hath, not now alone,
> But sundry times, raised me, in several shapes,
> And, but this morning, like a mountebank,
> To see thee at thy window. (III.vii.145–50)

As these lines suggest, Volpone unites in himself the two aspects of humours we have been tracing in this section: the performative and the pathological. Chapman's play *The Blinde Beggar of Alexandria* had adapted 'humours' to the theme of shape-shifting (see the beginning of this chapter), and now Volpone boasts of his flair for assuming 'varying figures' to astonish and woo Celia. But there also seems to be a genuine pathology of the mind behind this translation of amorous intent into a myriad of guises, suggested when he boasts to Celia that 'I am, now, as fresh / As hot, as high, and in as jovial plight' as when he himself was once an actor of comedies before the great (III.vii.157–8). To be jovial – to be ruled by the planet Jupiter – is to have the humour of blood reign in the body, and thus to incline towards high spirits generally and erotic desire in particular.

Volpone has, of course, been characterised throughout the play as a thoroughgoing sensualist, living solely for pleasure and amusing himself between visitations from his gulls via various elaborate entertainments (he employs a motley collection of dwarf, hermaphrodite and eunuch for this purpose). But it is only at this halfway point in the play that a question mark arises over the soundness of his judgement – his ability to understand the world from a perspective outside that of his own narrowly circumscribed humoral bias. He cannot conceive of Celia as other than a kindred spirit, one who will willingly join him in a kind of erotic masque in which they impersonate the fabled seductions of the gods: Jove and Europa, Mars and Venus. Celia's integrity has been sorely tested: her tyrannically jealous husband, Corvino, having kept her more or less under house arrest for the early part of the play, has been easily persuaded by Mosca to use his wife's body in a ploy to gain the 'decrepit' Volpone's favour. Volpone is thus on persuasive ground when he offers himself as 'worthy lover' in place of 'a base husband'. But her virtue cannot be corrupted. She opposes her 'mind' against the 'sensual baits' which Volpone proffers: pearls, diamonds, drinks of 'preparèd gold', baths of 'the milk of unicorns, and panthers' breath', dishes of exotic birds which, if he could only purloin it, would even include the phoenix.

Volpone's imaginative overreaching dazzlingly re-energises an otherwise stale Marlovian form of word-painting (the kind audiences might have remembered from *Tamburlaine*), but it proves unable to engage with the abstract concepts countered by Celia: honour, conscience, chastity. Even the song he sings to her, despite addressing her by name, seems oddly detached from its addressee, more wrapped up with its own exquisite imitation of a classical poetics of seduction. Each character speaks from within a circle of language which is absolutely separated from and unable to touch the other, and Volpone quickly surmises that rape is the only possible conclusion to such a one-sided seduction. Celia escapes his assault by the timely intervention of Corbaccio's son Bonario, the other paragon of abused virtue in the narrative (his father is disinheriting him in favour of Volpone), and Volpone's response to this reversal of fortune is that of the stereotypical voluptuary, lurching from extreme cupidity to extreme despair: 'Fall on me roof, and bury me in ruin … I am unmasked, unspirited, undone.'

It is Mosca's ingenuity which restores the status quo, if only temporarily. He prevails upon the three 'birds of prey' to defame Bonario and Celia before they can expose the subterfuges emanating from Volpone's house. Throughout the play, we see Mosca taking a delight in invention comparable to that of his master. Unlike Volpone, however, Mosca is not a sensualist. As a development of the parasite-figure Brainworm from *Every Man in His Humour*, his energies are channelled instead into the witty manipulation of others, usually (and predictably) achieved through the medium of flattery. But in the self-congratulatory soliloquy he delivers moments after managing the seemingly impossible – persuading the ultra-possessive Corvino to prostitute his wife to Volpone – he is not averse to including himself among the objects of his flattery:

> I fear I shall begin to grow in love
> With my dear self and my most prosp'rous parts
> They do so spring and burgeon; I can feel
> A whimsy in my blood. I know not how,
> Success hath made me wanton … (III.i.1–5)

Mosca seems almost literally to grow on the stage in front of us: the exploration of his 'prosp'rous parts' teeters on the brink of an auto-eroticism which balances out the homoerotic attention he has occasionally received from others – his dupes, and Volpone – over the course of the play. But his self-love quickly turns into a species of professional pride:

> O! Your parasite
> Is a most precious thing, dropped from above,
> Not bred 'mongst clods and clotpolls here on earth.
> [...]
> Almost
> All the wise world is little else in nature
> But parasites or sub-parasites. (III.i.7–13)

The difference between parasite and sub-parasite hinges less on the degree of self-abasement to which each is obliged to stoop (Mosca now professes to despise those who 'fawn, and fleer' and 'Make their rèvenue out of legs and faces') than on a peculiar claim to omnipresence:

> But your fine, elegant rascal, that can rise,
> And stoop, almost together, like an arrow;
> Shoot through the air, as nimbly as a star;
> Turn short, as doth a swallow; and be here,
> And there, and here, and yonder, all at once;
> Present to any humour, all occasion;
> And change a visor swifter than a thought! (III.i.23–9)

Mosca imagines himself a natural occupant of the same rarefied element that Ariel will later grace in Shakespeare's *The Tempest* (appropriately so, if we wish to pursue the contemporary line of thought that allied the humour of blood with the element of air). Yet despite this highly appealing encomium to his trade, Mosca here reveals himself to be just as much a creature of humour as any of his monomaniacal victims. He resorts to a totalising statement ('all the "wise world" is parasitic – just like me!') and then proceeds to sub-divide that world into superior and inferior examples. It suggests a reductive grasp of his social environment on a par with Volpone's: unable to read itself in relation to difference, to the Other, beyond what a grasp of people's humours can afford in the way of exploitation. When his powers of persuasion find they have no weakness to work upon, as in the case of the sceptical Bonario whom he encounters immediately after his soliloquy, he is obliged to fall back – literally – upon his own resources, translating that heady flux of 'wanton' humour into a display of physical tears which both appals and convinces the young man.

As the play moves into its later stages, we find that Mosca's ambitions are indeed oriented solely towards himself, with his attempt to double-cross Volpone into giving him half his property or face the exposure of his scheme before the judges:

> My fox
> Is out on his hole, and ere he shall re-enter,
> I'll make him languish in his borrowed case,
> Except he come to composition with me. (V.vi.6–9)

Mosca's betrayal of his master is a harsh but logical development of the witty servant exemplified by Brainworm in *Every Man in His Humour*, whose shift of allegiance from bumbling older master to vibrant youthful one was motivated primarily by self-interest. His success in countering the accusations of Celia and Bonario has ensured that the escapees now face the law's full vengeance for adultery and attempted parricide respectively; and while this has rescued the play's original pattern of gulling from the eccentric shape it took after the attempted rape of Celia, it is a growing sign that master and servant have shifted themselves onto the wrong side of an allowable comic resolution. There has also been a shift in the degree of self-possession demonstrated by Volpone, one which serves to question for the first time his proficiency as an actor, at least as far as a 'public' audience goes:

> I ne'er was in dislike with my disguise
> Till this fled moment. Here 'twas good, in private;
> But in your public – *cavé* whilst I breathe.
> [...]
> Give me a bowl of lusty wine to fright
> This humour from my heart. (V.i.2–12)

Mosca eagerly picks up on this failure of nerve, re-interpreting Volpone's professions of jocundity in the midst of danger – 'I had much ado / To forbear laughing' – in suitably humoral terms as expressions of innate cowardice:

> MOSCA: 'T seemed to me you sweat, sir.
> VOLPONE: In troth I did a little.
> MOSCA: But confess, sir,
> Were you not daunted?
> VOLPONE: In good faith, I was
> A little in a mist, but not dejected... (V.ii.36–40)

With the plot now brought back under the control of the two schemers, the sense that Volpone remains to a degree unbalanced by preceding events is confirmed when he spontaneously decides to torment his victims via the pretence of dying and leaving Mosca sole heir to his fortune.

Although the theoretical concept of hubris had a direct application to tragedy rather than to comedy, Volpone's gratuitous, self-hazarding display of cruelty seems neatly designed around that concept at the start of this final act; and indeed Jonson's recent literary venture in the genre of Roman tragedy with *Sejanus* (1605) may have prompted its clever application here. It begins a chain of events which, although strictly comic in form and moral architecture, arrives at an unprecedentedly painful conclusion. Mosca's decision to stay in his newly elevated persona and to blackmail Volpone into sharing his goods precipitates the latter's discovery of the entire plot to the court. Wit is not rewarded here in mitigation of its offences (as it is in *Every Man in His Humour*), nor is the law shown to be anything other than a highly fallible medium for distributing impersonal vengeance. The judges have shown no more penetration of Mosca's designs than crow, rook or raven, and indeed have attempted to curry favour with him when at the height of his apparent success. Now they sentence him to life as a galley slave, his master (protected from a comparable fate by virtue of birth and blood) to being 'cramped with irons' in a Venetian prison – the intent being not to reform but to prosecute a savage irony, rendering the erstwhile malingerer 'sick and lame indeed' (V.xii.123–4).

The play's sub-plot involving Peregrine's exposure of Sir Politic Would-Be's pathetic intrigues underscores the gap between *Volpone*'s dominant method of distributing moral justice and the more familiar practices of comical satire. Calling upon the English knight in disguise and pretending to arrest him for treason against the Venetian state ('my ambition is to fright him only'), Peregrine produces the kind of purgation aimed for in the earlier satiric mode, forcing Sir Politic to such an extremity of mannered behaviour, persuaded to hide himself under the 'engine' of a tortoise-shell, that the knight is necessarily shocked into self-awareness when the deception is revealed. Sir Politic hints that he will join his wife – similarly mortified after attempting to offer Mosca her sexual favours – in fleeing Venice and taking 'physic' for the humiliations they have suffered. The main plot, by contrast, exchanges the purgative for the punitive, compelling the miscreants, '[w]hen crimes are done and past and to be punished / To think what your crimes are' (V.xii.147–8). The play's final word makes explicit the impact of the 'beast fable' approach upon the older logic of relieving humoral excess: 'Mischiefs feed / Like beasts till they be fat, and then they bleed.'

Notes

1   See the introduction by Robert S. Miola to Ben Jonson's *Every Man in His Humour*, Revels Plays (Manchester: Manchester University Press, 2000), pp. 11–18, for further discussion of Shakespeare's relation to the humours movement in drama. In addition to the history plays, comedies such as *The Merry Wives of Windsor* (1597) and *Twelfth Night* (1601) are sometimes discussed as contributions to the genre. Despite a number of correspondences in terms of content, however, these plays retain a Romantic/New Comedy form overall.

2   *Every Man out of His Humour*, Prologue, in *The Complete Plays of Ben Jonson*, ed. Felix E. Schelling, 2 vols (London: J. M. Dent 7 Sons Ltd., 1936), vol. 1. Spelling modernised.

3   David Riggs, *Ben Jonson: A Life* (Cambridge, MA: Harvard University Press, 1989), p. 40. See ch. 2 on 'The Comedy of Humours' in general for an illuminating analysis of Jonson's approach.

4   Galen, the Roman doctor and medical theorist who provided the ultimate source for Renaissance ideas on the body, wrote that 'A particular humour might on occasion metamorphose into one or another sort of humour according to temperature, time, place, age and diet: for all humours arise and increase at every moment and season', *Galen on Food and Diet*, trans. Mark Grant (London: Routledge, 2000), p. 15.

5   For the shift towards satire which *Every Man out of His Humour* represents, see O. J. Campbell, *Comicall Satyre and Shakespeare's 'Troilus and Cressida'* (San Marino, CA : Henry E. Huntingdon Library and Art Gallery, 1938), pp. 1–8.

6   William Shakespeare, *Hamlet*, ed. Harold Jenkins, Arden, 2nd series, II.ii.336–58. An 'eyas' is a young hawk, famed for its screeching.

7   Ben Jonson, *Every Man in His Humour*, ed. Martin Seymour-Smith, New Mermaids (London: A&C Black, 1966), Prologue, l.21.

8   On this piece of formal irony see especially the comments by Anne Barton in *Ben Jonson, Dramatist* (Cambridge: Cambridge University Press, 1984), p. 53.

9   For discussion of identity in the play see James Loxley, *The Complete Critical Guide to Ben Jonson* (London: Routledge, 2002), pp. 46–8.

10   For a helpful discussion of the play's construction of gentility in terms of the humours, see Richard Allen Cave, *Ben Jonson*, English Dramatists (Houndmills: Macmillan, 1991), pp. 20–30.

11   John Marston, *Parasitaster, or The Fawn*, ed. David A. Blostein, Revels Plays (Manchester: Manchester University Press, 1978), I.ii.347–8.

12   The 'Ship of Fools', in which various examples of folly are loaded onto a ship and sent off to a fool's paradise, was a theme especially popularised by the German poet Sebastian Brant's satirical allegory *Narrenschiff* of 1494.

13   See Joel Kaplan, 'John Marston's "Fawn": A Saturnalian Satire', in *Studies in English Literature*, vol. 9, no. 2 (1969), pp. 335–50.

14   Kaplan, p. 347.

15   For a discussion of *The Courtier*'s centrality to Renaissance discourse about manners and taste see Peter Burke, *The Fortunes of the Courtier: The European Reception of Castiglione's 'Cortegiano'* (Cambridge: Polity Press, 1995).

16   For a reading of Hercules's speech and subsequent behaviour at Urbino in terms of 'sublimated libido', see in particular Frank Whigham, 'Flattering Courtly Desire', in David L. Smith, *The Theatrical City: Culture, Theatre and Politics in London, 1576–1649* (Cambridge: Cambridge University Press, 1995), pp. 137–56.

17   Ben Jonson, *Volpone, or The Fox*, ed. Brian Parker, Revels Plays, revised edn (Manchester: Manchester University Press), I.iii.16–20.

Jacobean Revenge Drama: *The Revenger's Tragedy* and *Women Beware Women*

The appeal of revenge as a dramatic concept is a complex one, both universal and highly specific to its moment. Arguments for the primal, universal attractions of the theme are strong, with revenge being central to much of ancient Greek tragedy as early as Aeschylus (*The Oresteia*) and enjoying a similarly powerful purchase in imperial Roman and early modern English and Spanish drama. Beyond these periods, it can be seen to have retained its appeal even after the decline of formal tragedy, including in our own period. While the drama of the twentieth and twenty-first centuries has tended to treat the idea parodically, if at all (as for example in Alan Ayckbourn's black comedy sequence, *The Revenger's Comedies*), film has found the subject much more amenable (it is a prominent motif in many Hollywood Westerns).

A consistent identifying characteristic through these periods is the status of revenge as an action which is at its heart a counteraction: its shape and purpose in some measure already defined by the provocative act which has set it on. In dramatic terms it thus includes a pleasing predictability – the audience has a sense of where it is going – but also the thrill of variation through augmentation, as the revenge in many cases outstrips in scale and horror the deed it answers. However, the evaluation of revenge is widely different in every epoch's theatre: mythically linked to the foundation of the state in Greek drama, closely tied to critiques of tyranny in Seneca's Roman plays, bound up with codes of family honour in the Spanish. Where the English drama was concerned, any evaluation of revenge had to take account of the act's widely assumed unlawfulness,

180

both from a temporal perspective and from a Christian one in St Paul's widely quoted insistence on the Old Testament injunctions: 'avenge not yourselves, but rather give place unto wrath, for it is unwritten, Vengeance is mine; I will repay, saith the Lord' (Romans 12.19).

Revenge as a general theme features in countless plays of the English Renaissance, and in that informal sense can be seen to span a variety of genres and sub-genres: romantic comedy (the revellers' revenge on Malvolio in *Twelfth Night*), domestic tragedy (Othello pledges to avenge himself on Desdemona), and history (Queen Margaret's verbal 'vengeance' on just about everyone in *Richard III*) are a few often-encountered Shakespearean examples. Our discussion here, however, will focus on something more specific: revenge narratives that can be identified as part of a separate sub-genre within tragedy, and in particular those revenge plays of the Jacobean period, where the accent on extremism becomes stronger and the role of women in the tragedy more central.

The accession of James I has often been seen as contributing towards a new tone and emphasis in the period's literature, with developing attitudes towards court life playing a key role in this. Although there is always a danger of over-emphasis on the so-called decadence of the Jacobean court, it is true that James did much less than Elizabeth to disguise luxury and corruption at the centre of the nation's political and cultural activity.[1] This led to a sharpening of the satire and stoicism which had already been circulating in the last years of his predecessor, while the passing of Elizabeth and the fading of her personal cult of virginity introduced a newer set of attitudes towards the role of women in that court.* The drama of this period has become notorious for both its violent content and its sexual themes, and while the portrayal of violence itself was hardly uncommon on the English stage, where the influence

---

* Both satire and stoicism (the classical philosophy that stressed self-sufficiency and freedom from the passions) became popular during the later Elizabethan years. Both lent themselves to the formation of a political position, in the sense of providing ways of dealing with corruption and injustice in public life. After Elizabeth, James I's court was notoriously one of favouritism, and satire and stoicism represented ways of attacking or maintaining equanimity in the face of exclusion from the centres of power. The poet and dramatist Ben Jonson, who pursued a career at court while promoting the image of the poet as the exemplar of virtue, was a notable exponent of both.

of Seneca was pervasive, these Jacobean dramas introduce that violence into social spheres where its appearance is shockingly incongruous or invasive. One of these spheres is that of the bonds formed through female activity, where personal relationships between women and women, and sexual relationships between women and men, develop within enclosed domestic and courtly environments. When these go awry through betrayal and deceit, a sense of the (male or female) victim's vulnerability to the irrational impulses of revenge is heightened.

There continues to be some debate, however, as to how far the 'sub-genre' designation is a meaningful one. In her recent study of revenge-themed tragedies Janet Clare rejects the 'genre' tag, arguing that there is insufficient formal unity between the plays to justify the idea of a coherent category. She points to the fact that 'few Renaissance plays in their titles or sub-titles … call attention to the revenge theme, or to the role of the protagonist as a revenger'.[2] This is a fair point: the two most famous and influential tragedies involving revenge in the Elizabethan period, Kyd's *The Spanish Tragedy* and Shakespeare's *Hamlet*, do not use the word in their published titles (although the Stationer's Register does refer to *Hamlet* as a 'booke called the Revenge of Hamlett Prince Denmarke'). To this we can add an absence of anecdotal references to 'plays of revenge' of the kind we encountered for the 'play of humours'. Nevertheless, it is tempting to think in terms of genre for many of these works, particularly once 'Elizabethan' becomes 'Jacobean' and some of the newer attitudes and concerns noted above coalesce around stable and persistent features of the earlier revenge dramas. One such feature, the play/entertainment/masque/staged combat which descends into massacre at the tragedy's conclusion, is so favoured that it continues to be used despite an awareness of its own redundancy, as we will see below when we look at the late Jacobean *Women Beware Women*. If the ending of a play can help to define its genre, then this trope of the duplicitous entertainment has some claim to doing so for revenge tragedy, although it of course is no more a 'universal' feature within that genre than any other feature.

The idea of the avenging entertainment was first employed by Thomas Kyd in *The Spanish Tragedy*, where Hieronimo uses it as a cover for assassinating the murderers of his son. Kyd's play is often cited as the seminal work for English revenge drama, and many of its most striking features were adapted with great invention by later dramatists. To begin with, these were often utilised en masse, but in later plays the elements became more diffusely associated, and sometimes the appearance of only one or two together would be sufficient to signify indebtedness to the Kydian 'formula'.[3] The protracted nature of the revenge, in Hieronimo's case explicitly linked to the concept of doubt and delay, is reworked most obviously in *Hamlet*, but also figures in plays as diverse as Marston's *Antonio's Revenge*, where it is linked to the stoic sufferance of wrong, and Henry Chettle's *Hoffman*, where it is a product of the sheer extensiveness of the hero-villain's avenging scope. In *The Revenger's Tragedy*, we discover at one point that the hero has waited nine years for his moment of retribution – although there is little sign of procrastination within the narrative frame itself.

Kyd's play makes use of madness as an adjunct to this delay, as both Hieronimo and his wife Isabella feel the bonds of reason slip owing to grief over the injustice of their son's death.* While plays like *Hamlet* and *Hoffman* retained the pathetic image of the woman distressed by madness, the motif became less common in the Jacobean-era revenge dramas, with the striking exception of its use in *The Duchess of Malfi*, where, however, as we will see, it is recast as an aspect of the revenge itself. Another favoured component from the earlier plays which subsequently became de-emphasised was the use of a Ghost as the initiating cause of vengeance – a feature directly borrowed from the revenge plots of Senecan drama. In *The Spanish Tragedy* the Ghost features in a Morality-style pairing with the allegorical figure of Revenge, and merely comments on the action from his position in the underworld. *Hamlet* and *Antonio's Revenge* give it a fuller part in the action; but by the time of *Hoffman*, where the 'dead remembrance of ... the living father' is now restricted to a corpse, the supernatural element is already declining.[4]

---

* This feature will be discussed in more detail in Part Four: 'Madness and Subjectivity'.

As this emphasis on the figure of the male spirit recedes, we find an increasing focus on the female body as an actuating cause of vengeance: sometimes as corpse, sometimes as sexual or maternal object, and sometimes (more rarely) as agent. By putting women at the fulcrum of their plots, these Jacobean revenge tragedies were in part following a narrative trajectory which had been suppressed in the earlier plays. In the Prologue to *The Spanish Tragedy*, the figure of Revenge prepares the Ghost of Don Andrea to witness how his murderer will be '[d]eprived of life by Bel-Imperia', the Spanish royal lady who was his lover in life and later becomes the lover of Hieronimo's son, Horatio. An audience is thus whetted in the first instance to the theme of a female-driven revenge, but that prospect is quickly countered by masculine prerogative, as Bel-Imperia's revenge becomes absorbed into Hieronimo's over the course of the action. It remains part of the play's appeal, however, that it seems to offer two revenges in one, male and female; and Bel-Imperia is essential both for providing verbal admonishment to Hieronimo's flagging vengeance and for personally despatching Don Andrea's murderer at the conclusion.

The Jacobean reinstatement of female figures to central positions in the revenge narratives should not be seen as a consciously empowering one, however. In line with the sexist ideologies of Renaissance England, where women are automatically equated with the body, nature, irrationality, it becomes a way of giving these revenge stories a material focus which can supersede the spiritual concerns of the Elizabethan revenge dramas. Where Hamlet repeatedly seeks for answers to the problem of a morally perplexing universe in comparably uncertain beliefs about the afterlife, these Jacobean plays locate their obsessive questioning in the 'why?' of the female body. Is it chaste? Is it a source of temptation? Is it threatening in its very fertility?

Giving Revenge her Due: *The Revenger's Tragedy*

The Revengers's Tragedy (performed 1606) was written for performance by the King's Men at the Globe theatre, the big open-air playhouse built in 1599 which retained a broad and socially eclectic clientele. Yet the play reads in many ways like an indoor theatre work, with its restricted cast of characters sporting precise allegorical names, claustrophobic use of space, and special emphasis on the effects of torchlight in its creation of an atmosphere of court luxury and depravity. This was still the period of ascendancy among the boy player companies, young occupants of the vastly more expensive and exclusive indoor theatres, and *The Revenger's Tragedy* often looks like a conscious appropriation of boy company theatrical styles and strategies by the adult company – a 'can't beat 'em, join 'em' tactic which brings the acerbic tone of a play like *The Fawn* (1604) to bear on the spectacles of blood and retribution historically handled by the bigger stages. In fact, the boy companies had already performed an ingenious parody of revenge tragedy in Marston's *Antonio's Revenge* in 1601, which deliberately pushed the conventions of onstage violence (already flexible enough) to the edge of acceptability with its sustained torture of its antagonist, Piero. This accent on excess, played out in a generically Italian court setting, was to be worked back into the adult plays, beginning with *The Revenger's Tragedy* with its comparably harrowing (but at the same time exhilarating) tormenting of a villainous duke as its dramatic centrepiece.

The play's opening moments signal the theatrical strategy which will predominate throughout – stacking the tropes of revenge one upon another for richness of effect ('three-piled', to use one of the play's favourite adjectives of opulence) in preference to stringing them out over a longer narrative arc. The play's hero, Vindice, watches from a distance as '*the Duke, Duchess, Lussurioso her son, Spurio the bastard, with a train, pass over the stage with torchlight*'.[5] Unseen by the ducal family, he unleashes an extended monologue against the sinfulness of their regime while holding in his hands the skull of Gloriana – the woman to whom he was once betrothed and whom we learn was poisoned by the duke because her 'purer part would not consent / Unto his palsey-lust':

> Duke, royal lecher; go, grey haired Adultery,
> And thou his son, as impious steeped as he:
> And thou his bastard, true-begot in evil:

And thou his duchess, that will do with devil:
Four ex'lent characters! (I.i.1–5)

The arresting, staccato delivery of the first line immediately sets the tone of crimes and misdemeanours mounting up uncontrollably. The device of a procession commented upon at length by an unseen observer, along with the tart reference to its participants as 'characters' (with the contemporary meaning of stereotypes, or thumbnail sketches rather than rounded individuals) suggests an exercise in boy player-style satire. But the satirist did not normally hold a skull when delivering his envenomed speeches: that office was performed by the preacher, often standing in front of his congregation and pointing to a skull to remind the listeners of their mortality, in what was called the 'memento mori' tradition. Vindice enlists this tradition by turning directly to the skull, once the procession has past, and apostrophising it as a 'sallow picture', his 'study's ornament' and a 'shell of Death' (l. 15). The classic revenger's task, to 'remember' the dead, is thus invoked, with ingenious economy, through the use of a particular stage property, rather than (as with *Hamlet*) the drawn-out narrative interventions of a Ghost. Vindice's business with the skull is very obviously adapted from *Hamlet*, but where Prince Hamlet's memento mori musings in the graveyard scene sit somewhat outside the dramatic action, in *The Revenger's Tragedy* they are made a part of it from the very beginning. As if to underscore this new link that has been forged, Vindice turns from the skull at once and explicitly announces his task of revenge, employing a flourish of personifications:

Vengeance, thou Murder's quit-rent, and whereby
Thou show'st thyself tenant to Tragedy,
Oh keep thy day, hour, minute I beseech,
For those thou hast determined. Hum, who e'er knew
Murder unpaid? Faith, give Revenge her due,
She's kept touch hitherto … (ll. 39–44)

The play revels in this personifying practice, one which extends to the naming of many of the key parts: 'Vindice' itself, for example, simply means 'vengeance', while his antagonists sport names such as 'Lussurioso' – lustfulness – and 'Spurio' – bastardry. This can give a pleasing sense of individuals who are 'determined', to use Vindice's phrase; that is, pre-ordained in their behaviour by the stereotypical logic of dramatic 'character' stamped upon them by virtue of their place in the plot. In that sense the play works as a kind of stripped-down, cleverly reassembled version of the classic revenge narrative, pointedly acknowledging the ground rules underlying the form and manipulating its participants like pieces in a board game. But in many cases these names are introduced late in the play: Vindice identifies himself as Vindice, for example, only at the moment of his revenge against the duke. As a personification of vengeance he therefore cedes place to the abstraction used in this opening soliloquy: and, unlike in *The Spanish Tragedy*, the audience are warned from the outset that Revenge in this play will have a female face.

The play's treatment of the revenge theme is too exuberant to confine it to one individual, however. We find revenge plots multiplying from the outset, so much so that some critics have found the main strand in danger of being submerged under the mass of subsidiary retributions.[6] No sooner have we heard of Vindice's plan to infiltrate the court by joining the louche entourage of the duke's eldest son, Lussurioso (who is seeking the services of a pimp), than the focus shifts to the aftermath of the rape and suicide of the Lord Antonio's wife. The youngest of the duchess's three sons (by a previous marriage) is responsible, and a trial in the play's second scene sees his mother pleading for his life against the seemingly inevitable death sentence, only for the duke to defer judgement at the last minute (ll. 83–5). It is a solution which satisfies no one: the law is made a mockery of (another perennial revenge drama theme); the duke's own sons – who despise their step-mother's progeny – are secretly disgusted, and the duchess herself confirmed in her contempt for her husband.

Two additional vectors of revenge thus develop as a result. A group of disaffected lords gathers around the dead body of Antonio's wife (I.iv), swearing on their swords to revenge the outrage on her body (they are prompted in this, significantly, by Vindice's brother, Hippolito, rather than by Antonio himself, who only consents passively to the idea). At the same time, the duchess seduces her stepson, the duke's bastard Spurio, in a policy of vengeance-by-cuckolding: 'Who would not be revenged of such a father / E'en in the worst way?' she asks him, aggravating his sense of malaise over his bastardry in a manner recalling that of Edmund in *King Lear* (I.ii.154–5).

Thus by the end of the first act, at a comparable stage in the action to that in *Hamlet*,* a plethora of familiar constituents of revenge drama are in place – an oath taken on swords, not one but two corpses enforcing the task of remembrance, and a scandalous suggestion of incestuous lust; all taking place in a polluted court through which a revenging agent stalks in disguise, awaiting his moment. Unlike in *Hamlet* and *The Spanish Tragedy*, however, where the play's digressions into sexual and moral concerns complicate the straightforward task of exacting 'wild justice', all these dramatic indices point towards vengeance and vengeance alone.[7]

The play develops its own special slant on the revenge theme by implicating the female body more directly in its retributive logic than had been the case in earlier plays. The skull of Gloriana and the body of Antonio's wife are the obvious shock-tactic replacements for the 'dead corse' of Hamlet's father, or the strung-up body of Horatio in *The Spanish Tragedy*. These female mortal remains encroach on a space ordinarily reserved for the masculine victims of the slaughter which usually begins the revenge drama. This generates some tensions in the dramatic language used by the play, as when Antonio describes his wife's body in an oddly de-sexualised, martial metaphor as 'a fair comely building newly fallen / Being falsely undermined' (the undermining of fortifications was a favoured military tactic). Vindice may seem to go to the opposite extreme in his first soliloquy with the terms he uses to describe Gloriana, at whose very purity and chastity

> the uprightest man – if such there be,
> That sin but seven times a day – broke custom
> And made up eight with looking after her. (I.i.23–5)

---

* *The Revenger's Tragedy*'s first printed edition has divisions into acts only (or acts with one scene to be precise), which are divided into scenes in modern editions. *Hamlet*, of course, originally had no act or scene divisions.

Yet through this relentless sexualising of his lost beloved – his acknowledgement of her unwitting power as a temptress – her status as a thing rather than a person is underscored. Her role in life was characterised by a kind of providential instrumentality in exposing the wicked and the weak (which is to say, in Vindice's cynical generalisation, everyone). Her function in death will be no less instrumental in providing both the memento for and, subsequently, the actual tool of vengeance against the duke. This is accomplished by the mid-point of the play, when Vindice lures the duke into a pretended assignation with a willing lady in an 'unsunned lodge / Wherein 'tis night at noon' (III.v.18–19). In reality the 'lady' is the skull of Gloriana, *'dressed up in tires'* (elaborate headwear) and poisoned on the lips – a bait which the duke takes at once (l. 141 ff.). But Vindice's revenge is, in true Senecan fashion, asymmetrical. Not only is a poisoning answered with a poisoning but also psychological agony – 'the torturing of his soul' (l. 20) – is added to the moment of death, with the duke forced by the two revenging brothers to watch as his wife and bastard son complete their assignation nearby in the same place, audibly fomenting their own plots against him. In this one excruciating sequence the female body is doubled as an instrument of vengeance, a grotesque and deadly rendering of the classic Morality pairing of virgin and whore.[8]

That pairing also works itself out in the sub-plot involving Lussurioso's attempt to debauch Vindice's sister, Castiza. Vindice himself, in his disguised persona, is despatched to act as Lussurioso's go-between, and he seizes upon the opportunity to test the moral fibre not just of his sister but also of his mother, whom the duke's son is certain (correctly, as it turns out) can be persuaded 'with gifts' to corrupt her own daughter. Castiza is, of course, the embodiment of chastity in the play, although she is no mere one-dimensional representation of virtue, since she acknowledges in soliloquy that her poverty makes her vulnerable to sexual approaches from the powerful (II.i.1–8). Yet when her disguised brother and her mother throw temptation into her path she quickly becomes an instrument of chastisement, fetching Vindice a blow on the ear and bitterly rebuking her mother as a bawd (at both of which her brother is secretly delighted).

This whole, extensive sub-plot is important in establishing from the early stages of the play that the primary target of retribution in *The Revenger's Tragedy* is not murder but lust, in all the varied and gaudy forms in which it appears. The duke's poisoning of Gloriana for refusing him her favours merely provides the rationalising gloss on a moral outlook which insidiously links sex and criminality throughout. Two instances in particular show how outrage at sexual depravity rather than at murder engages the conventional postures of revenge. Vindice's prevarication in II.ii over whether or not to kill Lussurioso – 'Oh shall I kill him o' the wrong-side now? No / Sword thou wast never a back-biter yet' – recalls Hamlet's fateful decision to spare Claudius at prayer ('Up sword, and know thou a more horrid hent'); but here it is prompted by Lussurioso's threat to seduce Castiza in person, and even includes a witty allusion to the homosexual proclivities of the duke's son (ll. 89–90). Then in IV.iv Vindice and Hippolito enter *'bringing out their mother, one by one shoulder, one by the other, with daggers in their hands'*, in a scenario which reproduces an attitude of menace similar to that which they adopted during their torture and murder of the duke.

Although the mother is forgiven for her attempt to debauch Castiza, Lussurioso is assassinated in classic revenge tragedy fashion, during a masque performed for his investiture as the new duke (V.iii). Lussurioso has by this stage supplied the protagonist with a valid motive for revenge, hiring the protagonist in his own shape to murder his disguised persona, but it remains a hatred of Lussurioso's sexual transgressions which preoccupies Vindice. Stabbing him clandestinely during the dance, Vindice exults that 'no power is angry when the lustful die', a view seemingly upheld by the host of strange phenomena which appear to mark the assassination (thunder, a blazing star). Lussurioso has already remarked on these with deep foreboding (ll. 15–20); but if they are omens, Vindice's own jocular attitude towards them – 'When thunder claps, heaven likes the tragedy' – compromises any sense that they can be enlisted to the avengers' interpretation of events.[9]

Ultimately, it is secular, rather than heavenly power which has the final word: in one of the big shock reversals of Jacobean drama, after installing him in power Vindice confidently confesses his murders to

Lord Antonio, who promptly despatches both brothers to execution. The move may arguably be necessitated by moral closure. Vindice himself acknowledges that he has by this time become a kind of revenging engine run out of control: ''Tis time to die when we are ourselves our foes' (l. 112). But Antonio's reasoning in the aftermath of Lussurioso's slaying is alarmingly doddery nonetheless – 'Such an old man as he! / You that would murder him would murder me' (l. 107) – and it returns us full circle to the image of a weak and capricious government by old men with which the play began. The court may now be purged of the lust personified in the duke's 'grey haired Adultery', but Vindice's hope that Antonio's 'hair will make the silver age again / When there was fewer, but more honest men' finds only a despondent irony instead of a cathartic endorsement.

Deadly Entertainments: *Women Beware Women*

The Revenger's Tragedy was *probably* written by Thomas Middleton, a younger contemporary of Shakespeare's who had been writing for the drama from the last years of Elizabeth's reign. *Women Beware Women* was certainly by him, and by the time of its (probable) late-Jacobean date of 1621 Middleton was well established as one of the most versatile writers in the capital. Pamphlets, satiric poems, occasional speeches but above all plays comprised an output which allied an attractive fluency of style to immense overall productivity. In terms of generic range his dramatic writing was on a par with Shakespeare's; but unlike Shakespeare he was not tied to any particular company. This meant his plays could shift more freely between very different theatrical idioms: boy-player satire, breathtaking urban farce and full-blown tragedy in the increasingly popular realistic (i.e. journalistic) mode.[10]

Among the many points of interest for present-day audiences and readers are the parts Middleton wrote for female tragic protagonists. These often demonstrate a special tension between sympathy for a female sexual autonomy equal to that of the male, and fatalism about the disastrous consequences which unfold when women are compelled to seize that autonomy for themselves. In *Women Beware Women* this fatalism terminates in a spectacular 'masqueing' finale where the revenges of three different women, thwarted in their sexual choices, collide to produce bloody carnage. Yet this denouement feels strangely – even wilfully – tacked on to the rich psychological drama which Middleton had built up behind it. Where most revenge dramas establish the revenging imperative from an early stage, in this play it arises only as a sudden, violent spasm at the end. Does the lurch into artifice indicate an awkward attempt to find new possibilities for a forty-year-old set of theatrical conventions? Or does it say something about the need to modify the tone of the narrative when women are the primary agents of destruction?

The play's title might have been conjured out of a line from *The Revenger's Tragedy* uttered by Castiza's mother: 'Women with women can work best alone.' The implication, worked out in detail in this later play, is that women's defences against male sexual advances are vulnerable primarily to the arguments and strategies of fellow women. This may be – as Martin White asserts – a traditional misogynistic theme refreshed through its expression by a female character; but it is a double-edged one nonetheless.[11] Male rhetorical power over women – the ability to persuade rather than to coerce – is limited. In supplying this deficiency women take control over a key link in what has been called the circulation of women within a patriarchal society.[12] Such control carves out a space for an exclusively female agency within this process, although it allies that agency with Eve's original sin of temptation. In the case of Castiza's mother, it is the prospect of exchanging a life of poverty for one of wealth which prompts her to try to corrupt her own daughter.

Women Beware Women provides a less straightforwardly mercenary picture, in which the debauchment of chastity arises from powerful social and familial longings. These are dealt with respectively over the course of two separate plot lines. In the first of these, the desire of the Duke of Florence for Bianca, newly eloped with her husband into his dukedom, shows ideals of marital love and loyalty succumbing to entrenched attitudes about social class. In the second storyline, the forced marriage of a young gentlewoman, Isabella, to a rich but idiotic heir (simply known as the Ward) sees her taking as a lover the man who has always desired her, her uncle Hippolito. These two storylines converge in the compelling character of Livia, a twice-widowed, well-off lady of Florence, now thirty-nine years of age, who takes it upon herself to resolve the impasses presented by each situation. In narratological terms she functions as the play's enabling agent, overturning impediments to the fulfilment of desires. Where in comedy these tend to be of an external kind (parental disapproval, for example, in romantic comedy), in tragedy they are more often moral in nature, and the consequences of their being overturned is inevitably catastrophic.

It is significant that we see Livia dealing first with the problem of the arranged marriage, since this gives her the necessary scope to outline her philosophy of equality in sexual choice. The young girl being pressed into marriage is her brother's daughter, and Livia remonstrates with him, determined to 'take [her] niece's part, and call't injustice / To force her love to one she never saw'.[13] Livia's appeal to a kind of 'natural justice' in affairs of the heart, it can be noted, already shares an argumentative basis with that used by the revenger of personal or familial outrage. The terms of that argument become explicit with Livia's ironic use of legal language to mock her brother's unbending exercise of patriarchal will:

> Though you be a justice,
> Your warrant cannot be served out of your liberty;
> You may compel out of the power of a father,
> Things merely harsh to a maid's flesh and blood,
> But when you come to love, there the soil alters;
> Y'are in another country, where your laws
> Are no more set by than the cacklings of geese
> In Rome's great Capitol. (ll. 131–8)

Yet there is a far deeper irony in the way Livia ensures the dictates of 'flesh and blood' are to be fulfilled in Isabella. When her adored second brother, Hippolito, confesses an incestuous passion for Isabella which has driven him to despair and threatened the exceptionally close bond between uncle and niece, Livia seizes the opportunity for a double resolution to the unhappiness of both. Falsely persuading her niece that she has been fathered by another man and that she is not kin to those she thought her family, she dangles the prospect of free sexual choice in front of her:

> How weak his commands now, whom you call father?
> How vain all his enforcements, your obedience?
> And what a largeness in your will and liberty,
> To take, or to reject, or to do both? (II.i.158–61)

The possibility of 'taking and rejecting' within the marriage contract – of marrying the Ward but enjoying Hippolito as her lover – is immediately understood and acted upon by Isabella. Both parties remain ignorant of Livia's deception until the very end of the play. Hippolito is fully conscious of the violation of the incest taboo, assuming his niece has overcome her aversion to it by herself. Isabella, however, merely assumes she is pursuing a clandestine affair with a man she finds attractive, a valid course of action given her ill fortune in having to marry a fool: 'how can I obey and honour him / But I must needs commit idolatry?' (I.ii.164–5).

The Ward's hopelessness as a prospective husband is made apparent in his preoccupation with petty game-playing, shown on his very first appearance before Isabella '*with a trap-stick*'. The play's opposition between wit and folly, however, is not based on a rejection of game-playing as such, but on a distinction between the kinds of game played, with women marked out as excelling at the more cerebral sort. Act II Scene ii develops this theme by intercutting further illustrations of the Ward's frivolity (he reappears at one point bandying about a '*shuttlecock*') with a series of key developments in the play's main narrative strand, brilliantly unfolded around a game of chess between Livia and Bianca's mother-in-law.

Bianca has been spotted at her window by the duke in his procession through Florence, despite the best efforts of her doting husband, Leantio, to hide her from the gaze of the world, and Livia promises to arrange an assignation at her home or 'shut up shop in cunning', as she puts it (II.ii.28). The phrase is cruelly appropriate to the lower-middle-class circumstances of her scheme's victims, for Leantio and his mother are tradespeople, nervously aware in their different ways of the mismatch between the superior social background Bianca forsook to marry him and their own more humble situation. Livia's strategy is to play shrewdly on the class consciousness of both women, flattering the mother into a 'neighbourly' visit while arranging for the 'gentlewoman' Bianca to tour her 'rooms and pictures' in the company of one of the duke's courtiers (ll. 271–3). In a particularly vivid utilisation of open theatre performance space we witness the ensuing sexual coercion of Bianca taking place on the upper stage (usually a gallery or walkway) while Livia simultaneously distracts the mother by engaging her in a chess game on the lower stage. Finding herself alone and surprised by the duke, Bianca begs to be spared his advances, but his appeals both to his elevated social station – 'I can command. Think upon that' – and her own compromised one – 'Do not I know y'have cast away your life / Upon necessities, means merely doubtful' – are forceful enough to silence her, and he leads her away (ll. 363–77). Their encounter is bracketed and heavily underscored by Livia's exultant commentary on her own chess-playing prowess, as she manoeuvres her 'duke' about the board to inflict a heavy defeat on the mother-in-law:

> LIVIA: Has not my duke bestirred himself?
> MOTHER: Yes 'faith, madam.
> Has done me all the mischief in this game.

The chess game functions as an ironic counterpoint to the physical and spiritual peril Bianca is in, and from the soliloquy she delivers on her re-appearance it becomes apparent that she has been forced by the Duke:

> Now bless me from a blasting; I saw that now
> Fearful for any woman's eye to look on.
> Infectious mists and mildews hang at 's eyes,
> The weather of a doomsday dwells upon him.
> Yet since mine honour's leprous, why should I
> Preserve that fair that caused the leprosy?
> Come poison all at once. (ll. 421–7)

It is a deeply unsettling speech, generating in the listener an initial uncertainty as to what Bianca might mean by the disease imagery she associates with the duke. Ultimately, it emerges that the speech is pointing towards his moral rather than physical corruption (i.e. in the sense of venereal disease), but further discomfort arises with Bianca's acceptance of her own future corruption as a consequence of the rape. A Calvinist ideology often noted in Middleton – a subscription to the idea that the saved and the damned are pre-ordained to their fates – may partly account for this, and it is notable that Bianca identifies her own beauty rather than the rape itself as the initiating cause of her 'leprosy'.[14] But her acceptance can also perhaps be seen as a kind of narrative acquiescence – a recognition of her role as a piece in a deadly game which she now understands is unfolding around her.

Livia's comfortable, upper-middle-class household is one of superficially enrapturing entertainments: of rooms and pictures (the courtier had shown Bianca erotic paintings on the way to see the duke to whet her 'appetite') and diverting games, behind which are concealed objects which poison the sight. These beguilements are summed up in Livia's request to the courtier that he take Bianca to see 'the monument' (l. 277) – her code word, laden with priapic meaning, for the waiting duke. The motif of the deceptive art work, the serpent beneath the rose, is, as we have seen, a favoured one of revenge tragedy, where innocuous pleasures erupt into violence as part of the denouement. *Women Beware Women* anticipates that conclusion by showing a leisurely gathering veering into sexual intrigue and rape, at a mid-point in the play from which all the subsequent tragedies will develop.

This fully integrated use of deadly game-playing is perhaps one reason why the final masque itself has a contrived air about it, inviting some critics to speak of its 'staginess' and 'extreme stylisation'.[15] But the shift in the play's tone in the last act also mimics the radical changes in women's affections which the latter half of the play details. The fallout from Livia's schemes sees the once-loving Bianca rejecting Leantio in favour of enjoying the sexual and social advantages of becoming the duke's mistress, while Livia herself, originally the confirmed single woman, takes the distressed Leantio as her lover. When this latter liaison becomes a matter of family honour for her brother Hippolito, his murder of the young man begins the series of female-initiated revenges which congregate in the masque. Bianca, watching the masque with the duke, contrives to poison his brother, a cardinal who has publicly condemned their affair; Livia attempts to take the life of her own brother, Fabritio, via a hidden trapdoor on the stage; and Isabella, now fully aware of the incest she has been tricked into committing, conspires to murder Livia through the use of poisoned incense in their masqueing roles as nymph and goddess respectively. After the fashion of *Hamlet*, all these efforts go awry, but in such a way as to destroy those guilty of lust and homicide anyway, with the duke, Hippolito and Guardiano perishing along with Bianca, Livia and Isabella.* Hippolito's dying testament sums up the catastrophe:

> Lust and forgetfulness has been amongst us,
> And we are brought to nothing.
> [...]
> vengeance met vengeance
> In a set match, as if the plagues of sin
> Had been agreed to meet here altogether. (V.ii.146 ff.)

The suddenness, incongruity and near-farcical nature of the conclusion have implications for the litany of all-female revenges it portrays. In contradistinction to Hieronimo's mastery over events in the finale to *The Spanish Tragedy* (heavily reliant though it is on Bel-Imperia's assistance), the unwinding stratagems of the masque in *Women Beware Women* offer a misogynistic rebuke to the control we have seen Livia exercise over the games and entertainments earlier in the play, and perhaps include a reassertion of masculine prerogative in that area. Perhaps most importantly of all, in having the play take the shape of a revenge drama at only the most belated stage, the female protagonists are obliged to take the maximum amount of responsibility for its disastrous outcome while being denied the sympathy that develops for the male avenger over the longer arc of the narrative.

The Revenger's Tragedy and *Women Beware Women* sat at either end of the Jacobean period which, we have argued, saw an increased narrative

---

* In an interesting inversion of the gender roles in the denouement to *Hamlet*, the duke accidentally tastes from a poisoned cup which Bianca prepares for his brother the cardinal, and in her despair she drinks from it and follows him in death.

(rather than simply thematic) emphasis on women and women's sexuality in revenge plays.* In the next part of this discussion we will look in more detail at *The Duchess of Malfi*, a tragedy which falls in the middle years of this period, and which combines the motif of a relentless interrogation of female chastity with that of the terrifying consequences of a woman's attempts to control her own sexual destiny.

Extended Commentary: *The Duchess of Malfi* (1614)

Middleton's success in bringing female protagonists to the centre of revenge dramas in plays like *Women Beware Women* (and *The Changeling* of a year later, 1622) may have owed something to the example of John Webster's *The Duchess of Malfi*, acted in 1614 by the King's Men – the company Shakespeare worked for. Middleton was among a number of writers who penned admiring commendatory verses to the printed version of Webster's play (a gesture not repeated by Middleton for any other playwright), where he confidently asserted that for Webster's epitaph:

> Write, 'Duchess', that will fetch a tear for thee,
> For who e'er saw this duchess live, and die,
> That could get off under a bleeding eye?[16]

The image of the 'bleeding eye' – tears saturated with blood – suggests an imaginative way of sub-dividing revenge-themed drama within the 'tearful' responses aroused by tragedy as a whole, although there is no indication from any of the prefatory verses that revenge was explicitly construed as a generic feature of the play. The verses tend to focus more on the dramatic impact of the duchess herself – 'lively bodied', as another

---

* Comparison with Shakespeare's *Hamlet* is helpful here: where that play may have made the focus on the sexuality of Gertrude and Ophelia important at a thematic level, neither character becomes a key part of the action in the way Gratiana, Castiza, Livia and Bianca do.

playwright, William Rowley, put it: an artistic compliment meaning that she has been convincingly represented 'to the life', but also surely acknowledging the vitality of the character herself. Webster took his characters and plot from an English retelling of a story of Italian intrigue and murder found in Belleforest's *Histoires Tragiques* – the same collection of narrative sources that lay behind Shakespeare's *Hamlet*. Although there is no specific call by any one figure to avenge another that sets the events of *The Duchess of Malfi* in motion, vengeance nonetheless pervades the play in forms which inventively rework such key revenge motifs as intra-familial strife, the outrage to honour, dark hints of incestuous affection and the deadly climax of the masque.

The play's opening scene shows the Duchess of Malfi, young and recently widowed, being forbidden to remarry by her two brothers: her twin, Ferdinand, the Duke of Calabria, and her elder brother, the Cardinal of Aragon. No clear or consistent reason beyond an ingrained hostility towards the idea is given by the two men for this prohibition, and their insistence swings between the weakly rationalised policing of family honour offered by the cardinal to an ill-defined mistrust of the calibre of female desire on the part of Ferdinand:

> FERDINAND: You are a widow:
> You know already what man is, and therefore
> Let not youth, high promotion, eloquence –
> CARDINAL: No, nor anything without the addition, honour,
> Sway your high blood.
> FERDINAND: Marry? They are most luxurious
> Will wed twice.
> CARDINAL: O fie!
> FERDINAND: Their livers are more spotted
> Than Laban's sheep. (1.1.284–90)

The two brothers are established from an early phase as acting in concert despite the inherent contradiction in their advice, with one allowing marriage with provisos about the social class of the husband while the other forbids it altogether. Of the two, it is the twin Ferdinand's demands which carry the more personal edge, one which spills over into physical threat when he harangues his sister privately: 'This was my father's poniard: do you see? / I'd be loth to see't look rusty, 'cause 'twas his' (ll. 322–3). The phallic quality of the threat embedded in this relentless focus on his sister's sexuality is made more overt still with his departing double entendre:

FERDINAND: And women like that part which, like the lamprey,
Hath ne'er a bone in't.
DUCHESS: Fie, sir!
FERDINAND: Nay,
I mean the tongue: variety of courtship.
What cannot a neat knave with a smooth tale
Make a woman believe? Farewell, lusty widow.
(ll. 327–31)

An atmosphere of revelry is allowed to permeate – without ever becoming joyous – these opening scenes, one which partly bears out Ferdinand's obsession with the temptations offered by court life but also sets the precedent for the ironic inversion of the masque which will later be used to torment the duchess. The key figure in the midst of this revelry is Antonio, occupant of two rather contradictory roles: realistic observer/ commentator on the degeneracy of the Italian court in comparison to the French one he has recently returned from, and steward of the duchess's household. This latter role might seem to place him on a class footing similar to that of Malvolio in relation to Olivia in *Twelfth Night*: a respectable, middle-ranking position which is defined by its service to the aristocratic members of the court. The boundaries of this 'personal secretarial' role are complicated, however, by the courtly accomplishments with which Antonio is associated from the start, including his success in jousting at the revels and, perhaps more importantly, his understanding of the display of courtly manners and virtues in others.

The ability to distinguish between true courtship and its mere impersonation was one of the essential qualities of the courtier, and in the opening exchanges we see Antonio exercising this ability in his assessments of the two brothers. The cardinal is noted as one on whom the 'flashes' of courtly accomplishment 'superficially hang, for form', while his 'inward character' (his true form, as perceived by the adroit courtier) is that of a 'melancholy churchman' – one whose rise to religious high office belies the grubby practice of bribery and political jockeying which has got him there (ll.149–50). The same inward/outward distinction is applied to Ferdinand, whose 'mirth', according to Antonio, 'is merely outside', but whose deceptive manner is less the result of Machiavellian policy, as it is with his brother, than of a gratuitous desire to 'entrap offenders' in the Law (ll. 162–7).

Against these character sketches of a perverted display of courtly virtue Antonio sets his description of their sister, 'the right noble Duchess'. Significantly, Antonio begins not with a description of her looks, as he had with the brothers, but with her 'discourse': the mode of speech which characterises her and which blends formal beauty with inspirational matter to fulfil one of the highest courtly attainments for either sex. It is, says Antonio:

> so full of rapture,
> You only will begin then to be sorry
> When she doth end her speech; and wish, in wonder,
> She held it less vainglory to talk much ... (ll. 181–4).

Only after this does Antonio go on to praise her physical beauty, but his description follows a movement the reverse of that which outlines the hidden corruption of her brothers: her discourse illuminates her physically from within, and the enchanting 'look' which she 'throws upon a man' while she speaks serves primarily to reinforce what she has to say. Antonio's star-struck encomium misses out some of the more informal aspects of the duchess's appeal, most notably the wit with which she asserts her own point of view about remarriage against her brothers'. But this emphasis on the integrity of the duchess's speech is an important one, nonetheless, because by the end of this first, busy scene of the play she has flouted her brothers' commandment and gone on to 'woo' (ordinarily the male prerogative in romantic discourse) Antonio for her husband. This sequence is both poignant and comic in its mood, with the duchess obliged to make the running and to contrive a way of putting the ring on Antonio's finger to make her intentions clear; but it also signals a shift in the play's prioritisation of social space. The rather unwholesome public world of courtly backbiting and staged activities is replaced by one intimate and private, with the duchess's maidservant, Cariola, the only other participant, hidden behind the arras to provide the witness for the troth-pledging.

Some critics have seen this shift as defining a set of bourgeois characters who emerge in opposition to the aristocratic ones embodied in the cardinal and the duke: characters whose sense of identity is inward and self-sufficient rather than formed through theatrical displays of courtly accomplishment.[17] Even if these labels are a matter more of personal values than of material circumstance, we should certainly be sensitive to the frissons about social status which this particular sequence includes, for in the presence of the duchess Antonio is a very different character from the majestically detached observer of court affairs he had been at the start of the scene – highly aware of his steward's rank and anxious (very unlike Malvolio) not to allow 'Ambition' to breach the social distinctions between the two of them (l. 410). The duchess compares his personal modesty favourably with the trick of dim lighting used by 'tradesmen i' th' city' to 'rid bad wares off': to her Antonio is the 'complete man', defined solely by his virtue. But the thoroughly bourgeois, mercantile analogy is a telling one, as the awkward matter of redefining their social relationship is left hanging in the air, exacerbated by their need to keep the marriage a secret. Does the duchess herself accept a nominal, if not actual, diminishment in status in order to accommodate Antonio's good fortune? Perceiving his anxiety, she reassures him that:

> This is flesh, and blood, sir;
> 'Tis not the figure cut in alabaster
> Kneels at my husband's tomb ...

> I here do put off all vain ceremony,
> And only do appear to you a young widow
> That claims you for her husband ... (ll. 443–8)

This too describes a shift away from the language she uses in soliloquy at the start of the wooing sequence, where a lofty martial discourse, equating forbidden marriage with a 'dangerous venture' and 'impossible actions', keyed us in to the expectation of some great act of elevation to be performed on her part. Instead, the quiet intimacy of her chamber, where marriage is self-sufficient and the church's ceremonial sanction deemed unnecessary, provides the setting in which the duchess retains her dominance of personality while eagerly meeting Antonio halfway socially. It is left to Cariola to encapsulate the troubling contradictions of this new position:

> Whether the spirit of greatness or of woman
> Reign in her, I know not, but it shows
> A fearful madness; I owe her much of pity. (ll. 494–6)

Although neither brother had explicitly threatened vengeance against the duchess should she defy their wishes and choose for herself in marriage, Ferdinand had intimated as much in the sinister business with the dagger and in his warning that the duchess's 'darkest action ... privat'st thoughts / Will come to light' (I.i.306–7). This latter notion is another important motif of the revenge drama, also expressed in Hamlet's *sententia* that 'Foul deeds will rise / Though all the earth o'erwhelm them to men's eyes'. In the difference between *Hamlet*'s and *The Duchess of Malfi*'s use of the motif, however, we can see the generic development from an emphasis on the male spirit towards the female body as a catalyst for vengeance. Where the Ghost of King Hamlet had burst the 'ponderous and marble jaws' of his tomb to testify to the 'foul, strange and unnatural' act which had cut off his life, the duchess's own female bodily nature will now become the means to bear witness to the transgression (at least as her brothers see it) of choosing sexually for herself. Hence it is that Ferdinand's prophetic warning to her is fulfilled, as we next see the duchess heavily pregnant by Antonio and struggling to keep the matter hidden. Her predicament has, however, become apparent to Bosola, the 'railing' (i.e. satirically abusive) malcontent figure whose overriding desire for employment at court has led him to accept the position of Ferdinand's spy in the duchess's household. It is a position which allows him ample space to impose his jaundiced satirical caricatures of humanity on everyone around him, with a particular victim in the Old Lady whom he targets with such aggression for her 'scurvy face-physic' that he breathes some temporary life back into the hackneyed diatribes favoured by Elizabethan and Jacobean moralists on the theme of cosmetics (see the set of exchanges at II.i.20–40). But Bosola's misogynistic caricaturing has a narrative role to play as well, as he draws on various stereotypes about women in pregnancy to tempt the duchess into publicly revealing her condition:

> I observe our Duchess
> Is sick o' days, she pukes, her stomach seethes
> [...]
> I have a trick may chance discover it ... (ll. 59–65)

Offering her fresh apricots in the hope of inducing a display of 'craving', his crude ruse surpasses expectations as her 'vulturous eating' (II.ii.2.) suddenly puts her into labour and she withdraws in panic. Despite Antonio's direct involvement in the scene and his later discovery by Bosola at night casting a nativity horoscope for the child, his status as her husband remains undetected by Bosola – in part because of its very implausibility – and he is at worst suspected by him of being her 'bawd' (II.iii.66).

Bosola's subsequent revelation to the two brothers of the duchess's pregnancy has the predictable effect on them, with Ferdinand in particular flying into a display of such intemperate rage that even the cardinal is shocked. The pathological habit of mind lying behind his attitude towards his sister's freedom of sexual choice is emphasised by the intrusive ideas he experiences of her copulating with a string of imagined (and socially inferior lovers): 'some strong thighed bargeman / Or one o' th' wood-yard, that can quoit the sledge' (II.v.42–3). The effect is both comic and deeply alarming, as if the excessive fantasising of Hotspur's speech on honour in *Henry IV Part 1* was being combined with the mad ravings of King Lear against women's sexuality. It also recalls the excessive investment of Vindice in his sister's chastity in *The Revenger's Tragedy*.

The play certainly allows the oddity of Ferdinand's obsession to chime with revenge drama's frequent excursions into the theme of incest although, as Kathleen McLuskie points out, this cannot be construed as a consistent aspect of character psychology given Ferdinand's orthodox speeches elsewhere on reputation and morality.[18] It is perhaps best seen as one of a number of features which aggregate at this point in the play to allow the revenge aspects of the narrative to come to the fore. Ferdinand's threats now include generically recognisable allusions to dismemberment ('When I have hewed her to pieces', l. 31) and the even more explicitly Senecan wish to 'boil their bastard to a cullis [i.e. a soup]' and feed it to the yet undiscovered father 'to renew / The sin of his back' (ll. 73–5). Yet it is significant that the first open reference to the revenge concept occurs in the passive voice, when he wonders if '[i]t is some sin in us heaven doth revenge / By her' (ll. 66–7). Ferdinand is speaking hyperbolically here – he cannot sincerely be claiming that his sister's behaviour is some kind of divine punishment on the two men. Nonetheless, a characteristically Jacobean emphasis on the woman's role as instrument in revenge here connects with the one unambiguous Judaeo-Christian statement on the morality of vengeance, cited at the start of this chapter – 'Vengeance is mine, saith the Lord: I will repay' – to point up the lack of moral authority which the brothers have had in all of their dealings with the duchess.

Subsequent scenes between Ferdinand and the duchess settle the matter of where she is to be located in this unstable economy of vengeance, manoeuvring her by degrees into the position of its principal object. Ferdinand's sudden, night-time appearance in her chamber in III.ii, where she had only moments before been conversing with Antonio in an atmosphere of domestic intimacy, shows her brother toying sardonically with the idea of her as agent in her own affairs by handing her a dagger and encouraging her to use it on herself. During these middle scenes of the play Ferdinand's threatened revenge is held up in a kind of dreadful pause as the brothers await intelligence of who her husband is, intending to deal with him first. Yet once Antonio is revealed by Bosola to be the man, interest shifts remorselessly to the duchess, in part because her husband is construed as too mean an object to carry the full weight of their anger. The couple are publicly humiliated and banished as a result of the cardinal's increasing political power, but become separated, leaving the duchess to face her brothers alone.

It is at this stage of the play, rather than at its conclusion, that *The Duchess of Malfi* makes its boldly original use of the motif of the masque. Although the very opposite of a formal, courtly entertainment – it takes place in a prison-house where the duchess is incarcerated by Ferdinand – it remains typical in forming a part of the enactment of revenge against its victim. Indeed, it becomes the chosen instrument, rather than merely the appropriate setting, for that vengeance, as Ferdinand makes use of various forms of representation to try to drive his sister into madness before having her strangled. A desire for mental disintegration thus replaces the earlier, more conventional emphasis on physical dismemberment, and it is significant that this shift towards a non-physical revenge is made appropriate to a female rather than a male victim.

Finding that the captive duchess's 'melancholy seems fortified / With a strange disdain' (IV.i.11–12), Ferdinand first confronts her with an object designed to remove all hope, presenting *'behind a traverse, the figures of Antonio and his children, appearing as if they were dead'* (SD l. 56). These are merely wax figures, but the duchess is at once persuaded of their reality, in a manner which perhaps draws on misogynistic tropes about women's credulity in response to representation.* Ferdinand's scoffing delight in the way in which she is 'plagued in art' by his device goes some way to supporting this reading (l. 111). Ferdinand then follows this supreme shock by sending a masque of madmen to parade themselves before her, with Bosola in disguise as master of the 'revels'. Most important is the duchess's response to these torments, as she soon

---

* A notorious instance of this trope is offered by the character of the Citizen's Wife in Beaumont and Fletcher's satiric comedy *The Knight of the Burning Pestle*, who proves unable to distinguish real from represented incidents, asking the actors of a play if they have slept well following a 'night' scene.

reveals a capacity for suffering – and for articulating that suffering – which makes of her a direct inheritrix of the tradition of Christian Stoic endurance which had come to exemplify the heroic response in revenge tragedy. Indeed, by having a female protagonist co-opt this tradition the play allows it a refinement which could not be achieved in the case of a male protagonist.

Where the male hero is often shown to work through the Stoic position exhaustively before switching to the role of revenger (thereby either endorsing or challenging conventional ethics, according to one's perspective), the duchess cannot have that option. Instead, a rather tired formula (at least by mid-Jacobean times) receives fresh impetus as themes of endurance in the face of horror become manifestations of gendered behaviour rather than religious dogma. Stoicism is softened by showing it first passing through its opposite stage, with her fruitless, and stereotypically feminine, cursing of the stars and self-destructive wish to be bound to the corpse of her husband (1. 68, 1. 96). She then welcomes the masque of madmen with an inversion of traditional philosophical norms which privilege reason:

> nothing but noise and folly
> Can keep me in my right wits, whereas reason
> And silence make me stark mad. (IV.ii.5–7)

Within a few lines she is able to assert:

> I am not mad yet, to my cause of sorrow.
> [...]
> I am acquainted with sad misery,
> As the tanned galley-slave is with his oar.
> Necessity makes me suffer constantly,
> And custom makes it easy. (ll. 24–30)

The position of endurance emerges progressively, rather than simply being asserted, and unlike traditional displays of stoic impassivity it is fully compatible with such emotional inflexions as her last request to Cariola that her remaining children be given syrup for their colds and made to say their prayers (ll. 195–7).

Immediately after the duchess is strangled by Bosola, Ferdinand becomes aware of the terrible gap between 'her innocence and my revenge', and attempts to shuffle responsibility onto his spy/factotum (ll. 265–70). If, as has been argued here, revenge can usually be construed as one long counteraction (which may be singular or involve several revenges, but which is fundamentally linear), *The Duchess of Malfi* describes a more complex patterning, where this narrative itself opens out into an action and its counteraction: Ferdinand's against his sister, and then Bosola's against him. The acme of asymmetrical revenge had been reached with Ferdinand's victimisation of the duchess, and in what follows the play broaches the question of whether or not it is possible to restore the symmetries of counteraction to action through human agency.[19] The self-inflicted damage of the avenger upon himself seems to answer the question one way. With Ferdinand now forced to confront his revenge as the fathomless, senseless act it is, he succumbs to the very madness he had attempted to induce, without success, in his sister – manifesting the lycanthropic form of the disease, or 'wolf-madness', appropriate to his frequent recourse to wolf imagery in earlier scenes.*

The disowned Bosola himself feels compelled to take 'a most just revenge' on Antonio's behalf against those who had sought his and the duchess's life, and hunts down the cardinal to that end (V.ii.338). He eventually dispatches him in a chaotic brawl in a darkened street which also brings down the deranged Ferdinand, each as wretchedly involved with the other in death as they had been in life. But the accidental stabbing of Antonio in the build-up to the revenge seems to defy these endeavours towards rebalancing, and we are left with Bosola's dying verdict, after he has now been stabbed by mischance at Ferdinand's hands, that 'We are only like dead walls, or vaulted graves / That, ruined, yield no echo' (V.v.96–7).

One way of interpreting this is that action cannot meaningfully answer action; that the responses of one human being to another will always be senseless, in the way this final revenge has been. It is a verdict which the play crafts as gendered, rather than universal, however, since it has already shown that the duchess herself may operate outside this

---

* The scholar Robert Burton described it as 'wolf-madness, when men run howling about graves and fields in the night, and will not be persuaded but that they are wolves, or some such beasts'.

terrifying cycle, not just in the stoicism of her death but in a haunting scene shortly after she has been murdered. The fugitive Antonio, unaware that his wife is dead, hears her voice returning his own words to him as an echo from some nearby ruins where she has been buried, warning him against an attempt at peace-making with the cardinal (V.iii). Her words are, as echoes, perfectly symmetrical with his own, and richly significant in their efforts to secure his safety. Yet the scene ends with him dismissing the voice as a 'dead thing' not worth listening to, and proceeding to his own death (l. 39). By means of such moments the play shows masculine attempts at finding responses to a treacherous world to be continually working in the dark. In direct contrast is the figure of the duchess, who has countered all the violent and destructive acts against her with an 'integrity of life' (l. 119) – an absolute clarity of purpose and feeling – which has been enough to send some men mad.

Notes

1   See Barry Coward, *The Stuart Age: England 1603–1714*, 3rd edn (London: Pearson Education Ltd, 2003), p. 122.
2   Janet Clare, *Revenge Tragedies of the Renaissance* (Hornden: Northcote Publishing, 2006), p. 15,
3   The idea of *The Spanish Tragedy* as a template for the revenge dramas that followed was put most forcefully by Fredson Bowers in his *Elizabethan Revenge Tragedy 1587–1959* (Gloucester, MA: Peter Smith, 1959).
4   See the opening soliloquy from Henry Chettle's *The Tragedy of Hoffman*, 1631 (first performed 1600).
5   Anonymous, *The Revenger's Tragedy*, ed. Brian Gibbons, New Mermaids (London: A & C Black, 1991), I.i.1 SD.
6   See Bowers, *Elizabethan Revenge Tragedy*, p. 136.
7   Francis Bacon's famous formulation for revenge in his essay 'Of Revenge': 'Revenge is a kind of wild justice; which the more man's nature runs to, the more ought law to weed it out', in *The Essays: or Counsels Civil and Moral*, ed. Brian Vickers, Oxford World Classics (Oxford: Oxford University Press, 1999), pp. 10–11. Often quoted alongside discussions of revenge themes in the drama, Bacon's essay really discusses the subject more as an ethical and philosophical problem than as a sociological phenomenon.
8   Samuel Schoenbaum was deeply impressed by the concentration of the moment, describing it as 'the essence of *The Revenger's Tragedy* – the union of cruelty and sexuality, the blending of the motif of lust and the motif

of death', *Middleton's Tragedies: A Critical Study* (Columbia: Columbia University Studies, 1955, p. 16).

9 Jonathan Dollimore in particular regards this as the play's invitation to the audience to read ideas of providential and divine justice ironically. See *Radical Tragedy*, pp. 138–43.

10 For the boy companies Middleton's comedies included *A Trick to Catch the Old One* and *A Mad World, My Masters*; among his tragedies (in addition to those of revenge discussed here) were *The Second Maiden's Tragedy* and *Hengist, King of Kent*; his city comedies included *Michaelmas Term* and *A Chaste Maid in Cheapside*; comedy of a more romantic and tragicomic temper appears in *No Wit, No Help Like a Woman's* and *The Witch*; among a great many co-authored works there is a strong argument that he co-wrote *Timon of Athens* with William Shakespeare (see *Wells, Shakespeare & Co.*, pp. 184–8); his career drew to a close in 1624 with the unique, anti-Spanish political satire of *A Game at Chess*, probably the most scandalous – as well as lucrative – play of this entire period. For the oeuvre and accompanying scholarly discussion see *Thomas Middleton: The Collected Works and Companion*, 2 vols, ed. Gary Taylor and John Lavagnino (Oxford: Oxford University Press, 2007).

11 See the discussion of this play in Martin White, *Middleton and Tourneur* (Basingstoke: Macmillan, 1992), pp. 111–23, esp. pp. 112–14.

12 For a key discussion of this argument, see Gayle Rubin, 'The Traffic in Women: Notes on the "Political Economy" of Sex' (1984).

13 Thomas Middleton, *Women Beware Women*, ed. Roma Gill, New Mermaids (London: A & C Black Ltd, 1968), I.ii.30–1.

14 On Middleton's Calvinism and its relation to the play, see John Stachniewski, 'Calvinist Psychology in Middleton's Tragedies', in *Three Jacobean Revenge Tragedies: The Revenger's Tragedy, Women Beware Women, The Changeling: A Casebook*, ed. Roger Victor Holdsworth (Basingstoke: Macmillan, 1990), pp. 226–47, and Holdsworth's own introduction to the volume, esp. pp. 18–23.

15 For a good résumé of these objections, see Lisa Hopkins, *The Female Hero in English Renaissance Tragedy* (Houndmills: Palgrave, 2002), p. 38.

16 John Webster, "The Duchess of Malfi", Commendatory Verses, lines 16–18, in *The Duchess of Malfi and Other Plays*, ed. René Weis, Oxford World Classics (Oxford: Oxford University Press, 1996).

17 See Andrea Henderson, 'Death on Stage, Death of the Stage: The Antitheatricality of 'The Duchess of Malfi', in *The Duchess of Malfi*, New Casebooks, ed. Dympna Callaghan (Basingstoke: Macmillan, 2000), pp. 61–79.

18 See Kathleen McLuskie, 'Drama and Sexual Politics: The Case of Webster's Duchess', in *Duchess of Malfi*, New Casebooks, pp. 104–21.

19 For the play's depiction of a 'perversion of this notion of a wrong outweighed by reprisal', see the discussion in Janet Clare, *Revenge Tragedies of the Renaissance*, pp. 101–6.

Part Four
Critical Theories and Debates

Madness and Subjectivity

Madness was an extremely popular subject among Elizabethan and Jacobean dramatists. Its portrayal cut with ease across different genres – most obviously in the cases of comedy and tragedy, where an important kind of theatrical pleasure could be gained from witnessing 'normal' behaviours being either distorted or held up for comparison with 'abnormal' ones. More broadly, madness as a theme (as opposed to its actual, direct representation) is very commonly employed in the form of a kind of social commentary – 'the world has gone mad', 'it's a mad world', and so on – which would have equal familiarity for us, for the Renaissance playwrights, and for the Greek and Roman authors they often drew on to elaborate the point. As a subject suitable for the theatre, we could say that madness was multi-valent – having different significance depending on its context – while for the working playwright it was also multi-purpose, and could provide a reliable, adaptable and visually striking piece of stage business.

For the student of playwrights of this period, madness can likewise provide a useful field of analysis for several reasons. In the first place, it helps us to question how 'genre' actually functions on the early modern stage, in terms of the fidelity plays showed to the critical and commercial categories which they worked with. Madness has a shock value in many productions which stems in part from the kind of violation it can inflict on notions of dramatic form. Is the torture of the duchess in *The Duchess*

211

of Malfi by means of a parade of madmen, sent to drive her mad in her turn, almost too comical-satirical for its distressing and tragic context? Similarly, is the incarceration and examination of Malvolio as 'mad' by the clown Feste in *Twelfth Night* pushed a little bit too far for a comfortable comic denouement? Perhaps these features needn't bother a twenty-first-century audience, accustomed as we are now to endless variants on the Quentin Tarantino formula routinely presenting us with scenes of mental and physical torture to be enjoyed as exercises in comic panache. But films such as these tend to deliver their 'extreme' moments largely on a single note, whereas the playwrights of Shakespeare's day had to perform the trickier job of generating multiple tonal effects through similar scenes. In doing so, they are often daring the tension between comedy and tragedy to collapse – sometimes to demonstrate virtuosity in holding the whole thing together; sometimes to create enjoyment through the very act of aesthetic breakdown.

Madness on the Renaissance stage also focuses attention on the issue of gender in this period: the way in which differences between men and women could be fashioned and represented within a specific culture. There is a good argument for suggesting that such differences become accentuated through the representation of the madwoman: female sufferers such as Ophelia can be seen to occupy exaggerated versions of the roles that others have insisted they play in society. In such instances, however, the constructed (which is to say artificial) means by which these roles come into being are offered up to wider inspection. For example, Ophelia's 'madness' is noticeably figured as a tissue of quotations from songs and sayings which refer back to ideas of the loyal daughter, the faithful lover, the fallen maiden – fragments that are not ultimately her own and that are no longer capable of easy coherence. At the same time, those roles are challenged in an overt, unabashed way that could only be licensed through the condition of madness. As Duncan Salkeld argues in his full-length study of madness on the stage, 'It is through madness that Ophelia eventually "comes out" and insanity makes of her an importunate, assertive and dangerous figure … Ophelia breaks from the subjection of a vehemently patriarchal society and makes public display, in her verses, of the body she has been taught to suppress.'[1]

Such considerations suggest a final, and important, area to which a study of madness on the early modern stage can lead us: a reading of 'subjectivity' in this period. This is a much discussed topic, so much so that most criticism of the plays since the 1990s has needed to take some cognisance of it – at least where it touches on what used to go under the rubric of 'character criticism'. For our purposes, it addresses the notion that the plays of Shakespeare and his contemporaries mark for the first time the portrayal of strongly individuated identities in literature – a practice which is itself held to reflect the development of a greater emphasis on selfhood in the period. These 'selves' as we encounter them in the form of Hamlet, Lear, Richard II or the Duchess of Malfi are seen as 'true to life' in a way which has encouraged later ages to explore them as personalities – often by detaching them from the play in the process. This fact is all the more striking given that, as Elizabeth Freund has remarked, 'drama is not the literary mode best suited to embody subjectivity'.[2] The complex representation of personhood really belongs with the novel, the innovation of a later period, in which the thoughts and feelings of characters constantly require an explicit logical precedent (motivation and justification) in the story. This is less the requirement of drama which – at least in its natural milieu, the theatre – moves too quickly for prolonged examination of such issues. Nevertheless, we can legitimately ask why characters such as those listed above, who seem more than most others to imply a 'deep' psychology, do so in conditions where madness is a serious threat, and sometimes an actuality. Jonathan Dollimore, whose cultural materialist readings of the plays have done as much as anyone's to set the tone of our understanding of subjectivity in the Shakespearean era, sees personal identity as inextricably connected to political power, while politics itself is in a state of crisis in the English Renaissance.[3] Hence, perhaps, the emphasis on 'subjection' in Salkeld's quotation on Ophelia. To be a subject is in part to be 'subjected' to a set of political circumstances beyond one's own control (in Ophelia's case, patriarchy), which set a limit to who, and how, you can be. When those break down, as they do for Ophelia when her father dies, there is both release and, at the same time, traumatic disorientation. It may prove very useful for us to consider the degree to which strongly individuated characters become so by means of a tension with their political circumstances which is articulated through the 'medium' of madness.

Materialist Readings of Madness in *The Changeling*

We will start by asking what relationship the drama's representation of madness had to the social reality it claimed to depict. A non-Shakespearean example of madness in the drama can be useful here, one which may be less familiar to readers of the plays and may thus be historically and critically 'alienating'; that is to say, it should be less easy for us to identify in an unreflective fashion with the situation and the characters, so challenging our tendency to read the scenario from our own present-day assumptions. It can have the added benefit of providing an opportunity to examine in more detail how choices about genre assist in guiding audience responses to particular kinds of narrative detail. The scene is from Middleton and Rowley's *The Changeling* (1622), and forms part of an extended sub-plot involving the infiltration of a madhouse by an oversexed city gentleman who is trying to gain access to the youthful wife of its owner, an elderly doctor. It's a fairly stock, 'cuckolding' (i.e. infidelity) scenario, one which offsets in ironic fashion the sinister and ultimately tragic seductions taking place during the main plot, and which in its comic form allows for a transparently London atmosphere to peer through the nominally Italian setting.[4] In the young man's use of a 'lunatic' disguise, however, it does something rather unusual for a play of this era: it proffers a rare glimpse into the madhouse itself. The moment that could perhaps most disconcert the modern reader comes in an early exchange between the doctor, Alibius, and his servant, Lollio, as the former frets about his wife's physical attractions:

> ALIBIUS: But here's the care that mixes with my thrift:
> The daily visitants, that come to see
> My brainsick patients, I would not have
> To see my wife: gallants I do observe
> Of quick enticing eyes, rich in habits,

Of stature and proportion very comely:
These are most shrewd temptations, Lollio.
[...]
       come they to see
Our madmen and our fools, let 'em see no more
Than what they come for ...⁵

The references here to young 'gallants' who find entertainment in coming to watch the madmen provides something of a jolt. Isn't this a pleasure in watching suffering (these inmates are 'sick', after all)? And isn't that rather akin to indulging the passion for bear-baiting which, we often conveniently forget, was one of the companion amusements offered by the playhouses? Yet hasn't the doctor just acknowledged the humanity of the madmen by calling them his 'patients' (he earlier avers that their 'cure' is '[m]y trade, my living ... I thrive by it')? What kind of category do they occupy in society, seemingly to be treated for their affliction but also exposed as spectacles?

Our first encounter with the madmen is as a set of cacophonous voices calling from offstage. It is a position which unavoidably bestows on them a marginal, 'neither-here-nor-there' status. The utterances we hear are regular in their syntax, but closely associated with the animal world in their lexis:

> 1 MADMAN WITHIN: Put's head i' the pillory, the bread's too little.
> 2 MADMAN WITHIN: Fly, fly and he catches the swallow.
> 3 MADMAN WITHIN: Give her more onion, or the devil put the rope about her crag ... Cat whore, cat whore, her parmasant, her parmasant!
>
> (I.ii.207–16)

When they later make a physical appearance onstage, it is to appear in the madhouse dressed *some as birds, other as beasts* and acting out fantasies of bestial identity (III.iii.197). It subsequently transpires that the madmen are to be co-opted by the doctor into a masque to be performed at the wedding of Beatrice-Joanna, the protagonist of the play's main plot.

There seems to be a clear trajectory throughout the play which locates the mad firmly within the category of the 'theatrical', even if that category is not seen to overlap completely with that of the 'human'. Since, moreover, the 'madmen' sub-narrative never fully intersects with the principal tragic narrative (we don't actually see the masque performed), as characters they remain embedded within the sub-plot's comic idiom. Their comic representation remains consistent even where expressions of sympathy for the mad are allowed to occur, principally from the mouth of the doctor's wife, Isabella: 'Afford me … the pleasure of your bedlam,' she demands of Lollio at one point, and then goes on to speak of the 'pitiful delight' and 'mirth in madness' which their spectacle can arouse (III.iii.24–30).

Isabella's use of the term 'bedlam' – adjectival in its context here, and not denoting an actual location used by the play – nonetheless refers to a place which would have been familiar to Londoners, and which is also alluded to by Edgar in his role as 'poor Tom of Bedlam' in *King Lear*. The Hospital of St Mary of Bethlehem (colloquially shortened to 'Bethlem', or 'Bedlam') had by Shakespeare's day become the specific preserve of inmates who were mentally ill. While the place had historically been under the care of a porter or keeper, around the very time that *The Changeling* was being written in 1622 King James I had been showing an active interest in trying to appoint a doctor – his own personal physician, Helkiah Crooke – to take charge.[6] It does not ultimately seem to have mattered who ran the hospital, however, as it made no difference to its condition; it was invariably described as filthy and poorly run.[7] The number of inmates was, moreover, consistently very small – sometimes a handful, sometimes around thirty – individuals who are most aptly described as being 'kept' rather than 'cured' during their incarceration. Despite some obvious correspondences with the scenario as outlined in Middleton and Rowley's play, then, there are evidently some large mismatches with the historical data as well, most particularly in the play's stated emphasis on the mad as 'patients'. How, therefore, are we to understand the inference from *The Changeling* that 'daily visitants' trooped through a London asylum to gawp at the inmates, or indeed that the mad could be treated primarily as a spectacle for the enjoyment of fashionable society?

It can be shown that towards the later part of the seventeenth century, and much more during the eighteenth century, this kind of voyeuristic behaviour became common among the citizens of London, and was widely documented as being so. Bethlem Hospital attracted large and regular quantities of visitors who were permitted, for a fee, not only to observe the inmates but also to aggravate them to some kind of display of 'frenzied' or lunatic behaviour. Such treatment became a scandal to those of compassionate leanings – a widely read novel from the 1770s, Mackenzie's *The Man Of Feeling*, openly deplored it – but in general this attitude to the display of the insane had by the eighteenth century become a systematically commercialised one. This emphasis on display went hand in hand, moreover, with an increased move to make sure that the mad were locked up. One very influential account of this trend is provided by the French cultural historian Michel Foucault, who perceives a Europe-wide social pressure to incarcerate the insane instead of letting them either intermingle freely with the populace or be ejected from society altogether (as lepers were in the Middle Ages). In Foucault's view this pressure resulted in a quite sudden shift, happening all over Europe from the 1650s on, which he titled 'The Great Confinement'.[8] Rather intriguingly, in this theory medicine – the actual care for the sick – had less to do with the new policy than the development of a distinct work ethic, coinciding with the growth of Industry and the Age of Reason. The mad were no longer symbolic of anything, such as divine punishment or divine 'wisdom': they were more akin to automata or machines that had gone wrong. To confine them in a special place, and to display them to public view was to make sense of them via a more secular, scientific world view.

What, then, are we to make of a sub-plot like that of *The Changeling*, which seems to hint at both of these procedures a good many decades before they became the widespread historical norm? Foucault does point out that sporadic, small-scale 'confinements' of the mad were going on in England at least a century before the Great Confinement got underway, and his argument implies a 'tacit assessment of Bethlem Hospital as an English precursor to the eighteenth-century "hopitaux generaux"'.[9] But his desire for a 'turning-point' in history is so strong that he points nonetheless to c. 1650 as a moment of general 'reorganization'. The following suggests a way of reconciling the issue. We know that at least some of the insane in the English capital are being incarcerated well before this date (the historical records tell us so); and we know that in 1622 the idea of parading these unfortunate individuals to a curious public is being canvassed in the sub-plot of *The Changeling*. Taking both of these together suggests that a blend of fact and fiction is working to anticipate what subsequently happens in society over the next 200 years. The play is showing a kind of institutional approach to the treatment of mad people prior to the proper development of such institutions. It can do so because all the elements that eventually coalesce to create the later eighteenth-century madhouses have been 'lying around', as it were, in that culture for some time. The scenes merely bring these elements together in a fictional context, as society will later bring them together in an institutional one.

The play, one might say, is thus giving us access to the language used about certain aspects of society as (or even before) that language hardens into practice. To take such an approach to the portrayal of the madhouse in *The Changeling* is to read it along materialist lines (cultural materialism is more specifically the method adopted here). This may sound a rather odd appellation if we believe that language is about the most immaterial thing possible, but that is to suppose that language simply reflects something that is already there, or has already happened, rather than forming a part of the material that contributes to our world. Talk, discussion, fantasy can ultimately create the conditions by which historical phenomena are made possible. A sobering present-day example might be the notion of 'ground zero' as it was utilised over several years in the 1980s and 1990s in numerous mainstream disaster films, or some of the more subversive Hollywood productions (think the denouement to 1999's *Fight Club*). Fictional scenes of anarchic, apocalyptic, anti-capitalistic destruction of buildings and established institutions, sometimes using the 'ground zero' tag explicitly, seem to have created the conceptual space for what was to follow in the terrorist attacks in New York in September 2001. There is a similar argument to be made here for *The Changeling*'s sub-plot: the fantasy precedes the reality, rather than subsequently reflecting it.

It is emphasised that *The Changeling*'s madhouse scenes must be taken as fiction rather than historical evidence, not to imply that one is 'true' whereas the other is 'false', but because we have to treat this particular idea of displaying the mad first and foremost as a theatrical device. More specifically, it is being self-referential, or 'meta-theatrical', about the very business of performing. The use of the mad in masques, their appearance in bird or animal garb, their tendency to 'act their fantasies in any shapes / Suiting their present thoughts' (Isabella, III.iii.200–1) are clearly theatrical fictions, and we have to see the notion of 'gallants' crowding into the madhouses as a similar kind of expedient. It may have actually happened like that; it may not have happened like that at all, or it may have happened to a rather different degree than is suggested in the sub-plot. The important point is that it functions here as a kind of wish-fulfilment for the company staging *The Changeling*. 'Gallants' (young, moneyed men of a leisured class) formed the optimum desired audience members for a commercial drama, and to portray them flocking to a madhouse is to spin a scenario which partly invites, partly incites, their real-world counterparts to follow suit in terms of playhouse attendance. To that extent, we can see the play combining what amounts to a witty piece of marketing in the service of an existing institution (the theatre) with local knowledge about the small and sad reality of the Bethlem hospital, to generate a pleasing fiction about a quasi-institutional insane asylum at the heart of a bustling capital city.

'Madness in Great Ones': *Hamlet, Twelfth Night, King Lear*

The theatre, then, is not giving us a straightforward depiction of the social reality of madness in England at this time; but neither is it disconnected from the social forces that were already starting to shape the treatment of its sufferers. A brief look at an earlier and more familiar play, Shakespeare's *Hamlet*, can help us to see how some of the prevalent tropes about the observation and confinement of madness are in circulation before *The Changeling* makes use of them, albeit in a much less systematised fashion. At the conclusion of III.i, we hear Claudius voicing his concern over Hamlet's increasingly volatile behaviour, which he and Polonius have been overhearing from their hiding places behind the arras.[10] The interview they have carefully stage-managed between the prince and Ophelia has just culminated in an outburst of misogynistic accusation aimed at her and her sex ('you jig, you amble, and you lisp'), and has also contained a veiled but perceptible threat towards the king himself ('Those that are married already – all but one! – shall live'). After Hamlet's exit the two eavesdroppers compare their diagnoses of his mental state and exchange advice about the best way to treat the problem. For Claudius it seems the preferred option is to 'confine' Hamlet (although it is left to Polonius to use that word explicitly: see line 185). As the concept is being used here, this means to put him out of the way somewhere where the immediate causes of his aggravation will be removed. For Polonius, a little more probing is needed by way of another arranged interview, this time with Hamlet's mother, to confirm beyond doubt his belief that 'erotomania', or sexual frustration, is the cause of the prince's madness. Both men are in agreement, however, that observation – 'watching' – is the most appropriate procedure; indeed, as Claudius says at the scene's close, it is mandatory in the case of Hamlet: 'Madness in great ones must not unwatched go' (III.i.187). The reasons do not need to be spelt out: Prince Hamlet is simply too important a figure to be left alone, where his madness could be allowed to follow its own course. It must be 'watched' – both in the sense of being directly scrutinised for signs which might reveal its cause and meaning, and in the sense of being compassionately overseen for his own safety.

It may seem a little odd that this concluding utterance of Claudius – 'madness in great ones must not unwatched go' – should contradict his own opinion, expressed only a few lines earlier, that madness is *not* the correct diagnosis for Hamlet's behaviour: 'what he spake, though it lacked form a little / Was not like madness'. Why should the King disagree with himself in so short a space of time? Perhaps we shouldn't ask for too much consistency here. This is the post-climactic moment of the scene, after all: events are drawing hastily to a close, with the participants in a state of some disarray. And Claudius does maintain the view that Hamlet is, if nothing else, 'melancholy' – a condition which could invite inclusion with other kinds of madness.[11] Yet the impression persists that a distinction has been created between a specific idea which Claudius holds of Hamlet's unstable state ('it's not madness, but it's dangerous – and to me in particular'), and a general notion to which he tips his hat at the scene's close ('it *is* madness, by no means unknown among the high and mighty, and there are established ways of dealing with it'). Perhaps we could account for this gap in the following way: for its final word on the subject, the scene gathers together the troubling, individuated and so far inexplicable details of Hamlet's mental condition, and puts them back – as it were for safe storage – into some more familiar categories of understanding. It is, from the king's point of view, a sensible, pragmatic way of dealing with the matter: 'I don't know what's wrong with him, I have my doubts and suspicions, but the expedient course lies in using some recognisable terms to talk about it.' For Claudius, the 'truth' of the matter about Hamlet is less important than swift recourse to various socially prescribed methods of describing, containing and curing madness.

These strategies for dealing with 'mad Hamlet' – confinement on the one hand and observation on the other – are on their own terms self-explanatory ones. They are, in any case, partly suggested by the source material on which the play is (directly or indirectly) drawing: the original Amleth legend had spies set to watch the hero and trick him into revealing his true state of mind, and his journey to England under guard follows his murder of one of these. Used in combination in the way they are here, however, they become curiously anticipatory of a later set of practices which define what we have detailed as the institutional approach to madness. What brings them together is the problem of Hamlet's status as a prince and a ruler-in-waiting – a 'great one' in Claudius's own phrasing. It is noticeable how careful and circumlocutory the king is in edging towards his policy of containing the threat posed by Hamlet, covering his initial betrayal of the fear of 'danger' with a solicitous approach towards the prince's health. It is Polonius who – alive to the shades of meaning in Claudius's rapid deliberations – articulates the idea of confinement and introduces the notion of further close observation on which the king seizes at the scene's end. What their decision amounts to can be described as a sort of political strategy for action in relation to

Hamlet, and this is all the more remarkable in a narrative which has as yet given only domestic imperatives for them to consider. Since there are no overt reasons to suspect a design on Claudius's life, their approach almost amounts to an overkill. We could frame the problem this way: although temporarily usurped by Claudius, Hamlet as a prince remains crucial to the running of the state, and his apparently dysfunctional behaviour is enough to invite the elaborate strategies for surveillance which the two men settle on here. A later and more democratic age, the one Foucault refers to in terms of its remodelled work ethic (he tends to use the catch-all label 'bourgeois' to categorise it, but there were many social elements involved), would attempt to make all levels of the state crucial to its productive functioning, thus extending the social control of its delinquent elements much further through the classes.

Comparison with an earlier instance of a 'mad' figure in a similar genre – the 'Knight Marshall' Hieronimo in Kyd's *The Spanish Tragedy* (1587) – is instructive in pointing up some of these nuances. Hieronimo has lost his son to murder and is seeking revenge under conditions of far greater political intrigue than Hamlet. Yet his frenzied behaviour, especially when petitioning the Spanish king for justice (at one point he digs up the earth with a dagger to try to bring back his son from 'Elysium'), never sees him subjected to any kind of close observation or closeted removal.[12] If one adopts Foucault's categories and understands a shift between historical conceptions of madness, Hieronimo seems rather to look back to a tradition in which the mad roam free, or are excluded from society (in his case the Spanish court), rather than face imprisonment and/or perusal. While *The Spanish Tragedy*'s representation of madness is spectacular in the sense of being a spectacle for audiences (Hieronimo's scenes of escalating madness quickly became notorious for their theatricality), in *Hamlet* it is spectacular in seeing that process of watching recessed into the play itself. The audience watches the watchers of madmen, and by normalising that process of observation a space is carved out for the treatment of the mad as a formal object of an institution's scrutiny or – as it is often termed – 'gaze'.

The Mad under the Gaze

When we use this term 'gaze', we are speaking about an action on the part of the observer which has a particular power, one which extends beyond the idea of simply looking at something in order to gain information about it. Rather, it goes some way towards defining that object, towards determining how it is evaluated in the eyes of others and, crucially, in its own eyes as well. Theorists from various disciplines have spoken of different kinds of gaze as having a 'controlling' or 'objectifying' effect, at the heart of which is the production of an inequality in power relations between observed and observer.[13] In some circumstances, such an inequality can challenge the recipient's sense of their subjectivity rather than just rendering them a passive or inert version of themselves. In the discussion that follows we will extend these ideas to the domain of mental illness, adapting them in particular to the representation of insanity in the Elizabethan drama. There are interesting repercussions in doing so. Arguably, the subject is disintegrated in madness, so might be thought to be beyond the reach of the objectifying power of the gaze directed at it. But provided some level of communicative contact remains between the mad person and the outside world, it could just as well be argued that they are rendered irrationally (because uncritically) receptive to that gaze – that they are more suggestible to its power to shape subjectivity than those who are sane. Once again, it is possible to see the theatre as anticipating in some of its fictional contexts the social practice that will later become current. We could see the bird- and animal-costumed mad patients of *The Changeling* as expressing just this notion, acting out fantasies not of their own but of their observers, doctors and prospective revellers, who for their own pleasure have construed these sufferers as non-human.[14]

In *Hamlet*, the gaze of the court generally and of the king and his cronies specifically bears down on Hamlet to try to produce, by way of confirmation, the symptoms it associates with his supposed madness. These efforts are of a quite various nature. Polonius tries crudely to elicit from Hamlet a display of the desire for Ophelia which he thinks lies at the root of the prince's irrational behaviour. More subtly, but no less insistently, Rosencrantz and Guildenstern attempt to produce the signs of thwarted ambition which will consort with their own, more politically oriented reading of his madness. That Hamlet, who is of course only feigning madness, nonetheless feels the pressure of this collective investment in establishing and demonstrating the 'heart of his mystery' is suggested by his aside to the audience that '[t]hey fool me to the top of my bent' (III.ii.375). But he remains proof against these efforts, at one and the same time the privileged object of a set of procedures which anticipate later practices for the social control of madness and the occupant of a class position – that of a 'great one' – which preserves the deference of those around him. A different picture emerges with Ophelia, who is not only an exemplar of 'true madness', in Polonius's unhappily prescient phrase, but is also obliged to refract that experience through a somewhat lower social status, that of an 'unvalued person' (i.e. not crucial to the functioning of the state), as her brother Laertes reminds her in the play's early stages (I.iii.18).

Like both Hieronimo and his wife Isabella, who *'runs lunatic'* in the aftermath of her son's murder (III.viii), Ophelia is suffered to wander abroad, her madness given its scope, and efforts to alleviate it restricted to a few helplessly soothing blandishments – 'How do you, pretty lady?', 'Pretty Ophelia' (IV.v.41 ff.). Her behaviour is, however, closely observed: 'give her good watch, I pray', begs the king. Initially it seems there is no sense of an unequal power relation in this process of observation. Indeed, one could argue that the older practice of reading the mad for a deeper significance – which here surfaces in an uneasy fashion with the admission that her speech moves the 'hearers to collection', who 'botch the words up fit to their own thoughts' (IV.v.7–10) – momentarily tips such a relation in her favour. As Duncan Salkeld argues, from the 'passively obedient' Ophelia of the earlier part of the play she becomes someone newly empowered, a woman whom 'no one dare touch' in her act of roaming, and whose mad discourse powerfully affects those who are exposed to it.[15] But the report of Ophelia's death by drowning which the queen subsequently gives is both strangely impersonal and second-hand in the subject position it adopts, and restores the sense of a gaze which takes narrative control of the insane person being observed (IV.vii.165–82). The queen's tale concludes by aligning Ophelia with 'a creature native and indued / Unto that element [i.e. of water]' (ll. 178–9), thus rounding off an association of the mad with 'mere beasts' that had been initiated earlier by the king (IV.v.86), and which can perhaps be seen as pre-empting the fate she suffers.

Hideous Darkness: The Plight of Malvolio

Another perspective on these ideas about madness and the social forces which were shaping its treatment during Shakespeare's period is provided by the case of Malvolio in *Twelfth Night*. Differences in genre and the degree of sympathy invited for the two characters need not obscure the recognition that both Ophelia and Malvolio are figures of middling rank who are hopeful of marrying above their station, and for whom a form of madness awaits as a bitter repudiation of their desires. Malvolio, of course, at no stage becomes mad in the literal sense, but his 'overweening' presumption in seeking to become a 'great one' by marriage to Olivia (one who has 'greatness thrust upon them', II.v.143) allows him to be construed as socially insane by the offended revellers. They go on to elicit from the steward what for them is simply the outward manifestation of this diseased fantasy (the smiling and the yellow stockings in front of Olivia), and once Malvolio's insanity is widely agreed upon they take the appropriate course of action and confine him (he is, after all, an important functionary in Olivia's household). This confinement, however, takes place in a space of 'hideous darkness', where the madhouse is a place of imprisonment rather than cure, and where observation is neither possible nor, from the point of view of the prank's perpetrators, desirable (IV. ii.30). The manner in which this enacts their revenge upon the steward is instructive. Malvolio can be seen as one incarnation of that ordering and monitoring tendency in society which we noted earlier, complete with its bourgeois work ethic (this tendency has also been associated with the growth of Puritanism, another aspect of Malvolio to which the play – briefly – alludes).[16]

Part of the joke in having him exposed as a madman lies in curtailing the particular gaze of sanity, which he bends so witheringly upon others

('My masters, are you mad?', II.iii.85). That Malvolio has been able to produce real and disintegrating effects through that gaze is suggested in his first exchange with Feste, where he succeeds in 'gagging' the clown through his hostile appraisal of his talents ('Look you now, he's out of his guard already', I.v.82). Once Feste has him incarcerated, he goes as far as (or perhaps just a little further than) the comic genre will allow him in trying to turn the madness that Malvolio has descried in others back upon him, adding insult to injury by parodying the form of a Calvinist curate (someone that Malvolio would expect to be able to trust). The clown's 'treatment' of Malvolio thus inverts on every point the approach to madness which a rationalist ideology was in the process of developing: it uses the language of exorcism ('Out, hyperbolical fiend!', IV.ii.25), which was notoriously the favoured approach of religious extremists of the day; it repudiates the power of direct observation by confining the 'patient' in absolute darkness; and, of course, it attempts to 'face [him] out of his wits' rather than cure him. That Malvolio does not succumb to these efforts should not necessarily lead us to assume that the play finds a dignity in his sufferings. What is being pointed up here, as so often in comedy, is not the potential fragility of a disagreeable character's sense of self but that character's obstinate resistance to the force of suggestion – to any idea that it could, or should, be altered from what it is.[17]

Troubling the Microcosm in *King Lear*

In *King Lear* (1605) the audience is obliged to watch as, shockingly, 'madness in great ones' goes decidedly unattended by its surrounding society. A consistent and convincingly represented pre-Christian world instead shows the mad in their anciently understood vagrant and unconfined state, but combines this with newer ideas objectifying the mad as animals, emblems of unreason. As is common in the tragedies of the Jacobean period, a story set in an apparently ancient world is in this way used to elucidate some very contemporary fears and concerns. Lear, king of ancient Britain and now advanced in age, decides, to the consternation of his loyal subjects, to divide his kingdom among his three daughters and their husbands, only demanding a little competitive test of their love to settle the largest portion of land. When the favoured daughter, Cordelia, fails this test by answering sincerely instead of flattering the old man ('I love your majesty according to my bond, neither more nor less'), his enraged rejection and banishment of her leaves him now solely in the care of his unscrupulous two remaining daughters.[18] Their subsequent course in stripping him of all remaining trappings of power and turning him, quite literally, from their doors is paralleled in a sub-plot in which the ambitious illegitimate son of the Earl of Gloucester deludes his father and cheats his legitimate brother of his inheritance.

The two principal victims of these acts of dispossession, Lear and Edgar, are thus forced out of human society and undergo the experience of madness, albeit in very different ways. Lear, roaming the wilderness, genuinely loses his wits and descends into a kind of monomania where everything he sees is subdued to the image of his two daughters' ingratitude. Edgar, the cheated elder son, feigns for his own safety (but also relief of heart?) the madness of a 'Bedlam beggar', one who is 'whipped from tithing to tithing and stocked, punished and imprisoned' – a harsh reminder of the realities that lay behind Foucault's sometimes rather poetic notions of the experience of madness in its older social incarnation (III.iv.130–1). Edgar's mad discourse is, however, terrifyingly convincing to its hearers, crammed as it is with references to the 'foul fiend' that drives him onward to his own destruction, and in bringing both Lear and Edgar together in a filthy hovel on the heath, the play forces the audience to see them in a mirrored relation to each other. Edgar himself draws a parallel between their sufferings when, in soliloquy, he observes of Lear that 'He childed as I fathered' (III.vi.107). Is this primarily, then, a moral being drawn about the shattering effects of familial rejection on the individual psyche (a perfectly valid reading given the play's repeated and overt references to the bonds of nature being cracked)? Or is there more to be mined here about the way madness figures as product of some very specific historical and social developments?

Many of the more recent critical readings of the play focus on the way that the breakdown of Lear's reason both shadows and comments upon the breakdown in social order that sets family members against one another. There is, of course, nothing very obscure about the play's presentation of a symbolic relationship between the protagonist and the world surrounding him, and *King Lear* in many ways marks one of the more conspicuous uses of a favoured Renaissance trope of subjectivity: man as the microcosm, the world in miniature, whose feelings and actions demonstrate correspondences with the macrocosm, or world at large. The scenes showing Lear in the storm on the heath, where, as a horrified observer describes it, he 'Strives in his little world of man to outscorn / The to and fro conflicting wind and rain' (III.i.10–11), are a particularly deft example of how this trope can be used to illustrate the multi-directionality of this relationship. Disintegration of the natural bonds within the family, as the newly empowered daughters turn on their father and drive him from their care and company, is figured inwardly in the increasing disorder of Lear's mind, and this mental upheaval is in turn re-figured externally by means of the surrounding chaos in nature. Yet it is notable that Lear's enraged addresses to the elements shift alarmingly in their explication of the meaning of this symbolic relationship, in a way that anticipates his slide into fully disconnected thought:

> Rumble thy bellyful! Spit fire, spout rain!
> Nor rain, wind, thunder, fire are my daughters;
> I tax not you, you elements, with unkindness.
> I never gave you kingdom, called you children;
> You owe me no subscription. Why then, let fall
> Your horrible pleasure. Here I stand your slave,
> A poor, infirm, weak and despised old man.
> But yet I call you servile ministers
> That will with two pernicious daughters join
> Your high-engendered battles 'gainst a head
> So old and white as this. (III.ii.14–24)

What begins as an outright encouragement and declaration of his identification with the furious elements (this continues the trend of the previous soliloquy, where he had called on the storm to enact vengeance against 'ingrateful man') shifts by the speech's conclusion to an accusation of their complicity with his daughters as their 'servile ministers'. Through the use of such unstable, shifting standpoints a sense emerges that the familiar microcosm/macrocosm model, a symbol of order and meaning in the cosmos, is itself starting to come apart, and that a different idea of the relationship between nature, society and the individual is taking its place.

The Edgar/Edmund subplot addresses head-on the implications of the sceptical and materialist ideas which were inviting an increasing amount of attention around the time when *King Lear* was written. In his opening soliloquy the younger, illegitimate brother rejects all ideas of religion and morality by assuming their straightforward entanglement with the maintenance of social order and hierarchy:

> Thou, Nature, art my goddess; to thy laws
> My services are bound. Wherefore should I
> Stand in the plague of custom, and permit
> The curiosity of nations to deprive me? (I.ii.1–4)

Like his invocation to the gods to 'stand up for bastards' at the soliloquy's close, Edmund's claim that nature is his 'goddess' is a piece of studied irony bordering on impudence, effective in setting off his subscription to purely natural 'laws' which reward youth, physical vigour and cunning – what he calls 'the lusty stealth of nature' (l. 11). His personal philosophy, enlarged at length over the course of the sub-plot, is one of the fullest expressions of self-determination (the individual as master of his self and his fortune) against belief in a 'divine thrusting on' (l. 126, the influence of the gods and/or the connection to the macrocosm) in Shakespeare's plays. With social structures, in particular those of 'legitimacy' (i.e. primogeniture), thereby exposed as things of convenience rather than products of a divinely appointed order, the way is clear for Edmund to supplant, at dizzying speed, first his brother in his father's affections, and then his father in his earldom. For all his refreshing perspective and engaging confidentiality with the audience (he delivers soliloquies and

229

drops asides in the manner of a well-rounded Vice),* what Edmund desires is little more than property and status – land and titles – so the alliance he demonstrates between materialist philosophy and acquisitive motive principle has led many commentators to see in him an embodiment of the new spirit of capitalist enterprise. Whether or not we choose to agree with this, the manner in which he works through these existing social structures in order to secure his own devious ends goes some way to exposing them as essentially means of exploitation.[19]

Between Subjectivities: The Madness of Poor Tom

When Lear, who is mad, and Edgar (Poor Tom), who is feigning madness, meet on the heath, the community of suffering which develops from the exchanges that pass between them focuses to a large degree on the failures, corruptions and oppressions of a variety of social institutions. When exposed to the storm, Lear, clinging to his sanity, has already begun to lament his neglect as ruler of the 'poor naked wretches' of his kingdom, whom a fair distribution of wealth could have seen housed and fed. The sight of Poor Tom marks his descent into full-blown madness (seemingly through an access of misdirected sympathy – 'Have his daughters brought him to this pass?', III.iv.62), and he later leagues with the beggar in trying to 'arraign' an imaginary Goneril and Regan in a makeshift trial in the hovel, which only ends with their 'escape':

> Arms, arms, sword, fire, corruption in the place!
> False justicier, why hast thou let her scape? (III.vi.54–5)

This particular fixation with corrupt institutions extends into later scenes of Lear's madness, where he berates the now blinded and refugee Gloucester on the topic:

> Thou hast seen a farmer's dog bark at a beggar? ... And the
> creature run from the cur – there thou mightst behold the great

---

* For more detailed discussion of the Vice, see the section on *Richard III* in Part Three: 'Shakespeare's History Plays'.

image of authority: a dog's obeyed in office.
Thou, rascal beadle, hold thy bloody hand;
Why dost thou lash that whore? Strip thine own back,
Thou hotly lusts to use her in that kind
> For which thou whipp'st her. The usurer hangs the cozener.
> (IV.vi.150–9)

This theme can even be applied, less formally, to Edgar's fictive 'mad' persona, that of a 'serving-man, proud in heart and mind, that curled my hair, wore gloves in my cap, served the lust of my mistress' heart and did the act of darkness with her' (III.iv.83–6) – one whom, in short, has sunk into misfortune and madness through lecherous abuse of the tradition of service. Through the eyes of mad king and beggar, all such institutions of society appear not so much in breakdown as in their true light: voracious in their feeding on the weak and vulnerable, and nakedly self-serving. Part of the power lies in the fact of madness's own pre-institutional moment. The 'bedlam beggar' remains in this play utterly unincorporated into society, beyond any form of gaze that could define, categorise or relieve it. When Lear remarks, on the first appearance of a naked and grovelling Edgar, that he is 'the thing itself ... a poor, bare forked animal' (III.iv.103–6), he is speaking not of a human being's return to 'nature' in any positive, identifiable sense, but of a thing which remains harrowingly indefinable because it falls outside the perimeter of institutional recognition (the tradition in Shakespeare's time of the 'Abraham's Men' – fraudsters who counterfeited madness in order to beg alms from passers-by – doubtless assisted the sense of Poor Tom as a 'thing' resisting social identity). In the play-world of *King Lear* the mad are a portion of humanity that has no positively defined subjectivity: they are understood through neither the older symbolic patterns of thought nor the emergent scientific ones. Yet the perspective which the play establishes for them over its central scenes is one which allows the pitiless operations of existing social institutions to be thrown into harsh relief – to show that they, like the gods, exist not to protect, but to destroy.

Notes

1   Duncan Salkeld, *Madness and Drama in the Age of Shakespeare* (Manchester: Manchester University Press, 1993), pp. 94–5.

2   Elizabeth Freund, "'Ariachne's Broken Woof'": The Rhetoric of Citation in *Troilus and Cressida*', in *Shakespeare and the Question of Theory*, ed. Patricia Parker and Geoffrey Hartman (New York: Methuen, 1985), pp. 19–36, p. 21.

3   See Jonathan Dollimore, *Radical Tragedy: Religion, Ideology and Power in the Drama of Shakespeare and his Contemporaries*, 2nd edn (New York: Harvester Wheatsheaf, 1989).

4   For a good account of the relation of sub-plot to main plot, which draws out some of the subtexts also explored here, see Marion Wynne-Davies, *Sidney to Milton 1580–1660*, pp. 129–32.

5   Thomas Middleton and William Rowley, *The Changeling*, ed. Patricia Thomson (London: A&C Black, 1987), I.ii.52–64.

6   Ken Jackson, 'Bedlam, The Changeling, The Pilgrim, and the Protestant critique of Catholic good works' http://findarticles.com/p/articles/mi_hb3362/is_n4_v74/ai_n28669845/.

7   Robert S. Kinsman, *'The Darker Vision of the Renaissance': Beyond the Fields of Reason* (Berkeley: University of California, 1974), pp. 287 ff.

8   See Michel Foucault, *Madness and Civilization: A History of Insanity in the Age of Reason* (London: Routledge, 1999; first published in French in 1961).

9   Review of Ken Jackson's *Separate Theaters* http://www.accessmylibrary.com/article-1G1-155476030/ken-jackson-separate-theaters.html.

10   William Shakespeare, *Hamlet*; first published in French in 1961 ed. Ann Thompson and Neil Taylor, Arden, 3rd series (London: Thomson, 2006).

11   See Kinsman, *Darker Vision*, pp. 303 ff.

12   Thomas Kyd, *The Spanish Tragedy* (London: A & C Black, 1989), III.xii.72.

13   In film theory, the classic essay on the narrative objectification of women through the 'male gaze' is Laura Mulvey's 'Visual Pleasure and Narrative Cinema' (see *Norton Anthology of Theory and Criticism*, pp. 2181–92), which explores the operations of this gaze through the interacting perspectives provided by the film form. For the social repercussions of the gaze (again, male) on standards of beauty and feminist strategies for countering it see Ann J. Cahill, 'Feminist Pleasure and Feminist Beautification' in *Hypatia*, vol. 18, no. 4, *Women, Art and Aesthetics* (Autumn–Winter 2003), pp. 42–64. A somewhat different analysis of the gaze in its more institutional form was provided by Michel Foucault in his discussion of the 'clinical gaze' in *The Birth of the Clinic: An Archaeology of Medical Perception* (New York: Pantheon,

1973), where it has an important role in producing the subject's moral evaluation of their particular disease.

14 The co-opting of this idea of the gaze from its non-verbal usage, e.g. in film criticism, to the broader one of 'perspective and voice' appropriate to literary criticism, is acknowledged in the entry under 'gaze' in Jeremy Hawthorn, *A Glossary of Contemporary Literary Theory* (London: Arnold, 2000).

15 Salkeld, *Madness and Drama*, p. 95.

16 For further discussion on the links between Puritanism and the rise of the bourgeoisie, see Christopher Hill, *The World Turned Upside Down: Radical Ideas During the English Revolution* (London: Penguin, 1984). For Malvolio's associations with Puritanism, see *Twelfth Night*, II.iii.136.

17 Lady Macbeth can be seen, at least in structural terms, as occupying the position of the mad woman in drama, with her disintegration of personality towards the close of *Macbeth*. Where Malvolio had been construed to be socially insane by his tormentors, Lady Macbeth can be understood (as Duncan Salkeld suggests) as an emblem of *political* insanity in the play (see Salkeld, pp. 111–13) – recklessly exposing the secretive operations of power. To that extent, the gaze of the doctor and gentlewoman, initially directed towards making a diagnosis, suddenly finds itself in the position of over-exposure to unexpected and appalling forbidden knowledge.

18 William Shakespeare, *King Lear*, ed. R. A. Foakes, Arden, 3rd series (London: Thomson: 1997; 2003), I.i.92–3.

19 For an argument that develops this point in much more detail, see Jonathan Dollimore, *Radical Tragedy*, pp. 195–202.

Rhetoric and Performance

[D]elight is the reason, that men commonly tarry the end of a merry Play, and cannot abide the half hearing of a sour checking Sermon.

Thomas Wilson, *The Arte of Rhetorique* (1553)

The term 'rhetoric' refers today, just as it did from classical through to Elizabethan times, to the ability to persuade people through the artful use of language. The relative standing of the concept has, however, altered dramatically over the millennia. Use the word 'rhetoric' in ordinary discussion nowadays, and the associations are quite often negative. We are cautioned, for example, to be suspicious of its presence in political debate, where the accusation 'empty rhetoric' is a standard formula for implying that eloquence and generalisation are being used to distract the listener from deficiencies in argument or evidence. An accusation such as this is more or less interchangeable with the phrase 'style over substance', which likewise implies an over-investment in the surface detail of speech at the expense of the underlying meaning. 'Style' and 'rhetoric' are here made synonymous, and involve a kind of back-handed compliment. It may be uplifting to hear what is being said – a 'delight' as Thomas Wilson suggested public speaking should be – but pleasure is ultimately in lieu of genuine content, and we can quietly congratulate ourselves on being able to tell the difference and to 'see through' the speaker to the political hollowness inside.

234

The kind of opposition that puts rhetoric on the wrong side of the moral argument has been a feature of both British and American political discourse over the last three decades. A preference for the supposedly straight-talking, feet-on-the-ground, judge-me-by-my-deeds-not-my-words politician has seen the elevation to office of some candidates whose lack of concern with elegant phrasing was construed in some quarters as a mark of sincerity and a repudiation of glib professionalism. A fascinating element of the US elections of 2008 was their reversal of these expectations: for the first time in two decades, a presidential candidate actually used eloquence to assist him towards victory, rather than avoiding it in order not to arouse mistrust. It could be argued that Barack Obama's candidacy emerged from a particular cultural milieu (African American) in which a heightened style has retained its validity as an acceptable political tool rather than being avoided as evidence of window-dressing. In such circumstances, Obama's rhetoric – his attention to the skilful manipulation of words – could be favourably revalued as 'oratory': a more neutral and respectable term reserved for the art of political speech-making.*

The modern sense that rhetoric is a dangerous and misleading practice, often obscuring access to the truth, can be contrasted with the premium put on it by our Renaissance forebears. For Elizabethans and Jacobeans generally (not just writers), rhetoric was a cardinal part – perhaps the most important part – of the re-introduction of classical, pre-Christian letters and learning into intellectual life. This in itself comprised a rejection of the centuries-old emphasis on writing primarily as a philosophical tool. The schools and academies of medieval Europe had prioritised the use of logic in debate, again drawing on classical thought (especially Aristotle's works), and taught a highly systematised form of argument which aimed at the demonstration of proofs within abstract contexts. Medieval and early modern schoolchildren would all have known of the 'syllogism', which was the standard method for arriving at logical conclusions from

---

* Martin Luther King's 'I have a dream' speech from 28 August 1963, addressing a civil rights march in Washington, remains the best-known example, and benchmark, of this mode of oratory within African American culture.

general premises.*[1] It was not only dry and inelegant in expression, but also could lend itself to various absurdities which only an indifference to real-life examples could allow.

The Renaissance emphasis on language as a tool for persuasion rather than for proof was part of that humanist enthusiasm, which we touched on in Part Two, for making education practical in terms of the individual's engagement with the public world. The speeches and techniques of Greek and Latin statesmen, above all Cicero, now became the key legacy from the ancient world, and were admired and imitated for their aesthetic appeal as much as for their sentiments. As an exponent of this newly rediscovered craft, Thomas Wilson declared (in a statement itself thoroughly rhetorical in its use of antitheses): 'by plain teaching the Logician shows himself, by large amplification, and beautifying of his cause, the Rhetorician is always known'.[2] The humanist Roger Ascham likewise defended the project on aesthetic grounds, and more importantly made aesthetics central to the pursuit of knowledge: 'Ye know not what hurt ye do to learning that care not for words but for matter and so make a divorce twixt the tongue and the heart'.[3] Language is here recovered as something which has access to the heart, to the emotions, promising a relation to truth which goes beyond that of abstract philosophical demonstration. A more homely grasp of the new parameters is suggested by Tranio's advice to Lucentio in *The Taming of the Shrew*: 'Balk logic with acquaintance that you have / And practice rhetoric in your common talk' (I.i.34–5).

In order to achieve their ends in persuading the listener, orators were able to draw on a huge repertoire of argumentative and stylistic resources. Rhetorical manuals and guide-books appeared in England in increasing abundance from the mid-sixteenth century on, cataloguing and describing the various components of rhetoric: from the setting out of the argument (generally known as the invention and disposition, i.e. finding and ordering, of 'matter'), through the deployment of an array of figurative devices to ornament or 'beautify' one's sayings (known as

---

* The syllogism typically derived a specific conclusion from two general statements by means of a common feature (or 'middle term') between them: e.g. 'all animals have bodies; all people are animals; all people have bodies', with 'animals' as the middle term.

elecutio), to the actual vocal and gestural delivery of the speech (these last, physical aspects of rhetoric being rather confusingly encompassed under the general heading of 'pronunciation'). The figures of rhetoric were taught in a detailed fashion in schools as part of the study of Latin and Greek texts, and can seem to us astonishing in their variety and quaintness. Today we all more or less understand what a *metaphor* is, and how to use it in common speech; we have probably heard of *metonymy* (at least, if we are students of literature) and recognise it when it's used; but it is when we get to the intricate subdivisions within these types of figure (*catachresis* in the case of metaphor; *transumption* in the case of metonymy) and the plethora of figures which deal with form and patterning in word usage (*anaphora*, *epistrophe*, *epizeuxis*) that the gap between our own perceptual grasp of language and that of the Elizabethans begins to open up. Unlike them, we are not taught to apprehend these devices from an early age, although they remain available to us for cold analysis. As a consequence we would seem to hear, as it were, in monochrome against the psychedelic 'colouring' of the Elizabethan discursive world. To such reflections it is perfectly reasonable to counter, 'So what?'. Even so conscientious a commentator on Elizabethan language and rhetoric as Frank Kermode can characterise present-day, exhaustive attempts to recover all its figurative content as so much 'archaeology'.[4] Nevertheless, for the period that re-opened this Pandora's box of classical rhetoric and revelled in its possibilities, its figures, schemes and tropes were evidence of language as something fully alive, and the endless combinations which they promised were seen as a force for novelty and for creativity.

The emphasis on variety and on the need to 'colour' speech through the use of linguistic ornamentation (*elecutio*) meant that oratory shared a common ground with literary language throughout history. As the editors of *Renaissance Figures of Speech* point out, 'it can be hard to draw the line between literary and rhetorical theory in the classical and Renaissance periods', despite the fact that Aristotelian theory had dealt with each as distinct branches of study in the *Ars Poetica* and the *Ars Rhetorica*.[5] Both poetry and rhetoric were understood as tools for moving people (in the sense of being moved to some kind of action or response), and the Renaissance grasp of this connection ensured that the 'portrait of the ideal orator' derived from classical constructions of the art 'underlay the humanist portrayal of the ideal poet'.[6] It is a connection made almost casually by George Puttenham in his much-read manual *The Arte of English Poesie*, when he honours poetry as the starting-point of civilisation among human beings: 'Poesie was th'originall cause and occasion of their first assemblies.'[7] This simply transposes a point Thomas Wilson had already made about the socialising power of 'art and eloquence' to induce people 'to live together in fellowship of life, to maintaine Cities, to deale truly, and willingly obeye one an other'.[8]

This sense of a natural cross-over between poetry and rhetoric was even more true of the practice of writing in Elizabethan and Jacobean England, where heterogeneity – the mixing of forms and styles – was so widespread. A highly representative work in that respect was Philip Sidney's *The Countess of Pembroke's Arcadia*, which fused prose romance and poetry with extended rhetorical passages. Characters often express (perhaps we should say declare) their emotions in heightened, artificial styles, employing elaborate figures of speech in ways that draw attention to the beauty of their language and hence, by implication, the skill of the writer. Sidney's *Arcadia* was self-evidently a literary pursuit, begun with the aim of providing a private entertainment for his sister Mary (who completed and expanded it after his death). It was as a work of poetry that he conceived it, in that broad sense of the term which he employs in his *Apology* as the creation of a fictive 'image' or 'speaking picture', rather than just as something done in verse. Yet it was as a rhetorical exercise that much of it was executed, and this makes sense if we consider that both poet and orator shared an investment in persuading the listener/reader: the one in the field of argument and the other in that of artistic imitation, mimesis.

The overlapping of rhetorical and literary modes was at its most sophisticated in the drama, which as a medium frequently combined the artistic aims of mimesis with the oratorical ones of the set speech. The addresses of Brutus and Antony to the Roman people after the assassination of Caesar in Shakespeare's *Julius Caesar* (III.ii.13–34, 74–223) are two of the more obvious cases in point, since here we have a dramatisation of oratory itself. The speeches given to the two men are quite self-consciously rhetorical, both making use of different techniques in order to appeal to the reason of the populace on the one hand (Brutus) and to their emotions on the other (Antony). While Brutus uses examples of what rhetorical theory often defined as figures of speech (that is, modes of verbal patterning), employing evenly weighted parallelisms to generate a sense of calm and balance, Antony prefers to use figures of thought such as apostrophe (addressing an abstract or non-present individual) to appeal directly to the imagination and work up the feelings of the crowd.[9] Rhetorical distinctions such as these, however, are also couched in literary form: Brutus's prose pointedly contrasts with Antony's blank verse, underlining his fatal attempt to engage with the listeners at a conversational level rather than elevating his discourse above them. Literary form here intervenes to create dramatic excitement out of the competing orations themselves.

What about the soliloquy, which was such a ubiquitous feature of English Renaissance drama? Here is another mode of declamation, often drawing on oratorical techniques and developing in the manner of an argument. But who is the addressee, exactly, in a speech like Hamlet's 'To be or not to be'? The speaker, self-reflexively? Or the audience, implicitly? If the latter is made too obviously the recipient, the illusion of the speaker's solitariness is in danger of being broken (it is already compromised by the presence of Ophelia onstage); but if the actor aims for a highly introspective delivery then the force of the general examples in the speech's second half can become vitiated. We will look in more detail at this problem below, but from a first glance it seems that, in terms of their power to persuade, soliloquies hover somewhere between the poles of the mimetic, through their creation of a believable fictional space around the speaker, and the oratorical, in their attempt to win the audience over to their point of view.

Rhetoric, we can conclude, pervades some of the most public as well as the most private aspects of drama, sometimes openly framed as oratory and sometimes adapting the figures and tropes of public declamation to the most intimate and interior of contexts. To this we can add one further, very important consideration: the actor's craft was itself conceptualised in terms of rhetoric, or more specifically that part of it which dealt with vocal and gestural delivery – what was referred to above as 'pronunciation'. The following discussion will therefore address the contribution of rhetoric from two angles. The first examines the way rhetorical figures underlie the dramatic poem, embedded within speech, within action, and even within scenic structure. The second considers the way that rhetoric underlies the dramatic performance, and how far we can regard oratorical theory as a substitute for a theory of acting – a thing which was itself non-existent in the plays of Shakespeare's period.

Figures in Speech

Where and how do we find this combination of representational and rhetorical modes in English Renaissance drama? We can begin by looking at a (different) Hamlet soliloquy, his first of the play, beginning 'Oh that this too too sallied flesh would melt' (I.ii.129 ff.). Wolfgang Clemen thought that these lines represented 'a new kind of dramatic speech' which was able to 'follow the quickly changing reactions of a sensitive mind better than speech in dialogue ever could'.[10] Many others have likewise seen its halting, recursive mode of expression – self-questioning, self-answering, self-defeating – as a completely convincing portrayal of a mind under intolerable internal pressure. It comes as something of a jolt, then, to find another critic, Jan H. Blits, characterising the soliloquy as 'ranting Roman rhetoric' employing a mass of text-book figures in the Ciceronian 'grand style'.[11] Yet these figures are indisputably there. As well as apostrophe ('Frailty, thy name is woman'), metaphor ('unweeded garden', 'Hyperion to a satyr') and metonymy (Niobe who is 'all tears'), all of which we noted above, Blits finds, among others, hyperbole, reduplication, interruption, synecdoche, personification, and a few which don't even have a direct English translation: 'commoratio' and 'notatio'. Some of these figures combine in the same piece of phrasing: so that 'Frailty, thy name is woman' is not only an example of apostrophe, but also of what was called a 'sentence' (i.e. moralising statement), as well as – from a feminist perspective – hyperbole (overstatement). If all this seems to be taking us into *very* specialist territory, we can be reassured by the fact that a good, modern-day A/AS-level guide would cover about half of these figures, applying them to contemporary literary contexts. However, the sheer concentration of these figures into a single speech, which unfolds as an apparently private, spontaneous register of thought and feeling (what later came to be characterised as 'stream of consciousness' in modernist writing), requires some explanation. If these lines are the product of artifice and literary convention, how is it that they read so naturally? Are we supposed to recognise in their rhetoric a way of establishing the speaker's personality (Hamlet is after all a scholar, on leave from the archetypal humanist university of Wittenburg)? Or are these figures so well disguised that they manage to create something fresh out of familiar rhetorical materials?

We could try to answer some of these questions by looking at one of the more straightforward figures used in the speech: repetition. At its simplest this involves the use of a single word twice or more in a phrase, sometimes consecutively, as in 'too too sallied flesh' and 'Oh God, God', sometimes with the separation of a few words, as with 'Fie on't! Ah fie!'. The obvious rhetorical effect in each case is that of emphasis: of intensification through reduplication. Thomas Wilson called this figure 'doublets', and gave a vivid description of its effect which works rather well with a revenge tragedy such as *Hamlet*: 'the oft repeating of one worde, doth much stirre the hearer, and makes the worde seeme greater, as though a sword were oft digged and thrust twice, or thrice in one place of the body'.[12] The rhetorical potency of a simple repetition like this, with its capacity to force itself upon the listener and to 'stirre' up a response, might be thought enough in itself; but it also has a representational effect in assisting the creation of the fictional character that is Hamlet. An example of the use of iteration in this way is afforded by Shylock in *The Merchant of Venice*, discussed by Stephen Greenblatt as an early Shakespearean triumph of subjective characterisation, that is to say the suggestion of an inner life. As Shylock loses his composure on the news of his daughter's elopement with a Venetian Christian, taking a huge store of money with her, his speech descends into a 'numb repetition' of the single word 'there'.[13] It is part self-consolation ('there, there'), part vain wish-fulfilment over locating her; but ultimately these duplications function as 'placeholders for silent thinking', creating a linguistic 'surface' beneath which emotional or unconscious depths can be construed. In Hamlet's case, then, we can add the effect of depth, created in the way Greenblatt describes, to the effect of emphasis. The repetition of words conveys not just the speaker's desire for intensification but also his sense that there is no intensifier sufficient to the purpose. We appreciate the point perfectly well without the duplication that Hamlet feels his flesh to be in some way contaminated; but with it we begin to sense there is something so awful about this feeling that it eludes expression – that it lurks 'beyond' even Hamlet's considerable linguistic resources (as an example of these, we heard him make exceptionally rich use of the punning figure in his dialogue with the king and queen earlier).

If this kind of repetition comes under the heading of word-patterning, another kind which Hamlet uses evokes the 'figure of sense' category, where the same thing is said in a number of different ways (known to rhetoricians as *synonymia*, i.e. the piling up of synonyms). So the first part of 'How weary, stale, flat and unprofitable / Seem to me all the uses of this world' registers an overplus of lexical alternatives rather than a poverty of them. Coming so soon after the two instances of doublets in the opening lines of the soliloquy, they throw the listener from one rhetorical extreme to the other, perhaps generating a sense of disconnect between the speaker and his world. Hidden psychological depth – 'that within which passes show' – is fostered by the narrow repetition of certain words, while a sense of the world's all-too-transparent worthlessness is created by the varied use of adjectives ('weary, stale, flat', etc.). The poet and critic T. S. Eliot is well known for arguing that there seemed to be a mismatch between Hamlet's emotions and the circumstances which give rise to them. Eliot found in this lack of an 'objective correlative' sufficient evidence to pronounce *Hamlet* 'an artistic failure'.[14] Yet the problematic 'excess' of emotion which Eliot refers to may be no more than an effect of the bold range of rhetorical devices being used in the soliloquy: a range which reflects dramatic *decorum* in being appropriate to Hamlet's youthful and scholarly persona.

When Hamlet declares 'That it should come to this! But two months dead / Nay not so much, not two', he goes on to use another figure identified in the rhetoric manuals: that of correction (*correctio*). By revising his first statement as soon as he has uttered it, in a kind of 'did I say that?' fashion, he makes a subtle comparison between the two estimates of time (two months, less than two months) which reflects negatively on the queen, who has remarried in that speedy interval. In the dialogue Hamlet is holding with himself this 'mistake' and its correction sound sincere enough; but the effect of the figure on the audience is to persuade them of his mother's wickedness (or depravity, or however we choose to read it). A more overt use of this same device can be seen in one of the most famous soliloquies from the drama prior to *Hamlet*, Kyd's *The Spanish Tragedy*. Hieronimo, beginning to despair of ever tracking down the murderers of his son Horatio, opens his speech at the start of III.ii. thus:

> O eyes, no eyes, but fountains fraught with tears;
> O life, no life, but lively form of death;
> O world, no world, but mass of public wrongs,
> Confused and filled with murder and misdeeds!
> O sacred heavens! if this unhallowed deed,
>> If this inhuman and barbarous attempt,
>> If this incomparable murder thus
>> Of mine, but now no more my son,
>> Shall unrevealed and unrevengéd pass,
>> How should we term your dealings to be just,
>> If you unjustly deal with those that in your justice trust?[15]

The first three lines all begin with a figure of correction: eyes that are not eyes, life that is not life, world not a world (they are bound together more tightly still by the additional figure of *anaphora*, the use of the same word to begin each consecutive line). The effect is of a series of verbal gestures which reach out, only to double back upon themselves, cancelling their own premise. They point towards the crux of the passage in line 8, identifying the cause of all this misery in the son who is no longer a son, having himself been cancelled out through the act of murder (the line's inverted syntax, beginning with the possessive pronoun and ending with the noun, powerfully marks this instance of *correctio* off from the preceding three and establishes it as a kind of climax to them). The overall impression is again that of comparison: we see a juxtaposition between how things once were (and should still be) and the negations that have taken their place, and this state of affairs is laid at the feet of the 'sacred heavens', who are made culpable by their failure to avenge it. As a piece of rhetoric the passage is, in contrast to Hamlet's soliloquy, highly formal and heavily patterned, and consequently easy to mock as 'over the top' (as Ben Jonson, self-appointed arbiter of poetic taste and learning, did in his comedies). But it can also be seen as another successful instance of dramatic decorum, since the speech is appropriate in its heightened style to its addressee: the powers above.

Figures in Speech 2: Competitive Rhetoric

The mockery of self-consciously rhetorical styles such as Hieronimo's in the speech quoted above was a feature of the boy player companies after their reopening in 1599. Not only did the writers for this particular repertoire have a preference for satire but they wrote with an eye to the debunking effects of having heroic adult roles played by young children. The kind of parody which this allowed created further possibilities for the use of rhetorical modes of address within a fictional context. In John Marston's romantic comedy for the Paul's Boys, *Antonio and Mellida* (1599), the hero, Antonio, escapes from a court where his beloved, Mellida, is held prisoner, shouting out his own name to confuse his pursuers, before stopping in mid-flight to deliver an impromptu speech on the ironic implications of this strategy:

> Alas, this that you see is not Antonio.
> His spirit hovers in Piero's court,
> Hurling about his agile faculties
> To apprehend the sight of Mellida
> [...]
> 'Tis so. I'll give you instance that 'tis so.
> Conceit you me as, having clasped a rose
> Within my palm, the rose being ta'en away,

My hand retains a little breath of sweet;
So may man's trunk, his spirit slipped away,
Hold still a faint perfume of his sweet guest.
[...]
            what was't I said?
O, this is nought but speckling melancholy
That morphews tender skin. I have been
Cousin german – bear with me, good Mellida –[16]

Antonio is saying that this whole little game of pretending he is not where he is points towards a bigger paradox: that his soul has indeed been left behind at court, casting about for his true love, Mellida. Instead of just leaving this as an elaborate metaphor in the vein of the Petrarchan lover, however, he suddenly steps out of the fiction and, addressing the audience directly, offers a specific 'instance' to argue his case. The reasoning Antonio goes on to use is highly sophistical, in the sense of employing subtle but fallacious argument. His 'conceit' of a soul that leaves its traces in the body the way a rose leaves its scent in the hand is actually lifted from a passage in Erasmus in which two lovers argue like 'Sophister' and 'Sophistress' over the theme that 'the soul is not where it giveth life, but where it loves'.[17] Sophistry sat on the blurred line between philosophy and rhetoric, offering arguments that dressed themselves up as logic but in fact operated through verbal persuasion and tendentious analogy. Antonio's speech makes comic capital out of this by showing a lover's pretensions to arguing logically about love doomed to collapse into incoherence. To reinforce the point, the last couple of lines employ the rhetorical figure of *aposiopesis*: a literal breaking off of speech before it is finished. The figure was very commonly employed in the drama for its powerfully arresting effects, but was used with particular relish by Marston's boy performers to ridicule the extravagant language often associated with adult company plays and players, and to show grandstanding heroic figures tripping over their own verbal feet, as it were. One could argue that aposiopesis serves a further purpose here in disrupting the effects of regular speech just as Antonio's direct address to the audience had disrupted the fictional barrier between speaker and audience. There is a constant unsettling of the effects of character from the start to the finish of the soliloquy (which over its course arguably becomes a monologue in form). It is one which cleverly develops Antonio's initial claim that he is 'not Antonio' in a direction that tests the cohesiveness of the theatrical illusion itself.

If Antonio's speech plays with the fuzzy line between philosophy and rhetoric, the dialogue between Volpone and Celia in the seduction scene of Jonson's *Volpone* plays with the tension between rhetoric and poetry. Volpone has been masquerading as an invalid, steadily extracting gifts from those desperate to benefit in his will, and has fallen in love (or at any rate lust) with the wife of one of his dupes. Tricking her husband into leaving Celia alone with him as a kind of sexual offering, Volpone leaps out of his disguise and attempts to woo her via a series of spellbinding speeches promising her limitless wealth and luxury. Celia, however, is impervious to these blandishments, desiring only to retain her chastity, and tries to argue her way around Volpone's verbal onslaught. The scenario is thus set for a kind of combat in persuasion, in which rhetorical force meets rhetorical counter-force. The clash is heightened by the heavy reliance of both speakers on the figure of *hyperbole* in their speeches – that is, patent exaggeration. Henry Peacham's definition of the figure seems apt here, when he speaks of it as a 'saying surmounting the truth ... not with purpose to deceive by speaking untruly, but with desire to amplifie the greatnesse or smalnesse of things by the exceeding similitude'.[18] In Volpone's case, the amplification is directed at the sensual delights he wants to shower on Celia:

> The heads of parrots, tongues of nightingales,
> The brains of peacocks, and of ostriches
> Shall be our food: and, could we get the phoenix,
> Though nature lost her kind, she were our dish.
> [...]
> Thy baths shall be the juice of July flowers,
> Spirits of roses, and of violets,
> The milk of unicorns, and panthers' breath

Gathered in bags, and mixed with Cretan wines.
Our drink shall be prepared gold, and amber ...[19]

The examples clearly outstrip credibility, but this is deliberate since exaggeration is employed by the speaker to convey his own inordinate desire for Celia. More significant, however, is the fact that Volpone's use of hyperbole has a predominantly poetic function. It aims to persuade, but by a process of enchantment – by the conjuring up of an imaginative world of objects so powerful that the speech either soars above speaker and addressee into a purely fictive dimension, or spills over into song (as it does twice). Against this use of hyperbole to fire the imagination Celia sets her own use of hyperbole in the interests of a rhetorical appeal to clemency. First begging either to be released or to be killed, Celia then goes on:

> If you will deign me neither of these graces,
> Yet feed your wrath, sir, rather than your lust;
> (It is a vice, comes nearer manliness)
> And punish that unhappy crime of nature,
> Which you miscall my beauty: flay my face,
> Or poison it, with ointments, for seducing
> Your blood to this rebellion. Rub these hands,
> With what may cause an eating leprosy,
> E'en to my bones, and marrow: anything,
> That may disfavour me, save in my honour.
> And I will kneel to you, pray for you, pay down
> A thousand hourly vows, sir, for your health,
> Report, and think you virtuous ... (III.vii.248–60)

Faced with a situation that can only end in rape, Celia's exaggerated illustrations of physical disfigurement make the point that the violation of her chastity would be a fate worse than death. These examples are balanced by an equally exaggerated form of compliment to Volpone. She tries to promote in him an awareness of the hierarchy of manly attributes which should lead him to prefer rage (one of the irascible emotions) over lust (one of the concupiscible ones), even offering to praise him before

God and the world if he will do so. While Volpone's use of hyperbole seems to have the character of 'immoderate excess' given it by Puttenham in his poetic categorisation of the figure, Celia's usage retains its oratorical quality in attempting a commendation of the addressee. The figure's use in two such closely related but nonetheless distinct contexts helps to give the exchange in this scene its particular edge. It brings the speakers close together but at the same time shows them so far apart in the character of their speeches that, as some critics have suggested, each seems to belong in a different genre of play.

Figures in Speech 3: Poetic Persuasions

For a final example of the use of rhetorical form within dramatic speech we can return to *Hamlet*, and to an exchange between Laertes and Ophelia (an appreciably more one-sided one than that between Volpone and Celia). Laertes is gently but firmly admonishing his sister against trusting too far in Hamlet's romantic attentions, insisting that class distinctions between prince and gentlewoman leave her vulnerable to rejection by Hamlet after he has seduced her:

> For Hamlet and the trifling of his favour,
> Hold it a fashion and a toy in blood
> [...]
> The perfume and suppliance of a minute
> [...]
>> For nature crescent does not grow alone
>> In thews and bulks, but as this temple waxes
>> The inward service of the mind and soul
>> Grows wide withal. Perhaps he loves you now,
>> And now no soil nor cautel doth besmirch
>> The virtue of his will; but you must fear,
>> His greatness weighed his will is not his own.[20]

In other words, Ophelia should fear Hamlet's very youthfulness itself; for as Hamlet's body grows into manhood – as his 'nature' continues 'crescent' – so his mental and emotional state will mature too, and his affection for Ophelia wane, particularly under the demands of public life. Laertes's sentiments are homely and solicitous for his sister's well-being, yet his advice seems devoid of anything we would recognise as dramatic character. The tone is formal, even impersonal, and seems akin to another area associated with the use of rhetorical speech, that of a sermon or homily delivered in church (Ophelia herself picks up on this tone at the speech's close when she wryly warns her brother against being an 'ungracious pastor'). To give his rhetorical arguments the emphasis they need, Laertes makes use throughout of a rather obscure figure of speech, glimpsed in such formulations as 'a fashion and a toy', 'perfume and suppliance', 'thews and bulks'. Known as *hendiadys*, a Greek term meaning 'one by means of two', it sounds on first hearing like the use of repetition or synonym, but on closer inspection turns out to involve the use of two separate ideas linked together to make us think we've heard a single one. So when Laertes describes Hamlet's attentions to Ophelia in terms of a fashionable dalliance, he rather oddly expresses it as a 'fashion' and a dalliance ('toy') – two distinct nouns, if you like, instead of a noun plus adjective. The same with the other two phrases given here, which convey the notions of 'perfume-filled' and 'physical bulk' by expressing each single, complex thought as two individuated ones: perfume and supply, physicality ('thews') and bulk. George T. Wright, who made a thorough and fascinating study of Shakespeare's use of hendiadys, finds that Laertes uses the figure 'at least' seven times in this speech.[21] Clearly, some specific effect is being striven for: but what exactly is it? One could begin by pointing out that hendiadys is a highly poetic figure, in the sense that it would seem fairly out of place in ordinary speech and perhaps doesn't even comfortably belong in rhetoric, with the latter's emphasis on clarity of expression. Rather, it does that peculiar thing that only poetry can do, which is to create an alternative, imaginative world of meaning through the use of non-logical connections. Wright defines these as 'false conjunctions': the second term is syntactically related to the first by the means of the conjunction 'and', but it seems to develop the initial thought in an unexpected direction. We grasp that there is a connection between the thoughts, but find that we are supplying it ourselves in some measure, rather as our imaginations fill in the blind spot in our field of vision. One possible interpretation of Laertes's prodigious use of the figure throughout the speech, then, lies in the way this sense of unpredictability assists the argument he is making about Hamlet's own personal development. He is thinking of the haphazard and disconcerting changes of direction characteristic of emotional growth in early manhood. Laertes's homily to his sister is thus rhetorical in its character – it is designed to persuade her against too readily surrendering her virginity to Hamlet – but it enlists a poetic figure to do much of its work, appealing to a subliminal level of fear within her about the very instability of affection in a young man.

Figures in Action

One good reason for treating hendiadys as more than just a curiosity of Elizabethan literary language lies in its status as a kind of rhetorical signature of Shakespeare's. He uses the figure far more often, and with far greater range, than any other English writer of this period, seemingly throughout his play-writing career, but especially around the turn of the century (when the Globe theatre was built), and above all in *Hamlet*.[22] Noting the capacity of hendiadys to conjoin ideas, Wright argues that *Hamlet*'s particular investment in the figure is part of the play's overall obsession with doubles and doubling, an obsession that works itself out on the psychological, thematic and even structural levels. Psychologically, Laertes's homily to Ophelia, which we have just been looking at, discloses the speaker's 'perception of doubleness in everything', as well as his own 'uncertain and divided sensibility'. Thematically, hendiadys suits the play's abiding concern with deceptive doublings: appearances of unity between people, like the marriage of Claudius and Gertrude, may conceal criminal origins and unstable foundations. Structurally, the play keeps bringing about parallels within plot and characterisation, only to reveal profound differences lying behind the surface similarities. So the mirrored relationship between Laertes and Hamlet as avengers of their fathers' deaths only serves to point up the stark contrast between the approach of each to his task (Laertes the hot-blooded avenger, Hamlet the procrastinator). All in all, Wright sees hendiadys as acting as more than just an aspect of rhetorical speech in the play: it has the status of a master trope, which underpins key elements of narrative and character. This, however, is by no means the only instance of a rhetorical figure shaping aspects of a play's drama as well as its poetic language.

We saw in the chapter on comedy how Bottom in *A Midsummer Night's Dream* became a walking metaphor after his transformation into an ass at the hands of Puck. Shakespeare's making him the living embodiment of that particular figure of speech works so well in part because the play itself is filled with references to imagination and change, two necessary components in the creation of metaphoric effect. If this example supplies evidence of how rhetorical figures can become dramatic ones, Shakespeare's *Julius Caesar* shows how they can inform larger patterns of action within the narrative. The play itself can be regarded as belonging to either the tragic or the history genre: if we treat it as history, we can see how it registers the same kind of tension between present predicament and past example as the plays examined in Part Three: 'Shakespeare's History Plays'. As the Roman nobles debate what to do about Caesar's growing power, they constantly cast their thoughts back, as Nashe might have advised them to do, to an earlier history of the Roman Republic, and in particular to their ancestors' example in refusing to tolerate tyranny. The relationship between past and present becomes particularly acute in the case of Caesar himself. Ageing, deaf, suspicious and superstitious, his great achievements are cleverly presented in the play as *already* being historical, however recently so, seeming not to emanate from him so much as to serve as models for his own vain emulation. The play accordingly shows Caesar constantly trying to fit himself to the image of 'Caesar' in both the public and the private sphere: the opening games, where he suffers a humiliating fit of 'the falling sickness'; his home and private conversation with his wife, where he hesitates over her advice to avoid the Senate; and the assembly itself, where he disdains all appeals to clemency with the insistence that he is 'constant as the northern star' of whom '[t]here is no fellow in the firmament'. Indeed, this last example shows him gesturing towards a form of apotheosis, with this peculiar difference: it arrives prior to (rather than after) his actual death (III.i.60–2).

This kind of back-to-front logic is the product of someone who has already decided on their place in history before that history has been fully written. However, Caesar is not the only person to employ it, for a kind of back-to-frontness is endemic throughout the play as a whole. In an intriguing close reading of key poetic terms in *Julius Caesar*, Nicholas Royle focuses on the play's use of the trope of *hysteron proteron*, by which events are described in the reverse of their natural order for rhetorical effect.[23] So, for example, when he is agonising over the justice of assassinating Caesar, Brutus characterises his emotional state as being caught '[b]etween the acting of a dreadful thing / And the first motion' (II.i.63–4). In terms of the logical order of the actions being described, the 'first motion' (which has already begun with the fomenting of the conspiracy) should precede 'the acting' of the assassination, but here it comes afterwards. George Puttenham described this figure as a 'manner of disordered speech, when ye misplace your words or clauses and set that before which should be behind ... we call it in English proverb, the cart before the horse'. He also christened it as 'the Preposterous' – which means, literally, going behind foremost. Like the anachronistic clock that chimes at the end of the scene, there is something deliberately disconcerting in the way it disrupts our sense of temporality.

The sense of inversion it generates in this particular instance seems to be figured in wider narrative and structural terms throughout *Julius Caesar*. An often noted point, for example, is that Caesar exerts more influence over the play in its second half, after he is dead. Where beforehand he had come across as a seriocomic, ineffectual parody of his own greatness, he subsequently becomes, through the memory others have of him, a much more sinister and powerful agent. Extend this reasoning to the play's pattern of historical examples and one frequently finds the dead (in the form of Caesar's ghost, Pompey's statue) appearing later to admonish the present rather than earlier to direct it (as in *Hamlet*, for example). Similarly back-to-front is the behaviour of the enraged crowd who run to tear down Rome before they have a reason to do so. In this last instance,

Mark Antony, having whipped his hearers into a homicidal frenzy over the mere report of Caesar's slaying, has to call them back, saying to them 'you go to do you know not what' (III.ii.228), before then going on to give them a specific incentive in the sight of Caesar's body. One could see the play's use of this trope in various ways: as the embodiment of carnival, for example – the 'topsy-turvy', holiday spirit of the plebeians which Richard Wilson, in an influential reading, sees as the key political discourse of the play, over which the pro- and anti-Caesar factions must fight for control of Rome.[24] Caesar, like a tragicomic Sir Toby Belch, is a Lord of Misrule who has the aim of absolute rule, and the conspirators the puritanical Malvolios who wish to curtail his ambitions in the name of republican virtue, while in their own hypocritical fashion 'revelling' in his bloodshed. The immediate beneficiary is, of course, Mark Antony, who knows precisely how to enlist the rage and power of the plebeians to manoeuvre himself towards the position Caesar has vacated, although it is Caesar's adopted son, Augustus, who will ultimately seal Rome's slide into dictatorship.

Figures in Action 2: Performance and Pronunciation

One final area in which we can argue for rhetoric's impact on the early modern drama is ultimately irrecoverable: the physical aspect of oratorical delivery. This would nonetheless have lain at the heart of the kinds of pleasure offered by the theatre, as a remark from the English rhetorician Thomas Wright suggests: 'in the substance of external action for most part orators and stage-players agree; and only they differ in this, that these act feignedly, those really; these only to delight, those to stir up all sorts of passions according to the exigency of the matter'.[25] Rhetorical guide books of the period did not forget that the ultimate domain of the orator was public speech, where the aim was to move the listeners to agreement by eloquence. Hence it was not much use plying readers with involved discussions of schemes and tropes without also giving guidance for the delivery of speeches on the podium. This aspect of rhetoric, which Wright calls 'external action', was more commonly known as 'pronunciation', and encompassed the impact made on the listener by the speaker's voice, gesture and posture. For orators, the gestural side of their art was conceived of as an accompaniment to the arguments they were constructing and to the figures of speech with which they were ornamenting those arguments. Verbal composition and gesture went together, emanating from the same single source, and in the hands of a capable practitioner the bodily aspect of oratorical performance was another kind of ornamentation or, as Thomas Wilson described it, 'a certain comely moderation of the countenance, and all other parts of mans body, aptly agreeing to those things which are spoken'; for 'like as the speech must agree to the matter, so must also the gesture agree to the mind'.[26] That, at least, was the ideal: but in practice the orator was not expected to provide some free and unmediated expression of thoughts and emotions through action. The vocal and gestural accompaniments to the words would have been taken from a repertoire of pre-given physical signs which the speaker's knowledge of decorum – of what was appropriate – would fit to the content of the speech.[27]

In the absence of anything in Shakespeare's period approaching the formal training for performers encountered today (RADA, the Guildhall, and so on), it is this physical aspect of rhetoric, mediated through a humanist curriculum, which comes closest to giving us a sense of what the actor was doing on stage by way of 'acting'.[28] It certainly cannot tell us about everything that was going on: the Clown's repartee, the quick-fire banter of young sophisticates in urban comedy, the unintentionally comic exchanges between the 'mechanicals' in *A Midsummer Night's Dream*, all seem to demand something far more flexible and informal. But the speeches and extended passages we have been looking at above, with their rich use of figurative language, would seem obvious areas for the use of stylised gesture to heighten their impact on audiences. Hamlet seems to be operating on this assumption when, in a famous commentary on the business of performance, he insists to the actors at Elsinore, prior to their staging of *The Murder of Gonzago*, that they 'suit the word to the action, the action to the word'.[29] To Hamlet this is what creates a 'natural' performance: playing, after all, 'hold[s] the mirror up to nature'. Yet it is quite clear that this effect of naturalness is the result of two distinct things being brought together; it is in itself an artificial union of word and action, rather than a spontaneous expression of emotion by the body. This issue is accentuated in the case of theatrical performance, because here speakers are using words that are obviously not their own, having been provided by the dramatist(s), who have themselves often taken them from a prose or historical source. Nonetheless, suiting word to action was the common requirement of both professions.

Hamlet's advice to the players proceeds partly from a nervousness about what they will do to the words which he himself has provided as an addition to their play. If they stress too much the 'pronunciation', which is to say both the vocal and the gestural side of their performance, then those words may get lost in the process of their own delivery. Accordingly he implores them to '[s]peak the speech … as I pronounced it to you, trippingly on the tongue', and not to 'saw the air too much' with the hand in an effort to emphasise the words and feelings of the character. To the extent that this suggests a tendency among actors to prioritise the physical aspect of their performance, perhaps sensing that this was the surest way to create a powerful impact on audiences, we can place Hamlet's nervousness in a wider set of attitudes about the power of the theatrical body to overpower words, to overpower meaning, and to overpower the senses (see, for example, the introduction to Part Three: 'Comedies of Eros' for comments on the capacity of theatrical performance to induce 'wantonness' in the audience). The earlier styles of playing (particularly where Marlovian tragedy was concerned) were notorious for their striving after effect through volume and mannered gesture, and Hamlet, the educated student of humanities, is trying to bring such styles under the control of correct oratorical 'moderation' by making the relationship between word and action an equal one. After all, Hamlet needs the actors to do more than just 'delight' with *The Murder of Gonzago*; he needs them to 'stir up all sorts of passions' in the king as part of his plan to spring the trap upon Claudius's conscience. But this, of course, serves to obscure the neat separation of actor from orator, of acting 'feignedly' from acting 'really', that Wright had tried to draw. By the time of Francis Bacon's opinion on the matter, we can see how far the success of the theatre had made this aspect of rhetoric entirely its own: 'A strange thing, that that part of an orator which is but superficial, and rather the virtue of a player, should be placed so high, above those other noble parts of invention, elocution, and the rest; nay almost alone, as if it were all in all'.[30] As we have seen throughout this discussion, however, the stage made use of rhetoric at the deepest as well as the most 'superficial' levels of dramatic practice, blending each craft with such subtlety and confidence that it is sometimes difficult to see where one ends and the other begins.

Notes

1 An example of the syllogism is provided in a parodic form by the clown Feste in *Twelfth Night*, 1.5.44 ff., when he attempts to cheer up Olivia: 'Anything that's mended is but patched: virtue that transgresses is but patched with sin, and sin that amends is but patched with virtue.' This *resembles* the argument by stages which the syllogism purported to give, but in fact works as a specious if witty example of moral equivalence.

2 Thomas Wilson, *The Arte of Rhetorique* (1553), Book 1.

3 Roger Ascham, *The Schoolmaster* (1570), Book 2.

4 Frank Kermode, *Forms of Attention* (Chicago: Chicago University Press, 1985), p. 48.

5 *Renaissance Figures of Speech*, ed. Sylvia Adamson, Gavin Alexander and Katrin Ettenhuber (Cambridge: Cambridge University Press, 2007), p. 4.

6 Isabel Rivers, *Classical and Christian Ideas in English Renaissance Poetry: A Student's Guide*, 2nd edn (London: Routledge, 1994), p. 131.

7 George Puttenham, *The Arte of English Poesie* (London: 1589), Book 1, ch. 3.

8 Wilson, *Arte of Rhetorique*, Prologue.

9 See the discussion of the contrast in Adamson et al., *Renaissance Figures of Speech*, pp. 8–9.

10 Wolfgang Clemen, *Shakespeare's Dramatic Art: Collected Essays* (London: Methuen & Co. Ltd, 1972), p. 160.

11 Jan H. Blits, *Deadly Thought: 'Hamlet' and the Human Soul* (Lanham, MD: Lexington Books, 2001).

12 Wilson, *Arte of Rhetorique*, Book 3.

13 Greenblatt, *Will in the World*, pp. 281–2.

14 See T. S. Eliot, *The Sacred Wood: Essays on Poetry and Criticism* (1922).

15 Kyd, *Spanish Tragedy*, III.ii.1–11.

16 John Marston, *Antonio and Mellida*, Revels Plays, ed. Reavley Gair (Manchester: Manchester University Press, 2004), IV.iv.27. The opening conceit of Antonio's speech, that he has lost himself, is a parody of Romeo's similar claim to Mercutio in *Romeo and Juliet*, I.i.195–6.

17 Erasmus, *Colloquies*, trans. H. M. (London: 1671), pp. 129–39. For discussion of this attribution see Reavley Gair's footnote on the passage in *Antonio and Mellida*.

18 Henry Peacham, *The Garden of Eloquence* (London: 1593), p. 31. In characteristic fashion George Puttenham personified the figure as follows: 'when we speake in the superlative and beyond the limites of credit ... I for his immoderate excesse cal him the over reacher', *Arte of English Poesie*, p. 159.

19 Ben Jonson, *Volpone*, III.vii.202–17.

20 Shakespeare, *Hamlet*, I.iii.5–20.

21 George T. Wright 'Hendiadys and *Hamlet*', *PMLA*, Vol. 96, no. 2 (March 1981), pp. 168–93, p. 176).

22 Wright counts sixty-six instances in *Hamlet*; others have suggested more.

23 Nicholas Royle, *How to Read Shakespeare* (London: Granta, 2005), pp. 24–37.

24 See Richard Wilson, 'Shakespeare's Roman Carnival', in *New Historicism & Renaissance Drama*, ed. Richard Wilson and Richard Dutton (London: Longman, 1992), pp. 145–56. For a sensible critique of this article see David Daniell's introduction to the Arden 3 *Julius Caesar*, pp. 97–8; Wilson's argument remains attractive, however, for relating this 'carnivalesque' reading of the play to the social control of Elizabethan audiences following the erection of the Globe in 1599.

25 Thomas Wright, *The Passions of the Mind in General* (1601), Book 5, ch. 3.

26 Thomas Wilson, *Arte of Rhetorique*.

27 Followers of the TV series *Rome* may recall the imposing figure of the official newsreader played by Ian McNeice, who employs a range of highly stylised gestures to accompany his pronouncements, the exact meaning of which seem to find no obvious parallel today. That kind of 'meaning' is an approximation (a rather extreme one) of the kind of thing we need to be imagining in relation to the ancient art of rhetorical pronunciation. For a list of episodes in which the newsreader appears, see the record at The Internet Movie Database, www.imdb.com/character/ch0099816/

28 See in particular, B. L. Joseph, *Elizabethan Acting* (Oxford: Oxford University Press, 1951). For a discussion which makes the important qualifying point about there being a plurality of performance modes, see Peter Thompson, 'Rogues and Rhetoricians: Acting Styles in Early English Drama', in Cox and Kastan, pp. 321–35.

29 For Hamlet's advice to the Players and exposition of the purpose of acting, see *Hamlet*, III.ii.1 ff.

30 Francis Bacon, 'Of Boldness', in *The Essays or Counsels Civil and Moral*, ed. Brian Vickers, Oxford World's Classics (Oxford: Oxford University Press, 1999), pp. 26–8, p.26.

Women at the Margins

A movement towards marriage was a key feature of the social role of women as represented in the comedies of Shakespeare's period (see Part Three: 'Comedies of Eros'). Although the sub-genre of romantic comedy had a specific investment in the idea of a happy and harmonious conclusion in marriage, we also noted that many comedies which fell outside that categorisation wound up their proceedings via wedlock. In Shakespeare's case this practice arguably amounted to a signature conclusion, designating a comic ending in spite of the sometimes decidedly unromantic story elements which unfolded prior to it. Thus a complex and tragicomic work like *Measure for Measure*, with its strong tones of satire and atmosphere of corruption, finishes almost jarringly on a note of marriage: the duke emerges from disguise to pardon miscreants and declare that he himself will claim the apprentice nun Isabella, whose attempted sexual coercion at the hands of Angelo has been the play's major focus. To the dismay of some modern audiences and readers, this declaration neither seeks nor receives a word of consent from Isabella herself. As a result, it can appear to be extending the theme of coercion beyond the play's conclusion. Like a much earlier but comparably unsettling comic ending, that of *The Taming of the Shrew*, marriage in comedy can be presented as emerging out of social necessity, rather than mutual agreement.

By contrast, a movement away from harmony within marriage provides the main trajectory for the social role of women as they are represented in tragic contexts, whether this disruption is figured as internal, arising from within that marriage, or as the product of external circumstances. So Desdemona, the Duchess of Malfi, Juliet, Beatrice-Joanna in *The Changeling* and to some degree even Lady Macbeth all figure their sufferings in terms of damage within this specific sphere. This is even true of a narrative of incestuous love such as that in *'Tis Pity She's a Whore*, where it is the fact of the heroine's arranged marriage to another man (himself a bigamist) which destroys the boldly presented vision of unmarried sexual happiness between brother and sister. We could be forgiven, then, for forming the view that marriage provided the key narrative domain for the representation of female action and agency in the period's drama – a simplistic but telling way of defining women's social identities that was recognisable, comprehensible and pleasurable to audiences. The many constraints on women in early modern society made this approach to some degree inevitable. Despite (or possibly because of) the consecutive reigns of two female monarchs from the middle of the sixteenth century, one of whom remained unmarried, women's social position throughout that century and well into the seventeenth remained understood as subordinated entirely to their male counterparts – a social relation legitimated by the institutions of marriage and its concomitant, family life. Katherine in Shakespeare's *The Taming of the Shrew* (1592), once she has to all appearances submitted to this ideal of subordination after her initial fierce resistance to it, gives it utterance in her concluding speech:

> Thy husband is thy lord, thy life, thy keeper,
> Thy head, thy sovereign; one that cares for thee,
> And for thy maintenance; commits his body
> To painful labour both by sea and land,
> To watch the night in storms, the day in cold,
> Whilst thou liest warm at home, secure and safe …[1]

As a way of qualifying this cosy picture of an exchange of absolute obedience for absolute security, we can suggest that as a dramatic speech it represents an attempt to stabilise a much more complex and shifting set of social factors. Catherine Belsey has pointed to the way in which the major upheavals of the period leading up to the 1650s – a move to an economy based on profit-making rather than patronage, religious disagreement and division, and experimentations with democracy – included a comparable, radical shift in the understanding of marriage. Women began to be understood as equal partners within a relationship based on love and freedom of choice of marital partner, rather than as merely silent reproducers of the dynastic family unit. Ultimately, however, this amounted to an equality subsisting only within that sphere, as the original relationship of subordination was re-stated in different terms. The female partner in marriage exerted control over this domestic unit, but it was on behalf of the male partner, as a 'newly defined place of retreat' for him from the worlds of business and politics, which carried on outside and from which women were more excluded than ever.[2] But, as Belsey also points out, this very process of social reorganisation, despite its orthodox outcome in terms of gender hierarchies, initially provoked crises of consternation and uncertainty as gender norms were put under strain. The literature of the period absorbed and shaped these crises in various ways: '[t]he period of Shakespeare's plays is also the period of an explosion of interest in Amazons, female warriors, roaring girls ... and women disguised as pages' (p. 178).

These were female figures whose relationship to the conjugal sphere ranged from the uncertain (as in the disguised pages) through the highly problematic (the roaring girls) to the non-existent (Amazons). To these can be added other figures such as the witch and the courtesan who again, to varying degrees, disrupted the basic understanding that marriage and family delimited female experience, and even raised the possibility of a measure of financial and intellectual independence. These are, it should be stressed, figures, which is to say figments, sometimes bordering on caricatures, embedded within the thought and literature about women in these times. They will (mostly) have had their counterparts in the social world, but that is not quite the same thing as assuming a social reality for all of the claims made for them. Precisely because there was such an investment in the creation of the domestic sphere in this period, all departures from this norm-in-the-making were liable to cause particular anxiety or fascination. And these anxieties could snowball, as anxieties will, taking in other kinds of destabilising social phenomena such as class mobility and dress codes, which thus served to over-determine the behaviourally different, socially marginal woman.[3] Unmarried, unaffiliated women had always existed in society, just as their male equivalents had; but in this period there is a particular sense that no one knew quite what or how to think of them, and hence the urge to spin fantasies and fictions about them becomes peculiarly strong.

In what follows we will look at a number of female figures from the drama who occupy this marginal social status with regard to the norms of love and marriage. Although some of these figures (e.g. the witch) lent themselves to established historical stereotype, the dramatists' sense of the inadequacy of these stereotypes is an important part of the attraction and the pleasure that these figures bring to the English Renaissance stage. This can be seen as partly consonant with historical innovations which were separate from those of the development of the 'affective' domestic sphere. Elizabeth I had notably encouraged a cult around her status as a Virgin Queen, which can be seen as a form of crossing two established figurations of femininity – those of the female ruler and the immaculate virgin – into one novel composite. But the requirement to remodel or overturn stereotypes was under more immediate pressure from the requirements of a fully commercialised drama that offered novelty – or at any rate the semblance of novelty – as one of its staples. The discussion that follows will draw on the now very substantial feminist scholarship that exists by way of commentary on these marginal female characters, but it also proposes a less ideological consideration alongside it. These characters were played by male actors, boys in some cases but in others more probably young men, and would have presented special challenges in terms of the performance of gender. Not being conventional emblems of femininity, these characters would have obliged the male actor to find means of signifying their femaleness other than the established gestural and vocal ones. We can't recover how this was done, deriving as it did from the evanescent moment of performance. But we can acknowledge its implications for the *re*coding skills of the actor and the decoding skills of the audience, just as much as for the pointed commentary on power relations between the sexes that arose out of it. We will begin by looking at what to modern readers is probably the least familiar of the categories mentioned above by Belsey, that of the 'roaring girl'.

Mad Moll: *The Roaring Girl*

The 'roaring girl' tag is really only associated with one historical figure, an unattached (except for a brief, sham marriage) London woman named Mary Frith, who was continually in trouble with the law over the first decade of the seventeenth century. Some of the offences for which she was brought before magistrates were of the petty kind rife in Jacobean London – purse-stealing and house burglary – and she seems to have been acquitted for these frequently enough. Her association of some kind with the criminal underworld was nonetheless obvious to many and persisted through much of her life, with an additional note of complexity (which had significance for the quasi-heroic status she developed) in that she often acted as an informant on thieves and the whereabouts of stolen goods. In these associations Mary was not greatly distinguishable from the broader class of women who pieced together an independent living on the margins of legality and respectability. What made her stand out from the crowd, and exacerbated her problems with the law, was her recorded habit of adopting behaviour, mannerisms and above all clothing ordinarily reserved for men. She scandalised and fascinated Londoners in equal measure over the course of two decades by often going in fully masculine attire, visiting ale houses, smoking tobacco, swearing, and at one point famously visiting a London playhouse in this get-up and providing the performance's concluding 'jig'.* This was emphatically not the use of a disguise to inveigle herself into male preserves: it was quite open behaviour. By the same token, it was not in itself law-breaking activity. There had been 'sumptuary' laws in the Elizabethan era (statutes regulating what people wore) which were concerned to ensure that

---

* It can't be known for sure, but since the visit took place at the Fortune theatre in 1611, and since the Epilogue itself alludes to such an event, it is highly likely that this was an honorary attendance of *The Roaring Girl* itself.

the social classes remained distinct via their dress codes; but these had nothing to say about gender and had in any case been repealed in 1603.

Mary was undeniably flouting convention, however, and via the oddly associative logic of the time such an activity could always find itself being mapped onto the actual illegalities for which she was prosecuted. A case in point is the charge of public immorality levelled at her by an ecclesiastical court in 1612. Admitting freely to the court her cross-dressing, her visits to 'disorderly and licentious places in this city' and even the risqué repartees she indulged in with those men who barracked her (she jokingly invited them to 'come to her lodging [that] they should find that she is a woman'), she nonetheless 'absolutely denied that she was chargeable with ... these imputations' of prostitution and bawdry. Her denials seem fair: such imputations fail to tally with her repeated offences, and seem to come about instead as a corollary to her outrageous behaviour in crossing the clothing divide between the sexes. As Stephen Orgel puts it, 'this was considered not dangerously masculine, but dangerously feminine', in the sense that to enter the male domain of brazen self-advertisement and loose talk was to stress her own female immodesty rather than bear witness to the presence of 'masculine' desires.[4] It was a short, if illogical, step from here to presuming that her body was therefore being offered for sale: an accusation which frequently attached itself to other reported cases of woman dressing as men in the period.[5] According to the correspondent on London affairs John Chamberlain, who refers to her as 'Moll Cutpurse, a notorious baggage', the subsequent public penance ordered by the authorities saw her weeping ruefully (while dressed in conventional feminine attire) and vowing to reform her ways, while arousing the suspicion that she was merely 'maudlin drunk, being discovered to have tippled of three quarts of sack before she came'. Finding one supposedly exclusive domain of male activity blocked off, Mary cunningly deploys another (excessive drinking) to leave the sincerity of her repentance in doubt; and we find her back in court several times over the following decade on similar charges of 'immorality' and petty crime.

Such behavioural traits could be class-specific as well as gender-specific, however: the designation 'roaring boy' was often applied to the swaggering, drinking, expensively dressed young gentleman frequenter of the city's wide array of leisure pursuits[6] – precursor of the Hooray Henry of later ages – and Mary Frith's encroachment into this territory added further levels of confusion in a culture which relied on clear demarcations along its different social axes. When Thomas Middleton and Thomas Dekker collaborated on a comedy called *The Roaring Girl* (1611), capitalising on her celebrity only a year before her public 'penance', their application of the 'roaring' label to Mary (or Moll) herself conveniently brought all of her socially transgressive actions under one available category of understanding. But far from this normalising Moll, the writers are at pains to ensure that the label enhances her mystery, her lack of fixity in the eyes of the audience. The play's prologue sets the auditors a little conundrum on this theme, baiting them with the desire '[t]o know what girl this roaring girl should be':

> For of that tribe are many. One is she
> That roars at midnight in deep tavern bowels,
> That beats the watch, and constables controls;
> Another roars i' th' daytime, swears, stabs, gives braves,
> Yet sells her soul to the lust of fools and slaves:
> Both of these are suburb-roarers. Then there's besides
> A civil, city-roaring girl, whose pride,
> Feasting and riding, shakes her husband's state,
> And leaves him roaring through an iron grate.
> None of these roaring girls is ours; she flies
> With wings more lofty.[7]

The passage industriously populates this newly defined 'tribe' with an apparently wide membership, many of whom read like straightforward, if inverted, images of the familiar male 'roarer'. 'Mad Moll', we are told, is to be none of the above, and is notably characterised through a kind of geographical indeterminacy, being neither 'city' not 'suburb', rather than the cross-dressing for which her historical counterpart was notorious. Part of *The Roaring Girl*'s appeal lies in the way it continually displaces expectations, making theatrical capital out of the idea that Moll is a force for the resistance of easy categorisation.

Moll's ostensible narrative function is to provide a novel intervention into an updated New Comedy plot of thwarted romance. The choice of comic form thus neatly allows a recent, contemporary phenomenon of female-to-male transvestism to be juxtaposed with a set of conventional comedic tropes which includes its own (rather cursory) instance of a girl disguised as a boy. Unable to marry Mary Fitzallard, the girl he loves, because of his father's intransigence over her dowry, Sebastian Wengrave resorts to the expedient of declaring a 'counterfeit passion' for Moll to concentrate his father's mind on a scandalous alternative and force his acquiescence (I.i.96–8). He continues to see Mary Fitzallard in secret, meanwhile, through her visits to his house in a page's outfit. His father is appalled at the threatened match, but not enough to lift his bar to his son's original choice, and instead uses the opportunity to complain about the iniquity of youth in doting on an 'unnatural' object:

> It is a thing
> One knows not how to name: her birth began
> Ere she was all made. 'Tis woman more than man,
> Man more than woman, and – which to none can hap –
> The sun gives her two shadows to one shape;
> Nay, more, let this strange thing walk, stand, or sit,
> No blazing star draws more eyes after it. (I.ii.129–35)

That this choice is seen to reflect on Sebastian socially rather than sexually is suggested by Wengrave senior's emphasis on Moll's high public profile: she is the centre of a widespread and objectifying gaze which is sufficient to define her as a 'drab', or whore, and convict his son of ungoverned 'lust'. By contrast, his contention that Moll herself is neither man nor woman (or rather, a self-contradictory overplus of both) is located by him in a fault of 'birth' rather than of behaviour, and his characterisation of her draws haphazardly on Renaissance theories about sexual abnormalities (such as hermaphroditism) which can arise when the sexes are 'decided' in the 'womb'.[8] Yet even this attempt to characterise

Moll as 'in between' the sexes escapes the fixity to which it pretends, as Wengrave senior goes on to declare Moll a physical impossibility rather than just a freak, someone who has 'two shadows to one shape'.

The audience has not yet seen Moll, however, and our introduction to her comes in the context of the play's subplot involving an array of city merchants and their wives, and the 'gallants' who hang about their shops and attempt sexual intrigues with the women. (This sexual exploitation of citizen wives by raffish younger gentlemen was a perennial feature of city comedies.) The sub-plot provides the opportunity for substantial character development of the play's heroine, chiefly via her encounters with one of the gallants, Laxton, who provides an important dramatic counterpart to her. Carrying on an intrigue with the wife of one of the merchants, Mrs Gallipot (which he keeps unconsummated to ensure an expectant stream of financial favours from the smitten lady), Laxton at first appears asexual, less interested in pleasure than in the monetary advantages his physical attractions can bring. But he is aroused at once by the sight of Moll appearing among the shops dressed '*in a frieze jerkin and a black safeguard*' and accepting the offer of the admiring gallants to '*take … tobacco and smoke*':

> [*Aside*] Heart, I would give but too much money to be nibbling with that wench. Life, sh' has the spirit of four great parishes, and a voice that will drown all the city! Methinks a brave captain might get all his soldiers upon her … I'll lay hard siege to her. Money is that aquafortis that eats into many a maidenhead …
> (II.i.170–8)

This initial glimpse of Moll, and Laxton's commentary on her, emphasises her sexuality in feminine terms, but in ways that ask audiences momentarily to rethink the feminine. Her clothing bucks cross-dressing expectations (as well as helping the male performer clearly establish the character's gender) by signifying as female rather than male (a '*safeguard*' indicates that she is wearing a skirt). But this clothing nonetheless emphasises decidedly non-domestic, outdoor activities, and perhaps conveys a witty hint of the hermaphroditism which figured in Wengrave senior's paranoid fantasy earlier (Moll, we find out later, is carrying the stock phallic signifier of a sword). Likewise, her effect on Laxton is to galvanise him from sexual apathy into talk about breeding (male) children. Rather as in Macbeth's compliment to Lady Macbeth 'Bring forth men children only', Laxton sees Moll as the ideal reproducer of a specifically masculine world. He also crucially acknowledges her 'maidenhead': her virginity is known, even as, contradictorily, her promiscuity is assumed. In these early, busy scenes focused around Moll, we see her resisting offers of both sex (from Laxton, who offers her money for an out-of-town assignation) and marriage (the younger Wengrave, purely in order to further his scheme, proposes to Moll within his father's hearing).

These overtures, in different ways bespeaking Moll's attractions, are compatible with the Amazon stereotype – that of the female warrior who frequently overpowers men in combat – which is conveyed through such incidents as the physical assaults Moll metes out to two separate men in the open streets. A notable use of this stereotype occurs in Shakespeare's (and Nashe's?) presentation of Joan of Arc, in *Henry VI Part 1*, where it overlaps with the additional stereotypes of the whore and the witch (Joan, as a Catholic reclaimer of French lands from the English during the period of the Hundred Years War, was a figure of villainy in Protestant early modern England). In a memorable first entrance into the play, after Joan's announcement that she has been sent by the Virgin Mary to raise the siege of Orleans, Joan offers to make proof of her divine calling by urging the dauphin (the French heir to the throne) to try her in hand-to-hand combat:

> My courage try by combat if thou dar'st,
> And thou shalt find that I exceed my sex.
> Resolve on this: thou shalt be fortunate
> If thou receive me for thy warlike mate.[9]

If audiences and readers immediately pick up on an unexpected nuance in that final word 'mate', they are right to do so, for the play makes a point of forcing into equivalence the martial prowess of this female-in-arms and the theme of sexual availability (here implied by the play on 'mate' as 'marital partner'). The motif recurs when the dauphin accepts the offer of combat and is greeted with the rejoinder 'while I live I'll ne'er fly from a man', at which *they fight and Joan ... overcomes* (l. 103). Such linkages between combat and Joan's sexuality are introduced insidiously at the start of her influence in the narrative, to generate doubts about the chastity which she explicitly professes. Hailing her after his defeat as an 'Amazon' and a 'Deborah' (expressly virtuous figures from classical and biblical legend, both sometimes counted among the female 'nine worthies') the dauphin then spoils the effect by begging her for her sexual favours: 'Impatiently I burn with thy desire / My heart and hands thou hast at once subdued' (ll. 108–9). This is straightforward male submission to female sexual conquest, a parody of conventional Petrarchan rhetoric (where the man is romantically subordinated to the woman) which underscores the inversion of gender roles by which Joan's influence is marked out as pernicious in the play. But it is clear that the dauphin is mesmerised, as Laxton is later to be, by the same heady eroticisation of a woman through combat and of combat through a woman. While on this occasion Joan maintains the façade of chastity by refusing his offer, the play later makes it clear that she continues to exercise power over the dauphin by giving him the body sexually that has vanquished him in combat (see, for example, the accusation at V.ii.58–9). In Moll's case the theme of success in combat over men is allowed to overlap more strongly still with ideas of gender inversion and confusion, as male commentators commend her for actions 'Gallantly performed ... and manfully' (II.i.240) and remark jocularly on her 'heroic spirit and masculine womanhood' (ll. 325–6). The context in each case nonetheless shows these remarks delivered in a spirit of sexual admiration which is only partly ironic.

Moll courteously turns down Sebastian's proposal of marriage with a set of prosaic if comic dissuasions stressing her 'headstrong' unsuitability to wedlock (II.ii.37). Her subsequent rebuttal of Laxton's efforts at seduction in III.i takes a different form, as she appears at the place of assignation now fully dressed *like a man* and at first unrecognisable to him. She confuses Laxton by teasing him with the prospect of having sex openly in the street before then drawing a sword and threatening him. A long monologue in verse provides a general defence of women's capacity to behave freely and openly in public, which men wilfully misconstrue as sexual provocation ('I'm given to sport, I'm often merry, jest / Had mirth no kindred in the world but lust?', ll. 101–2). But Moll also inveighs more specifically against the habits of Laxton's class in defaming women merely on the basis of harmless flirtation:

> How many of our sex by such as thou
> Have their good thoughts paid with a blasted name
> That never deserved loosely or did trip
> In oath of whoredom beyond cup and lip? (ll. 78–81)

The competitive in-group behaviour of the city's gallants in seeking the (mostly empty) reputation of seducers is humiliatingly exposed, and its cost counted in the ruined names of innocent city women. Moll then pushes this argument further by linking the plight of these victims of defamation to those '[d]istressèd needlewomen and trade-fall'n wives' whose descent into prostitution arises from the genuinely competitive conditions experienced by the city's merchant classes (l. 92).

Following a brief sword-fight with Laxton, which Moll wins by wounding him, her triumphant soliloquy initially offers to provide the moment of self-definition in fully feminist terms towards which the play had seemed to be working: 'she that has wit and spirit / May scorn to live beholding to her body for meat' (ll. 132–3). The principal alternative for women outside a dependency on their husbands, whether this dependency figures as domestic or involves the shop work undertaken by the citizen's wives, is understood by Laxton's class to be that of prostitution; and this is in itself always finally referred back to male pleasures and prerogatives, with prostitutes constructed as the consumed rather than the producer in the commercial relationship. Indeed, in a play like John Marston's *The Dutch Courtesan* the prostitute is shown as ultimately hungering after the normative ideal of marriage and respectability (which, of course, she must be denied). Moll seems to offer defiance to such restrictive choices by fully adopting the stance of independent consumer assured by the possession of the 'wit and spirit' which characterise Laxton's class. Yet she then goes on to frame this stance in terms that draw on traditional metaphors of subjectivity which, wittingly or not, reinforce gender hierarchies and female subjection: 'Base is that mind that kneels unto her body / As if a husband stood in awe on's wife!' (ll. 136–7). Even in her most ideologically outspoken moment, Moll continues to defy expectations and categorisations.

That Moll can be seen as standing in for marginal positionality per se, not just for that of women struggling to lead independent lives, is suggested by her separation from the citizen sphere of work at the beginning of the play, where she is shown openly exercising purchasing power and meeting the active hostility of the tradeswomen, and by later developments in which she has a full part in the narrative resolutions but only a muted one in the comic ending.[10] In the play's conclusion, after Moll has resolved a number of conflicts – most importantly the one between Sebastian and his father over the young man's love for Mary – she is presented as pointedly in defiance of narrative convention when a male character fatuously asks her when she herself will marry. The joke is turned back on the person who delivers it as Moll more or less implies that she won't marry until 'doomsday'. At the same time, it underlines the fact that self-exclusion on this particular point, at this particular moment, leaves her, as one critic puts it, 'isolated from the very social structure that her courage and vitality have done so much to enliven and renew'.[11] Moll's hovering at the margins of comic closure is just one more instance of the continual slippage her character undergoes – between genders, between social groups, between fictional and historical personae.

The Grotesque Body of the Fair: Ursula in *Bartholomew Fair*

The Roaring Girl was open and direct about its efforts to soften some of Mary Frith's reputed criminal associations when presenting the dramatic character of Moll.* In Ben Jonson's *Bartholomew Fair*, performed at the Hope theatre in 1614, an entirely fictional female character, Ursula *'a pig-woman'* (i.e. seller of pigs), is by contrast made an unabashed representative of London's underworld. Indeed, she is the focus for many of the kinds of activity for which Mary Frith had been repeatedly hauled before the courts: associating with rogues and cutpurses, 'fencing' for stolen goods, and pimping for prostitutes. That Ursula's self-sufficiency as a working woman is partly secured through such amoral activities is testament to patriarchal assumptions about the value of a woman's pursuit of independent means in the first place. These assumptions were particularly nuanced in early modern England by the period's special emphasis on the creation of a domestic sphere and the 'enclosure', as it has been called, of women into it.[12] As we shall see in what follows, Ursula's status as self-sufficient woman, making an independent living by whatever dubious means, becomes associated during the play with a world passing out of fashion, rather than with something challenging in its novelty. The play in that sense builds her up into one of the more memorable figures in Jacobean comedy, only to bring her crashing down.

Bartholomew Fair dates from Jonson's later, less acerbic phase of dramatic satire, gathering together an amazingly rich (in some ways proto-Dickensian) cast of rich idiots, incompetents, hypocrites and grotesques, and publicly exposing their personal and moral flaws at the venue of London's annual summer fair. As well as hosting a dazzling array of amusements, the Fair as Jonson presents it is a byword for gluttony, debauchery and drunkenness, and the main locus for these activities is Ursula's 'booth' where she roasts the pigs and sells them to customers, and provides a kind of thoroughfare for the petty criminals who in turn prey on these visitors.[13] She thus provides a central figure in terms of the play's dramatic space; but a number of important aspects of characterisation also combine to separate her from all the other

---

* See in particular the Epistle to the play's printed version, in which Middleton admits that '[w]orse things ... the world has taxed her for than has been written of her; but 'tis the excellency of a writer to leave things better than he finds 'em'.

participants in the Fair, both consumers and hawkers. In the first place, she is not a central character in terms of the play's narrative logic: for all the raucous comedy that surrounds her and takes place in her booth, her role in the plot remains an insignificant one and it is possible to summarise the events of the play without reference to her. Second, she is, like Moll, alienated from prescriptive gender norms by reference to her body, although in this instance it is not via sartorial differentiation but by the fact of her gross physical corpulence. Typically, we find her situated in exclusively male company throughout the scenes in which she appears, and she converses with them on free and equal terms. Third, her confinement to an indoor domain, her place of work, with its seething ovens and sweaty mass of visitors who constantly keep the place teetering on the edge of chaos, functions as a parody of the normative idealisation of female domestic space – of home, hearth and family – through which Ursula appears as both 'enclosed' and uncontainable. In this respect Ursula's booth presents a parallel instance of the parodic use of space in *The Roaring Girl*, where Moll both invited and mocked the stereotype of the prostitute by being almost always found on the streets.

Ursula is from her first appearance defined by and through her physique, but she herself is responsible for much of this definition, vividly articulating her work-space and her body's relation to it:

> Fie upon't! Who would wear out their youth and prime thus in roasting of pigs, that had any cooler vocation? Hell's a kind of cold cellar to 't … I am all fire and fat … I shall e'en melt away to the first woman, a rib, again, I am afraid. I do water the ground in knots as I go, like a great garden-pot; you may follow me by the S's I make.[14]

Comparisons of Ursula with Falstaff are inevitable and perhaps deliberately invited; but these extend not just to the phenomenon of her girth and the accommodations others must make for it (she rounds on her tapster for not letting out the sides of her chair) but also in her control over simile and metaphor: she herself outdoes, like Falstaff, all comparisons that others can venture about her shape and size, often making familiar use of biblical analogy to do so. This particular mode of rhetorical assertiveness is unusual for a female character, and the sense of Ursula's easy incursion into male preserves of activity is furthered by her nonchalant smoking of tobacco and her connoisseur's understanding of the bottling and drinking of ale. There is no suggestion here of gender confusion, however. The observation of Justice Overdo, sitting disguised in her booth to observe the misdemeanours of the Fair, that Ursula's entire operation is the 'very womb and bed of enormity, gross as herself' reinforces the sense that this an emphatically female space, and Ursula herself literally marks it out as such by watering it – rendering the ground fertile – with her sweat.

Other references to her physique expand on the theme of its seemingly fluid physical properties – a conventional feature of 'humours'-based satire, but one with added misogynistic resonance in a belief system that construed women as less physically continent and more liable to overflow their bodily boundaries than men (compare Count Orsino's conviction in *Twelfth Night* that women's bodies 'lack retention'). One stage direction requires Ursula to '*come … in again dropping*', that is to say sweating profusely; and one wonders how far the male performer relied on the power of inference to create this effect and how far he went to mimic its physical actuality. Women's toil in the workplace was not normally characterised so overtly in terms of the by-products of its physical labour, even if the effect here is to mystify her sweat as a property of the woman's physique rather than of her work at the roasting-spit.[15] In a later scene she is singled out by two of the play's young protagonists, fortune-hunting 'gallants', for a litany of disparaging physical comparisons:

> QUARLOUS: Is she your quagmire? Is this your bog? … he that would venture for 't, I assure him, might sink into her, and be drowned for a week … 'Twere like falling into a whole shire of butter … (II.v.82–9)

The range of similes explored throughout the exchange between the men ('too fat to be a Fury', 'some walking sow of tallow', 'an inspired vessel of kitchen stuff'), in a frequently interrogative tone, bespeaks the lack of fixity to which her physical presence gives rise in their minds. This creates a sense not of ambivalence, however, as in *The Roaring Girl*, but of the 'grotesque' – a much commented-on comic idiom in the Renaissance which represents bodies as fundamentally unstable entities and provokes mingled responses of disgust and mirth.[16] Ursula's reaction to these taunts is to fix her physical identity in her own terms, in a way which eroticises her – 'Ay, ay, gamesters, mock a plain plump soft wench o' the suburbs, do, because she's juicy and wholesome' – and opposes an appetising sexual plenitude to the meagre fare offered by the courtesans obtainable at a rival leisure institution, the 'lean playhouse poultry, that has the bony rump sticking out' (II.v.75–95).

Attempts by Ursula to fend off the dehumanising insults of the gallants begin to founder when she loses control of the rhetorical high ground on which she constructs her own metaphors of self. As an observer of the incident comments, 'Where's thy Bartholomew-wit, now? Urs ...?' (II.v.91). In its place she resorts to scolding followed by physical attack, with the use of a red-hot 'pig-pan' taken from the fire; an action in which she comes off the worse, scalding her own leg as the men flee. This defeat functions partly as satirical comeuppance for one who is known, after all, to have been 'punk, pinnace, and bawd' in her career (II.ii.69–70), and partly as a typical Jonsonian quashing of female assertiveness. But the play requires us to read it as rather more than that, too, given the heavy investment it has made throughout these scenes in Ursula's symbolic presence. Much of this symbolism works to keep nudging her outside the frame of Jonson's realistic social commentary and towards an older form of dramatic representation, in which stage figures have allegorical and mythological functions. So the booth where she roasts the pigs, which makes 'Hell ... a cold cellar' by comparison, may well have been positioned on stage to comically evoke the 'hell-mouth' of medieval stage tradition. By the same token, classical references abound in others' descriptions of her: as a 'pillar of the fair' she is kind of female Atlas; as a 'pig-woman' she may have associations with the goddess of fertility, Demeter, but also, as the inhabitant of a somewhat sinister 'bower', Circe, who turned men to swine; and after she is wounded there is even a mock apotheosis (the fate of classical heroes) with the promise that she will return to 'shine Ursa Major'.

Ursula thus seems suspended midway between the emblematic and the grittily everyday: apparently irreconcilable qualities which are nonetheless well encompassed in her 'grotesque' person. As commentators on the play agree, Ursula functions most obviously as an embodiment of the Fair itself, presiding over its saturnalian overindulgence and its general relaxation of bodily inhibitions, as well as its unsavoury underworld which lurks to take advantage of the festivity. At the time Jonson was writing, the Fair was beginning to change its character, adapting to the commercialisation and privatisation of many areas of city life, and losing some of its flavour as a domain of spontaneous, communal exchange. The traditional market was, as Susan Wells puts it, 'becoming marginal, slowly being replaced by the private shop' and morphing into a 'location of exchange and profit rather than a gathering space, a common space'.[17] The figure of Ursula can perhaps be seen as freezing this moment of change, its contradictory forces physically articulated in a private space which is also a public confluence and a woman who is at the fount of the Fair's primal activities of enjoyment as well as its most sordid exploitative mechanisms. Her defeat in the confrontation with the two gallants thus has the suggestions of a self-defeat. As she collapses under her own weight and is shunted offstage, she cedes ground to the savvy young men who properly understand how to seek a fortune in this rapacious new environment.

Domestic Inversions: *The Witch of Edmonton*

Both Moll and Ursula resist assimilation to the domestic sphere, instead operating freely – in the first instance as inveterate consumer, in the second as consummate producer – through civic spaces ordinarily marked out for the activities of the city's male population. At the same time, they pose no definitive challenge to the ideologies that lay behind the creation of that sphere, and in Moll's case she is even (rather improbably) co-opted into reinforcing them. As eccentric, marginal figures in Jacobean city comedies, both women can suggest exciting and subversive possibilities about female independence and self-sufficiency without these ideas issuing into genuine narrative threat. Tragedy (or in the case of the play we will look at next, tragicomedy) presents a rather different case since threats are inevitably realised, this time through the agency of a witch who revenges herself on her village. At the same time, she attracts the blame for an act of murder within a marital unit of the kind frequently idealised in comedy: that of a rich yeoman's daughter to a young if impoverished man of the gentry class. In dramatising this narrative of breakdown and recrimination, the play exposes the victimisation of socially marginal figures which drove the mania for witch-hunting, but it also sets out an inversion of bourgeois domestic norms which is at times sharply satirical, at others deeply disquieting.

The Witch of Edmonton, written for performance both at the public theatre and at court in 1621, was the work of at least three dramatists (the names Thomas Dekker, William Rowley and John Ford are followed by an '&C.' on the title page), combining their efforts in order to capitalise on a sensational witch trial documented that same year in a pamphlet, *The Wonderful Discovery of Elizabeth Sawyer a Witch, late of Edmonton*. The play dramatises some of the events related in Sawyer's 'confession' (she had already been convicted and was in jail awaiting execution by the time this was extracted from her), in particular the bewitching to death of a neighbour, Agnes Ratcleife, with whom she had had a local dispute, and her conference with the Devil in the form of black dog whom she entertained as her 'familiar'. These documentary elements are worked into a larger, invented narrative framework involving an unusual angle on the forced marriage theme: Frank Thorney has already secretly married a serving girl, Winnifride, but reluctantly succumbs to pressure from his father to marry where the family estate can be salvaged from debt. When the young man murders his new wife, Susan, to escape the perils of bigamy (assisted in his task by the devil-dog, who keeps a canine eye out for anyone tempted to do evil), the two strands are brought together, but without any knowledge or positive intervention from Sawyer herself. It is the Dog, not the witch, who provides the narrative bridge here. Nonetheless, at the play's conclusion, when she is being taken off to execution, we watch as her own crimes become run together with those of the bigamist's in the accusations of the villagers:

> OLD CARTER: Did you not bewitch Frank to kill his wife? He could never have done 't without the devil.
> ELIZABETH SAWYER: Who doubts it? But is every devil mine?
> […]
> OLD CARTER: Thou didst bewitch Anne Ratcliffe to kill herself.
> ELIZABETH SAWYER: Churl, thou liest! I never did her hurt.[18]

Sawyer denies all accusations indifferently: it no longer matters what she says since the villagers are now evidently projecting onto her the rage and guilt they feel towards their own part in fomenting the social conditions which have led to the wife murder. A further plot element which leads nowhere in dramatic terms – the young man's first wife has already been seduced by a local squire – only serves to reinforce the theme of youth exploited by an unscrupulous older generation. In some powerful but not easily defined way, it is the old woman, Elizabeth Sawyer, who, despite her negligible bearing on these particular events, ends up the scapegoat for the socially destructive tendencies circulating within the community.

Sawyer's entry into the play only occurs once all the principal characters and narrative complications relating to the marital arrangements have been introduced. She appears immediately after the main protagonist, now secretly committed to bigamy, closes the previous scene with his forlorn aside: 'No man can hide his shame from heaven that views him / In vain he flees whose destiny pursues him' (I.ii.235–6). The play's shift in tone from romantic comedy towards domestic tragedy, rapidly effected over the two opening scenes, transfers ominously onto our first view of the solitary old woman, and assists the impression of a manufactured link between the two narratives. Her poverty, isolation and vulnerability are all neatly encapsulated in the single action of her '*gathering sticks*' for firewood, which she performs while rehearsing the injustices which have set her against the local community:

> And why on me? Why should the envious world
> Throw all their scandalous malice upon me?
> 'Cause I am poor, deformed and ignorant,
> And like a bow buckled and bent together
> By some more strong in mischiefs than myself,
> Must I for that be made a common sink
> For all the filth and rubbish of men's tongues
> To fall and run into? Some call me a witch,
> And, being ignorant of myself, they go
> About to teach me how to be one ... (II.i.1–10)

The speech creates sympathy for its speaker by generating a powerful sense of dramatic subjectivity, drawing close attention to her physical frame – 'deformed' and 'bent' – and connecting this with her own sense of subjection in the face of the constructions others put on her body. More powerfully still, although Sawyer retains a clear sense of her own selfhood (l. 9), she goes on to admit that the relentless accusations of bewitching cattle and babies, which 'they enforce upon me', partly prompt her to 'credit it', that is to say to believe them herself (ll. 11–15).

That these are specifically patriarchal assumptions is suggested not just by the reference to 'men's tongues' but also by the beating which follows at the hands of a hostile local landowner, Banks, who will not suffer her to '[g]ather a few rotten sticks' from his land. He blames the old woman's habit of '[c]ursing' for the physical violence which he inflicts on her, but at this stage the curses she levels at him are clearly scolds and not magical imprecations, for all their fulsome malice ('convulsions stretch and crack thy sinews!').[19] The episode sorely points up the privilege of patriarchy in being able to ignore the distinction between these two categories in the case of female utterance – to perceive 'swearing and cursing blended', as the source pamphlet puts it – while maintaining a separation in terms of its own utterances.* Bank's ready assumption that he is being cursed in earnest ignores the fact that neither the name of God nor that of any other supernatural entity is on Elizabeth Sawyer's lips at this point. A 'bad tongue' (l. 11) in the case of a solitary (and therefore ungovernable) woman is imbued with a magical effectiveness; yet it is the power of male verbal abuse which makes someone what they are in the eyes of society, which names them and identifies them, as Sawyer herself recognises in her soliloquy.+ The extent to which it is the scolding aspect of her behaviour which remains her chief affront to patriarchy is suggested by a much later scene when she is interviewed by a local Justice. He is initially sceptical of the villagers' claims of witchcraft and is willing to act as her protector, but subsequently becomes wary of her when she continues to heap 'saucy and bitter' abuse on her accusers (IV.i.93). The fact that Sawyer at the same time indulges in the kind of satirical rhetoric usually associated with the male malcontent – making witchcraft a global metaphor for corruption in all levels of society (ll. 116–59) – only arouses suspicions further.

The episode of her beating in II.i. culminates in Sawyer turning her thoughts towards entering into the very role that society has defined for her:

> What is the name? Where and by what art learned?
> What spells, what charms or invocations
> May the thing called Familiar be purchased? (II.i.34–6)

---

* Shakespeare's *The Taming of the Shrew*, about as anti-feminist a work as could be expected in this regard, perhaps acknowledges this association in its very adoption of the 'shrew' epithet over that of the 'scold', since there existed a long-established association of the shrew with influences that were malignant and satanic.

+ Again, we may compare Petruchio's primary tactic for subduing Kate in *The Taming of the Shrew* in his contradictory naming of objects, the moon as the sun and then the sun as the moon, in order to force her acquiescence: 'What you will have it named, even that it is / And so it shall be so for Katherine', IV.v.21–2. Male prerogative in naming things is usually referred back to Adam in the Garden of Eden – 'whatsoever Adam called every living creature, that was the name thereof' – and in Shakespeare's play this right of naming can be read as a kind of counteraction to the independent verbal power wielded by Katherine before she is 'tamed'.

After a further unpleasant encounter with the landowner's clottish son, the 'Familiar' in the form of the Dog duly appears before Sawyer, making use of a cue similar to the one which led to her beating – 'Ho! Have I found thee cursing? Now thou art mine own' – although it is her specific descent into blaspheming which allows him to be brought into league with her (II.i.119–22, 128). There follows the now standard Faustian bargain exchanging magical powers for the possession of her soul, although it is in keeping with her socially disempowered state that, unlike Faustus, this choice is forced upon her. Again, sympathy for Sawyer's distressed economic situation is allowed to guide the audience's understanding of her motive and circumstance, with the play drawing a metaphorical link between her tormentor Banks, whom she describes as a 'black cur / That barks and bites, and sucks the very blood / Of me and of my credit' (II.i.123–5) and the physical form of the devil when he appears immediately afterwards. It was a staple of the domestic tragedy genre, best exemplified in *Arden of Faversham*, that the economic abuse of the poor is made a root cause of social discontent, and the momentary equation the play makes here between the cruel landowner and the devil which will shortly become her 'familiar' allows the audience to grasp that relationship in moral terms. This does not turn into any sustained challenge to the social order itself, however: when Sawyer demands the devil's assistance in revenge, the Dog claims – in defiance of the play's presentation of the man's character – that the landowner is 'loving to the world / And charitable to the poor', and cannot be harmed by infernal powers. The old woman's justifiable complaint is thus speedily revised as an individual instance of antipathy.

Sawyer's relationship with the Dog is to be central in orchestrating audience responses towards her during her subsequent career in witchcraft. He himself is a great dramatic creation: wryly articulate (in between a chorus of Bow, wows), independent and unpredictable, his appeal is conveyed to us not just through Sawyer but also through Banks's clownish son, who semi-adopts him despite being on the receiving end of much of his mischief. This helps give a wider dimensionality to the character than, for example, Marlowe's Mephostophilis had enjoyed, but also points up distinctions in the handling of class and gender that will have implications for the fates of his victims. Dog's deceitful leading of young Banks into a bog during a pretended assignation with a local maid in III.i is played with strong elements of physical comedy, and towards the end of the play Dog defines their relationship as one which has 'used [Banks] doggedly, not devilishly' (V.i.118). Dog's part in the drama's central act of domestic violence, Frank Thorney's stabbing to death of Susan, is not in itself experienced as terrifying because it plays comically on themes of canine loyalty and assistance (e.g. helping Frank's alibi by tying him to a tree) and because it presents him as merely enabling the evil deeds of others rather than actively setting them on ('The mind's about it now. One touch from me / Soon sets the body forward', III.iii.2–3).

These scenes of Dog's diabolic interaction with young, gentry-class males turn out to be either dismissive or evasive about the young men's spiritual fates, and contrast strongly with his relationship with the socially marginalised and impoverished old woman. Not only is the spiritual outcome of this established from the start, but Sawyer's oft commented-upon personal 'ignorance' assists the sense of inevitability in the final outcome. Crucial here in manipulating audience sympathies is the play's head-on engagement with some of the most unsavoury aspects of witchcraft lore, particularly the female witch's 'suckling' of her familiar with blood drawn from an unnaturally positioned teat on the body.[20] One scene shows the Dog begging for this favour and, when he is denied (it would be off-limits for the stage to show any such thing), invited to 'tickle', that is to say embrace lasciviously, with Sawyer instead (IV.i.166 ff.). Her language towards him furthers the sense of an erotic doting upon the Dog, perhaps drawing on satirical tropes about courtly women's affection for their pet animals: 'my dainty / My little pearl! No lady loves her hound / Monkey or parakeet, as I do thee' (ll. 175–7). It is language that becomes even more fully eroticised in the scene where the Dog finally abandons her to her fate (see V.i.1–23).

The conflation of maternal and sexual behaviour in the space of this short sequence has the effect of creating for Elizabeth Sawyer the conjugal and domestic sphere which the play has so pointedly alienated her from.* It does so, of course, as a transgressive imitation of that sphere, taking the form partly of parody, as we suggested Ursula's pig-booth did, and partly of inversion. Dog is rather like the newly equable master, returning from the public world to feign parity with his partner and to be catered for by her. Inversion – the upending of the natural order – was what witches did, and by putting increasing emphasis on Sawyer's violations in this respect the play can position her as the principal transgressor of the family unit rather than Frank Thorney or the exploitative older generation of men.[21] At such points the play's shifting of the locus of blame onto the female violator of domestic order seems to evoke another work also using the theme of witchcraft: Shakespeare's *Macbeth*. In this latter play the witches' chant, 'fair is foul and foul is fair', and their unsettling, half male, half female appearance in the early stages of the play, function to wipe clean the existence of natural distinctions, creating a blank slate in preparation for the full inversion of the norms of domesticity which Lady Macbeth will go on to perform.[22] She, like Sawyer, confounds maternal and sexual impulses, invoking the forces of darkness both to 'unsex me here' and to come to her 'woman's breasts / And take my milk for gall' (I.v.40–54). She seems guided not by the desire to be sex*less*, but to reverse what she recognises as her woman's natural state and to usurp the masculine prerogative of seizing the crown by 'the nearest way' – murder – which, as she correctly anticipates, her husband will be too reluctant to follow. Although it is of course Macbeth who ultimately does the deed, the play hints strongly in these early stages that she would perform the murder herself, so long as her 'keen knife see not the wound it makes' in the darkness (l. 52).

The final scene of *The Witch of Edmonton* sees both witch and wife murderer taken off to execution, and while both are heard to repent

---

* \Those who knew the pamphlet on Elizabeth's Sawyer's trial would have been aware of its references to her husband and children – brief ones, but important in establishing someone who was part of a family group and whose career in witchcraft represented a violation of established domestic relationships. The play, as several critics point out, makes Sawyer a completely isolated and solitary figure from the start, with no hint of a family around her.

of their evil deeds, Sawyer is hounded to the last by the unforgiving mob who seem only interested in provoking her towards fresh cursing, despite her efforts at public penitance:

> These dogs will mad me. I was well resolved
> To die in my repentance.
> [...]
> Have I scarce breath enough to say my prayers,
> And would you force me to spend that in bawling?
> (V.iii.42–50)

Thorney, by contrast, is allowed a fulsome repentance and forgiveness by all those he has wronged, and he is even granted the privilege of restoring the damaged family ideal when he asks (and receives) his father's blessing and entrusts Winnifride into the care of his second wife's family. The play's 'enforced marriage' narrative thus ends on a tragicomic note – a triumph over death and a hostile fate – made possible by transferring all of its malaise onto the muted tragedy of Elizabeth Sawyer.

Notes

1   William Shakespeare, *The Taming of the Shrew*, ed. G.R. Hibbard, in *Four Comedies* (London: Penguin, 1996), V.ii.145–50. Many readers will be relieved to know that modern-day actresses have found inventive ways of getting round any hint of sincerity in this speech: for example, Paola Dionisotti's rendition in a 1978 RSC production, when it became clear that her character had been lobotomised. See *Cambridge Companion to English Renaissance Drama*, p. 114.

2   Catherine Belsey, 'Disrupting Sexual Difference: Meaning and Gender in the Comedies', in *Alternative Shakespeares*, New Accents Series (London: Routledge, 1985), pp. 167–89, p. 177.

3   On the way in which gender issues can become entangled with wider social concerns, see Mary Beth Rose, *The Expense of Spirit: Love and Sexuality in English Renaissance Drama* (London: Cornell University Press, 1988), ch. 2. 'Sexual Disguise and Social Mobility in Jacobean City Comedy'.

4   Stephen Orgel, 'The subtexts of "The Roaring Girl"', in *Erotic Politics: Desire on the Renaissance Stage*, ed. Susan Zimmerman (London: Routledge, 1992), pp. 12–26, p. 21.

5   See Jean Howard, 'Cross-dressing, The Theatre, and Gender Struggle in Early Modern England', in *Shakespeare Quarterly*, vol. 39, no. 4 (Winter 1988), pp. 418–40, pp. 420–1.

6   See Orgel, p. 13.

7   Thomas Middleton and Thomas Dekker, *The Roaring Girl* in *Plays on Women*, Revels Student Editions, ed. Kathleen E. McLuskie and David Bevington (Manchester: Manchester University Press, 1999), Prologue, lines 15–26.

8   For a cogent resume of the scientific beliefs about the body and the formation of the sexes see the introduction to *Plays on Women*, pp. 52–4.

9   William Shakespeare, *King Henry VI, Part 1*, ed. Edward Burns, Arden, 3rd series (London: Cengage Learning, 2000), I.ii.89–93.

10   On this point see in particular the discussion in Mary Beth Rose, *The Expense of Spirit*, pp. 86–92.

11   Rose, *The Expense of Spirit*, p. 91.

12   See Peter Stallybrass, 'Patriarchal Territories: The Body Enclosed', in *Rewriting the Renaissance: The Discourse of Sexual Difference in Early Modern Europe*, ed. Margaret Ferguson, Maureen Quilligan and Nancy Vickers (Chicago: University of Chicago Press), pp. 123–42.

13   For a discussion of Jonson's inevitable focus on the 'pleasure fair' rather than the commercial fair in which most of the business was transacted, see Jonathan Haynes, *The Social Relations of Jonson's Theatre* (Cambridge: Cambridge University Press, 1992), pp. 122 ff.

14   Ben Jonson, *Bartholomew Fair*, New Mermaids, ed. G.R. Hibbard (London: A & C Black, 1994), II.ii.41–52.

15   Michael Hattaway makes the point that it was rare enough to acknowledge this kind of labour at all: 'The productive work that women might do (like that done by men) tended not to be portrayed in the drama, and the only available indices of female virtue were modesty, sexual chastity, and wifely constancy', in 'Drama and Society', *The Cambridge Companion to English Renaissance Drama*, pp. 91–126, p. 107.

16   See Neil Rhodes, *Elizabethan Grotesque* (London: Routledge & Kegan Paul, 1980) in general, and ch. 7 on 'Jonsonian grotesque' in particular for discussion of the theme's use in this play. For the political, rather than just the literary and moral, implications of the grotesque, now frequently explored on literature courses, see Michael Bakhtin, *Rabelais and His World*, trans. Hélène Iswolsky (Indiana: Indiana University Press, 1984).

17   Susan Wells, 'Jacobean City Comedy and the Ideology of the City', in *English Literary History*, vol. 48, 1981, pp. 37–69, p. 38.

18   William Rowley, Thomas Dekker and John Ford, *The Witch of Edmonton*, Revels Student Editions, ed. Peter Corbin and Douglas Sedge (Manchester: University of Manchester Press, 1999), V.iii.26–33.

19   On the relationship between witchcraft and cursing, see Keith Thomas, *Religion and the Decline of Magic: Studies in Popular beliefs in Sixteenth- and Seventeenth-Century England* (Harmondsworth: Penguin, 1991; 1971) pp. 599–611. As Thomas points out, although Protestantism characteristically denied the magical properties of the curses themselves, it upheld the view that they could nonetheless act as petitions to the Almighty who might go on to enact them, especially in the case of injuries to the poor.

20   This was, inevitably, the cue for much degrading surveillance of the bodies of women (especially elderly ones) for growths or marks which could be deemed an unnatural duct for the nourishment of familiars. See Thomas, *Religion and Decline of Magic*, p. 530.

21   See in particular, Stuart Clark, *Thinking With Demons: The Idea of Witchcraft in Early Modern Europe* (Oxford: Clarendon Press, 1997), pp. 69–79.

22   William Shakespeare, *Macbeth*, ed. Kenneth Muir, Arden, 2nd series (London: Routledge, 1984), I.i.11.

Nation-Building

In the discussion that follows we will look at the possibility that the literature of Shakespeare's day, including some of his own plays, could be involved in the process of 'nation-building' – that is, the fostering of a national identity among the people of England. There are complexities involved with this approach. The idea of nation as used by Renaissance writers does not precisely overlap with the one in currency today. Plays, poems, treatises and proclamations in sixteenth-century England frequently refer to the English as a 'nation' in a way that closely parallels what we think of now as an ethnic identity. Thus when English Renaissance writers refer to this or that 'nation' they are often drawing on the word's Latin sense, *natio*, implying a fantasy (it could hardly be a fact) of a community united by birth (i.e. common descent).* This is at some distance from the abstraction implied by the modern idea of the nation state, which describes a political, linguistic and geographical entity which only secondarily (or speciously) includes a common ethnic identity.+ Some historians and commentators have argued that this more abstract definition is the product of a later, post-revolutionary age in

---

* This sense would be readily grasped from its transmission through the Bible, with its readings of the Jews as a single 'nation' (who significantly lacked a common territory), traceable back to a common progenitor.
+ The twentieth and twenty-first centuries have been familiar with a kind of nationalism that attempts to collapse the idea of national identity back into that of ethnic identity.

which the nation-state replaces older forces commanding the loyalty of the populace, such as royal or religious authority.* Pointing to the monarchical government and the less defined sense of community in Shakespeare's England, such historians have felt that the period accordingly lacked a true idea of nationhood.

This viewpoint has been challenged by cultural historians working in the early modern field who find that there is much going on in the Tudor and Stuart periods which points towards a conception of English nationhood along recognisably modern lines. In particular, the upheavals of the 1530s created the need for an English collective identity which went further in establishing unity than the older, vaguer sense of *natio* could manage. This was the period which saw Henry VIII break from submission to papal authority and launch the country as a whole on its turbulent journey away from Catholicism and towards a reformed style of religion. (For discussion see Part Two: 'A Cultural Overview'.) Two formative pieces of legislature lay at the heart of these events. The Act in Restraint of Appeals of 1533 declared that 'this realm of England is an empire ... governed by one supreme head and King' to whom a 'body politic, compact of all sorts and degrees of people' owed absolute obedience. There would henceforth be no sources of authority outside those of the English state. The Act of Supremacy of the following year, 1534, declared that Henry was 'the only supreme head on earth of the Church in England', thus explicitly bringing the country's institutions of belief directly under the jurisdiction of the crown. Both Acts hailed into being an England that was exclusive (it had 'always' existed in an independent condition) and exclusionary (it was opposed to foreign, and particularly papal, forms of control). One consequence of this move was that it more closely identified the ruler with the country, the state with the nation: England and its monarch were suddenly bound together in a way that suggested a mutual dependence and a mutual definition.

Early Protestant defenders of the break with Rome seized on this identification of the state with the nation to urge the sovereign's absolute

---

* By 'post-revolutionary' is meant the period following the American and French revolutions of the late eighteenth century, which occurred in 1776 and 1789 respectively.

authority over his or her subjects. Rebellion against the monarch was seen as rebellion against God's divinely ordained plan for the people of England as they moved, under the ruler's initiative, towards reformation in the church. Infused with a belief in God's special election of a chosen few for salvation, the idea developed over the course of the century that this plan encompassed England as an elect nation. A crucial text in providing the impetus to this line of thinking was John Foxe's *Acts and Monuments of these Latter and Perilous Days* of 1563, informally known as the 'Book of Martyrs', which told of the struggles of English Protestants during the middle part of the sixteenth century under Mary I. As the country swung from Protestantism to Catholicism and back again, belief was strengthened among the prevailing reformist side that their trials were evidence of England's special status. Later, with England's independence affirmed by the spectacular victory over the Spanish Armada in 1588, this was to develop into the view that the English were *the* elect nation, God's Chosen People appointed to deliver all other nations from bondage to Rome and superstition.[1] A point of tension arising out this set of ideas, which we will need to bear in mind for what follows, is that England felt itself bound to assist the other Protestant populations of Europe who were imperilled by Counter-Reformation forces, in part through accepting them as immigrants (as in the case, for example, of the French Huguenots fleeing persecution in France). This incorporation of a foreign presence – of 'strangers', as they were called – into the English body politic as a matter of state policy ran up against the anti-foreign ethos generated by the initial break with Catholic Europe.

For students of literature, another key aspect of the changes in this period is the elevation of the vernacular – of the native English language – to a position of greater ideological significance than it had previously held. The 'universal' language of Latin, upheld by Roman Catholicism throughout Western Christendom as the medium for worship and for reading of the Bible, was decisively rejected by religious reformers in favour of the translation of sacred and liturgical books into the specific languages of Protestant countries: English, German, Dutch and so forth. Medieval Latin was now seen as a corrupt and unnecessary mediator between the original biblical texts (in Hebrew and Greek) and the native tongues which God had provided for the perfection of each nation.* The language of England's native literature and the language of its state religion now became one and the same, and the virtue of the one could be held to demonstrate the virtue of the other. Hence, for example, Edmund Spenser's *The Faerie Queene* (published 1590 onwards) promoted Protestant ideology through a verse form which was an attempt to surpass continental epic poetry (such as that of Dante) using the English native idiom. This issue of the promotion of the vernacular will come frequently to the fore in the plays we will look at in this discussion, where it also describes an antagonistic stance towards a mistrusted foreign influence. Taken together, the points mentioned here about the forces driving English nation-building suggest a process which has a number of facets, but which is founded on a sense of collective unity in the face of external threat and an increasing emphasis on self-sufficiency.

Land and Language: Negotiating English Nationhood in the Plays of the 1590s

The plays we will be looking at in this section emerge out of the heightened triumphalism and heightened anxiety of the post-Armada years, when England under Elizabeth seemed both more favoured by God's providence and more isolated from the Continent than ever before. This was the period that saw most of Shakespeare's history plays written and performed, with their (eventual) construction of a continuous narrative of English chronicle history leading up to the advent of the Tudors. It also included developments in city comedy which explored the possibilities of using native and parochial locations. Here we will look at examples from both genres to suggest that the plays of the 1590s negotiate a particular problem arising out of England's endeavours to affirm its separateness from other European countries. In the construction for the English of a

---

* One can compare this attitude with what was going on in the fields of rhetoric and poetry, where medieval Latin was seen as the degenerated version of the original, classical Latin.

national identity various factors, including ethnic and geographical ones, could be invoked to suggest their natural distinctiveness as a people, but a sense of their cultural distinctiveness remained a nagging doubt, since such borders were necessarily less easily policed than physical ones. The plays raise this doubt, and then answer it by reinforcing claims about the superiority of the English language over other tongues, demonstrating in a secular, theatrical context the integrity of the vernacular, which thus becomes the crucial mark of English identity.

Shakespeare's *Richard II* (1595) tells the story of the crisis of deposition which lay at the root of the narrative of late medieval English history dramatised by Shakespeare in his two tetralogies.* The England it depicts is denominationally Catholic, dynastically Plantagenet, feudal in its power structures (it sports a strong, competitive nobility) and chivalric in its culture (the play begins with a trial by combat between two nobles). The play is much concerned with the issue of 'sacred majesty' – the monarch's supposedly divine sanction for his or her office – and the consequences which follow from abuse of that office. Yet despite its focus on high-level politics, the play does not let us forget that the king's actions affect the country at large, and the narrative makes continual use of short exchanges and theatrical vignettes involving secondary characters to provide a summing-up of domestic affairs. In one of these, in the early stages of the play, two of Richard's uncles, the Duke of York and the now dying Duke of Lancaster, John of Gaunt, share their thoughts on the disaster which is hurtling towards the king and which they find they are powerless to prevent.[2] For the Duke of York, Richard's great problem is the company he keeps: young courtiers who encourage the king in a lavish lifestyle and reckless expenditure of money. Instead of restraining him with wise counsel, these courtiers ensure that his royal ear:

---

* See Part Three: 'Shakespeare's History Plays' for further discussion of the two tetralogies. The first in historical order includes *Richard II*, *Henry IV Part 1*, *Henry IV Part 2* and *Henry V*. The second includes *Henry VI Parts 1, 2* and *3*, and *Richard III*.

is stopped with other, flatt'ring sounds,
[...]
Lascivious metres, to whose venom sound
The open ear of youth doth always listen;
Report of fashions in proud Italy,
Whose manners still our tardy-apish nation
Limps after in base imitation. (II.i.17–23)

Extravagant investment in the latest continental fashions and cultural diversions ('lascivious metres' perhaps refers to erotic poetry) is supported in the time-honoured way: by taxing a population until they groan under the burden. While this is bad enough, for John of Gaunt the particular outrage is that Richard has raised money by effectively becoming the national landlord, leasing the country out to these same young courtiers who then tax the inhabitants as they please. His disgust at this 'farming' of his native land is expressed in what has become perhaps the most famous of all encomiums on England, endlessly anthologised and reproduced out of dramatic context:

This royal throne of kings, this sceptred isle,
This earth of majesty, this seat of Mars,
This other Eden, demi-paradise,
This fortress built by Nature for herself
Against infection and the hand of war,
This happy breed of men, this little world,
This precious stone set in the silver sea,
Which serves it in the office of a wall
Or as a moat defensive to a house
Against the envy of less happier lands,
This blessed plot, this earth, this realm, this England,
[...]
This land of such dear souls, this dear dear land,
Dear for her reputation through the world,
Is now leased out – I die pronouncing it –
Like to a tenement or pelting farm. (ll. 40–60)

While the complaints of both men are ostensibly rooted in the concerns of a particular historical moment 200 years before the writing of the play, they resonate with the fears and concerns of the late-Elizabethan England in which these lines were written.[3]

The Duke of York's remarks about English 'imitation' of foreign cultural influences echoes one of the talking points of the second half of the sixteenth century in England, when travellers returning from abroad, particularly Italy, were held in contempt for supposedly bringing new fashions in dress, new ideas about religion and politics (including atheism and Machiavellianism) and a whole 'new' repertoire of sexual habits (sodomy was a favourite accusation). Italy was, however, only the most prominent of a range of foreign targets, the cultural emulation of which was held to have an unwholesome, effeminising influence on the native culture at large. In 1588 a polemicist named William Rankins published a tract with the title *The English Ape, the Italian imitation, the Footsteps of France*, which lambasted 'our Englishmen [who] blinded with an Italian disguise and disfiguring themselves with every French fashion corrupt their natural manners, by their climate created perfect'.[4] York's remark about England as a 'tardy-apish nation' is evidently couched in this same caustic vein of late-Elizabethan complaint. The English are seen as not merely 'apish' in their ludicrous addiction to the fashions of other countries, but also as 'tardy' – that is, late – in their endeavours to keep up with them. As a country in an archipelago on the fringes of the continent, at some distance from the epicentres of innovation in fashion (Italy in particular), England was an irregular recipient in the process of European cultural transmission. As a consequence, a good deal of amusement was had at the caricature this produced of an Englishman who was an amalgam of fashions from all countries at once.[5] Rankins had at least assumed the existence of English 'natural manners' which lay submerged beneath the mania for emulation; but for Shakespeare's Duke of York it seems that the nation of 'base' imitators to which he belongs does not have a clearly fixed identity of its own.

As if in response to York's disappointment with a nation of 'limping' cultural copycats, John of Gaunt presents an England which is distinctive by virtue of its natural gifts, gifts which in turn create the character of the people who dwell in it. Rankins had maintained that the English were 'by their climate [i.e. general environment] created perfect', and in Gaunt's speech a comparable idea is traced in the notion of England as Nature's special preserve which, being proof against disease and war, generates a 'breed' who are 'happy' not merely in body but also in mind (possessors of 'dear souls'). The keynote in this differentiation of England from all other countries (one which quietly elides any mention of the Celtic nations who necessarily enjoy the same benefits) is that of self-sufficiency. England is, to use an image from later in the play, a 'sea-walled garden' (III.iv.43) which protects and nurtures its inhabitants while serving as a launching point for warlike endeavours and conquest of other countries (see l. 65). Gaunt's enumeration of England's attributes is wonderfully lyrical, yet it also helps to mystify a sense running throughout the speech of a nation which is under siege. England is a 'fortress', the sea a 'moat defensive' against the 'envy' of hostile powers, the country 'bound in' for its better good against immensely powerful assaults from outside (see l. 61 ff.). Late Elizabethan audiences would have recalled through such language the threat which they had faced less than a decade earlier in the attempted Spanish invasion and occupation of 1588. Acknowledgement of victory over the Armada was inseparable from an ever-present terror that a larger assault could occur at any time. As they watched the play, the fourteenth-century medieval Catholic world of Richard II would thus readily dissolve into a contemporary awareness of a collective identity which was defined defensively – through a sense of being separated, isolated, 'bound in'.

Race, Nation, Impersonation

Gaunt's argument about a political distinctiveness of the English which is founded on the natural advantages of their country points us towards a way of naturalising ideas about national characteristics through what has been called 'climate theory'. As Rankins implies when he uses the term, 'climate' here meant the whole physical surroundings of one's native country and its impact on the temperament of the people who lived in the hot, cold and intermediate zones of the world. The idea, and its close association with humoral theory, emerges clearly in Shakespeare's *Othello*, when Desdemona defends her husband from the accusation of jealousy: 'I think the sun where he was born / Drew all such humours from him'.[6] Physical environment is here seen to have a crucial effect on a person's character, but it is an effect that would be shared by all inhabitants equally rather than form part of an individual matrix of traits. As used in this particular play, of course, the concept is imbued with dramatic irony: Othello is in the process of transforming himself (via Iago's influence) from a man whom passion could not shake into the stereotype of the hot-blooded and possessive Moor from African climes. But this irony merely underscores the fact that climate theory could be used to support directly opposing arguments about national character while using precisely the same pieces of evidence. In Desdemona's view the heat of his native land makes of Othello an especially worthy – one might argue a superior – creature, since it evaporates the harmful humours that are not dispelled in cooler lands. In Iago's diabolic understanding, by contrast, Othello's hot country background has instilled a natural volatility ('these Moors are changeable in their wills') which can easily be manipulated towards murderous rage. Although there can be little doubt which point of view is expressly calculated to engage audience sympathy, the play nonetheless makes important tragic capital out of the idea of a difference of bodies between Othello and Desdemona. It is a difference which would be readily explicable in terms of the climate theory alluded to above, and which would carry the implication of a kind of natural incompatibility which was founded on their diverse origins. Iago again seems to be alluding to this idea when he insinuates to Roderigo that Desdemona's passion for him is merely a transient erotic phase, that soon she will find herself literally trying to expel him from her system, to begin to 'heave the gorge, disrelish and abhor the Moor' (II.i.230–1).

Iago's comments are about broad ethnic differences, comments that would nowadays be put within the framework of racist thinking. However, the same kind of ideology could percolate down into the construction of national differences. To the cocktail of factors which we have argued were combining to create the idea of nationhood in this period, we can add what might be called a protectionist tendency when it came to urging Englishmen and women to use native rather than foreign products. For example, in 1580 a physician named Timothy Bright published a tract arguing against the use of imported herbs and other plants in the preparation of drugs given that there was a 'diversity of complexion of our bodies from those of strange nations'.[7] God's providence, the argument went, had planted each country with what was good for its own particular inhabitants, and the impact of non-native produce on English bodies could be only either very weak or actively harmful. (One can see this argument becoming doomed in practical terms during an age of colonial expansion and 'plantation' in overseas colonies such as Ireland and the Americas, but as a theory it had no less validity than the arguments against foreign fashions.) Both Bright and Iago adopt the same kind of theoretical standpoint, arguing that some things are natural and appropriate for some bodies while others are not. Where Bright, however, is involved in firming up the sense of English nationhood by trying to nullify the effects of foreign trade, Iago gives this idea a racialised application by making it appear that Othello's *own* body is the indigestible toxin which Desdemona will soon find herself physically unable to tolerate. Seen this way, that is to say from a 'climatological' perspective, distinctions of race and nation emerge as differences of degree rather than kind, both ultimately explicable on the same theoretical basis. Indeed, one of the epithets used by Roderigo to describe Othello, 'stranger' (the full insult is 'an extravagant and wheeling stranger / Of here and everywhere', I.i.134–5), was the term typically used to describe foreigners in general.

The plays of the Elizabethan and Jacobean periods found the use of romantic plots highly amenable to the representation and reinforcement of racial and national differences. Moreover, distinctions of genre were frequently used to reflect the degree of difference between the principals that drives the narrative complications within the fiction. So while a tragedy such as *Othello* is played out across large geographic distances and through a romantic conflict charged with a sense of European and African alterity, just as *Antony and Cleopatra* is later to be, the genre of comedy tended to explore ideas of national identity through love plots operating within a more local framework. Operating somewhere between these two poles is a play like Shakespeare's *Merchant of Venice* (1596), where a foreign (i.e. Italian) setting is used to work out plots traversing problems of racial and national distinction. Not only is Portia contemptuous of her non-Venetian suitors (see the dialogue with Nerissa at I.ii.35-101), but she is openly dismissive of the first of them to attempt the challenge of the caskets on account of his (Moroccan) 'complexion' (II.vii.79). Through such stereotyping the satire of the English imitation of foreigners of the kind already used in *Richard II* could also be introduced, as when the young English suitor Falconbridge is described as 'oddly suited' in a mixture of European fashions (I.ii.70). The Englishman's inability to speak any foreign tongue – he has 'neither Latin, French, nor Italian' – is glanced at in similarly negative tones although, as we shall see in what follows, this will not always remain an insufficiency. The play locates much of its uneasy comedy in resolving the sexual tensions generated by the wooing of native women by foreign men, while endorsing the wooing of foreign women (such as Jessica) by Italian men.

A play by William Haughton from 1598, *Englishmen for My Money*, broaches the theme of national differences in a theatrically daring way. The play is the first in a long line of racy, sexy, City of London comedies which held the stage well into Jacobean times, and it takes the disguise and cross-dressing motifs which were endemic to the genre into fresh territory by allying them directly to anti-foreign sentiment. One of the by-products of this, as we shall argue below, is the unexpectedly favourable light which the play throws on ideas about English habits of 'imitation' of foreigners: that much-criticised tendency towards 'disfiguring' English 'manners' with a foreign exterior. The play itself readily invites a structural analysis, given its neat balancing of oppositions between groups of characters, and its clever manipulation of the polarities of national difference by the introduction of a median point between them. A wealthy Portuguese merchant named Pisaro, resident in London, has had three daughters by a (now deceased) Englishwoman and is determined to marry off the girls to an array of wealthy foreign suitors: a Dutchman, a Frenchman and an Italian. His daughters, however, are interested only in their English suitors, a fact which exasperates their father because his fortune has been built on exploiting these same young gentlemen, charging hefty interest on lands which they have mortgaged to him for spending money (a practice becoming increasingly notorious among gentry in the city). The mathematical symmetry of foreign to native suitors acts as more than just a pleasant conceit: it provides the opportunity for the girls, precisely balanced between each category in terms of their dual backgrounds, to express a clear bias which must be construed in nationalistic terms foremost (with class terms, i.e. breeding over wealth, coming second). As one of the girls declares fervently:

> Though I am Portingale [i.e. Portuguese] by the Father's side
> And therefore should be lustful, wanton, light;
> Yet Goodman Goosecap, I will let you know,
> That I have so much English by the Mother,
> That no base slavering French shall make me stoop.[8]

If any residual sexual tension attaches itself to the Portuguese merchant's marrying and propagating by an English woman, that situation is to be fully reclaimed by having his daughters first reject their Portuguese side and then go on to marry Englishmen. Although specific characters and pairings are strongly drawn in the play, it is clear that the daughters' preference for the Englishmen is not in itself an individuated one: the men are selected because of a generically perceived 'difference … / Betwixt an English Gentleman' and everyone else (ll. 1889–90).

These neat character groupings with their clearly demarcated identities are complemented by two individuals who demonstrate less overall fixity of character and who act as key initiators of stratagems and counter-stratagems. Pisaro himself, while self-identifying as Portuguese, is allowed to shift between different manifestations of foreignness, making of him a composite of characteristics associated with the untrustworthiness of strangers. At times, for example, he overlaps with the stereotype of the

Jew, announcing himself in boldly Marlovian terms as one who profits by 'the sweet loved trade of usury / Letting for Interest and on Mortgages' (ll. 19–20) and being lampooned by the English for his 'bottle nose' (l. 1423). Such characteristics, however, operate more as cases of opportunistic theatrical referencing (to Barabas from *The Jew of Malta*, to Shylock from *The Merchant of Venice*) than as specific markers of identity. In contrast to Pisaro's inadvertent character slippage, his main English antagonist in the play, Anthony, tutor to the three girls, deliberately occupies the role of master of disguise after he is fired by Pisaro for encouraging the match with the Englishmen, re-entering the merchant's service as a tutor of French. From this vantage point he can initiate the set of highly successful disguises which enable the girls to marry the Englishmen, including dressing one up as himself to let her out of the merchant's house, and dressing one of the Englishmen as a woman to let him in.* Anthony spends most of his time as an imitation foreigner, nominally a Frenchman, but dressed in the black cloak, black beard and black hat which provided the stereotype of continental 'not-us' attire equally associated with Spanish and Italians. He is thus a laudable 'English Ape', performing the role not of base imitator but of sly trickster out-tricking the strangers who are themselves conniving with Pisaro to get the girls by foul means.

Anthony's replacement role as tutor of language points up the key differential which enables the comic conclusion of the play: the ability to speak English properly. The three foreigners are represented as being as much a threat to the native language as to Pisaro's daughters, botching it (as the French doctor, Dr Caius, from Shakespeare's *Merry Wives of Windsor* (1597), also does) with 'rustic Phrases', 'Dutch French terms' and '[s]tammering half sentences' (ll. 958–9), but also raising the prospect of a kind of cultural miscegenation: as the clown Frisco begs the gentlemen in their pursuit of the girls, 'do not suffer a litter of Languages to spring up among us' (ll. 357–8). From his position inside the household Anthony discovers that the three foreign suitors have been primed by Pisaro to imitate the Englishmen in an underhand ruse to trick their way

---

* This male-to-female transvestism scenario was a lot less common an aspect of the fiction on the Renaissance stage than the girl-to-boy one. Here it is exploited to the full for its suggestive possibilities, e.g. when Pisaro lecherously courts 'her', and when 'she' emerges, still in female dress, married to one of the daughters and boasting of a consummation already performed.

into his daughters' bedchambers and decide the matter of who marries whom through sexual deception. Anthony's revelation of this plot to the girls relaxes any suspense that may attach to it, so that much of the comedy generated from here on can focus on the inept efforts of the three foreigners to approximate a passable English diction. This has been well prepared for by the play's depiction from an early stage of their impenetrable accents and mangling of the English language. The idea that they may succeed in deceiving the girls merely by changing their names is thus comically doomed from the start, as the Italian's excited response to the stratagem reveals:

> And I sall name me de signor Harvey, end monsieur Delion sall be de piculo signor Ned, end when madona Laurentia sall say, who be dare? mister Vandalle sall say, Oh my sout Laide, hier be your love Mestro Heigham: Is not dis bravissime, maister Vandalle? (ll. 1215–19).

Yet the play operates an outrageous double standard when it makes fun of the foreigners' linguistic struggles, for the English are almost universally represented as being unable to attempt any foreign tongue at all.* Anthony's disguise requires him to be master of languages, yet he is very nearly exposed when the Frenchman tries to converse with him in his mother tongue, only for the daughters to rescue him at the last minute. It is a key moment in the play, for it involves an important ideological crux. Anthony's imitation of a foreigner must be shown to be masterful (and it is), but this must not include any suggestion of acceptance of languages other than English. The normative point of view in the play involves an elevation of English via the rejection of other tongues, and particularly the half-breed languages gasped out by the foreign suitors: as Laurentia puts it to the Dutchman, 'you must learn sweeter English or I shall never understand your suit' (ll. 1090–1). This rejection manifests itself as a species of linguistic inviolability, a ring-fencing of the English language against an outside threat both through Anthony's providentially protected

---

* There is one exception, during the courting of one of the girls by an Englishman, where the context is, however, plainly parodic.

ignorance and through the girls' determination to retain a barrier between themselves and the strangers: 'If I speak English (as I can none other) / They cannot understand me, nor my welcome' (ll. 779–80).

We could say that Haughton's play reverses the idea expressed in *Richard II*, whereby the English are held to have strong natural advantages but an as yet unstable sense of their own cultural identity. In *Englishmen for My Money*, the English show a more secure collective identity, provided above all by their vernacular language, even as the main plot dissolves into a chaos of interchangeable, exchangeable bodies. The play's jaw-dropping finale, in which an Englishman appears in full '*Woman's attire*' with his new wife alongside him, underscores this sense of confidence, while also managing to stabilise things in time-honoured comedic fashion by pointing to the generation of new life:

> Nay stare not, look you here, no monster I,
> But even plain Ned: and here stands Matt[ea] my wife.
> Know you her Frenchman? But she knows me better.
> Father, pray father, let me have your blessing,
> For I have blest you with a goodly Son;
> Tis breeding here i'faith, a jolly Boy. (ll. 2655–62)

Ned does not need to step out of his disguise to assert his identity as an English gentleman before Pisaro and the others foreigners. Superior English wit has been demonstrated in the successful carrying-out of all deceptions leading to the marriages, and perhaps most importantly in the gentlemen's triumphant effort to 'work our lands out of Pisaro's Daughters / And cancel all our bonds in their great Bellies' (ll. 1921–2). This rush among the young men for territorial reclamation through the impregnation of the foreign merchant's daughters will doubtless strike modern readers as an unseemly one. However, it finds an echo in a play of the following year which is also much concerned with issues of nationhood, Shakespeare's *Henry V* (1599).

Laws of Nature and of Nations: *Henry V*

Henry V tends to invite the label 'nationalistic', and its corollary 'patriotic', more than any other of Shakespeare's plays (see the extended discussion of *Henry V* in Part Three: 'Shakespeare's History Plays'). As with *Richard II*, the play works into its portrayal of late medieval territorial disputes a specifically early modern idea of national identity which is anachronistic to the period it depicts.[9] In its portrayal of English martial prowess against the numerically superior French forces in the victory at Agincourt, and in its repeated stress on a 'band of brothers' which unites king, nobles and commoners against a foreign foe, the play can be seen as turning outwards the trope of self-sufficiency which, we have been suggesting, marked the positive construction of English nationhood in the period in which Shakespeare was writing. Henry's designs on the French crown are nominally dynastic in their origin, deriving from the ancestry of the English Plantagenet line in France. 'No king of England if not king of France,' he proclaims boldly at the beginning of the play, supplying the watchword by which he rehearses this ancestral claim and by which he establishes himself within the chivalric and honour-obsessed tradition of his forbears. Yet the play does not allow us to forget that Henry himself has come to the throne by his father's usurpation of the crown from Richard II. Moreover, it manages to compound this problematic situation by presenting a decidedly flimsy pretext for the conquest (or re-conquest, as the dynastic claim would rather see it) of French land in the dispute over the validity of the French Salic law which is used to debar English claims. Critics have thus frequently been tempted to read the play in terms of its fulfilment of the advice of Henry's father at the end of *Henry IV Part 1* to quell internal political dissension in the kingdom (especially among aggrieved nobles) by the use of a 'distraction agenda': to 'busy giddy minds / With foreign quarrels' (IV.v.213–14). This imposition of an artificial unity by means of outwardly directed aggression is an important tool in the process of nation-building.

Although the play disposes of any internal political opposition to the king himself early on by the exposure of the Southampton plot to assassinate him, it does continue to make use of internal distinctions in Henry's army which the military adventure can serve to unify, amassing together a host of regional dialects (which is of course a different thing from foreign 'broken English') all speaking in a common English tongue. Most famously, there are scenes involving, Irish, Scottish, Welsh and English captains all united under Henry in the campaign against the

French. This scenario allows for much entertaining friction of an ethnic and linguistic kind, while maintaining the English claim to superior national status. The theme is neatly emblematised in a hot-headed exchange between the Welsh and Irish captains, significantly on the theme of nationhood. Fluellen's challenge to the Irishman Macmorris that 'there is not many of your nation' present in the king's army prompts the outburst: 'Of my nation? What ish my nation? Ish a villain, and a bastard, and a knave, and a rascal? What ish my nation? Who talks of my nation?' (III.ii.123–6). Macmorris's touchiness suggests that he understands the applicability of the word to his native homeland as an ethnic slur (we have already noted its pejorative associations in this context). The 'joke', as such, would have had some resonance for audiences of 1599 given the current embroilment of the Earl of Essex in Ireland in order to quell Hugh O'Neill's uprising against English colonial interests there (a campaign later alluded to directly by the Chorus in V.0.29–34). Placing a denial, however inadvertent, of Irish nationhood into the mouth of one the country's inhabitants helps legitimise the long-standing assumption of English royal dominion in Ireland, and reinforces the aggressive Tudor policy of imposing authority over the country. By way of slyly emphasising this point, it is the English captain, Gower, who breaks up the contention between the Irishman and Welshman. At the same time, the play manages an equally sly nod towards the Welsh ancestry of the Tudor dynasty who were in power during Shakespeare's day by letting the Welshman have the better of the argument in the exchange, and indeed in having Henry claim (without any supporting evidence from history) Welsh blood of his own during a later conversation with Fluellen.[10]

After the spectacular victory at Agincourt, with the French army effectively destroyed, Henry is able to command what terms he pleases in order to make good his dynastic claims. He does not, however, choose to take the title of King of France, but elects to keep that honour for his future heirs by marrying the French king's daughter, Katherine, who thus becomes the human seal on his possession of conquered lands. This decision to waive his personal claim to the crown, and then spend a large amount of time wooing a lady who is already won as the 'capital demand' of the peace treaty, enforces a sense throughout the scene of a distance to be overcome – of a persistent 'rub or impediment' (to borrow terms used by the Duke of Burgundy) to unity between the kingdoms. This *ought* to be the moment at which antagonisms collapse with a reassertion of shared dynastic identity between French and English royal bloods, and liberal usage of the terms 'cousin' and 'brother' by both kings during the early exchanges acknowledges this.* Yet in the scene between Henry and Katherine what we get is a protracted, awkward, comically fumbled display of courtship in which differences of language and culture stand determinedly in the path of romantic and political union. One way of reading this is as a demonstration of the *success* of the nation-building project which the campaign in France has promoted. So completely identified has Henry become with the 'modern culture of personal achievement and national identity' that he no longer has an easy point of contact with the 'ideology of chivalry and hereditary nobility' which he has overpowered.[11] It is not simply a case of love-combat between two different nations in this scene, then. Henry is the representative of a principle of self-sufficient nationhood, whereas Katherine is an embodiment of the rich, familial network of alliances appropriate to a feudal power structure. A marriage of two minds is unlikely, the scene seems to be suggesting, unless somebody can find a way to break the impasse.

The handling of the 'communication problems' between wooer and wooed in this scene helps shape the sense of key differences between Henry and Katherine which go beyond the simple lack of a common tongue. In a play performed on an English stage the courtship is for obvious reasons largely conducted in English, and this of course is the language Katherine must learn (and has been seen to be learning in an earlier scene, III.iv) now that she is the subordinate party in a political alliance. Nonetheless, in Henry's insistence on plain speaking in a language unembellished by courtly conceits we can perhaps catch a glimpse, behind the explicit protestations of honest soldierly values, of a promotion of the virtues of the vernacular language, with its supposedly readier access to the truth of the heart as defined in Reformation ideology. Henry's side of the dialogue with Katherine is prosaic in its quality, pointedly contrasting, as critics often remark, with his soaring eloquence

---

* The shared ancestry in this case goes back to Phillip III of France, great grandfather on the female side of Edward III, who was Henry V's great grandfather.

on the field of battle. Through this idiom he equates his status with that of a commoner, while in the Crispin's Day speech he had elevated all ranks to his own level:

> I' faith, Kate, my wooing is fit for thy understanding. I am glad thou canst speak no better English, for if thou couldst thou wouldst find me such a plain king that thou would think I had sold my farm to buy my crown. I know no ways to mince it in love but directly to say 'I love you.' Then if you urge me farther than to say 'Do you in faith?', I wear out my suit. Give me your answer, i' faith do, and so clap hands and a bargain. How say you, lady? (V.ii.123–32).*

Just as important, however, is the careful separation Henry maintains between French and English in his addresses to Katherine. His first attempt to speak French to her at ll. 181–5 is clearly marked off by him as a distinct phase in their courtship; and while he interrupts himself in his search for the right phrasing, French and English syntactical units are kept intact (as they are again at ll. 213–15). Despite some faulty grammar his French is broadly correct, yet he nonetheless quickly dismisses the francophone enterprise with the disarming appeal to a very different kind of prowess: 'It is as easy for me, Kate, to conquer the kingdom as to speak so much more French.' Both the material fact of his conquest and his apparent (if self-deprecating) grasp of French allow him to reject Kate's language. By contrast, her own efforts to speak English consistently produce the hybrid form which, as we have seen, provided the object of mirth in Elizabethan comedies featuring foreigners: 'Your majesty 'ave *fausse* French enough to deceive de most *sage demoiselle* dat is *en France*' (ll. 216–17). Henry shows himself no exception in finding humour in this when he discreetly mocks her 'broken' English (l. 106, l. 241). Kate's attempt to work in two languages is not, like the king's, a carefully differentiated one. It symbolises a mish-mash of tongues, which counterpoises Henry's awareness of distinctiveness.

---

* Compare 'he today that sheds his blood with me / Shall be my brother, be he ne'er so vile / This day shall gentle his condition' at IV.iii.61–2.

One way of reading this difference between wooer and wooed in the handling of each other's language is to extrapolate from it a France which lacks the national self-identity enjoyed by England and embodied in Henry. The term 'nation' is never directly applied to France in the play, and its one association with the concept, made in Exeter's threat to the French king, goes so far as to suggest that France is usurping that privilege from England in the form of 'borrowed glories' that by 'law of nature and of nations' should belong to King Henry (II.iv.79–80). The term is by contrast associated with England, where it concludes the Archbishop of Canterbury's long speech on the workings of a properly ordered 'state of man', or body politic (I.ii.183–221), in which sense it suggestively foreshadows the idea of a 'nation-state'. The 'hardiness and policy' associated with the English here stand as a testament to the successful development of a self-sufficiency which, we have argued, was voiced in the exchanges between John of Gaunt and York in *Richard II*. Gaunt's speech on England's natural boons in that earlier play has its French equivalent in *Henry V* just prior to the wooing of Katherine, when the Duke of Burgundy eulogises his native land as 'this best garden of the world / Our fertile France', and laments the squandering of these gifts by the descent into 'savagery' and 'wildness' which has come from the war (V.ii.23–62). It is striking, however, that the blame for this ruination is not laid at the feet of Henry the invader of France. It is blamed on France herself, who in the absence of peace lies '[c]orrupting in her own fertility', devoid of the 'husbandry' which would order the realm, and of the 'arts' and 'sciences' which should provide its culture. Through Burgundy's speech we gain a sense that it is not by an assertion of her own nationhood that France must recover these things. Rather than a rejection of foreign cultures in the name of self-sufficiency, France is to submit herself to the ordering influence of a vigorous English nation state, a process symbolised in Henry's marriage to Katherine. The point is driven home in the moment when Henry breaches French protocol by kissing Katherine, to the outcry from both the princess and her gentlewoman that it is 'not a fashion' in France to kiss before marriage (l. 248 ff.). The development from *Richard II* seems complete. Far from submission to the 'nice custom' of another culture, this English king asserts his power not merely to uphold his own customs but to determine foreign ones, and to take his French queen with him: 'you and

I cannot be confined within the weak list of a country's fashion. We are the makers of manners, Kate ...' (ll. 267–9).

Nation and Assassination: Jacobean Readings of the Body Politic

The plays looked at above were notable for the emphasis they placed on unity against an external, specifically foreign, threat as a condition for England's development of a sense of national identity. In this section we will look at how that representational strategy shifts after the accession of James I towards a focus on an internal threat. With the change of dynasty after Elizabeth's death in 1603 to that of the Stuarts, beginning with the reign of James I, the Tudor Myth promulgated in the history plays of the 1590s such as *Henry V* was no longer of much importance to the political status quo. Further complicating the picture was the fact that with the change of dynasty came a change of the nationality of the monarch, for James I of England was also (and had been since 1567, when he was just over a year old) James VI of Scotland. The Protestant son of the deposed Catholic monarch Mary, Queen of Scots, who had caused Elizabeth one of the biggest crises of her reign by helping to foment a Catholic plot against her, James was seen as a welcome successor to Elizabeth. After an early period of hostilities there had been no serious political tensions with Scotland itself during Elizabeth's reign, and the two countries shared a common commitment to a reformed religion. Indeed, Protestant hopes for renewed reformation in the English Church, dampened during the decades of the Elizabethan Settlement, now sprang up again in the belief that James would pursue the policies his predecessor had neglected. These hopes were to be very quickly dashed; but there were good secular reasons as well for the early optimism invested in James's reign. Chief among these was the new king's sizeable family, which included (at the time of his accession) two male heirs, thus allaying the kind of uncertainties about a future succession which had so bedevilled Elizabeth's reign.

James was eager to unite England and Scotland under his rule into one political state: to create the first manifestation of what would have been a united kingdom of Britain ruled from one parliament. He was never successful in this aim, since both countries desired to retain governmental independence from each other. However, the drive which James initiated towards creating an ideology of Britishness leaves its traces in the literature of the time, as Shakespeare's *King Lear* of 1605 (a 'King of Britain', whose troubles notably begin when he divides the kingdom) and his *Cymbeline, King of Britain* of 1609, both attest. Such 'imperial' endeavours, along with the mere fact of a Scottish royal family, necessarily affected the anti-foreign agenda which we have traced over the preceding discussion. To this can be added James's explicit gestures towards fomenting a peaceful reign in contrast to the sometimes belligerent stance of his predecessor Elizabeth, who as an excommunicate from the Catholic church and vanquisher of the Armada was a permanent target for the anti-Protestant cause. James, by contrast, made immediate and successful efforts at pursuing peace with the hated enemy Spain and built up an image of his reign as a generally pacific one which nurtured the arts and sciences – a realisation, we might suppose, of the Duke of Burgundy's misty-eyed eulogy of the benefits of a peaceful state in *Henry V*. How did this programmatic dismantling of anti-foreign sentiment affect the representation of nationhood in the drama? We can address this question by looking briefly at some plays on the theme of English history which emerged in the aftermath of Elizabeth's death.

One of the more significant theatrical repercussions of the dynastic succession was that it was now possible to represent Tudor monarchs themselves on stage. This had been forbidden by Elizabethan censorship laws while the dynasty was still extant, so that even the most effusive praise for the reigning monarch had to be transmitted through allegorical representation (as for example in the appearance of Cynthia in Jonson's *Cynthia's Revels* of 1600) or built into the representation of the kings and queens of the preceding dynasty: the Plantagenets. After 1603 it became possible to represent monarchs from Henry VII onwards, and in particular to broach the formative events of the preceding two reigns, those of Mary and Elizabeth, when England endured violent disruptions to its peace from both internal and external threats. Two highly popular plays by the dramatist Thomas Heywood from the early years of James I's reign, *If You Know Not Me You Know Nobody, Parts One and Two* (1604, 1605) depict some of the key historical highlights of Elizabeth's reign, as indicated by their respective subtitles: *The troubles of Queen Elizabeth* and *The Building of the Royal Exchange and The famous Victory of Queen Elizabeth anno 1588* (i.e. against the Armada). Both have been grouped by critics under the generic heading of 'Elect Nation' plays, by which is meant their return to the specifically Protestant ideological reading of the events of English national history which had characterised the middle years of the sixteenth century. The label is valuable up to a point, accurately describing an interpretive framework which closely corresponds to the martyrological approach of the Protestant writer John Foxe, one which could yield readings of history strikingly different from that of the plays of the 1590s that utilised the Tudor Myth.* Nonetheless, these plays need to be seen as bringing together a number of ideological concerns which gained prominence in the early years of James's reign: Protestant hopes for further reformation, but also a renewed emphasis on sacred, inviolable majesty and a relaxation of hostilities with Catholic countries which would have sat less well with the radical protestant cause in seventeenth-century England.

The first part of *If You Know Not Me You Know Nobody* traces Elizabeth's relationship with her elder sister Mary while the latter was reasserting Catholicism after the strides made towards a fully Protestant national religion in the reign of Edward VI. In incident after incident deriving from sisterly persecution – imprisonment, false accusation and attempted assassination – Princess Elizabeth is shown very much as a passive victim, surviving not by her own actions but by sometimes incredible reversals of fortune which are interpreted by commentators within the narrative as acts of divine protection. On a par with these are the intercessions of the Spanish king Philip II, Mary's husband and arch-proponent of Catholicism, as a peace-maker between the two women. As has been

---

* An example is afforded by an early Elect Nation play of 1599, *Sir John Oldcastle*, which represents a fifteenth-century knight of that name who provided the model for Shakespeare's supremely fat and licentious knight Falstaff, but who in the eyes of Protestant hagiographers was a hero for harbouring heretical and anti-papal beliefs (known as Lollardy) which anticipated those of Martin Luther. Henry V, whom the Tudor Myth elevated to the pinnacle of kingly virtue, was by contrast seen by those same hagiographers as a disappointment, being so orthodox in his religion that he was known as 'the prince of Priests' (John Foxe, *Acts and Monuments*, Book 5, p. 779).

pointed out, this positive portrayal of Philip is consistent with his presentation in Foxe's 'Book of Martyrs', where the very unlikelihood of Philip's assistance of a Protestant princess is held up as evidence of God's handiwork in assisting Elizabeth.[12] Yet Foxe's book was first published in 1563, shortly after Elizabeth's accession; and in the intervening decades before the play was written Philip had launched the Armada and relations with Spain had sunk to their nadir. The striking adoption of a flattering stance towards Philip in *1 If You Know Not Me You Know Nobody* assists the Jacobean emphasis on conciliation with the foreign foe as much as it assists the providential narrative. *2 If You Know Not Me You Know Nobody* splices together a local London narrative of major importance to the nation's commercial history – the founding of the Royal Exchange (the first stock exchange) in 1565 by Sir Thomas Gresham – with an urban comedy of sexual intrigue on a par with *Englishmen for My Money*. Haughton's play is explicitly referenced at one point in a dialogue between an English ne'er-do-well and a French courtesan, who is full of praises for the superiority of the English lover over the 'sweaty Spaniard', 'the carousing Dane', 'the foggy Dutch-man', and so forth, prompting the reply 'Well then the Englishman for thy money'.[13] But any genuinely provoking anti-foreign sentiment is nullified by having the Frenchwoman speaking in fluent English (and indeed blank verse) throughout their exchange, and matching the Englishman wit for wit.

The play shifts abruptly in its climactic scenes towards two of the more sensational events in Elizabeth's reign: her attempted assassination by the Catholic conspirator Dr William Parry, and the victory over the Armada. The former is more important in providing the play's moment of supreme danger to the queen, involving a direct attack on her private person while she is walking in a garden. It is providentially diverted, this time by the assailant's inability to perform the deed while in the presence of her sacred majesty. He begs her pardon as soon as he offers to kill her, and as the queen observes is 'dead already / Struck with remorse of that he was to do' even before he is wheeled off to a traitor's execution.[14] The historical narratives of Parry suggest a murky double agent whose innocence or guilt are not ultimately provable, like the Portuguese doctor, Lopez, later accused of an attempt on Elizabeth's life (see the discussion in Part Two).

Unlike Lopez, however, Parry was Welsh born and English bred, and the scope the play gives to this particular assassination attempt complicates the picture of national unity against an external foreign threat which the play goes on to consolidate in the Armada climax. This final 'battle' is itself a mere succession of reported skirmishes lacking full dramatic tension, in which the queen herself is shown as more concerned for the well-being of her subjects than with triumphing over her foes. The play's ideology of national unity under the new king is thus founded on an idealisation of national prosperity (through the Gresham narrative) which suggests a nation achieving an internally driven cohesion. The threat to that cohesion is also represented as internal, arising from one of the queen's own subjects. In the soliloquy Dr Parry delivers before his assassination attempt he admits a bond with the queen (who has already pardoned him for misdemeanours) which is organic in its kind – his limbs, he says, 'had life by her' – and which creates a powerful internal conflict with his Catholic and papal loyalties.

2 If You Know Not Me You Know Nobody's depiction of a native Catholic conspiracy against the monarch is remarkably prescient of events that were to happen later that year, when James was to have an assassination and famous victory combined, appropriately vanquishing an internal rather external threat to his rule. Hard-line Roman Catholic discontent, which had been simmering for decades under Elizabeth, culminated in the failed terrorist attempt of the Gunpowder Plot upon the new government in 1605. A cause of widespread national outrage, it also created profound relief that the hand of providence seemed to be protecting the new king, a view strengthened by the fact that he himself had a major role in uncovering the conspiracy. The whole event was a gift to James in terms of positioning him within an ideology of nationhood for the newly united crowns of England and Scotland. Any tensions arising from the idea of a Scottish king of England (and the inevitable influx this entailed of Scottish lords and commoners into the capital) were re-directed towards a threat which was extra-national (in the sense that the conspirators were acting without foreign backing), ensuring that English Catholics as a whole, however loyal, became a focus for national antagonism. At the same time the attempt to blow up the Houses of

Parliament during the State Opening was a uniquely corporate act which consolidated James's position within the nation *state*. Unlike Elizabeth, who had suffered attempts on her private person, James was targeted along with the whole of the body politic, strengthening the king's identification with his realm while reinforcing his particular emphasis on his divinely sanctioned position within it. This was well understood by the political theorist Edward Forset shortly after the event, when he expressed his horror at the 'storm' that was nearly 'raised for the blowing up, shivering into pieces, and whirling about of those honourable, anointed, and sacred bodies'.[15] Commons, clergy and king are here seen as members of a single body; but only one of these members is 'sacred'.

Shakespeare's *Macbeth* of 1606, written in part to honour James's accession, glances at the theme of Scottish–English relations, and perhaps also at the conspiracy of the year before. The play has one, notably extended, scene in England, in which the English court is shown as a safe harbour for Scottish thanes exiled from their country during Macbeth's reign of terror. Not only is the English king of the time, Edward the Confessor, described in terms which leave no doubt as to the sacred nature of his kingship (he performs miracles of healing), but his court provides the warriors who form an alliance with the Scottish exiles for their return to overthrow Macbeth (see the discussion in Part Three: 'Tyranny, Terror and Tragedy on the English Stage'). Such overtures towards a shared national destiny could be expected from the theatre company which James himself patronised almost immediately on coming to London as the King's Men. But in its tale of Macbeth's treacherous ascent to power through the murder of the rightful king Duncan the play also describes a narrative of threat from within, of a kinsman who turns out to be an assassin. Indeed *Macbeth*, a play in which the word 'assassination' occurs for the first time in English (and in connection with a Scottish king), has been grouped along with a spate of so-called 'gunpowder plays' which emerged in the immediate aftermath of the plot, and which attempted to capitalise on the emotions aroused by this would-be apocalyptic event by elaborating scenarios of witchcraft and conspiracy thought to surround the Catholic plotters.[16] If it does allude to the dynamic we have traced here of an internal threat which unites the whole country against it, then *Macbeth* is in its own way prescient of things to come, telling the double-edged (or, as the play would have it, equivocating) story of a king who becomes his nation's enemy, and is eventually beheaded as a tyrant, as a man of blood. Through his emphasis on the divine right of kings, James I set England on the path towards absolutism which was to culminate forty years later in his son Charles I's doomed war on Parliament, and trial and execution for high treason. In a way that would have astounded Shakespeare and his contemporaries, the nation had become fully independent of its king.

Notes

1   See William Haller, *Foxe's Book of Martyrs and the Elect Nation* (London: Cape, 1963), for the attribution of the idea of England as the elect nation directly to Foxe. This viewpoint has been criticised for ignoring Foxe's internationalist Protestant agenda and his attempts to position England as one elect nation among many. Edwin Jones, *The English Nation: The Great Myth* (Stroud: Sutton Publishing Ltd, 2000), argues that it is not until the seventeenth century and particularly the period of John Milton that the idea of England as *the* elect nation becomes explicit. However, Foxe was following the Protestant dramatist John Bale whose writings more openly privilege the special status of England (see Andrew Hadfield, *Literature, Politics and National Identity: Reformation to Renaissance* (Cambridge: Cambridge University Press, 1994), pp. 57–9).

2   William Shakespeare, *Richard II*, ed. Charles R. Forker, Arden, 3rd series (London: Thomson Learning, 2002), II.i.

3   Indeed, as Claire McEachern puts it, far from resembling a medieval notion of the realm, the England Gaunt describes is by the time the play is being written 'just beginning to be glimpsed', McEachern, *Poetics of English Nationhood*, p. 6.

4   William Rankins, *The English Ape, the Italian imitation, the Footsteps of France* (London, 1588). Spelling and punctuation modernised.

5   See Sara Warneke, *Images of Educational Travellers in Early Modern England* (Leiden: E. J. Brill, 1995), esp. ch. 6.

6   William Shakespeare, *Othello*, ed. E. A. J. Honigmann, Arden, 3rd series (London: Thomson Learning, 1999), III.iv.30–1.

7   Timothy Bright, *A Treatise, Wherein is declared the Sufficiency of English Medicines* (London: 1580), p. 11.

8   William Haughton (attributed), *Englishmen for My Money: Or, A pleasant Comedy, called, A Woman will have her Will* (London, 1616), 1840–4.

9   On this point, see Jean H. Howard and Phyllis Rackin, *Engendering a Nation: A Feminist Account of Shakespeare's English Histories* (London: Routledge, 1997), p. 187.

10 See *Henry V*, IV.vii. As Philip Schwyzer put it wryly, 'Henry "inherits" his Welshness not from his ancestors, but from his Tudor successors', *Literature, Nationalism, and Memory in Early Modern England and Wales* (Cambridge: Cambridge University Press, 2004), p. 127.

11 Howard and Rackin, *Engendering a Nation*, 207.

12 See Spikes, 'The Jacobean History Play', pp. 137–8.

13 Heywood, *2 If You Know Not Me You Know Nobody*, G1v.

14 Heywood, *2 If You Know Not Me You Know Nobody*, I1r.

15 Edward Forset, *A Comparative Discourse of the Bodies Natural and Politic* (London: 1606), pp. 52–3.

16 See in particular Garry Wills, *Witches and Jesuits: Shakespeare's Macbeth* (Oxford: Oxford University Press, 1995).

Part Five
References and Resources

Timeline

	Historical and Theatrical Events	Plays (First Performances) and Literary Events
1558	Death of Mary I, Roman Catholic queen of England and Ireland; accession of Elizabeth I, Protestant queen	
1563		John Foxe's *Acts and Monuments*, or 'Book of Martyrs', a key work of Protestant 'apocalyptic' history, is published
1564	William Shakespeare and Christopher Marlowe born	
1565	Founding of the Royal Exchange by Thomas Gresham	
1568	Exile of Mary, Queen of Scots, and beginning of long 'house arrest' in England	
1570	Elizabeth excommunicated by the pope in decree which also urges her subjects to revolt against her	
1576	The Theatre, built by James Burbage, opens in London	
1577	The Curtain theatre built	

Timeline

Historical and Theatrical Events	Plays (First Performances) and Literary Events
1581	Philip Sidney's *An Apology for Poetry* written (but not published until 1595, posthumously)
1585 Execution of William Parry for attempted plot on Elizabeth's life	*Galatea*, by John Lyly
1586 Death of Philip Sidney in the Netherlands on campaign against the Spanish	*The Famous Victories of Henry the fifth*, anonymous
1587 Rose theatre built, owned and managed by Henslowe. Execution of Mary, Queen of Scots	*The Spanish Tragedy*, by Thomas Kyd; *1 Tamburlaine*, by Christopher Marlowe
1588 The attempted Spanish invasion of England fails after the destruction of Philip II's Armada	*2 Tamburlaine*, by Christopher Marlowe
1589	*The Jew of Malta*, by Christopher Marlowe
1590 The Children of Paul's, a semi-professional troupe of child chorister-actors, are suppressed after their plays become mired in political scandal	*1 Henry VI*, by William Shakespeare (and Thomas Nashe?); *Henry VI*, by William Shakespeare (Other estimates suggest that the play is a 'prequel' to *2* and *3 Henry VI*, added in 1592)
1591	*Arden of Faversham* (anonymous); *3 Henry VI*, by William Shakespeare
1592 London theatres closed owing to severe outbreak of plague	*Doctor Faustus*, by Christopher Marlowe; *Comedy of Errors*, by William Shakespeare; *Richard III*, by William Shakespeare; *The Taming of the Shrew*, by William Shakespeare

Historical and Theatrical Events	Plays (First Performances) and Literary Events
1593 Christopher Marlowe stabbed to death, 30 May	Philip Sidney's *The Countess of Pembroke's Arcadia*, the main authorised edition of his work, is augmented and published by his sister Mary
1594 London theatres fully re-opened for business; the Lord Chamberlain's Men formed, with Shakespeare as a member; Roderigo Lopez executed, 7 June	*Titus Andronicus*, by William Shakespeare
1595 The Swan theatre built	*Richard II*, by William Shakespeare; *A Midsummer Night's Dream*, by William Shakespeare
1596 The Blackfriars theatre built by James Burbage, but legal problems ensure that Shakespeare's company cannot occupy it until 1608	*The Merchant of Venice*, by William Shakespeare
1597	*1 Henry IV*, by William Shakespeare; *2 Henry IV*, by William Shakespeare; *An Humourous Day's Mirth*, by George Chapman, begins the vogue for humours plays
1598	*Every Man in His Humour*, by Ben Jonson; *Englishmen for My Money*, by William Haughton; James VI of Scotland's (later James I of England) *Trew Law of Free Monarchies* published

Historical and Theatrical Events	Plays (First Performances) and Literary Events
1599 Earl of Essex leaves for Ireland to suppress the rebellion of Irish lords; the Globe, built by Burbage's company, the Lord Chamberlain's Men, is opened; Archbishop Whitgift orders the public burning of a number of satirical works in prose and poetry, and institutes a ban on the further publication of satire; boy actor companies – in the form of the revived Children of Paul's and the Children of the Chapel – resume performing, the latter group in the Blackfriars theatre	*Antonio and Mellida*, by John Marston; *Henry V*, by William Shakespeare; *As You Like It*, by William Shakespeare; *Every Man out of His Humour*, by Ben Jonson; *A Warning for Fair Women*, attributed to Thomas Heywood
1600 The Fortune theatre built, funded by Henslowe for the Admiral's Men	*Hamlet*, by William Shakespeare
1601	*Twelfth Night*, by William Shakespeare; *Antonio's Revenge*, by John Marston
1602	*Il Pastor Fido*, by Giambattista Guarini (English translation, originally written 1585); *Troilus and Cressida*, by William Shakespeare.
1603 Death of Elizabeth I; accession of James I of England, Scotland and Ireland; the Lord Chamberlain's Men become the King's Men and the Lord Admiral's Men become Prince Henry's Men	*All's Well That Ends Well*, by William Shakespeare

Historical and Theatrical Events	Plays (First Performances) and Literary Events
1604 James I concludes peace with Spain	*Othello*, by William Shakespeare. *Measure for Measure*, by William Shakespeare; *1 If You Know Not Me You Know Nobody*, by Thomas Heywood; *The Fawn*, by John Marston
1605 Attempted assassination of James I foiled in Gunpowder Plot of 5 November	*King Lear*, by William Shakespeare; *2 If You Know Not Me You Know Nobody*, by Thomas Heywood
1606	*Macbeth*, by William Shakespeare; *The Revenger's Tragedy*, attributed to Thomas Middleton; *Volpone*, by Ben Jonson
1608 The King's Men, Shakespeare's company, take over the Blackfriars theatre	*Pericles*, by William Shakespeare; *The Faithful Shepherdess*, by John Fletcher
1609	*Philaster*, by Francis Beaumont and John Fletcher; *Cymbeline*, by William Shakespeare
1610	*The Winter's Tale*, by William Shakespeare
1611	*The Tempest*, by William Shakespeare; *The Roaring Girl*, by Thomas Middleton and Thomas Dekker.
1614 The Hope theatre built (another Henslowe venture)	*Bartholomew Fair*, by Ben Jonson; *The Duchess of Malfi*, by John Webster
1616 William Shakespeare dies	*The Works of Ben Jonson* are published (under the poet's supervision): a groundbreaking act for a dramatist in this era

Timeline

Historical and Theatrical Events	Plays (First Performances) and Literary Events
1621	*Women Beware Women*, by Thomas Middleton; *The Witch of Edmonton*, by Thomas Dekker, William Rowley and John Ford (and others?)
1622	*The Changeling*, by Thomas Middleton and William Rowley
1623 Hostilities with Spain resume after failed effort of Charles, James I's eldest son and heir, to secure marriage with the Infanta	*Mr William Shakespeare's Comedies Histories and Tragedies* published by Isaac (and William) Jaggard and Edward Blount; later ages know it as the 'First Folio' – the first collected edition of his plays

Further Reading

General Resources

Chambers, E. K., *The Elizabethan Stage*, 4 vols (Oxford: Clarendon, 1923)
> This remains the key resource for historical and bibliographic data on the plays of Shakespeare and his contemporaries

Cox, John D. and David Kastan, *A New History of Early English Drama* (New York: Columbia University Press, 1997)
> A particularly useful collection of essays addressing a range of subjects on the English Renaissance theatre

Alternative Shakespeares ('New Accents' series), vol. 1, ed. John Drakakis (London: Routledge, 1985); vol. 2, ed. Terence Hawkes (London: Routledge, 1996); vol. 3, ed. Diane E. Henderson (London: Routledge, 2007)
> These collections of essays provide the best way of following the development of the various challenging perspectives on Shakespeare that have arisen over the past thirty years

Harbage, Alfred, *Annals of English Drama, 975–1700*, 3rd edn, revised by Sylvia Stoler Wagonheim (London: Routledge, 1989)
> A detailed chronology which provides the most accurate information on performance and publication dates

Norton Anthology of Theory and Criticism, ed. Vincent B. Leitch et al.
(London: W. W. Norton & Company)
> A number of the critical discussions on poetry and drama by sixteenth-century
> English and continental writers referred to in this volume are conveniently
> collected here

Penguin Book of Renaissance Verse 1509–1659, ed. David Norbrook and
H. R. Woudhuysen (Harmondsworth: Penguin, 1993)
> Very well arranged and helpfully edited collection of the non-dramatic poetry
> of the period, with a particularly good introduction

Whickham, Glynn, Herbert Berry and William Ingram, *English
Professional Theatre 1530–1660*, Theatre in Europe: A Documentary
History (Cambridge: Cambridge University Press, 2000)
> Contains an extensive range of primary sources in a single-volume format

Social and Political History

Brigden, Susan, *New Worlds, Lost Worlds: The Rule of the Tudors 1485–
1603* (Harmondsworth: Penguin, 2000)
> A thorough and entertaining introduction to the development of Tudor
> politics and culture up to the death of Elizabeth I

Coward, Barry, *The Stuart Age: England 1603–1714*, 3rd edn (London:
Pearson Education Ltd, 2003)
> Provides a solid historical foundation for understanding the changes wrought
> by the accession of James I

Parry, Graham, *The Seventeenth Century: The Intellectual and Cultural
Context of English Literature 1603–1700*
> Highly recommended as a starting point for contextualising the literature of
> the Stuart reigns

Greenblatt, Stephen, *Will in the World: How Shakespeare Became
Shakespeare* (London: Pimlico, 2005)
> Goes well beyond the standard biographical format in teasing out some
> fascinating connections between Shakespeare's plays and early modern English
> society

Rowse, A. L., *The England of Elizabeth: The Structure of Society* (London: Palgrave Macmillan, 2003)

> First published in 1950 but continually reprinted and reissued: remains an excellent analysis of society during this particular reign

Wynn-Davies, Marion, *Sidney to Milton 1580–1660*, Transitions Series (Houndmills: Palgrave Macmillan, 2003)

> Offers insightful readings of many dramatic and non-dramatic works in their social and political contexts

Theatre and Literary History

Bruster, Douglas, *Drama and the Market in the Age of Shakespeare* (Cambridge: Cambridge University Press, 1992)

> Makes a strong argument for the reading of the plays in their commercial contexts

Gurr, Andrew, *The Shakespearean Stage 1574–1642*, 3rd edn (Cambridge: Cambridge University Press, 1992, repr. 1994)

— *Playgoing in Shakespeare's London*, 2nd edn (Cambridge: Cambridge University Press, 1996)

> These two volumes are the starting points for any detailed discussion of Elizabethan and Jacobean theatre history, taking the perspectives of the theatre professionals and the consumers of plays respectively

Harbage, Alfred, *Shakespeare's Audience* (New York: Columbia University Press, 1941)

> Although some of its conclusions have been challenged during the intervening decades, this remains a valuable survey of the data, which overturns many assumptions about the composition of theatre audiences (including those put about the dramatists themselves)

Wells, Stanley, *Shakespeare & Co.* (London: Penguin, 2007)

> Provides a highly readable introduction to the working lives of key individual dramatists, including Shakespeare

Theatrical Genres

Cambridge Companion to Shakespearean Comedy, ed. Alexander Leggatt (Cambridge: Cambridge University Press, 2002)

Cambridge Companion to Shakespeare's History Plays, ed. Michael Hattaway (Cambridge: Cambridge University Press, 2002)

Cambridge Companion to Shakespearean Tragedy, ed. Claire McEachern (Cambridge: Cambridge University Press, 2002)
> Series of volumes on Shakespeare which contain a variety of essays from expert writers on the each of the three main Shakespearean genres

Miola, Robert S., *Shakespeare and Classical Comedy: The Influence of Plautus and Terence* (Oxford: Clarendon Press, 1994)
> Examines the importance of Roman New Comedy as a formative influence on Shakespeare and other playwrights of the period

Smith, Emma, *Shakespeare's Comedies: A Guide to Criticism*, Blackwell Guides to Criticism (Malden, MA: Blackwell, 2004)

— *Shakespeare's Histories: A Guide to Criticism*, Blackwell Guides to Criticism (Malden, MA: Blackwell, 2004)

— *Shakespeare's Tragedies: A Guide to Criticism*, Blackwell Guides to Criticism (Malden, MA: Blackwell, 2004)
> These three volumes have valuable prefatory discussions introducing a range of traditional and more recent critical readings of the plays

Approaches to Genre

Danson, Lawrence, *Shakespeare's Dramatic Genres* (Oxford: Oxford University Press, 2000; repr. 2007)
> Deals primarily with Shakespearean approaches to comedy, history and tragedy, but provides excellent groundwork for thinking about the problem of genre as a whole in this period's drama

Fowler, Alastair, *Kinds of Literature: An Introduction to the Theory of Genres and Modes* (Oxford: Clarendon Press, 1982)

> A thorough discussion outlining an approach to genres as flexible, continually developing forms rather than fixed categories – corresponds to much current critical thinking on the topic

Lennard, John and Mary Luckhurst, *The Drama Handbook: A Guide to Reading Plays* (Oxford: Oxford University Press, 2002)

> Has some helpful introductory discussion on the topic of genres and gives clear definitions of key terms

Comedy

Barber, C. L. *Shakespeare's Festive Comedy* (Princeton: Princeton University Press, 1959)

> On the carnivalesque, misrule element in Shakespeare's comedy in general, but particularly influential on studies of *Twelfth Night*

Frye, Northrop, *A Natural Perspective: The Development of Shakespearean Comedy and Romance* (New York: Columbia University Press, 1965)

> Very influential discussion of the folk and ritual aspects of Shakespearean early and late comedies (i.e. tragicomedies)

Greenblatt, Stephen, 'Fiction and Friction', in *Shakespearean Negotiations: The Circulation of Social Energy on Renaissance England* (Oxford: Clarendon, 1988)

> An essay which has strongly influenced readings of *Twelfth Night*'s homoerotic subtext

Happé, Peter, *English Drama Before Shakespeare* (Harlow: Longman, 1999)

> Contains a helpful discussion of Lyly's plays and generally very good context for the Elizabethan drama leading up to Shakespeare

Hunter, G. K., *John Lyly: The Humanist as Courtier* (London: Routledge & Kegan Paul, 1962)

> A thorough analysis of the intellectual background to Lyly's plays and gives some in-depth readings of the individual works

Kehler, Dorothea, ed. *'A Midsummer Night's Dream': Critical Essays* (London: Routledge, 1998)

> Volume of essays, particularly strong on themes of gender and sexuality in relation to Shakespeare's play

Laroque, François, *Shakespeare's Festive World: Elizabethan Seasonal Entertainment and the Professional Stage*, trans. Janet Lloyd (Cambridge: Cambridge University Press, 1991)

> Provides a more recent and thoroughly documented analysis of the festive and folk strands in Shakespearean comedy

Paster, Gail Kern and Skiles Howard (eds), *A Midsummer Night's Dream': Texts and Contexts* (Boston: Bedford/St Martin's, 1999)

> A good collection of essays, in which the festive and aristocratic contexts of the play are addressed

Zimmerman, Susan (ed.), *Erotic Politics: Desire on the Renaissance Stage* (London: Routledge, 1992)

> Excellent collection of essays which present challenging readings of the cross-dressing and gender confusions of Elizabethan and Jacobean comedy in general

History

Dollimore, Jonathan and Alan Sinfield (eds), *Political Shakespeare: Essays in Cultural Materialism*, 2nd edn (Manchester: Manchester University Press, 1994)

> Ranging more widely than the history plays, this nonetheless includes many valuable discussions, particularly on the *Henry IV/V* plays

Holderness, Graham, *Shakespeare Recycled: The Making of Historical Drama* (New York: Harvester, 1992)

> Important and well-argued challenge to earlier historicist readings of unity and orthodoxy in the history plays

Jones, Robert C. *These Valiant Dead: Renewing the Past in Shakespeare's Histories* (Iowa City: University of Iowa Press, 1991)

> Particularly well-written and closely argued analysis on the multiple uses of history for the Elizabethans

Leggatt, Alexander, *Shakespeare's Political Drama: The History Plays and the Roman Plays* (London: Routledge, 1988)

> Takes a more traditional (i.e. author-based) approach to the 'political' theme than some of the other critical discussions mentioned here, but puts forward many perceptive readings

Rackin, Phyllis, *Stages of History: Shakespeare's English Chronicles* (London: Routledge, 1990)

> Provides an excellent, stimulating reading of the plays from the standpoints of both genre and gender

Ribner, Irving, *The English History Play in the Age of Shakespeare* (Princeton: Princeton University Press, 1957)

> An influential mid-twentieth-century discussion examining different political ideologies within the history plays

Tillyard, E. M. W., *Shakespeare's History Plays* (London: Chatto & Windus, 1944)

> An early historicist reading very important in establishing the Tudor Myth approach to the plays, but which now provokes strong objections for its emphasis on the universality of this viewpoint

Tragedy

Aristotle's Poetics, trans. Richard Janko (Indianapolis: Hackett, 1987); also in the *Norton Anthology of Theory and Criticism* (without extensive annotations)

> Early Greek work of literary criticism which has had incalculable influence on the subsequent criticism and practice of the genre – the key caveat here is that early moderns recognised a highly diverse generic inheritance for tragedy not reducible to classical theory

Belsey, Catherine, *The Subject of Tragedy: Identity and Difference in Renaissance Drama* (London: Routledge, 1985)

> Valuable discussion probing the links between Renaissance tragedy and the construction of a unified idea of the self through the genre's conventions

Bradbrook, M. C., *Themes and Conventions of Elizabethan Tragedy*, 2nd edn (Cambridge: Cambridge University Press, 1980; originally published 1935)

> Detailed and wide-ranging discussion of Elizabethan and Jacobean tragic conventions and their articulation by different dramatists

Bradley, A. C., *Shakespearean Tragedy* (London: Macmillan, 1985; originally published 1904)

> Feted and dismissed in equal measure as monuments of 'character criticism', Bradley essays can still produce powerful individual readings despite their now-superseded approach

Clemen, Wolfgang, *English Tragedy before Shakespeare: The Development of Dramatic Speech* (London: Methuen, 1961)

> Important and influential discussion, especially on the development of the soliloquy

Callaghan, Dympna, *Woman and Gender in Renaissance Tragedy: A Study of 'King Lear', 'The Duchess of Malfi' and 'The White Devil'* (London: Harvester Wheatsheaf, 1989)

> Contains some very fine readings of tragedies which challenge traditional critical assumptions about the representation of women in these plays

Dollimore, Jonathan, *Radical Tragedy*, 2nd edn (Hemel Hempstead: Harvester Wheatsheaf, 1989)

> A key late-twentieth-century discussion, very important for placing Renaissance tragedy in its immediate social and historical moment and for attacking universalising readings of the plays.

Eagleton, Terry, *Sweet Violence: The Idea of the Tragic* (Oxford: Blackwell, 2003)

> A stimulating recent account of the broad historical development of the concept of tragedy

Greer, Germaine, *Shakespeare* (Oxford: Oxford University Press, 1986)

> Although not restricted to tragedy, some of the volume's readings serve as highly thought-provoking points of departure for discussion of the genre

Tragicomedy

Bliss, Lee, 'Pastiche, burlesque, tragicomedy', in *The Cambridge Companion to English Renaissance Drama*, ed. A. R. Braunmuller and Michael Hattaway (Cambridge: Cambridge University Press, 1990), pp. 237–61

>Provides a good introduction to English playwrights' adoption of the genre and sets it in the context of a number of experimental modes being utilised at the time

Foster, Verna A., *The Name and Nature of Tragicomedy* (Aldershot: Ashgate, 2004)

>Relates the 'dark' or 'problem' comedies of Shakespeare's middle years to the romances of his later years and treats the plays as differentiated experiments in the tragicomic genre

Gibbons, Brian, 'Romance and the heroic play', in *The Cambridge Companion to English Renaissance Drama*, pp. 207–36

>Relates some of Shakespeare's late plays to the native dramatic idiom

Guarini, Giambattista, 'The Compendium of Tragicomic Poetry', in Allan H. Gilbert, *Literary Criticism: Plato to Dryden* (New York: American Book Co., 1940)

>A key primary source for discussions of the genre in Shakespeare's time

Hathaway, Baxter, *The Age of Criticism: The Late Renaissance in Italy* (Ithaca, NY: Cornell University Press, 1962)

>For comprehensive discussions of the way tragicomic response was theorised by neoclassical critics

Henke, Robert, *Pastoral Transformations: Italian Tragicomedy and Shakespeare's Late Plays* (London: Associated University Presses, 1997)

>Provides a detailed assessment of the indebtedness of tragicomedy to Italian innovations

Rossiter, A. P., *Angel with Horns: Fifteen Lectures on Shakespeare* (London: Longman, 1961)

>Influential collection of essays on a number of Shakespearean genres, with some especially thought-provoking analyses of the middle-period comedies, which Rossiter designated tragicomedies in preference to the 'problem' label

Humours Plays

Campbell, O. J., *Comicall Satyre and Shakespeare's 'Trolius and Cressida'* (San Marino, CA: Henry E. Huntingdon Library and Art Gallery, 1938)

> Remains a valuable early discussion on the intersection of the humours theme with satire, even though its premise (that satire on the stage directly replaced satiric poetry when the latter was censored by the Elizabethan authorities) has long since been dismantled

Cave, Richard Allen, *Ben Jonson*, English Dramatists (Houndmills: Macmillan, 1991)

> Provides some helpful discussion of the manipulation of the humours theme in the direction of wider social commentary

Kernan, Alvin, *The Cankered Muse: Satire of the English Renaissance* (New Haven: Yale University Press, 1959)

> Explores the stylistic developments of Marston and Jonson in satire

Munro, Lucy, *Children of the Queen's Revels: A Jacobean Theatre Repertory* (Cambridge: Cambridge University Press, 2005)

> A recent examination of the main boy player company at the heart of the fashion for satire: very good on the theatrically innovative nature of this company and its writers

Paster, Gail Kern, *The Body Embarrassed: Drama and the Disciplines of Shame in Early Modern England* (New York: Cornell University Press, 1993)

> Provides a fascinating, gendered reading of the handling of the medical theory of the four humours in the drama of Shakespeare's day

Riggs, David, *Ben Jonson: A Life* (Cambridge, MA: Harvard University Press, 1989), ch. 2, 'The Comedy of Humours'

> Provides a good overview of the sub-genre and Jonson's contribution to it

Scott-Warren, Jason, 'When Theaters Were Bear-Gardens; or, What's at Stake in the Comedy of Humors', in *Shakespeare Quarterly*, 54:1 (Spring 2003), pp. 63–82

Recent discussion linking some of the structural motifs of humours comedy to the animal-baiting practices of the amphitheatres, and discussing Jonsonian and Shakespearean comedy (especially *Twelfth Night*) from this perspective

Shapiro, Michael, *Children of the Revels: The Boy Companies of Shakespeare's Time and Their Plays* (New York: Columbia University Press, 1977)

Discussion of the two all-boy acting companies which provided the principal theatrical platform for humours and satirical plays

Revenge Drama

Bowers, Fredson, *Elizabethan Revenge Tragedy 1587–1642* (Princeton: Princeton University Press, 1940)

Despite over-anatomising its subject in seeing a proliferation of different 'periods' and 'schools' of revenge drama, this remains a classic study of the revenge genre

Clare, Janet, *Revenge Tragedies of the Renaissance*, Writers and Their Work (Hornden: Northcote Publishing, 2006)

Recent, approachable guide which suggests that the application of the revenge theme among Elizabethan and Jacobean plays is too diffuse in the tragic drama to warrant a special category

Hallett, Charles A. and Elaine S. Hallett, *The Revenger's Madness: A Study of Revenge Tragedy Motifs* (Lincoln, NE: University of Nebraska Press, 1980)

Focuses on madness as one of an aggregate of generic conventions: like Bowers, these critics see revenge as a distinct genre

Hopkins, Lisa, *The Female Hero in English Renaissance Tragedy* (Houndmills: Palgrave, 2002)

Covers in detail many of the plays treated here and makes powerful points about their ideologies of social control, for those wishing to follow up the present volume's emphasis on the representation of women in Jacobean revenge plays

Kerrigan, John, *Revenge Tragedy: Aeschylus to Armageddon* (Oxford: University Press, 1996)

> See chapter 7 for a valuable discussion of Elizabethan revenge drama in a broad European literary context

Key Themes and Critical Approaches

Madness and Subjectivity

Belsey, Catherine, *The Subject of Tragedy: Identity and Difference in Renaissance Drama* (London: Routledge, 1985)

> A clear and helpful discussion of subjectivity – the ideas of selfhood, identity and agency – in the Renaissance and its articulation in the drama can be found in chapter 2

Coddon, Karin S., '"Suche Strange Desygns": Madness, Subjectivity and Treason in *Hamlet* and Elizabethan Culture', in *Renaissance Drama*, New Series: 20 (1989), pp. 51–75

> Discusses the way madness could be manipulated to carry a political message

Dollimore, Jonathan, *Radical Tragedy*, 2nd edn (Hemel Hempstead: Harvester Wheatsheaf, 1989)

> A founding text in the cultural materialist approach to literary studies, this explores some of the historical stresses on the idea of the self which the present volume has also addressed, and includes a (provocative) discussion of madness in *King Lear*

Kinsman, Robert S., *'The Darker vision of the Renaissance': Beyond the Fields of Reason* (Berkeley: University of California, 1974)

> Collection of essays on what one contributor calls 'the most psychically disturbed era in European history'; see especially the editor's own essay 'Folly, Melancholy, Madness' in this volume

Macdonald, Michael, *Mystical Bedlam: Madness, Anxiety, and Healing in Seventeenth-Century England* (Cambridge: Cambridge University Press, 1981)

A social history of madness much consulted by literary critics which, like the other studies on the theme, takes issue with Michel Foucault's *Madness and Civilisation: A History of Insanity in the Age of Reason*, trans. Richard Howard (London: Routledge, 1971, repr. 1999) while acknowledging the stimulus it has provided

Neely, Carol Thomas, '"Documents in Madness": Reading Madness and Gender in Shakespeare's Tragedies and Early Modern Culture', in *Shakespeare Quarterly*, 42:3 (Fall 1991), pp. 315–38

> Reads madness for its gendered construction in the plays: especially good discussion of Ophelia's insanity

Salkeld, Duncan, *Madness and Drama in the Age of Shakespeare* (Manchester: Manchester University Press, 1993)

> Uses Foucault and other critical theorists to set out some political readings of the dramatic representation of madness

Women in the English Renaissance

Aughterson, Kate (ed.), *Renaissance Woman: A Sourcebook, Constructions of Femininity in England* (London: Routledge, 1995)

> A very good collection of source materials

Belsey, Catherine, 'Disrupting Sexual Difference: Meaning and Gender in the Comedies', in *Alternative Shakespeares*, ed. John Drakakis, New Accents Series (London: Routledge, 1985)

> Excellent discussion of the way the plays of this era formed responses to social change

— *The Subject of Tragedy: Identity and Difference in Renaissance Drama* (London: Routledge, 1985)

> See especially the chapter 'Silence and Speech'

Callaghan, Dympna, *Woman and Gender in Renaissance Tragedy: A Study of 'King Lear', 'The Duchess of Malfi' and 'The White Devil'* (London: Harvester Wheatsheaf, 1989)

> A very good discussion of normative constructions of major female characters in the Shakespearean and non-Shakespearean drama

Ferguson, Margaret, Maureen Quilligan and Nancy Vickers (eds), *Rewriting the Renaissance: The Discourse of Sexual Difference in Early Modern Europe* (Chicago: University of Chicago Press, 1986)

> Provides detailed arguments about the generally marginal position of women in early modern England

Greer, Germaine, *Kissing the Rod* (London: Virago, 1988)

> Anthology of women's poetry in the period, with a good general introduction on the social status of women in early modern England

Newman, Karen, *Fashioning Femininity and English Renaissance Drama* (Chicago: University of Chicago Press, 1991)

> Brings a very broad range of non-dramatic sources to bear on the construction of the idea of the feminine in the drama

Rose, Mary Beth, *The Expense of Spirit: Love and Sexuality in English Renaissance Drama* (London: Cornell University Press, 1988)

> The socially transgressive act of cross-dressing is looked at in the context of broader discussions of sexual politics

Witchcraft

Clark, Stuart, *Thinking With Demons: The Idea of Witchcraft in Early Modern Europe* (Oxford: Clarendon Press, 1997)

> One of the most substantial and closely argued accounts available, for those who wish to understand the phenomenon from a European-wide perspective

Macdonald, Michael, *Witchcraft and Hysteria in Elizabethan London: Edward Jordan and the Mary Glover Case* (London: Routledge, 1990)

> A fascinating comparison of primary sources arguing for and against the use of witchcraft as an explanatory system

Thomas, Keith, *Religion and the Decline of Magic: Studies in Popular Beliefs in Sixteenth- and Seventeenth-Century England* (Harmondsworth: Penguin, 1971; repr. 1991)

> Contains a substantial discussion over several chapters, placing witchcraft in its social and religious contexts – a very good starting point

Sharpe, James, *Instruments of Darkness: Witchcraft in Early Modern England* (Philadelphia: University of Pennsylvania Press, 1996)

> Provides a detailed sociological study of the phenomenon in England with a focus on the legal status of witchcraft

Rhetoric in Elizabethan England

Adamson, Sylvia, Gavin Alexander and Katrin Ettenhuber (eds), *Renaissance Figures of Speech* (Cambridge: Cambridge University Press, 2007)

> Has some succinct remarks in the introduction and individual essays by expert writers on specific figures in the main body of this volume; Shakespearean dramatic examples are very well served throughout, although other playwrights come a rather distant second

Bevington, David, *Action is Eloquence: Shakespeare's Language of Gesture* (Cambridge, MA: Harvard University Press, 1984)

> A detailed and wide-ranging discussion on the theme of suiting action to word on the early modern stage

Joseph, B. L., *Elizabethan Acting* (Oxford: Oxford University Press, 1951)

> A clear and helpful starting point for the analysis of performance from a rhetorical standpoint

Kermode, Frank, *Shakespeare's Language* (London: Penguin, 2001)

> Written for the general reader, this includes analysis of the dramatist's rhetorical figures as well as his poetic language and has some excellent, clear explanations of both

Murphy, James J. (ed.), *Renaissance Eloquence: Studies in the Theory and Practice of Renaissance Rhetoric* (Berkeley, CA: University of California Press, 1983)

> A number of essays which suggest the range and extent of rhetorical learning and practice in early modern England.

Rivers, Isabel, *Classical and Christian Ideas in English Renaissance Poetry: A Student's Guide*, 2nd edn (London: Routledge, 1994)

> The brief but lucid discussion in the chapter on humanism can help orientate readers as to the importance of rhetoric to all areas of the period's literature

Vickers, Brian, *In Defence of Rhetoric* (Oxford: Clarendon, 1989)

> A forcefully argued and widely admired account of rhetoric from classical antiquity onwards, which makes the point about the centrality of the practice to Renaissance literature

Nationhood and National Identity

Gurr, Andrew, *Playgoing in Shakespeare's London*, 2nd edn (Cambridge: Cambridge University Press, 1996)

> Has some brief but interesting discussion of the role the so-called Elect Nation plays in the repertories of playing companies

Hadfield, Andrew, *Literature, Politics and National Identity: Reformation to Renaissance* (Cambridge: Cambridge University Press, 1994), pp. 57–9

> Focuses on the role of religion and the vernacular in the formation of national identity: an important study to which a number of later ones are indebted

Haller, William, *Foxe's Book of Martyrs and the Elect Nation* (London: Cape, 1963)

> The main proponent of the Elect Nation hypothesis, since the source of some dispute (the extent to which there really *was* an Elect Nation concept, which could therefore provide the basis of a mini-genre, as originally proposed, is discussed briefly by Hadfield (above), pp. 57–8)

Hoenselaars, A. J., *Images of Englishmen and Foreigners in the Drama of Shakespeare and His Contemporaries: A Study of Stage Characters and National Identity in English Renaissance Drama* (London: Associated University Presses, 1992)

> A substantial but very approachable discussion of the links between English self-identity and anti-foreign attitudes, and the drama's involvement in forging these links

Howard, Jean H. and Phyllis Rackin, *Engendering a Nation: A Feminist Account of Shakespeare's English Histories* (London: Routledge, 1997)

> Contains some excellent insights into the way Shakespeare's history plays deploy the tropes of gender to imagine an idea of English nationhood

Kermode, Edward, *Aliens and Englishness in Elizabethan Drama* (Cambridge: Cambridge University Press, 2009)

> A recent, nuanced reading of the familiar theme of English versus foreign identity

Maley, Willy, *Nation, State and Empire in English Renaissance Literature: Shakespeare* (London: Palgrave Macmillan, 2003)

> Examines the role of literature, including Shakespeare, in creating a national identity, with a particular focus on the complex engagements between Englishness and Britishness in that process

McEachern, Claire, *The Poetics of English Nationhood, 1590–1612* (Cambridge: Cambridge University Press, 1996)

> An analysis of how the literature of post-Armada decades crucially articulated the act of national 'birth' which had occurred fifty years prior to it in the break with Rome

Schwyzer, Philip, *Literature, Nationalism and Memory in Early Modern England and Wales* (Cambridge: Cambridge University Press, 2004)

> A recent discussion which also argues the case for centrality of the 'British' component in the formation of national identity in early modern England

Index

Index

YORK NOTES **COMPANIONS**

Texts, Contexts and Connections from York Notes
to help you through your literature degree ...

✔ **Medieval Literature**, Carole Maddern
ISBN: 9781408204757 | £10.99

✔ **Renaissance Poetry and Prose**, June Waudby
ISBN: 9781408204788 | £10.99

✔ **Shakespeare and Renaissance Drama**, Hugh Mackay
ISBN: 9781408204801 | £10.99

✔ **The Long Eighteenth Century: Literature from 1660 to 1790**
Penny Pritchard
ISBN: 9781408204733 | £10.99

✔ **Romantic Literature**, John Gilroy
ISBN: 9781408204795 | £10.99

✔ **Victorian Literature**, Beth Palmer
ISBN: 9781408204818 | £10.99

✔ **Modernist Literature: 1890 to 1950**, Gary Day
ISBN: 9781408204764 | £10.99

✔ **Postwar Literature: 1950 to 1990**, William May
ISBN: 9781408204740 | £10.99

✔ **New Directions: Writing Post 1990**, Fiona Tolan
ISBN: 9781408204771 | £10.99

Available from all good bookshops

For a 20% discount on any title in the series visit
www.yorknotes.com/companions and
enter discount code JB001A at the checkout!

The best books ever written

P E N G U I N C L A S S I C S

SINCE 1946

20% discount on your essential reading from
Penguin Classics, only with *York Notes Companions*

Volpone and Other Plays
Ben Jonson
Edited with an Introduction by Michael Jamieson
Paperback | 496 pages | ISBN 9780141441184 | 29 Apr 2004 | £9.99

A Midsummer Night's Dream
William Shakespeare
Edited with an Introduction by Helen Hackett
Paperback | 224 pages | ISBN 9780141012605 | 07 Apr 2005 | £7.99

The Tempest
William Shakespeare
Edited with an Introduction by Martin Butler
Paperback | 240 pages | ISBN 9780141016641 | 26 Apr 2007 | £7.99

Hamlet
William Shakespeare
Edited by Alan Sinfield with an Essay by Paul Prescott
Paperback | 400 pages | ISBN 9780141013077 | 07 Apr 2005 | £7.99

Henry V
William Shakespeare
Edited by A. R. Humphreys with an Essay by Michael Taylor
Paperback | 336 pages | ISBN 9780141013794 | 25 Feb 2010 | £7.99

Richard III
William Shakespeare
Edited with an Introduction by Michael Taylor
Paperback | 288 pages | ISBN 9780141013039 | 07 Apr 2005 | £7.99

To claim your 20% discount on any of these titles
visit **www.penguinclassics.co.uk** and use
discount code **YORK20**